Ocean Crossings

Spring 2020

Tagus Press
Center for Portuguese Studies and Culture
University of Massachusetts Dartmouth
Portuguese Literary & Cultural Studies (PLCS) 33

PREVIOUS ISSUES

Fronteiras/Borders (PLCS 1)
Edited by Victor J. Mendes, Paulo de Medeiros, and José N. Ornelas

Lídia Jorge in other words / por outras palavras (PLCS 2)
Edited by Cláudia Pazos Alonso

Pessoa's Alberto Caeiro (PLCS 3)
Edited by Victor J. Mendes

2001 Brazil: A Revisionary History of Brazilian Literature and Culture (PLCS 4/5)
Edited by João Cezar de Castro Rocha

On Saramago (PLCS 6)
Edited by Anna Klobucka

A Repertoire of Contemporary Portuguese Poetry (PLCS 7)
Edited by Victor K. Mendes

Cape Verde: Language, Literature & Music (PLCS 8)
Edited by Ana Mafalda Leite

Post-Imperial Camões (PLCS 9)
Edited by João R. Figueiredo

Reevaluating Mozambique (PLCS 10)
Edited by Phillip Rothwell

Vitorino Nemésio and the Azores (PLCS 11)
Edited by Francisco Cota Fagundes

The Other Nineteenth Century (PLCS 12)
Edited by Kathryn M. Sanchez

The Author as Plagiarist—The Case of Machado de Assis (PLCS 13/14)
Edited by João Cezar de Castro Rocha

Remembering Angola (PLCS 15/16)
Edited by Phillip Rothwell

Parts of Asia (PLCS 17/18)
Edited by Cristiana Bastos

Facts and Fictions of António Lobo Antunes (PLCS 19/20)
Edited by Victor K. Mendes

Garrett's Travels Revisited (PLCS 21/22)
Edited by Victor K. Mendes and Valéria M. Souza

Economies of Relation: Money and Personalism in the Lusophone World (PLCS 23/24)
Edited by Roger Sansi

Lusofonia and Its Futures (PLCS 25)
Edited by João Cezar de Castro Rocha

Literary Histories in Portuguese (PLCS 26)
Edited by João Cezar de Castro Rocha

The South Atlantic, Past and Present (PLCS 27)
Edited by Luiz Felipe de Alencastro

Fernando Pessoa as English Reader and Writer (PLCS 28)
Edited by Patricio Ferrari & Jerónimo Pizarro

The Eighteenth Century (PLCS 29)
Edited by Bruno Carvalho

Transnational Africas: Visual, Material and Sonic Cultures of Lusophone Africa (PLCS 30/31)
Edited by Christopher Larkosh, Mario Pereira & Memory Holloway

Luso-American Literatures and Cultures Today (PLCS 32)
Edited by Christopher Larkosh with Maggie Felisberto, Jo-Anne Ferreira and Emanuel da Silva

Ocean Crossings (PLCS 33)
Edited by André Nóvoa

Portuguese Literary & Cultural Studies (PLCS) is an interdisciplinary, peer-reviewed hybrid online and print journal that publishes original research related to the literatures and cultures of the diverse communities of the Portuguese-speaking world from a broad range of academic, critical and theoretical approaches. PLCS is published semi-annually by Tagus Press in the Center for Portuguese Studies and Culture at the University of Massachusetts Dartmouth.

Manuscript Policy

Portuguese Literary & Cultural Studies welcomes submission of original and unpublished manuscripts in English or Portuguese appropriate to the goals of the journal. Manuscripts should be between 6,000–8,500 words in length and must be accompanied by an abstract. Manuscripts should be in accordance with the *MLA Style Manual and Guide to Scholarly Publishing* (latest version) or *The Chicago Manual of Style* (latest version) with parenthetical documentation and a list of works cited. The author is responsible for the accuracy of all quotations, titles, names, and dates. Manuscripts should be double-spaced throughout. All of the information must be in the same language (e.g., abstract, body of the article, bio-blurb). Updated guidelines are available at https://ojs.lib.umassd.edu/index.php/plcs/index. PLCS encourages submission of manuscripts in the form of a single attached MS Word document. Please send submissions to Mario Pereira, Editor, at mpereira6@umassd.edu.

Portuguese Literary & Cultural Studies 33

Ocean Crossings

Edited by André Nóvoa

Tagus Press
UMass Dartmouth
Dartmouth, Massachusetts

Portuguese Literary and Cultural Studies 33
Center for Portuguese Studies and Culture/Tagus Press
University of Massachusetts Dartmouth

Manufactured in the United States of America
Copy edited by Dawn Potter
Designed by Richard Hendel
Cover design & typesetting by Inês Sena

For all inquiries, please contact:
Center for Portuguese Studies and Culture/ Tagus Press
University of Massachusetts Dartmouth
285 Old Westport Road
North Dartmouth MA 02747–2300
Tel. 508–999–8255 / Fax 508–999–9272
https://www.umassd.edu/portuguese-studies-center/

Cover Image: Watercolors from *Diário das Viagens do Comandante António Jervis de Atouguia Ferreira Pinto Basto*, 1879-1905. Biblioteca Nacional de Portugal.

This publication was supported in part by "The Colour of Labour- The Racialized Lives of Migrants," funded by the European Research Council (ERC) under the European Union's Horizon 2020 Research and Innovation programme (Advanced Grant No 695573 - PI Cristiana Bastos), hosted by the University of Lisbon/Universidade de Lisboa, Instituto de Ciências Sociais.

ISSN: 1521-804X (print)
ISSN: 2573-1432 (online)
ISBN: 978-1-933227-9-24 (pbk.: alk. paper)
ISBN: 978-1-951470-11-1 (Ebook)

Library of Congress Control Number: 2021938091

5 4 3 2 1

Contents

Interviews

Other Essays

Reviews

Editor's Note

March, 2021. This issue of *Portuguese Literary & Cultural Studies* dedicated to "Ocean Crossings" was not immune to the effects of the Covid-19 pandemic that has shaped our lives for the past year. We closed the issue in the fall of 2019 and were about to move into production in the spring of 2020 when the pandemic struck and work had to be halted. After a year of anxiety and devastation, we once again move forward as we mark the one year anniversary of lockdowns and *confinamentos* and bring this issue into print. I thank all of the contributors for their patience and understanding as we navigated the uncertainty of this pandemic.

I would like to acknowledge the excellent work of André Nóvoa as the guest editor of "Ocean Crossings." I would also like to express my gratitude to Cristiana Bastos for advice and support. This publication is supported in part by "The Colour of Labour - The Racialized Lives of Migrants," funded by the European Research Council (ERC) under the European Union's Horizon 2020 Research and Innovation Programme (Advanced Grant No. 695573 - PI Cristiana Bastos).

MARIO PEREIRA
Center for Portuguese Studies and Culture
University of Massachusetts Dartmouth

Ocean Crossings

Introduction: The Sword and the Shovel[1]

Tribute to António Hespanha

We would like to dedicate this special issue to António Hespanha, who passed away in July 2019. Professor Hespanha was one of the most important and original figures of not only Portuguese historiography but also Portuguese culture in a broader sense. His teachings in the fields of legal history and the history of the Portuguese Empire have been paramount in the shaping of our collective identity. Professor Hespanha kindly agreed to do an interview for this special issue. We honor his memory by publishing it here and dedicating the entire issue to his legacy.

The Portuguese have shown themselves for ages a restless and roving people; enterprising in spirit, and adventurous in their habits, we have already seen them, along with the Spaniards, exploring and visiting this country; behold them now again, but in a different capacity. Formerly they came to be masters; now they were satisfied to be servants and laborers. Formerly they came with the sword and the spear; now they were to wield the shovel and the cutlass.[2]

—Henry Dalton

The epigraph is from Henry Dalton's 1855 *History of British Guiana*. In it, he refers to the large contingents of Portuguese who landed on Guyanese soil, beginning in the 1830s and continuing until the end of the century. Over the course of almost seventy years, an estimated 40,000 Portuguese, mostly from Madeira, arrived in Demerara, a river city in what was then a British colony (Ferreira, J. 2006; Menezes 1986). As Cristiana Bastos notes (2018b), this number is much higher than the number of Portuguese in the Portuguese African colonies at that time.

The highlight of the Dalton quotation appears in the last sentence. With his metaphorical reference to "the sword" and "the shovel," Dalton highlights the duality, or ambiguity, of Portuguese ocean crossings throughout time. On the one hand, there were Portuguese who acted as agents of colonialism; they came bearing a sword and took territorial, political, and economic control of native, indigenous, and other local populations. On the other hand, there were

Portuguese who came prepared to wield a shovel, most of them poor migrants and laborers, often forcibly displaced, who joined the working ranks in unknown places and unfamiliar contexts.

Portuguese historiography, cultural studies, and social sciences have generally paid much more attention to the ocean crossings of the sword than to those of the shovel. In this issue, we turn the equation around and take a critical look at ocean crossings of the shovel, in line with Bastos's (2018a, 2018b, 2019) suggestions to reframe its role in Portuguese historiography. As she explains, "the identification of the Portuguese as intrepid sailors crossing oceans and bridging the world has been central to a historical narrative that merges sea travel, trade, conquest, knowledge, empire and nation." However, in many circumstances, "sailing overseas was a way to escape poverty, abuse, oppression, misery and distress" (2018b, 66). The paths of such travelers had little, if anything, to do with an imperial strategy.

The Sword

Until recently, the mainstream historiography of Portugal was very much a hagiography of the seas, which were treated as an avatar of bravery that metonymically translated into a certain stereotype of Portuguese identity. Within it, the maritime trope was systematically encoded as the place where the Portuguese fabricated themselves as agents of exploration, discovery, globalization, and cutting-edge science. In Portuguese culture (in a broad sense), the seas were a calling that the Portuguese ought to answer, one capable of pulling them from a state of relative insignificance in the grand theater of European politics toward an emancipation of the being and a full realization of a long-lost inner identity.

Consider Tim Cresswell's (2006) differentiation between movement and mobility. In his view, movement is mobility exempted from social meaning and relations of power, whereas mobility is its opposite: a dislocation or movement constrained by and embedded in meaning and contexts of power. Cresswell has built on this notion to theorize on what he calls the "production of mobilities": the meanings that have been ascribed to ideas and practices of movement in different cultural and historical contexts. He has used that theory as a basis for exploring how these meanings and narratives have affected the lives of people within these contexts.

As a performance of mobility, the practice of crossing the oceans lauds the grandeur of the Portuguese and their capacity to build an inclusive empire that was the forerunner of globalization, international trade, scientific exploration, and cultural exchange. As a mobility of empowerment, of self-representation, such crossings constructed a maritime trope as an enterprise of becoming. In the words of Eduardo Lourenço (1990), they produced the conception of Portugal as a "nation-ship" of civilization. The idea of sailing, itself a performance of mobility, was codified and produced as a movement of national glory. Since the nineteenth century, this has been deeply rooted in the history of Portuguese nationalism.

Since the construction of Portuguese national identity, the seas have been systematically mobilized as the place where the Portuguese found their vocation, their realization, and their place in the world. The ocean—most notably the Atlantic—has been treated as a fundamental aspect of Portuguese culture, of Portugueseness, of being Portuguese. We see this in the writings of Oliveira Martins (the nineteenth century), Jaime Cortesão (the first half of the twentieth century), and Eduardo Lourenço (the second half of the twentieth century), among many others. We see this in the neo-Manueline style, an architectonic trend of the 1800s that lauded the maritime "discoveries" of the fifteenth and sixteenth centuries—even if art historians have showed that the relation between the original Manueline and the theme of the seas is, at best, marginal (Pereira 1990). We see this later in the works of Gilberto Freyre (1953), who coined the idea of luso-tropicalism, wherein the oceans were metaphorized as bridges of cultures, milieus of hybridization, the passageway of the lethargic or passive colonizer. We see this in the rhetorics of the Estado Novo and the grand Exposition of the Portuguese World of 1940, symbolically located between the Jerónimos Monastery, the Tower of Belem, and the *Padrão dos Descobrimentos*, all celebrating the maritime grandeur of the nation.[3]

We need not travel further into the past than twenty years ago to unearth one of the most renowned examples of the seas as a celebration of Portuguese identity: the Lisbon World Exposition, known as EXPO 98 (Sieber 2001). Portugal's biggest public event since the Carnation Revolution of 1974, it was a celebration of Portuguese modernity and identity, a moment of nationalism for the world to see. Its entire iconography was based on the empire, the seas, and their capacity to help humankind build a world of globalization and intercultural prosperity. The Lisbon Oceanarium, the largest indoor aquarium in Europe, was built on site. The mascot was a wave. The streets of the exposition were named after Portuguese sailors of the so-called "discoveries." The largest arena was known as the Atlantic Pavilion. It was, in short, a celebration of the Portuguese with swords in their hands (Ferreira, C. 2006; Martins 2016).

The Shovel

The problem is that focusing on the notion of sailing as a cultural production contained within a nationalist rhetoric has pushed colonialism and slavery into the background. Discussions of colonialism and slavery were swept under the rug. The imagining of the maritime trope as an enterprise of becoming and Portugal as a nation-ship of civilization (Lourenço 1990) obliterated many other visions of the seas. First and foremost, it obliterated many attempts to come to terms with a colonial and slaver past. The replication of this trope through time silenced views of the seas as a place of exploitation, colonialism, suffering, killing and racism—this topic is analyzed in the interviews in this issue. Second, it has also overlooked other paths and trajectories in and within the lusophone world, other alternative ocean crossings, such as those in which the Portuguese were themselves the underdogs, targets of brutality in a world of persecutory labor and precarious living conditions.

The essays and papers in this special issue explore these other lusophone crossings—those involving the shovel and the cutlass, to return to Dalton's expression, in detriment of those of the sword—with the hope of showing new ways of understanding the performance of ocean crossing in the lusophone world that do not make an apologetic view of the seas and sailing, but rather one that reveals new understandings of labor, racialization, poverty, and despair (Bastos 2018b). The various papers, some more strongly than others, are in dialogue with this and have been included precisely for their attention to lesser visible ocean crossings in the lusophone world.

The issue kicks off with two special essays. The first is by Malyn Newitt, which aims to show an alternative history of the Portuguese at sea (see Newitt 2015). The essay's opening sentence sets the tone for the focus of the analysis: "there is another story to set alongside the grand narrative of the discoveries and the founding of Portugal's worldwide maritime empire." Newitt puts in perspective the history of Portuguese migration through the seas, by sharing examples set in Hawai'i, the Caribbean, and parts of Asia.

The other essay in the "Special Essays" section is by Kevin Brown. Brown focuses his analysis on the British Empire and the coolie trade from India and China. Many parallels can be drawn from his analysis for the Portuguese reality, but most importantly Brown shows how the Portuguese in the outpost of Macau were very much involved in this trade and how they contributed to a world marked by indentured servitude and labor.

The articles that follow help to deepen these topics. My paper "Sailors and Whalers" addresses the mobility of Portuguese whalers in the nineteenth century. It attempts to show that there were many Portuguese who joined the sailing ranks of whaling ships throughout the 1800s, mostly those from Madeira and the Azores. These men converged in the city that lit the world (a reference to how whale oil was primarily used as a source of lighting), New Bedford, Massachusetts, and from there ventured out into other parts of North America and the Pacific. In doing so, they created paths of migration for many other Portuguese that followed into New England, Hawai'i, and California.

Nicholas B. Miller's "Crossing Seas and Labels" focuses on the sea journeys of Portuguese labor migrants into Hawai'i. Miller emphasizes how the Portuguese arrived in British vessels under Hawaiian contracts, which complexified the various social and economic categories in place. The Portuguese were neither enslaved Africans, nor indentured Asians, nor exactly free migrants bounded to North America. This exploration of the Portuguese bearing the shovel is important to show that there are many realities that fall in-between pre-established categories, often with intricate social processes in terms of differentiation, hierarchizing, and even racialization.

Miguel Moniz's analysis in "The Day of Portugal, Social Exclusion, and Imagined Mobilities" centers on migratory experiences in New England in the first part of the twentieth century. The article deals with processes of racialization of labor migrants from the Portuguese islands, using data from public events, such as the annual Day of Portugal and others. Moniz shows how the Portuguese were able to use these events to lift themselves socially and politically, aiming at aspirational equality: "Annual celebrations of Portugal and Portuguese migrant communities known as the Day of Portugal take place in New England as part of longitudinal responses to the racialization of migrant labor and attempts among settler communities of these workers to achieve socio-economic mobility" (Moniz, this issue).

Diana Simões's article "A Diáspora como Base da Identidade Cabo-Verdiana em *Ilhéu dos Pássaros*, de Orlanda Amarílis, e *Chiquinho*, de Baltasar Lopes" shifts the analysis to Cabo Verde, highlighting a different facet of the lusophone world. Simões argues that Cabo Verdean migration can be seen as an escape from the physical conditions and geographical positioning of the archipelago, added to the lesser conditions of living and continuous hard labor. She then moves on to explore representations of the Cabo Verdean diaspora, showing how these are fundamentally linked to the seas. Simões does this through an interesting exploration of the works of Baltasar Lopes and Orlanda Amarílis, two Cabo Verdean writers. In doing so, she provides a fresh look at representations of the ocean contained within the lusophone world, ones that do not adhere to the stereotypical Portuguese-sword binomial.

Finally, in "The Maritime Micro-Gestures in Elizabeth Bishop's Brazil Poems and Translations," Magdalena Edward examines the writings of Elizabeth Bishop, a controversial author who was recently lauded as the main honoree of the 2019 edition of the famous International Literary Fair of Paraty (FLIP), which sparked anger amongst many Brazilians because it is generally known that Bishop supported the military coup of 1964 (which installed a militarized, dictatorial regime). Edwards' analysis is focused on what the author calls maritime gestures, creating a water imagery of Bishop's writings. The article offers a fascinating reading of Bishop's poetic use of the sea and connected bodies of water, showing a different (and more literary) facet of lusophone waters.

The issue closes with transcriptions of interviews with António Hespanha, Cristiana Bastos, Joacine Katar Moreira, Miguel Vale de Almeida, and Pedro Schacht Pereira, who discuss the importance of ocean crossings in Portuguese culture and consider how certain visions of the seas have contributed to the dynamics of racialization and segregation in Portuguese society. This topic is explored in order, once again, to challenge the more traditional visions of the seas as places of grandeur and braveness.

Conclusion

Much study and creative imagining of the Portuguese on the high seas have focused on the sword and, as a result, on whiteness.[4] Portuguese historiography has reinforced this line, for good or ill. Conservative historians continue to privilege the deeds of the Portuguese and the fabrication of a civilizing empire. Progressive historians have, naturally, questioned this, but did so whilst still focusing their works on the Portuguese under the Portuguese Empire, and not exactly beyond it. Which means that the Portuguese under analysis remained those of the sword. Whilst they have challenged assumptions of the Portuguese as civilizing agents and "good colonizers," trying to stop the naturalization of luso-tropicalism, these historians have still focused on the mobilities, the movements, and the ocean crossings of the sword.

Little has been written, at least from the perspective of Portuguese and lusophone mainstream historiography, about the other mobilities, the other seas, the other places in which the Portuguese were seen as underdogs, as nonwhite laborers, as a disposable workforce. In this issue, this is what we aim for: we aim to give voice and analyze a number of alternative trajectories and paths, certain "ocean crossings" that are hardly the subject of enquiry of mainstream historiography and that have seldom been the target of identity when "Portuguese" and "the seas" are put in the same sentence. The articles and essays in this issue are focused on achieving this. Some do it more incisively and others less so, though these still provide fresh perspectives on dimensions of ocean crossings that are not self-centered on white, sword-handling Portuguese men.

NOTES

1. This article results from research conducted within the project "The Colour of Labour- The Racialized Lives of Migrants", funded by the European Research Council (ERC) under the European Union's Horizon 2020 Research and Innovation programme (Advanced Grant No 695573 - PI Cristiana Bastos), hosted by the University of Lisbon/ Universidade de Lisboa, Instituto de Ciências Sociais. I am grateful for the invitation to serve as guest editor of this special issue of *Portuguese Literary & Cultural Studies*. I do so in my role as a team member in the European Research Commission's (ERC) Colour of Labour project. It is my goal to use my role as guest editor to create a conversation around the project's core concerns as outlined by Principal Investigator (PI) Cristiana Bastos. Colour, which has received funding from the ERC under the European Union's Horizon 2020 research and innovation program, focuses on the coproduction of racialization and labor. Some of its tracks examine the lusophone world beyond the Portuguese Empire, studying how the Portuguese were often racialized through the types of labor they performed. The essays in this special issue contribute to these explorations by addressing informal, less obvious, and often veiled ocean crossings within the lusophone world.

2. I was first introduced to Dalton by Marcelo Moura Mello in his presentation at the Mobile Labor Symposium, held at the Institute of Social Sciences, University of Lisbon, March 2019. Marcelo is a colleague and team-member of the Colour of Labour project. Portuguese migration to British Guyana in the nineteenth century is the central axis of ERC Colour of Labour.

3. The *Padrão dos Descobrimentos* (Monument to the Discoveries) was erected temporarily in 1940 for the Grand Exhibition. The current monument, built in 1960, is a replica of the original.

4. Innovative perspectives have surfaced in the recent years. Some scholars have argued that this idea may be a naturalization of certain historic projections rather than the actual experiences of Portuguese sailors and migrants, who had to thread their way carefully amid pre-established social, cultural, and racial hierarchies. See, for instance, António Hespanha's *Filhos da Terra* (2019).

REFERENCES

Bastos, Cristiana. 2018a. "Migrants, Inequalities, and Social Research in the 1920s: The Story of 'Two Portuguese Communities in New England.'" *History and Anthropology* 29 (2), 163–183.

______. 2018b. "Portuguese in the Cane: The Racialization of Labor in Hawaiian Plantations. In Aboim, Granjo, and Ramos (eds.), *Changing Societies: Legacies and Challenges*. Vol. 1, *Ambiguous Inclusions: Inside Out, Outside In*. Lisbon: Imprensa de Ciências Sociais, 65–96.

______ (2019). "Açúcar, ananases e ilhéus portugueses no Hawaii: dinâmicas de migração, etnicidade e racialização no terreno e no arquivo." *Etnográfica* 23 (3), 777–798.

Cresswell, Tim. 2006. *On the Move*. New York: Routledge.

Ferreira, Claudino Cristóvão. 2006. *A Expo'98 e os imaginários do Portugal contemporâneo: cultural, celebração e políticas de representação*. Coimbra: Faculdade de Economia da Universidade de Coimbra.

Ferreira, Jo Ann S. 2006. "Madeiran Portuguese Migration to Guyana, St. Vincent, Antigua, and Trinidad: A comparative overview." *Portuguese Studies Review* 14 (2), 63–85.

Freyre, Gilberto. 1953. *Um Brasileiro em terras Portuguesas: introdução a uma possível luso-tropicologia, acompanhada de conferências e discursos proferidos em Portugal e em terras lusitanas e ex-lusitanas da Ásia, da África e do Atlântico*. Lisbon: Livros do Brasil.

Hespanha, António. 2019. *Filhos da terra: identidades mestiças nos confins da expansão portuguesa*. Lisbon: Tinta da China.

Lourenço, Eduardo. 1990. *Nós e a Europa ou as duas razoes*. Lisbon: Imprensa Nacional–Casa da Moeda.

Martins, Nuno Gomes. 2016. "Da representação do mundo: as exposições internacionais e a Expo'98." *Cadernos do Arquivo Municipal* 2 (5), 357–382.

Menezes, Mary Noel. 1986. *Scenes from the History of the Portuguese in Guyana*. Self-published.

Newitt, Malyn. 2015. *Emigration and the Sea: An Alternative History of Portugal*. New York: Oxford University Press.

Pereira, Paulo. 1990. *A obra silvestre e a esfera do Rei*. Coimbra: Universidade de Coimbra.

Sieber, R. Timothy. 2001. "Remembering Vasco da Gama: Contested Histories and the Cultural Politics of Contemporary Nation-Building in Lisboa, Portugal." *Identities* 8 (4), 549–581.

ANDRÉ NÓVOA (PhD, Royal Holloway, 2014) is a geographer who previously trained as an historian and anthropologist. He was a researcher at Northeastern University (USA) and an assistant editor of *HAU Magazine: Journal of Ethnographic Theory*. His work has been published in journals such as *Mobilities* and *Environment & Planning*. In "The Colour of Labour" project, he is directly involved with the study of mobilities, addressing the movements of whalers, the journeys of indentured migrants, and the entanglements of labor and mobility.

Special Essays

The Portuguese Diaspora

There is another story to set alongside the grand narrative of the discoveries and the founding of Portugal's worldwide maritime empire. As the great navigators and conquistadores opened up the world, drew their maps and founded their empire which stretched across the globe, they set in motion a movement of the ordinary people, people who sailed their ships, manned their fortresses, and colonized the lands they discovered. They and their descendants founded new 'Portuguese' communities across the world which continued to flourish, even when the heroic age of exploration and conquest finally came to an end. Subaltern history, the history of ordinary people, does not always follow neatly in the wake of the activities of the politically powerful, indeed there is often significant divergence which it is important to understand to get a clearer picture of human development.

This story brings to the fore two aspects of European history which are not always given the importance they deserve. First, migration has always been a regular and accepted part of the life of very many ordinary people. Although, before the fifteenth century, most people were employed in agriculture, it was common for workers to migrate in search of seasonal employment, there was migration from the countryside to the towns and men from coastal communities would enlist as crew on fishing boats and merchant ships, being away from their communities for months at a time. The religious-minded went on pilgrimages and fighting men, like Chaucer's Knight, joined campaigns wherever they were being conducted. The educated moved between the courts and universities of Europe and there were movements of population to settle empty land as the frontiers of Europe expanded. Once new lands were discovered and new horizons opened for trade, conquest, and settlement, departures on ever more distant and speculative enterprises were greatly facilitated by networks and traditions of migration that already existed.

Just as migration was more common than is generally assumed, so also was the diversity of populations. The nationalist narrative that has people fitting neatly into boxes with nationally defined labels does not fit the realities of European history before nineteenth century politicians designed the nation states that appear on today's map. Before that century most states were multi-ethnic;

diverse languages and dialects were spoken and laws and customs differed, sometimes from one town to the next. People of all classes moved in search of employment, often resulting in a thoroughly polyglot population. Scottish and Swiss soldiers settled in countries where their contracts terminated; refugees from religious wars were scattered in dozens of different states; the crews of ships and populations of port-towns reflected a similar diversity, while at the other end of the social scale, the scholarly and scientific community and the royal courts attracted people of very diverse origins (McNeill 1978).

Three Streams of Migration

The spread throughout the world of communities that identified themselves as Portuguese was the first major expansion of European populations beyond Europe and it raises questions about cultural adjustment and the molding of identities, as cultures that had hitherto evolved largely in isolation from one another were brought into close contact.

This movement had a bewildering complexity, as three migratory streams with quite separate origins merged to form the 'Portuguese diaspora.' First, there were the migrants who left Portugal more or less voluntarily for employment or settlement overseas. Second was the forced migration of Africans who entered the Portuguese world as slaves and third was the migration of Jews from the Iberian peninsula which began toward the end of the fifteenth century. These three streams of migration, which continued to flow at least until the nineteenth century, merged with each other to create new Portuguese communities and these in turn mixed with the indigenous peoples in Africa, the New World, and Asia to form uniquely diverse Portuguese communities across the world.

The first phase of Portuguese expansion in the fifteenth century was characterized by conquests in Morocco, by slave raiding and trading on the African coast, and by the settlement of the islands of the eastern Atlantic (Vieira, 2007). The sailors who provided crews belonged to maritime communities in Portugal which made a living from fishing, gathering seaweed, and operating salt pans. When the Portuguese Crown began the settlement of the Atlantic Islands many men from the peasant communities of northern Portugal, who had traditionally moved in search of seasonal employment to supplement the incomes from family small holdings, took the opportunity to emigrate to cultivate the richly fertile volcanic soils of the islands. Not all those who availed themselves of these opportunities were from Portugal and settlers came from elsewhere in Europe when the opportunity arose. Those who settled in Madeira after 1419 and the Azores from the 1430s also turned to the sea, sending their own trading expeditions to Africa and mounting exploratory voyages of their own into the Atlantic.

Slaves

Meanwhile, to this stream of migrants from Portugal was added a second movement of population, as slaves were brought from Africa both for sale in Portugal itself and in the islands where their labor was employed on sugar plantations. Madeira and the Azores were attractive to settler families from Portugal who constituted the largest part of the populations of those islands but the Cabo Verde and the Guinea Islands were a long way from Europe and presented a more hostile environment. Fewer settlers came from Portugal and slaves played a more important part in the settlement, slave women becoming the mothers of a free mixed race population that characterized these island settlements (Santos, 1991-2002).

The Portuguese controlled the slave trade until the end of the sixteenth century and also supplied slaves for the Spanish communities in the New World. It is thought that at least 300,000 slaves were traded from Africa between 1450 and 1600 and a further 2 million between 1600 and 1700. Possibly 200,000 of these were shipped to Portuguese communities—rather less than 1,000 a year, though heavily concentrated in the seventeenth century. The slaves came almost exclusively from the upper Guinea region from Senegal to Sierre Leone and from the Kongo and Angola area of central Africa (Atlantic Slave trade database; Curtin, 1969).

The slaves, although separated violently from their communities, took with them many elements of their culture, as Gilberto Freyre emphasized in his famous study *Casa Grande e Senzala*, originally published in 1933, and which has been confirmed by so much recent research. Among these were social and religious relationships, music, dance and oral tradition, matters effecting the domestic economy in dress, diet, medicine, etc., craft skills, and a general adherence to the moral values of their homeland (Freyre, 1933; Sweet, 2003).

Jews and New Christians

Toward the end of the fifteenth century a third stream of migration began. The persecution of Jews in Spain intensified with the founding of the Inquisition in 1480 and in Portugal the expulsion of Jews who would not convert was decreed in 1495. Tens of thousands of Sephardic Jews left the peninsula, many heading for more tolerant regimes in Italy, the eastern Mediterranean or North Africa but many also going to Portuguese communities already established in the islands and on the west African mainland. It has been estimated that as many as 70,000 Jews were displaced from Spain and many also left Portugal in the final years of the fifteenth century, by far the biggest single exodus of population during that century. How many of these joined Portuguese communities overseas is not known, but migrants of Jewish or New Christian origin soon became an important element in the populations of Cabo Verde and the Guinea Islands(Saraiva 1964, 1969).

The exodus of people of Jewish origin did not cease with the new century. Although Jews who converted to Christianity (*Conversos* and New Christians) were able to remain in the Iberian peninsula, there was constant persecution as the Inquisition (which was established in Portugal in 1536) inquired into their orthodoxy. Whenever persecutions were intensified, there was a corresponding increase in the emigration of New Christians to join exile communities, and this stream of migration continued until the persecutions finally ended in the second half of the eighteenth century.

Jewish communities of Portuguese origin established themselves in many cities of the Mediterranean and in northern Europe. The largest and most prosperous communities were in Italy, Amsterdam, Hamburg, and London. These Sephardic communities kept their Portuguese identity, continuing to use the Portuguese language in religious ceremonies and their Portuguese names. They also retained their communal obligations to support the poor and to provide dowries for girls. They maintained links with families in Portugal and kept themselves very separate from Ashkenazi Jews coming from Germany and Eastern Europe. Their commercial investments extended to the New World where they were prominent in the sugar industry in Brazil and the Caribbean and in the early settlements in the United States (Bodian 1994, 1997).

The commercial networks of this early modern period were largely independent of the narrow, monopolistic policies of individual states. Merchant syndicates and commodity brokers did not belong to any one national group and in this international fraternity of finance and commerce, Jews of the Portuguese diaspora were prominent participants.

Numbers of Migrants

At the beginning of the sixteenth century, the discovery of Brazil and the founding of the Estado da India, coinciding with the first Spanish settlements in the Caribbean, began to divert the streams of migration. Migrants now looked beyond the Atlantic Islands and western Africa to opportunities in the New World and the East.

The numbers who left Portugal between 1500 and 1640 were estimated by Godinho to number 600,000, which would average at more than 4,000 a year, a number larger than the total who emigrated from Spain to the New World. This figure is very approximate as the patterns of emigration, return, and onward migration, are very complex. But this represented a major haemorrhage of population from a country whose total population was little more than one million (Godinho 1978).

This sustained migration was largely the result of economic opportunity: to farm better land in the islands or Brazil, to trade on the coast of Africa, to join Spanish expeditions in the New World or to endure the hardships of the long voyage to the Indian Ocean where there were many and varied opportunities to get rich, to marry and found families, and to acquire higher social status.

There is a massive literature on the impact of the slave trade on Africa, one aspect of which has been the impact of the loss of population, so it is interesting to compare the numbers involved in the slave trade with the emigration from Portugal over the same period. Over the period 1500 to 1850, 4.67 million slaves were sent to Brazil, mostly from the Kongo and Angola region—an average of 13,000 a year. Over the same period 2.9 million Portuguese emigrated, averaging approximately 8,000 a year. In the second half of the nineteenth century, a further 360,000 Portuguese emigrated to Brazil alone, part of the massive emigration from Europe which far exceeded the number of slaves exported from Africa during the whole of the slave trade (Newitt 2015, p.113).

Portuguese Migrants

At first most Portuguese migrants came from the populous northern provinces of Portugal, the Minho and Tras-os-Montes, but by the sixteenth century emigrants were also coming from the islands, which had been settled in the previous century. However, voluntary migration does not account for the totality of this population movement. Among those who left Portugal were convicts (*degredados*), men and women sentenced to exile by the Inquisition, and orphan children shipped overseas as servants or with dowries to enable them to marry (Coates 2001).

There was no gender balance to this exodus. Overwhelmingly it was men who joined the emigration from Portugal and very few women (except convicts and orphans and the occasional wife of some senior official) sailed to India or relocated to the African settlements, or even to Brazil. As a result, the migrants had to take wives from the slaves they imported or from the native populations where hey settled.

Migrants leaving Portugal or the islands took with them cultural baggage. As well as their language and Portuguese names, they took their particular form of Christianity—their Corpus Christi day celebration, their brotherhoods, their devotion to St Anthony and St Elmo, and those from the Azores their cult of the Holy Spirit. Throughout Africa and the East emigrants were subject to the *padroado real* which established a global Portuguese jurisdiction in all matters related to religious worship and became one of the main structures supporting this world-wide community. Migrants also took with them institutions—the *Misericórdias*, the local democracy of the town councils (*Senados da Câmara*), their acceptance of the social divisions between the married (*casados*) and the unmarried (*soldados*), and their particular forms of land tenure, the system of entailed property and the emphyteutic tenures which linked land use with social and political obligations. These were institutions which connected widely scattered populations and bound them together with a common understanding of the rights and duties of a member of a Portuguese community.

The Creation of Creole Societies in Africa

During the three centuries from 1450 to 1750 the Portuguese settled the Atlantic Islands and from there traded with most of the communities of the western African seaboard, establishing permanent settlements in the upper Guinea rivers, Elmina in modern Ghana, the Kongo, and Angola. While emigrants from Portugal (Christian and Jewish) carried with them their European Portuguese identity, their contacts with slaves and with the indigenous populations of the countries where they traded led to the adoption of elements of non-Portuguese culture which coalesced into a new creole identity. At the same time, their settlements became doors through which Atlantic trade and cultural influences entered Africa and spread widely among the peoples of the interior so that the early history of Atlantic trade is a story of cultural diversity and creolization.

The first areas to which migrants found their way were the Atlantic Islands. Although Madeira and the Azores largely replicated the society of Portugal, what happened in Cabo Verde and the Guinea Islands was very different. There the number of settlers who came from Europe was soon surpassed by the arrival of New Christians and by slaves. At first the society was very stratified with settlers from Portugal becoming a landowning class who held local office and controlled the economic resources, but within a comparatively short space of time a mixed race population emerged and a process of creolization began. The large number of slaves speaking African languages soon gave rise to a widely spoken creole language, while the social culture of the islands became heavily Africanized.

The process of creolization was intensified when traders from the islands moved to the mainland and established trading settlements along the rivers of upper Guinea and in the region south of the Zaire. These trading communities (founded by the so-called *lançados*) intermarried with women from local lineages, adopted elements of African religious belief and local commercial practices. Although traders from the islands continued to control the maritime trade, within two generations the Portuguese resident on the coast had become almost completely Africanized, keeping Portuguese names and a nominal Christianity, even building square 'Portuguese' style houses, but in most other respects merging with local populations. In upper Guinea a Portuguese creole language also took root. These creole societies became intermediaries in the growing Atlantic trade, and when Dutch, English, and French began trading for slaves in West Africa they found a class of black 'Portuguese' middlemen who acted as brokers in the commercial relations with African states (Brook 2003, Green 2012).

São Tomé and Príncipe followed a rather different trajectory, its slave-operated sugar plantations enjoying fifty years of prosperity. A Portuguese institutional structure was established, with a town council and a bishopric, but by the end of the century the cathedral canons, the militia officers, and the town councillors were all black, the descendants of African slave women, and spoke a distinctive creole language (Garfield 1992).

The Kongo kingdom and the Portuguese colony of Angola also experienced creolization, with Christianity and many aspects of Portuguese material culture being adopted and assimilated by populations that were either mixed race or of wholly African descent. The Atlantic influences were felt in the increasing use of firearms and the spread of American food crops. In Angola powerful creole families controlled the land and the slave trade. They provided town councillors and officers in the armed forces and many of them had close ties with the African slave traders. They also attracted to themselves a large following from the local African population. As the seventeenth century wore on they became increasingly Africanized, using the Kimbundu language and adopting the customs and practices of the Mbundu elite (Thornton, 1992, Pinto 2015).

Portuguese who sailed for the Estado da India also made settlements on the coast of East Africa where another creole society became established with the Portuguese traders acquiring large followings of hunters, porters for inland trade, canoemen, and fighters. Dominican and Jesuit missionaries established a structure of Christianity to which the creole society more or less conformed, while retaining the practices of the established local spirit cults.

In western Africa it was the creole communities of the islands which provided personnel, shipping, and capital for the trade, but in eastern Africa soldiers, traders, and settlers did not come directly from Portugal but from the Estado da India. Many of them were Indians or sons of Portuguese and Indian women. Indians were prominent in establishing the inland fairs and Indian capital financed the trade in gold and ivory. The influence of the Estado da India can also be seen in the way that one of its institutions was grafted onto the eastern African settlements. The idea of *prazos* had developed in India and the Portuguese-occupied regions of Sri Lanka. The *prazo* was a grant of land (and of the population resident on it) made to individual Portuguese who collected tribute and administered the land, in return paying a rent to the Crown and undertaking to provide soldiers for the Estado da India. By the middle of the seventeenth century, a large area of land south of the Zambesi had been granted as *prazos*, but in Africa they had one distinctive feature—that they should be inherited by women who were then obligated to marry a Portuguese husband. The *prazos* passed down for three generations before reverting to the Crown. The *prazos* went through many evolutions but in one form or another survived until 1930, showing the extraordinary resilience of the creole society that had been established in eastern Africa (Rodrigues 2001, Newitt 1995).

One striking characteristic of the creole societies that emerged from Portuguese contacts with Africa was the important role that women had as land-owners, traders, investors of capital, and ship owners. This is particularly striking as society in Portugal was very patriarchal. The explanation for the importance of women in creole society can be found first and foremost in the matrilineal African families into which the Portuguese married where women occupied prominent positions as owners of property and heads of families. However, there is also a functional explanation. Portuguese traders were often transient and local women formed multiple liaisons, inheriting property and remaining in the country while the men with whom they established partnerships, which were often very brief, moved on or died or returned whence they came (Havik 1995).

In eastern Africa the prominent position of the *senhoras* of the *prazos* had been institutionalized by the Portuguese in the largely vain attempt to establish European families as a feudal elite. However, the prevalence of matrilineal customs among the African population undoubtedly assisted the *prazo* inheritance laws to become indigenized and acceptable to local ideas.

Brazil

Settlement on the coast of Brazil took some time to get established. Although the coast was divided into twelve captaincies in 1530, it was not till the end of the sixteenth century that sugar plantations at last began to attract settlement and the import of large numbers of slaves. The society that emerged was again highly creolized. Although an upper elite of European Portuguese came to own most of the plantations and filled the official positions in the towns, the rest of society reflected the culture of the African slaves and the native Indian population. As in the islands, it was not long before a free population of mixed race emerged and distinctive Brazilian cultural forms began to appear in music, religion, marriage, and domestic customs. A local creolized language, the so-called *lingua geral*, was also widely used. In the seventeenth century, Brazil developed close links with the islands, West Africa, and Angola which, to some extent, bypassed Portugal itself and created a distinctive creole Atlantic community (Russell-Wood 2007).

The gold discoveries at the end of the seventeenth century resulted in renewed immigration from Portugal. In the first half of the eighteenth century, half a million Portuguese emigrated to Brazil and the Portuguese population there became the largest and, in many respects, the most dynamic settler population in the New World. At the end of the century, the gold mining center of Ouro Preto was larger and more populous than New York.

Luso Asiatic Communities

The early Portuguese voyages to India did not result in permanent settlements but, with the capture of Goa in 1510, the Estado da India had a fixed base in the East. Portuguese settled in the city which soon became the capital of what was a new kingdom of the Crown of Portugal. Goa was an episcopal See, had a town council modelled on that of Lisbon, and a *Misericórdia*. As there were few if any Portuguese women who went to the East, the Portuguese married Indian women and much of the 'Portuguese' population of Goa became in effect Luso-Indians. Alongside this Portuguese population, there grew up an increasing number of Indians who became Christian, entered the Portuguese community at some level and became Lusitanized, although most of them had no direct connection with Portugal itself.

From Goa, other Portuguese towns were founded until by the middle years of the sixteenth century there were as many as fifty Portuguese settlements that formed the Estado da India. In northern India the Portuguese established the so-called Provincia do Norte which was made up of a string of towns, including Bassein, Chaul and Damão; in Malabar the city of Cochin was the unofficial capital of a number of smaller towns under Portuguese control. Each of these Indian towns reflected the Portuguese culture of Goa with a ruling elite of Portuguese and Luso-Indians and a large indigenous population which became more or less Lusitanized. Although the Portuguese came to control considerable areas of land around these towns where they established the regime of *prazos*, these settlements were primarily urban and commercial (Ames 2007).

A similar process led to the founding of important Portuguese settlements at Ormuz, Malacca on the Malay peninsula and Colombo on the island of Sri Lanka from which the Portuguese proceeded to take control of much of the lowland areas of the island. These fortress towns and commercial factories were all part of the Portuguese Estado da India, subject to the viceroy. Although ships continued to arrive from Portugal with officials to occupy senior posts and with soldiers for the fortresses, increasingly the Estado da India became a Luso-Indian project (Subrahmanyam, 1993, Newitt 2005).

Alongside the Estado da India with its network of fortresses and towns, there also grew up an unofficial network of independent Portuguese communities. These were founded by independent merchants or by Portuguese who sold their services to Indian rulers as mercenaries. Many of them also took to piracy. Christian missionaries, working in areas not directly controlled by the Estado da India, also created the nuclei for unofficial Portuguese communities, although they recognized the jurisdiction of the *padroado real* in religious matters. Important communities, largely independent of Goa, were formed on the eastern coast of India, notably at São Tomé, the supposed burial place of the apostle Thomas, and in the Bay of Bengal. Portuguese soldiers in the service of Asian rulers were also to be found fighting in Cambodia and Myanmar (Burma) where more or less permanent Portuguese communities were formed by the soldiers and their followers.

The most important of all these independent Portuguese communities were in China and Japan. Macao was founded by traders in 1556 and settlements in Japan, notably at Nagasaki, grew up around the Jesuit missions from the 1570s.

In the seventeenth century, the Dutch and English began to attack the towns of the Estado da India and in the middle years of the seventeenth century captured Ormuz, Muscat, Malacca, Colombo and the Malabar ports. This led to a dispersal of the Portuguese populations of these towns. Many settled down under English or Dutch rule, so that Bombay had a large Portuguese population during its early years, as did the Dutch capital at Batavia. Sri Lanka also had a population which identified as Portuguese. Other Portuguese refugees settled in Indonesia, where Macassar became a center of Portuguese population. In the eastern part of the Indonesian archipelago 'Portuguese' Christian populations survived in Timor and Flores.

By the eighteenth century, although remnants of the old Estado da India survived on the East African coast and in Goa, Diu, and Macao, most of the 'Portuguese' populations in Asia are best described as a separate caste or tribe, distinguished by the use of Portuguese names, adherence to Catholicism, the use of Portuguese creole languages and, strangely, the wearing of hats. Few, if any, of these 'Portuguese' had any connection with Portugal at all and were, in fact, of Asian or African origin and had assumed a 'Portuguese' identity from among the diverse castes and cultures of maritime Asia.

The Portuguese soldiers, merchants, and settlers who had founded so many new communities across the globe had a profound influence on the course of human history. As a result of their activities, what is understood today as globalization had entered its first stage of development. Portuguese had become the first truly global language of maritime commerce and the silver that circulated as a result of Portuguese trade had become the first global currency. Missionaries of the *padroado real* had made Christianity the first truly global religion and Portuguese map-makers had made a scientific understanding of the nature of the world a possibility. For the first time, the products of Asia and the Americas reached global markets, while the food crops of the Americas were beginning to revolutionize the diet of Africans and Europeans and the cattle and horses of the Europeans were transforming the economy of the New World. Moreover, the slave trade, initiated by the Portuguese, constituted the first global migration of labor.

Portuguese Emigration in the Nineteenth and Twentieth Centuries

In the nineteenth century, emigration from Portugal and the Atlantic Islands began to increase again and by the end of the century had become a flood. However, as Miriam Halpern Pereira wrote, migration "came to acquire...new characteristics; it ceased to be predominantly integrated into an imperial project and became the result of distortions in the development of dependence capitalism" (Halpern Pereira, 1981, p7). Portugal had suffered widespread destruction during the Napoleonic Wars. In 1822 Brazil broke away from Portugal, threatening to sever the commercial ties that had kept the Portuguese economy afloat during the previous two hundred years and this was followed by a twenty-five year period, from 1826 to 1851, when there were three civil wars and constant rural unrest. Meanwhile, Madeira, the Azores, and the Cabo Verde Islands suffered from a deteriorating environment, overpopulation, a landowning system that was archaic, and an economy that was either controlled by foreign business or lacked entirely the means to modernize (Carreira 1962).

Driven by desperate poverty, ordinary Portuguese began to emigrate in large numbers. The most popular destination was Brazil where many had family connections and where the language and culture made relocation relatively easy. Most Portuguese immigrants settled in and around the main port cities and sought employment in the retail and commercial sectors.

However, other destinations were becoming increasingly popular.

Portuguese, both from mainland Portugal and the islands, joined the mass migration to the United States. The links between the islands and the United States went back to the time when American whalers called at the Azores and the Cabo Verde Islands to recruit crews. When the whalers returned to the New England ports, Portuguese crew members were paid off and many settled in the country. Family members crossed the Atlantic to join them and, by the end of the century, there were large communities of Azoreans, Cabo Verdians, and mainland Portuguese in many of the towns of New England (Serrão 1981).

Not all this migration was voluntary as there were hidden forms of pressure, and Portuguese emigration played out one of the great ironies of modern history. Portugal had been the biggest single participant in the slave trade from Africa. However, by the nineteenth century one country after another, including Portugal itself, abandoned the slave trade and freed the slave populations in their countries. Contract labor now replaced African slaves in the growing economies of the New World and laborers were sought from Portugal and its Atlantic Islands where there were large numbers of poor and underemployed people willing to be recruited. Agents engaged Portuguese for the Caribbean sugar plantations, for newly settled Hawaii, and for the *fazendas* of Brazil. The conditions under which these contract laborers worked was little better than slavery as the laborers were tied to their employers and could be subject to corporal punishment and other forms of coercion.

The former slavers now found themselves working in very similar conditions to the slaves they had once transported. Many died in unhealthy conditions, but for those who survived, once their contracts ended, there were opportunities to settle and Portuguese communities established themselves in many of the Caribbean countries, notably Trinidad, Bermuda, and Guiana, as well as Hawaii where they came to form a substantial part of the population.

If there is an unavoidable irony in Portuguese contract laborers being recruited to replace slaves who had been freed, there is further irony in the way the Portuguese were treated. Portuguese in the Caribbean and the United States were often considered to be a separate racial group, distinct from Asians and white Europeans. There are two reasons for this; it allowed white planters and colonial officials to treat Portuguese differently from other whites and subject them to a coercion which would not have been possible had they been seen as belonging to the white community. However, this treatment also recognized the fact that many of the Portuguese immigrants, especially from Cabo Verde, were of a mixed racial appearance.

Portuguese emigration reached a peak in the years 1909-1911 when over 200,000 legal emigrants were recorded. Emigrants also sought new destinations and began to settle in Argentina, Uruguay, and Venezuela. Partly this was in response to the United States and Brazil closing the doors to new migrants in the 1920s and 1930s. In the case of the U.S. this was largely racially motivated, in the case of Brazil it was a reflection of the downturn in the world economy (Baganha 1990). After the Second World War when the world's economy began to expand, migrants began to go to Canada and, after the 1952 earthquake in the Azores caused a widespread refugee crisis, the U.S. opened its doors again. In total, 1.6 million emigrated between 1901 and 1961.

However, the most momentous changes were experienced in Europe. There had always been emigration to the countries nearest to Portugal, to Morocco, Gibraltar, and, of course, Spain and France. This migration was often on a seasonal basis with workers returning at the end of short contracts. However, with the formation of the Common Market in 1956, the economies of Germany, France, the Low Countries, and Switzerland all experienced rapid growth. Large numbers of Portuguese came to these countries, not only seeking well-paid jobs but, in the 1960s, trying to escape military service in the colonies. Between 1961 and 1970,

680,000 Portuguese emigrated. Many of these were not permanent migrants and return visits to Portugal and retirement back home were a common feature of this movement. Even so, the numbers who settled permanently in France soon made Paris, after Lisbon, the second biggest 'Portuguese' city in Europe.

In the 1960s, Portuguese immigrants, especially from Madeira, found employment in the tourist industry in Britain and a large population established itself in Jersey as well as the British mainland. The African colonies had never attracted Portuguese migrants because they were penal colonies and had a reputation for being disease-ridden and primitive. However, in the 1950s, encouraged by the Salazar government, increasing numbers went to Angola and Mozambique and from there to South Africa where the growing economy provided job prospects for immigrant people of European origin (Castillo 2007).

A Worldwide Portuguese Community

Over the last hundred and fifty years the movement of populations around the word has created diasporic communities of almost every nationality. The Portuguese diaspora, however, has some unusual features which set it apart, for example, from the Irish or Italians.

First, it was part of a very old process that extended back to the fifteenth century. Seeking employment overseas, at sea, in the Atlantic islands, and in western Africa, and in the commercial cities of the East became part of the life pattern of generations of Portuguese. This emigration deeply marked Portuguese society where women were often left behind and rural parts of Portugal supported populations of widows and single women. Migrants tried to maintain a strong Portuguese identity through the church and other communal institutions and, particularly in recent times, many migrants returned to Portugal to find wives, to claim inheritances or to retire permanently.

The second characteristic was the growth of communities that called themselves 'Portuguese' but with no direct links back to Portugal itself. In West Africa, Sri Lanka, Indonesia, and elsewhere there were 'Portuguese' communities often made up of Catholics of local birth who adopted a Portuguese identity as a way of defining their status and identity in a world where caste was all important. It is not easy to find many parallels to this phenomenon in the diasporas of other European peoples.

A third characteristic is the way in which Portuguese diasporic communities generated their own emigration, independently of what was happening in Portugal. The most obvious example is the Atlantic Islands, settled in the first wave of migration in the fifteenth century, from which emigrants then left to settle in Africa and later, in the nineteenth century, generating a constant emigrant flow to the United States, the Caribbean, Canada, Hawaii, and other destinations.

Another example is provided by Goa. Goa was the capital of the Estado da India and for a century one of the most important commercial ports in India. It was also the ecclesiastical center of the *padroado real* and the base for the missionary orders. A large Christian population became established, made up of Portuguese, their children by Indian women, Indians who converted, slaves, and numerous other people who for one reason and another attached themselves to the Portuguese. By the eighteenth century, the great days of Goa were over and the old city was abandoned for the more healthy site of Panjim. The large Lusitanized population of Goa had achieved a relatively advanced level of education and a medical school had been established. Unable to find employment in the Goan territories, increasing numbers of Goans left for British India and eventually for British colonies in Africa where they occupied clerical and medical positions in the British colonies and enjoyed a status above that of Hindu and Muslim Indians. The Goan diaspora received a fresh impetus when India annexed Goa and the other Portuguese enclaves in 1961.

A Worldwide Community

After the final retreat from empire in 1974-1975, Portugal joined the EU in 1986, following the logic of the tens of thousands of Portuguese who had already settled elsewhere in Europe. But in 1996 the Comunidade dos Países de Língua Portuguesa (CPLP) was founded to bring together the eight members of the United Nations who recognized Portuguese as one of their official languages (Equatorial Guinea joined as a ninth member in 2014). The CPLP was dominated not by Portugal but by Brazil whose size and economic strength exerted a gravitational pull like a large planet. Language was the cement that bound together the members of the CPLP, but also their colonial past and this became more obvious as other countries which had been connected with Portugal in the era of its maritime empire also sought to join or become associate observers, among them Senegal and Morocco and territories such as Macau, Goa, and Malacca which were formerly Portuguese colonies but were now parts of other states.

BIBLIOGRAPHY

For a more extensive bibliography see Edward A. Alpers and Molly Ball, "'Portuguese' Diasporas: a Survey of the Scholarly Literature," in Eric Morier-Genoud and Michel Cahen, *Imperial Migrations. Colonial Communities and Diaspora in the Portuguese World*, Palgrave Macmillan (Basingstoke, 2012), 31–71 and Malyn Newitt, *Emigration and the Sea*, Hurst (London, 2015).

Ames, Glenn, "The Portuguese Province of the North: 'Creole' Power Groups in Urban Centres and their Hinterlands, c.1630-1680," in Philip J. Havik and Malyn Newitt, *Creole Societies in the Portuguese Colonial Empire*, Bristol University, (Bristol, 2007), republished Cambridge Scholars (Newcastle-upon-Tyne, 2015) pp. 212-234.

Baganha, Maria Ioannis, *Portuguese Emigration to the United States 1820–1930*, Garland Publishing (New York, 1990).

Bodian, Miriam, "'Men of the Nation': the Shaping of Converso Identity in Early Modern Europe," *Past and Present*, 143 (1994), pp. 48–76.

——— *Hebrews of the Portuguese Nation: Conversos and Community in Early Modern Amsterdam*, Indiana University Press (Bloomington, 1997).

Brooks, George E., *Eurafricans in Western Africa*, Oxford University Press (Oxford, 2003).

Carreira, António, *The People of the Cape Verde Islands*, Christopher Fyfe, trans., Hurst & Co. (London, 1962).

Castelo, Cláudia, *Passagens para África: O Povoamento de Angola e Moçambique com Naturais da Metrópole* (1920–1974), Edições Afrontamento (Porto, 2007).

Coates, Timothy J., *Convicts and Orphans: Forced and State-Sponsored Colonizers in the Portuguese Empire, 1550–1755*, Stanford University Press (Stanford, CA, 2001).

Curtin, Philip, *The Atlantic Slave Trade: A Census*, University of Wisconsin Press (Madison WI, 1969).

Freyre, Gilberto, *Casa Grande e Senzala* (1933); translated as *The Masters and the Slaves*, Alfred Knopf (New York, 1946).

Garfield, Robert, *A History of São Tomé Island*, Mellen (San Francisco, 1992).

Godinho, Vitorino Magahlães, "L'Emigration portugaise (XVe-XXe siècles), une constante structurale et les réponses aux changements du monde," *Revista de História Económica e Social*, 1, Jan.-June (1978), 5–32.

Green, Toby, *The Rise of the Trans-Atlantic Slave Trade in Western Africa, 1300–1589*, Cambridge University Press (Cambridge, 2012).

Halpern Pereira, Miriam, *A Política Portuguesa de Emigração 1850–1930*, Editora A Regra do Jogo (Lisboa, 1981).

Havik, Philip, "Sóciais, Intermediárias e Empresárias: o Género e a Expansão Colonial na Guiné," in *O Rosto Feminino da Expansão Portuguesa*, 2 vols., Comissão para a Igualdade e para os Direitos das Mulheres (Lisbon, 1995), vol. 2, 87–90.

McNeill, William H., "Human Migration: A Historical Overview," in W. H. McNeill and Ruth S. Adams, *Human Migration Patterns and Policies*, Indiana University Press (Bloomington, 1978), pp. 3–19.

Newitt, Malyn, *History of Mozambique*, Hurst (London, 1995).

Newitt, Malyn, *A History of Portuguese Overseas Expansion 1400-1668*, Routledge (London, 2005).

Newitt, Malyn, *Emigration and the Sea*, Hurst (London, 2015).

Pinto, Alberto Oliveira, *História de Angola*, Mercado de Letras (Lisbon, 2015).

Rodrigues, Eugénia, "Mercadores, Conquistadores e Foreiros: a Construcão dos prazos dos Rios de Cuama na primeira metade do seeculo XVII," J.R. Magalhães et al eds. *Vasco da Gama. Homens, Viagens e Culturas*, CNCDP (Lisbon, 2001) 443-480.

Russell-Wood, A. J. R., "Atlantic Bridge and Atlantic Divide: Africans and Creoles in Late olonial Brazil," in Philip J. Havik and Malyn Newitt, *Creole Societies in the Portuguese Colonial Empire*, Bristol University, (Bristol, 2007), republished Cambridge Scholars (Newcastle-upon-Tyne, 2015) pp. 142-183.

Santos, Maria Emília Madeira, *História Geral de Cabo Verde*, 3 vols., Centro de Estudos de História e Cartografia Antiga and Instituto de Investigação Científica Tropical (Lisbon, 1991–2002).

Saraiva, António José, *A Inquisição Portuguesa*, 3rd edn, Europa-América (Lisboa, 1964).

———*A Inquisição e Cristãos-Novos*, Editorial Nova (Porto, 1969).

Serrão, Joel, *A Emigração Portuguesa: Sondagem Histórica*, 2nd edn, Livros Horizonte (Lisbon, 1974).

Subrahmanyam, Sanjay, *The Portuguese Empire in Asia 1500-1700*, Longman (London, 1993).

Sweet, James H., *Recreating Africa*, University of North Carolina Press (Chapel Hill, NC, 2003).

Thornton, John, *Africa and Africans in the Making of the Atlantic World, 1400-1800*, Cambridge University Press (Cambridge, 1992).

Vieira, Alberto, "A Emigração portuguesa nos Descobrimentos: Do Littoral às Ilhas," *Portuguese Studies Review*, 15, nos. 1–2 (2007), pp. 63–101.

Slave trade database: http://slavevoyages.org/tast/assessment/estimates.faces

MALYN NEWITT taught at the universities of Rhodesia and Exeter where he became Deputy Vice Chancellor. From 1998 until he retired in 2005, he was the Charles Boxer Professor of History at King's College London. A specialist in Portuguese colonial history, he is the author of 20 books on the subject including *A History of* Mozambique (1995) and the recently published *A Short History of Mozambique*.

KEVIN BROWN

The Coolie Trade, 1838–1916: The Migration of Indentured Labor from India and China

Although the British have always liked to think of themselves as exceptional, however unfounded and delusional that may seem at times, any consideration of the migration of government-sponsored indentured labor following the abolition of slavery in the British Empire can only be understood in the context of similar migration patterns from other colonial powers.[1] In the case of the so-called coolie trade from Hong Kong, Portuguese Macau was a major rival to the British for Chinese emigrant labor, and the experience of Macau offers interesting parallels and contrasts to the experience of the British colony. At the same time, the British experience of exporting Chinese laborers to its colonies is only to be understood alongside the contemporary migration of labor from India to the British colonies. Such migration originated from economic needs as European powers built up their colonies and, in order to do so, exploited the availability of non-European peoples who saw migration as a route out of their poverty at home. Whatever their origin, the experiences of forced migrants were very similar.

The abolition of the slave trade in 1807 and of slavery in British colonies in 1833 meant that cheap labor could no longer be bought in Africa and shipped across the Atlantic to the colonies. Sugar planters in the West Indies saw their wealth threatened and put pressure on the British government for aid. Bringing indentured emigrant labor from India, China, and Polynesia to the West Indies, Mauritius, and South America was seen as the solution to this labor shortage. This new trade in the shipment of indentured labor began in 1834 when 41,056 workers sailed from Bengal to Mauritius.

European emigrants were generally not considered suitable for labor on plantations in the tropics (except as overseers) because of their delicate constitutions, whereas Africans were seen as much more resilient in the heat and so suitable for heavy plantation work.[2] However, with emancipation came the question of how to ensure a good supply of labor suited to work in sultry climates. In many respects, the resulting system of indentured labor differed little from the slavery system it replaced, but it greatly differed from previous systems of indentured labor in the British colonies, where many of the men on contract were white overseers or skilled tradesmen rather than replacements for slaves. Prospective workers now signed up for a fixed period of five to eight years, during which time they were supposed to receive a monthly wage, housing, food, and clothing. At the end of their first or second term of service, they were entitled to receive tickets home, paid for by their employers. During the period of their indentures, they may as well have been slaves. Nevertheless, many of the Indian migrants who had returned home after their first or second terms subsequently remigrated, often bringing new recruits with them. Other indentured laborers never returned home but settled in Mauritius, British Guiana, Trinidad, and Natal, creating substantial and visible Indian communities that reflected the burgeoning internationalization of the imperial labor market.[3]

Many of the early indentured laborers later complained that they had been lured on board ship under false pretenses. J. P. Woodcock, a Bombay civil servant, was a passenger on the *Drongan*, sailing to Mauritius in 1841, on a voyage lasting two months. According to him, the ship was carrying "a cargo of rice and sixty-six Coolies," and he commented that "Mauritius was described to them in glowing terms, and advantage taken of their ignorance to provoke the belief that every necessary of life was cheap, labour light, and that the voyage would only occupy them ten days." According to observers on the *Whitby* in 1838, many of "the men appeared to have no conception as to where they were going and the length of the voyage; they said they had been told...that they were to go on board for two or three days, and then land and march the remainder of their journey."[4]

The reality of conditions on board was a shock to these men, who came from "every variety of caste from the Brahmin to the Choman" and were mixed together without any sensitivity toward the caste system.[5] In particular, many of the coolies "complained of being seduced from their own country by fine promises; and, they had no idea, when they consented to come down, that they would of necessity lose caste."[6] Clearly, they were considered less valuable than the other cargo on board. Woodcock noted that "the lower decks of the *Drongan* were stowed with rice, and the Coolies were disposed in the waist between the gangways and the forecastle, where, if the weather had not been remarkably fine, they might have suffered, being unprotected from every change of weather."[7] In many instances "the proper allowance of food for the voyage has not been provided, medical inspection [had] not taken place previous to embarkation, nor medical attendance been furnished during the voyage," all of which contributed to the coolies' unhappiness.[8]

As early as 1837, Thomas Fowell Buxton and Lord Brougham, politicians prominent in the abolition of slavery, were condemning such abuses in the system. As a result, in 1838, the East India Company banned any further shipments of coolies. J. P. Grant, a member of the committee appointed to investigate the conditions under which the coolies were being shipped and employed, pressed for legislation to regulate the system so that emigration would be restricted to particular ports and supervised by a protector of emigrants. In 1842, an Order in Council provided for the appointment of responsible emigration agents in India and a protector of immigrants in Mauritius. In 1844, emigration to Jamaica, British Guiana, and Trinidad was also sanctioned. All laborers had to satisfy a magistrate that they had chosen to emigrate and understood their contracts. During the next decade 107,000 coolies were sent through the agency of East Indies government officers, mainly from Calcutta, to Mauritius.[9]

Before embarkation, the coolies were herded together in guarded depots so that they would not attempt to escape after having signed their contracts and where they could be examined by the protector of emigrants, who was charged with ensuring that they were well-looked-after, fed, and adequately clothed ahead of the long voyage. All laborers were weighed, and a record was kept of whether they had gained or lost weight during their stay in the depot.[10] Note was taken of "the slender form, lank limbs and obvious muscular weakness of most natives of India, as contrasted with Europeans."[11] A native doctor was employed to check the emigrants for signs of venereal disease or ruptures before they were examined by the ship's medical officer. It was also the responsibility of the protector of emigrants to make sure that the ship was seaworthy before it sailed.

In a large number of cases, the desire of families to emigrate together meant that sick or ailing emigrants and young children got through the medical inspections held just before embarkation. The able-bodied coolies would not leave their families behind, so the old and infirm were allowed to embark; otherwise, there would have been very few emigrants. When typhoid and dysentery killed ten men, eight women, and six children on the *Wellesley* on its voyage from Calcutta to Demerara in 1856, "it is believed that the evil originated in the depot at Calcutta," though the emigration agent, the assistant protector of emigrants, and the medical officer at the depot claimed that, "with the exception of a few old people, who were objected to, but embarked in consequence of their being members of families, the coolies were fair average lots, and in good health at the time of leaving Calcutta." Similarly when cholera struck aboard the *Bucephalus* a few weeks later, soon after it had sailed from Calcutta, officials argued that this was unrelated to conditions at the depot:

> The occurrence of cholera in the passage down the river is no proof that the emigrants were in a bad state of health when they embarked, as similar outbreaks of that inscrutable malady have happened in troop ships, and vessels of all kinds and class, among robust healthy Europeans, strong bodied Lascar crews, pilgrims to Mecca, and even in boats with natives on board, who constantly live on the river, and are proof against all the ordinary exhalations and miasmata incident to its banks.[12]

As the nineteenth century progressed, there was more rigorous selection at the depots, and increasing numbers of emigrants were rejected on medical grounds. In 1894, the protector of emigrants noted in his report that, out of 26,707 registered emigrants, only 14,865 actually embarked for the colonies. The few not dismissed on health grounds ran away, frightened by the harshness of the depot, where the slightest hint of infection could change it into "a place of sickness and death."[13] By 1897, the protector of migrants at Port-au-Prince could comment that "the immigrants that have arrived this year are an exceptionally good lot and indicate a more careful selection at Calcutta."[14]

Depots known as barracoons (a term originally used in the African slave trade for the enclosures in which the slaves were confined) were also established in Hong Kong and the Chinese ports for the collection of coolies before embarkation. Compared to the government-sponsored depots in India, conditions here were more akin to those that slaves had experienced. Once in the barracoons, the emigrants were sold to shipping companies or ship captains at so much a head and marked with a stamped or painted letter on their breasts to indicate their destination, such as C for California or P for Peru.[15] Since 1855, the Chinese Passengers Act had laid down that all British ships carrying passengers from Chinese ports should be inspected by an emigration officer to ensure that the migrants were emigrating of their free will and the ships were well ventilated and free of disease.[16] Yet the barracoons remained full of unwilling emigrants, kidnapped or conned into making unwitting agreements; and despite successive measures to stop abuses, the exploitation of the coolies remained a scandal. Emigrant brokers were required to be licensed and bonded, the barracoons had to be licensed and be operated under rules laid down by the governor of Hong Kong, permits were necessary for passengers and ships, and contract laborers leaving from Hong Kong could only be taken to British colonies.[17] Nevertheless, regulation of contract emigration from Hong Kong remained weak because the West Indian planters needed labor, and the city's merchants were involved in the supply and fitting up of ships sailing not only from the British colony of Hong Kong but also from Portuguese Macau and mainland China.[18]

Before the Opium War of 1839–42, Canton had been the only trading port open to foreign traders and served as imperial China's main point of contact with Europe. It had also developed as a center for emigration, at first mainly to Southeast Asia via Macau but later, after 1848, also to California and Peru. In the early years of the coolie trade, the Cantonese authorities had not interfered with emigration, which was openly advertized, but by the 1860s kidnapping by crimps was becoming common. Governor-General Lalou in Canton feared that this increase in enforced emigration was the "offspring of the receiving ship system." Smaller boats would deliver emigrants to receiving ships anchored off the coast. In 1859, there were three receiving ships flying the U.S. flag moored at Whampoa, the deep-water anchorage downstream from Canton, as well as individual vessels registered in Peru, Oldenburg, and the Netherlands. All of them acted as feeders for the barracoons of Macau. If an emigrant received by one of these ships insisted that he had been kidnapped, he would be returned to the crimps and tortured so brutally that, when presented to another ship, he would be too terrified of the crimps not to embark.[19]

Local Cantonese mobs, outraged by the growth in the number of kidnappings, took the law into their own hands if they found a crimp attempting to coerce someone into emigrating, often lynching or beating him to death.[20] As a result of pressure from the West, Peh-kwei, the governor of the province of Kwangtung, not only made kidnapping an offence punishable by death but also took the radical step of authorizing voluntary emigration for anyone compelled by poverty to seek work overseas. This was a complete reversal of the imperial government's long-standing policy but meant that an attempt could be made to prevent the horrors of the crimping system. Yet, as long as shipments of emigrants continued without adequate supervision at Macau and Hong Kong, crimps remained active.

At Macau, the Portuguese authorities attempted to enact ordinances to check these abuses committed by the crimps. In 1853, Governor Isidoro Francisco

Guimarães imposed sanitary regulations for both ships and depots and decreed that any emigrants rejected on the grounds of ill-health or old age should be returned to their homes at the expense of the crimps. In 1855, he directed that all contracts of emigration should be registered and that all emigrants should be inspected on shore by the procurator and on ship by the harbormaster. In 1856, he required all emigration brokers to be licensed. Nonetheless, he admitted to John Bowring, the governor of Hong Kong, that it was almost impossible to eliminate the existing abuses so long as the crimps remained in control of the business of emigration.[21]

In 1860, Guimarães created the post of superintendent of emigration at Macau, who was paid by the government and independent of vested interests. Moreover, he insisted that emigrants should not be confined to the barracoons but must be free to enter and leave as they wished. The British consul Charles Winchester was impressed by the Macau barracoons, calling them "exceedingly well arranged and worthy of imitation," Their 480 occupants were "stout men and boys well lodged and well clothed and looking clean and comfortable."[22] Nevertheless, the barracoons in Macau continued to be heavily guarded by sentries with heavy clubs.

Furthermore, the 1866 Emigration Convention signed by China, the United Kingdom, and France limited emigration to the treaty ports and prohibited emigrants from going to any country that did not have diplomatic relations with China. This should have ruled out trade from the Portuguese colony of Macau, but it continued to be a center of emigration for Chinese going to South America. Finally, in 1874, pressure from the Chinese government led to a Portuguese ban on emigration from Macau. Jui-lin, the governor of Kwangtung, had demanded the immediate closing of the Macau barracoons in 1873 after his war junks on patrol in the waters between Canton and Macau had stopped three ships with sixty kidnapped Chinese emigrants and the Portuguese captains had admitted to working for the barracoons.[23] Jui-lin had responded by issuing a proclamation warning against kidnapping and had blamed the Portuguese for this abuse.[24] The ending of emigration from Portuguese Macau removed a major rival to Britain's trade in Chinese emigrant labor.

For emigrants embarking for a new world, whether from India or China, the journey was painfully long. The average length of the voyage from Calcutta or Bombay to the West Indies was twenty weeks. The voyage took nineteen weeks from Madras, with ships usually calling at Cape of Good Hope and Saint Helena en route. Ships took twelve weeks to travel from Calcutta to Natal and ten weeks from Calcutta to Mauritius. Voyages from Hong Kong to Peru took about 110 days; to the West Indies, about 120 days. Steamers could have shortened these journeys by ten to twenty days, but the shipowners saw no profit in using newer or faster ships.[25] Often the coolies had no idea how long they would be at sea or indeed that they would be so far from land. Rahman Khan, travelling to Surinam in 1898, "had the impression that land would be more or less visible throughout our journey" but soon realized he was wrong. Succumbing to seasickness, he noted that "many of us became dizzy and had to vomit."[26]

The ships on which the Indian coolies sailed were more crowded and less comfortable than the ships on which European emigrants sailed to the Americas and Australia. It was widely accepted that the coolies were not accustomed to western ways and comforts and so did not need them.[27] There was little concern about how they would use most efficiently the limited space available to them. Women and children slept on bamboo-work platforms raised three feet above the deck, while the men slept below them on the deck. Western observers saw this as an unhealthy arrangement, claiming that "Indian women and children are more dirty in their personal habits than the men of the same race, and, their sleeping above the men must have been productive of nuisances injurious to health and destructive of cleanliness."[28] Don Aldus, a writer and adventurer, traveling on a coolie ship from Macau to Havana in the 1860s, noted that "each shelf simply represented one hundred and fifty in a bed." While the legal minimum of sleeping space allotted to each man was between twenty and twenty-four inches, "they are not over particular in this matter as they seldom exceed twenty one inches."[29] The space was enough to allow a passenger to lie on his back in discomfort. The 1852 Passenger Act regulation that British ships could carry only one passenger for every two tons registered was generally ignored, and the governor of Hong Kong admitted that any attempts to enforce this provision would drive shipping to non-British ports, to the detriment of the city's trade. Pressure from shipowners led to an 1853 amendment to the Act that allowed for "twelve instead of fifteen superficial feet to be sufficient space for natives of Asia and Africa who may be conveyed from Hong Kong through the Tropics."[30]

Ships transporting Chinese coolies from Hong Kong to South America were invariably cargo vessels modified for the purpose in a very similar manner to slave ships: "they are (to use the phrase known in slave ships) 'packed and sold,' and merely 'paddy' (unclean rice) and oil put on board for their food."[31] In Joseph Conrad's novella *Typhoon* (1899), Captain McWhirr, who is shipping two hundred Chinese coolies home from Southeast Asia, merely mirrors the views of many real-life captains when he says he has "never heard of coolies spoken of as passengers before." He regards them as little more than the sacks of rice and other commodities also crammed below deck.[32]

European tastes in food rarely appealed to Indians; observers thought that the Bengalese coolies suffered when fed on sea biscuits because they were more used to rice, just "as is often the case with Irish and Scotch Emigrants who have been accustomed to potatoes."[33] Moreover, these dry biscuits were considered "not suitable food for a woman nursing, as bread is considered most injurious for all emigrants, as being the main cause of bringing on dysentery." Rice and dried fish would have been acceptable to many of the passengers, but sago was more common, and most disliked it. There was also the danger that emigrants would eat too much at mealtimes or "hide what they cannot eat, and, before they eat it, it turns sour, and brings on diarrhoea; though every means were used to prevent them hiding any."[34]

Some British government tenders stipulated that salt fish, chilies, dal, ghee, and spices such as turmeric and tamarind should be carried on board to make the food palatable to the tastes of the emigrants and that dry provisions should be stocked for use when cooking was impossible in bad weather.[35] The supply of tinned milk was considered especially important for infants because, "from sea sickness, the unaccustomed life at sea and the total change in their habits, women, with children at the breast, rapidly lose, and, in the majority instances, do not again recover their milk."[36] Tinned mutton was provided in lieu of carrying live sheep on board because "the pens take up valuable space; the urine and dung get under the pens and are hard to remove and become very offensive."[37]

On ships carrying Chinese coolies, rice, tea, and salt fish and meat were supplied to the emigrants, which they could cook in their own fashion in "smelting pots" set up as communal galleys on the upper deck. However, this food soon became putrid, and diarrhea and scurvy were a common result. Some ships took on fresh vegetables and live pigs and sheep at ports en route; but for emigrants accustomed to lifelong starvation, a sudden change to a plentiful diet often caused dysentery, which they were unable to fight, given their weakened and emaciated state.[38]

Water supplies were as inadequate as the food, and the situation was made worse by the difficulties of obtaining fresh water in Indian and Chinese ports. Water was often taken on board at Anjer, Cape Hope, and Saint Helena. To conserve these supplies, passengers were rationed to between a pint and a gallon a day. Water was stored in casks with reeds inserted in them, which emigrants used as straws when they wanted a drink. On one ship, the water supplies were treated twice a week with six gallons of port wine and one gallon of "anti-scorbutic medicine." Officials claimed this prevented scurvy and wrote that the emigrants drank it with "great avidity and enjoyment."[39]

Ships from China were heavily armed to keep the passengers under control. The movement of passengers from the between-decks to the main deck was controlled by crossed iron bars, arched in the center with a small opening at the top, fitted over the hatchways. The hatches leading to the provisions stores of tea, fish, and rice in the hold were surrounded by iron bars fitted to both decks to prevent theft, and also serve as cages for armed guards in the event of a mutiny. The captain's cabin was protected by a barricade firmly bolted to the deck with sixteen-pound cannons poking through the defenses. This defensive structure resembled a "floating menagerie for wild beasts," and from it a small number of guards could command the entire deck and subdue the passengers.[40]

Crews sailing in the China seas had long feared piracy, and they widely believed that Chinese pirates were volunteering as emigrants to South America in order to hijack the ship.[41] As a result, "in the *Fei Ma*, the Chinese passengers are put down in the hold twelve feet deep and the ladder is taken away" while "a sailor keeps guard over them with a drawn cutlass." Similarly, "one of the Yankee ships has an iron cage on deck into which the Chinese passengers are invited to walk and are then locked up." There was only one way to feel secure from hijacking: "the Peninsular and Orient boat has a better but more costly precaution; she carries no Chinese passengers."[42]

There was a real danger of mutiny on these ships. Between 1850 and 1872 there were at least sixty-eight mutinies on ships carrying Chinese contract laborers bound for Cuba, Peru, British Guiana, Australia, India, and the United States. Some of the mutineers had been effectively kidnapped; others regretted having agreed to emigrate; some were reacting to the harsh treatment they received on board; a small number wished merely to plunder the ship.[43] E. Holden, a passenger on the *Norway*, which was carrying 1,038 Chinese laborers to Cuba in 1859, witnessed a mutiny in which the participants wrote, in blood, their demand to be taken to Siam. After an initial attack on the crew was repulsed, they attempted to set the ship on fire:

> The foiled wretches, maddened at defeat from the outset, rushed with furious yells from one hatch to another, swinging lighted firebrands or striving

> to wrench away the iron bars that covered them, or hurling bolts and clubs at every face that peered down at them from above. The red glare of the flames lit up the sky, reflecting grimly against the swelling sails, and in spite of a constant stream of water from the pumps seemed scarcely to diminish.[44]

As in the heyday of slavery, floggings were a common punishment. On ships carrying Chinese emigrants, they were also used as a deterrent to mutiny. A dozen lashes were given for smoking below deck, theft, or illegal gambling. Up to two dozen were given for perjury, fighting, or "depositing filth between decks." The worst punishments were reserved for challenges to authority: "any coolie or coolies discovered conspiring to mutiny, shall, when found guilty, be punished with the cats not exceeding four dozens and afterwards be handcuffed and chained to the ringbolts of the deck during the master's pleasure."[45]

A more effective way of keeping the coolies under control was to keep them "employed in any way to prevent them from thinking and drooping." Chinese coolies were notorious for spending their time on deck playing dominoes and cards, but arguments over gambling often ended in fighting. Music served as an alternative entertainment, with passengers playing one-stringed violins, clarinets, cymbals, gongs, drums, and trumpets. Sometimes these instruments were provided as part of a ship's equipment, but many passengers brought along their own.[46] On the *Salsette*, traveling from Calcutta to Trinidad in 1858, Captain Swinton and his wife Jane "found exercise, such as their native dances, very useful in keeping up a good state of health—an experiment which we tried. Music is also very desirable." However, they took care not to encourage immorality among the younger passengers, who "have no morality whatever: if they fancy each other they become man and wife for the time being, and change again when they please."[47]

Keeping the passengers entertained depended very much on the cultural characteristics of different groups of coolies. Emigrants from the Madras area were seen as sociable and eager to be involved in what was happening on board: "The Madrasee is a lively, singing merry fellow, who delights in remaining on deck, seldom stays below if he can help it, day or night, is always ready to bear a hand in pulling ropes or any other work going on in the ship, and is much less troubled with prejudices of any kind."[48] In contrast, emigrants from Bengal were seen as much less cheerful and active: "The Bengali is so much given to remaining below that compulsion is necessary to bring him on deck. He rapidly gives way to sea sickness and depression; when taken ill, always imagines that he must die; and remains in an apathetic state of torpid indifference, the very reversal of the mercurial propensities of the Malabar."[49] Europeans also applied such crude racial stereotyping to Chinese migrants. Jane Swinton preferred Indian coolies to the Chinese, whom she considered "a most determined and self-willed people, who thought a great deal of their joss, and were quite opposed to the others in character."[50]

Much depended upon the attitude of the captain and his crew to the passengers. It was in his interest to look after the migrants because the death of a coolie represented a loss of £13 from the shipowners' charter money as colonial authorities in Trinidad would only pay for coolies who landed alive.[51] Jane Swinton believed that it was "most unjust and illiberal to the owners of any Coolie-ship to be paid only for such as are landed alive, particularly when put on board in such a diseased state by the emigration office in Calcutta." She questioned "Why have one law for our Indian emigrants to the West India colonies, and another for our English emigrants to Australia?"[52] Yet the same system also applied to ships carrying Chinese emigrants.[53]

On British government–sponsored ships, as on emigrant ships from Britain to Australia, a qualified surgeon superintendent was always on board. The captain of a chartered ship was required to "on all occasions, when practicable, attend to any of the suggestions of the surgeon calculated to promote the health, comfort or well-being of the emigrants."[54] The surgeon superintendent was in charge of the coolies and responsible for keeping them under control and healthy. Inevitably, many of these appointees were not always of the highest quality. European doctors considered service on a coolie ship to be demeaning. Surgeons on these ships were also less well paid than their equivalents on government-assisted passages to Australia because the West Indian colonies could not afford such generous fees. Barbados officials recognized that "there can be no question as to the advantage of employing competent surgeons on board emigrant vessels...but I fear that the adoption of the Emigrant Commissioners' [advice]" to increase their remuneration and recruit a superior class of surgeon "would very materially increase the expenses of emigration, already high."[55]

As a result, many Indian-born and -educated doctors took these posts, and European officers and even Indian crew members tended to look down on them. Robert Sinclair, the surgeon superintendent on the *India*, shipping coolies from Calcutta to British Guiana in 1879, made himself unpopular with the captain and crew when trying to carry out his duties:

> It was mainly in insisting on the rights of the emigrants in my charge and endeavouring to control abuses that I got myself into disfavour with the crew and others aboard. The simple fact is that the commander and officers could not control the crew in their ill-treatment of the emigrants, the crew being an unruly lot, recruited from the back slums of Calcutta, and utterly beyond restraint; and their repugnance to me, in my efforts to defend the emigrants from their ill-treatment, is the surest proof of my determination not to tolerate abuses in spite of the odds against me.[56]

Sinclair was scorned as a "native surgeon," but highly placed government officials supported him in denying this label: "the Lieutenant Governor cannot understand how Mr Sinclair is spoken of as a native. He is in appearance a decidedly fair European, though his education was received in the Calcutta Medical College."[57]

Not all surgeon superintendents were as determined as Sinclair to stand up for their status and the rights of their charges. On the *Bucephalus*, "the surgeon was a mere boy, and unfit to be entrusted with so serious a duty." A fellow doctor commented on his inexperience: "I knew him during the whole period of his study in the Medical College of Calcutta and am aware that he was a lad of ability who was well acquainted with his profession; but I should not on that account have considered it right to entrust him with the management of so large a body of emigrants" as the 389 on board the *Bucephalus* in 1856. One of the reasons for sickness among the coolies was "the excessive and mistaken kindness which induced the surgeon to allow the people to remain below the greater part of the voyage."[58]

Although native surgeon superintendents were despised as inferior to European doctors, many did have the advantage of being able to speak to their charges in their own language depending upon which part of India they came from. On the *Blue Jacket* in 1857, "the surgeon was well accustomed to the management of natives and spoke their language fluently."[59] The ships did carry interpreters, known as *sirdars* or *chokedars*, who were essential for communication between the surgeon superintendent and the coolies. An Indian apothecary could be a helpful intermediary between the doctor and his charges, especially in helping them overcome prejudices against western medicines. Otherwise, "the ship [had to] be supplied with the herbs used by the natives in sickness, as it is next to an impossibility to get them to take our medicine."[60]

Chinese migrants were also suspicious of western medicine and preferred to treat dysentery, scurvy, dropsy, fever, and opium withdrawal with traditional

Chinese remedies. Although from the 1850s onward, emigrant ships were supposed to have qualified surgeons, a hospital, and adequate medical supplies, these regulations were often ignored. In many cases, the only doctors who could be obtained were Chinese practitioners unfamiliar with European medicine who often extorted money from the sick in return for favors or opium.[61]

Without coolie emigration from India and China, there undoubtedly would have been severe labor shortages in the colonies and in South America. Such emigration was also accepted by the Indian government as a safety valve for those of its people who could not be provided with work at home. However, by the beginning of the twentieth century, there was growing concern about the exploitation of Indian migrants. Within a year of his 1898 appointment as viceroy of India, Lord Curzon refused a petition from Caribbean planters for the general abolition of the Indian laborers' right to free return passage at the end of their five-year contracts. Meanwhile, the indentured community was protesting against some of the abuses of the system. In Natal, resistance was led by the young Indian lawyer Mohandas Gandhi, who convinced the Indian public that emigration was detrimental rather than beneficial for India. His fellow campaigner, the lawyer Henry Polak, described the treatment of Indians in South Africa as "a record of shame and cruelty that has no counterpart within the confines of the British Empire."[62]

The British government favored reform of the indenture system rather than its abolition. Joseph Chamberlain, Secretary of State for the Colonies, asserted in 1897 the right of the self-governing colonies to control the influx of Indian and Chinese migrants who were "alien in civilization, alien in religion, alien in customs" but insisted that it was necessary "also to bear in mind the traditions of the Empire, which makes no distinction in favour of, or against, race and colour."[63] Nevertheless, the days of the indenture system were numbered, thanks to a combination of exclusionist policies among the white dominions, rising Indian and Chinese nationalism, and the changing world economy in the aftermath of the First World War. Falls in the profits of sugar plantations made the importation of contract laborers less commercially viable, especially now that there was a pool of settled labor in those colonies. In 1916, indentured emigration was banned by the government of India, bringing to an end a far from glorious period of imperial migration but one in which the coolie ships had built up the economy of the British Empire and fostered a multicultural world.[64]

Conclusion

Portugal had ceased to be a major rival to Britain for Chinese emigrant labor since 1874, but there had been many similarities in its approach to the shipping of indentured labor with that adopted by the British in sending both Indian and Chinese coolies to its colonies. In many ways the treatment of the indentured laborers had differed little from the methods adopted by the defunct slave trade, most notably in the use of depots based on the barracoons of the slavers. In attempting to check the notorious abuses perpetrated by the crimps in Macau, the Portuguese authorities in the 1860s instituted the post of superintendent of emigration, which was very similar to the role of the protector of emigrants for Indian migrants. Very little consideration was given to the cultural and social customs and beliefs of the migrants, whether Indian or Chinese, in the rush for the cheapest transportation. Just as in the slave trade, the well-being of the migrants was a secondary consideration to their economic worth. The main difference between the Indian and Chinese experience was that the British ruled in India, whereas the colonial officials in both British Hong Kong and Portuguese Macau had to comply, sometimes reluctantly, with Imperial Chinese policies on the mainland. Whereas in India the British controlled the indentured labor market and its shipping, whether privately owned or state-sponsored, in China the trade in indentured labor was more international in nature with vessels of the United States, Germany, the Netherlands, and Peru all acting as feeders for Macau. Any consideration of the coolie trade has to look beyond national boundaries for it to be seen in its wider context in colonial development, just as its impact was to be multicultural.

NOTES

1. This essay revisits material discussed in Kevin Brown, *Passage to the World: The Emigrant Experience, 1807–1940*. Seaforth (Barnsley, 2013), 113–35.

2. J. Lind, *An Essay on Diseases Incidental to Europeans in Hot Climates* (1808), p. 8; J. Hunter, *Observations on Diseases of the Army in Jamaica and on the Best Means of Preserving the Health of Europeans in that Climate* (1788), p. 24.

3. I. M. Crumpson, 'A Survey of Indian Immigration to British Tropical Colonies to 1910', *Population Studies* 10 (1956), 158–65.

4. House of Commons Papers, 1841, vol. 16, p. 60, 1841

5. British and Foreign Anti-Slavery Society, *Emigration from India: The Export of Coolies and Other Labourers to Mauritius* (1842), p.33.

6. House of Commons Papers, 1841, vol. 16, p. 60, 1841

7. Ibid., p. 31.

8. Ibid., p. 33.

9. K. Brown, *Passage to the World: The Emigrant Experience 1807–1940* (2013), p. 118.

10. TNA, CO 384/107, register of emigrants waiting to board *Golden Fleece, British Empire, Essex, Brechin Castle* and *St. James* at Trinidad Depot, 1874.

11. TNA, Co 318/218, Report on Mortality of Emigrant Coolies on the Voyage to the West Indies, 1856–7.

12. TNA, Co 318/218, Report on Mortality of Emigrant Coolies on the Voyage to the West Indies, 1856–7.

13. H. Tinker, *A New System of' Slavery* (1974), p. 141

14. TNA, CO 295/387, Report of W.H. Combes, Protector of Migrants, Port-au-Spain, 7 January 1897.

15. TNA, FO 17/873, letter from Mayers to Alcock, 1 November 1866.

16. Ibid., FO 97/101, Chinese Passengers Act, 1855.

17. Ibid., FO 17/877, Foreign Office to Governor of Hong Kong, 14 December 1869.

18. A.J. Meagher, *The Coolie Trade* (2008), pp. 105–6.

19. Ibid.

20. TNA, FO 881/894, letter from Alcock to Bowring, 12 April 1859.

21. Ibid., FO 97/102A, letter from John Bowring to Lord Clarendon, 27 June 1856.

22. Ibid, FO 97/1023, letter from C.A. Winchester to J. Bowring, 22 July 1855.

23. Ibid., FO 17/882, letter from Robertson to Wade, 23 April 1873.

24. Ibid., FO 881/2445, proclamation against kidnapping, 6 August 1873.

25. TNA, FO 97/102B, letter from Parkes to Hammond, 21 May 1860.

26. R. Khan, *Autobiography of an Indian Indentured Labourer* (2005), p. 83.

27. 'Indian Emigration', *Chambers Journal*, 43 (1866), 395. 394–7.

28. TNA, Co 318/218, Report on Mortality of Emigrant Coolies on the Voyage to the West Indies, 1856–7.

29. D. Aldus, *Coolie Traffic and Kidnapping* (1876), p, 31.

30. A.J. Meagher, *The Coolie Trade* (2008), pp. 155.

31. Captain and Mrs Swinton, *Journal of a Voyage with Coolie Emigrants from Calcutta to Trinidad* (1859), p. 16.

32. J. Conrad, *Typhoon* (2003), p.23.

33. TNA, Co 318/220, letter from J.W. Murdoch to H. Merrivale, 11 August 1858.

34. Captain and Mrs Swinton, *Journal of a Voyage with Coolie Emigrants from Calcutta to Trinidad* (1859), p. 13.

35. TNA, CO 318/165, Dietary Scale for Emigrants from India to the West Indies, 1845.

36. TNA, Co 318/218, Report on Mortality of Emigrant Coolies on the Voyage to the West Indies, 1856–7.

37. TNA, CO 295/387, Report of W.H. Combes, Protector of Migrants, Port-au-Spain, 7 January 1897.

38. TNA, FO 881/744, Report to Emigration Commissioners, 10 December 1853.

39. D. Aldus, *Coolie Traffic and Kidnapping* (1876), p. 325.

40. Ibid., p. 46.

41. W. Speer, *The Oldest and the Newest Empire* (1870), p. 483.

42. G.W. Cooke, *China and Lower Bengal* (1861), 67.

43. A.J. Meagher, *The Coolie Trade* (2008), pp. 176–7.

44. E. Holden, 'A Chapter on the Coolie Trade', *Harper's New Monthly Magazine*, 29/169 (June 1864), 7.

45. D. Aldus, *Coolie Traffic and Kidnapping* (1876), pp. 51–2.

46. E. Holden, 'A Chapter on the Coolie Trade', *Harper's New Monthly Magazine*, 29/169 (June 1864), 5.

47. Captain and Mrs Swinton, *Journal of a Voyage with Coolie Emigrants from Calcutta to Trinidad* (1859), p. 14.

48. TNA, Co 318/218, Report on Mortality of Emigrant Coolies on the Voyage to the West Indies, 1856–7.

49. Ibid.

50. Captain and Mrs Swinton, *Journal of a Voyage with Coolie Emigrants from Calcutta to Trinidad* (1859), p. 14.

51. Ibid., p. 4.

52. Ibid., p. 15.

53. TNA, FO 97/102B, Testimony of Doctor on the Norwegian ship *Norma*, 1860.

54. TNA, Co 318/165, tender for the conveyance of Indian emigrants to the West Indies, 1845.

55. TNA, CO 101/117/28, dispatch from Lieutenant Governor Cartwright to the Governor of Barbados, 1 June 1861.

56. TNA, CO 318/261, Report on Mortality among Indian Emigrants Shipped from Calcutta to British Guiana, statement of Robert Sinclair, 15 March 1879.

57. Ibid, Lieutenant Governor's Comments, 15 March 1879.

58. TNA, Co 318/218, Report on Mortality of Emigrant Coolies on the Voyage to the West Indies, 1856–7.

59. Ibid.

60. Captain and Mrs Swinton, *Journal of a Voyage with Coolie Emigrants from Calcutta to Trinidad* (1859), p. 13.

61. D. Aldus, *Coolie Traffic and Kidnapping* (1876), p. 218.

62. H. Polak, *The Indians of South Africa* (1909), p. 90.

63. Proceedings of a Conference between the Secretary of State for the Colonies and the Premiers of the Self Governing Colonies, June and July 1897, C 8596, 1897, p. 12.

64. D. Northrup, *Indentured Labour in the Age of Imperialism, 1834–1922* (1995), p. 145.

KEVIN BROWN is an authority on the history of medicine, most recently concentrating on medicine and health at sea, and is the author of *Passage to the World: The Emigrant Experience 1807-1940*. A graduate of Hertford College, University of Oxford, and University College, London, he is Trust Archivist to Imperial College Healthcare NHS Trust and Alexander Fleming Laboratory Museum Curator at St Mary's Hospital, London, a museum and archives which he established. He was Chairman of the London Museums of Health and Medicine (2001-04) and is a Trustee of the charity St Mary's Hospital Association. He was awarded a Gladstone's Library Scholarship. He has lectured widely in the United Kingdom, Italy, Spain, Germany, Belgium, and the United States.

Essays

ANDRÉ NÓVOA

Sailors & Whalers: Forerunners of Portuguese Labor Migration to North America?[1]

The sea, the snotgreen sea, the scrotumtightening sea
–James Joyce, Ulysses

ABSTRACT: This paper sheds light on the importance of whaling paths and stations in the migration of Portuguese laborers to North America. Even though there are many factors influencing these migratory trails—the attraction that a country like the U.S. had on most prospective migrants in the 1800s, the American economic and political influence which made it a convergence point globally, and its geographical position—this study demonstrates that the Portuguese sailors and whalers, who were active in the Pacific and Atlantic North in the nineteenth century in search of turning a profit and better living conditions, can be seen as pioneers of sorts, having played a role in blazing the paths and trails for the Portuguese who followed. It is not a historical coincidence that the places where the Portuguese established themselves were precisely the places frequented years before by Portuguese whalers and fishing sailors. This line of analysis puts mobility first as an important theoretical and analytical tool to reveal the causes and consequences of migration.

KEYWORDS: mobility, whaling, ocean, nineteenth century

RESUMO: Este artigo lança luz sobre a importância dos percursos de baleação e respetivos portos na migração de trabalhadores portugueses para a América do Norte. Embora existam certamente muitos fatores que influenciaram tais migrações – nomeadamente a atração que um país como os EUA gerou na maioria dos migrantes do século XIX, ou o facto de os EUA serem um ponto de convergência global devido à sua influência político-económica, ou mesmo o seu posicionamento geográfico – este estudo demonstra que os baleeiros Portugueses, ativos no Pacífico e no Atlântico no século XIX, podem ser vistos como uma espécie de pioneiros, tendo desempenhado um papel fundamental na abertura de trilhos migratórios para aqueles que se seguiram. Não deve ser entendida como uma mera coincidência histórica que os locais onde os Portugueses se estabeleceram foram precisamente aqueles mais frequentemente visitados anos antes por baleeiros. Esta linha de análise coloca a mobilidade em primeiro lugar, como uma importante ferramenta teórica e analítica para revelar as causas e consequências da migração.

PALAVRAS-CHAVE: mobilidade, baleação, baleeiros, oceanos, século XIX

Introduction

In this article, we look at the influence that several whaling paths and stations had on the migration of Portuguese[2] laborers into North America. Naturally, this does not diminish other important factors, such as the demand for workforce, the attraction that a country like the US caused on most prospective migrants in the 1800s, the American economic and political influence which made it a convergence point globally, and its geographical positioning. These factors played a decisive role in luring and drawing Portuguese migrants into its ports and harbors. However, it is my argument that the Portuguese sailors and whalers who roamed the waters of the Pacific and Atlantic North in search of a profit played a role in blazing the paths and trails of the Portuguese that followed. It should not be treated as historical coincidence that, precisely in the places that had the most Portuguese whalers, other Portuguese followed their trails, producing migrant trails of their own. This line of enquiry puts mobility, mobile phenomena, a focus on movement, as an important theoretical and analytical tool to uncover the causes and consequences of migration.

A Mobility Lenses

Mobility has been in the academic spotlight at least since the early 2000s, following the advent of the so-called new mobilities paradigm or, as others prefer to label it, the *mobilities turn* (Sheller & Urry 2006). Naturally, it would be futile to claim that analysis of movement and mobility only became a novelty with the rise of this scholarly field—flows, paths, routes, metaphors of itinerancy, flaneurism, nomadology, and dromology were already part of mainstream social sciences and humanities research: for instance, in Hannerz (1992), Clifford (1997), Virilio (1986), Deleuze and Guattari (1987), and de Certeau (1984). Instead, what may be arguable is that the mobilities paradigm had the merits of turning mobility into a theoretical tool rather than making it simply an outcome or consequence of certain structures, practices, agencies, or social institutions. Mobility was changed from a product of interactions—a thing that happens because of other things—to a producer of the social: a thing that explains and crafts other things, such as certain practices, specific ideologies, different worldviews, and so on. Some within the disciplines of history, sociology, and anthropology may perceive this shift as only cosmetic, but it has been significant in the fields of geography, migration, and transport studies (Sheller 2013), opening a panoply of new theories, analyses, and methodologies.

To illustrate this, we can think of classic migration theory. There, the main theoretical frame was one of the dialectic struggle between push and pull factors, between country of origin and host country. The line between the two remained, to a large extent, uncharted (Cresswell 2006). Mobility appeared as a consequence of migration in itself, not as an axial feature of it, one that shaped the experiences of migrants, conditions of living, or perspectives of identity. It was only more recently that migration theorists started to center their analyses on the movements themselves, be they of individuals, groups, or the things these entities brought with them. There has been a burst of interest in this new approach, as revealed by a quick scan through the archive of the influential *Journal of Ethnic and Migration Studies*. Between 1980 and 1999, only fifteen papers had the word *mobility* in their title; between 2000 and 2018, the number rose to 141.

This paper borrows from these approaches. Here, mobility is taken as a key producer of the social. I argue that the movements, paths, and flows of Portuguese sailors and whalers were not just the consequence of internal politics or endogenous economics factors (such as a deterioration of living conditions, the pursuit of new lifestyles, the escape from political constraints). Just as importantly, they produced channels of migration, communal networks, and transnational events that in some cases have lingered for more than a century. Even as sailors and whalers moved because of certain political constraints, economic predicaments, and logics of territorial expansion (Arch 2018), they were opening up networks and channels both for themselves and for migrant communities that followed. That is, whaling is not only a *thing* that *happens because of* other things, but also a *thing* that creates and explains other things. Whilst the former is usually the lenses through which whaling and whalers are seen, the latter has remained relatively unmapped. This paper focuses on this aspect: on whaling mobilities as *producers* of the social.

In doing so, my thesis, perhaps incidentally, engages with Bruno Latour's (2005) actor-network theory, particularly in its consideration of the agency of non-humans. In the world of whalers, mobility is underpinned by the fundamental agency of a non-human: the whales themselves. The whales' motion very much dictates the mobility of the whalers. In fact, the entire portfolio of whaling logs is a Latourian exercise in whale agency. For the most part, the logs (one of this essay's primary sources) registered the movements and whereabouts of whales according to type, along with weather conditions and information related to natural harbors and islands. They decoded and encoded the wheres and whens of such a species in ways that affected the mobilities of the whalers, who were chasing an animal they did not control and that needed to remain untamed, if it was to continue profitable. The sailors followed the whales across the four oceans, from the iceberg-littered waters of the Arctic to the sun-glazed seas of the equator. As Herman Melville recorded in *Moby-Dick*, they signed up for the chase. They went to where the animals had moved, they picked up their trails, and they traveled with them. Movement was not only a product, but a producer guided by a non-human agency.

New England's Mills and Fisheries

The history of New England is one of close ties to the whaling industry. The industry peaked there in the mid-nineteenth century and gradually dwindled during the first quarter of the twentieth century (Dolin 2007). The last whaler out of New Bedford, the city at the heart of the trade, was the *John R. Mantra*, which made its final voyage in 1927. Whaling provided meat and whale bones that were used in several industries, but of particular importance were the oils and blubber, which were used for candles (sperm oil in particular, from sperm whales) and lamp fuel. In fact, the importance of whale oil in the sourcing of light in the 1800s was such that New Bedford was known, in the nineteenth century, as the "city that lit the world."[3]

During the peak of the industry, many Portuguese were attracted by the promise of new lifestyles and improved conditions, and they flocked to New England in search of adventure, money, or a fresh start. The reason why so many found their way to New England can be explained by simple cartography. The archipelagos of the Azores, Madeira, and Cabo Verde (now an independent and decolonized country, but not until the 1970s) are virtually the only ones located in the open waters of the Atlantic., particularly the Azores.[4] During the first half of the nineteenth century, the whaling industry was focused on the Atlantic grounds, and these Portuguese islands became a regular, if not compulsory, station for most vessels sailing out of New England, especially those in search of

Figure 1. Scrimshaw art with a scene from Horta, on the Azorean island of Faial, and a portrait of the ship *Herald*. Attributed to John Boston, 1866. According to the New Bedford Whaling Museum, Boston was born in the Azores in 1837 (Frank 2012, 100). Courtesy of the New Bedford Whaling Museum.

Figure 2. Women in typical Azorean cloaks made out of whale teeth. Presumably carved by an anonymous Portuguese artist (Frank 2012, 148). Courtesy of the New Bedford Whaling Museum.

the valuable sperm whales found close to the equator. As captains replenished their ships' ropes, tools, and provisions, they also added crewmen to their vessels. Hundreds, maybe thousands, of locals signed up. Given the poverty of the islands, many were desperate to go, at any cost (Warrin 2010).

It would be impossible—and not even the purpose of this paper—to track the entirety of the Portuguese whaling trajectory in New England, given its tremendous latitude and richness. Rather, a few selected snippets are provided here to illustrate the presence of the Portuguese amongst the communities in New England, especially in New Bedford.

To give a summary review of the numbers, Donald Warrin was able to trace as many as 363 whaling voyages—some of which undertaken with the same vessel—under Portuguese or Portuguese-American command in just over the span of a century, between 1824 and 1927 (2010: 328-350). The numbers of Portuguese crewmen involved is very hard to pin down, but the figure is definitively four-digit,

Figure 3. The Azorean Gallery display at the New Bedford Whaling Museum, tracing the histories and tales of the Portuguese in the American whaling industry.

if not five. As the New Bedford whaling captains sailed out into the open waters of the Atlantic, only to replenish their ships in the Portuguese Atlantic islands, the number of Portuguese would have been impressive. Soon, they would be scattered around the globe, providing a significant percentage of the manual labor of the whaling (and also the fishing) industry.

Donald Warrin (2010) traces the presence of Portuguese whalers in New Bedford between 1765 and 1927. According to him, this trajectory was initiated by Joseph Swazey, who sailed into the Atlantic and returned to Martha's Vineyard (a Massachusetts island with a strong whaling presence) with an Azorean crew, and ends with the last voyage of *John R. Manta*, captained by Joseph Edward in 1927. By the end of the industry, the Portuguese were dominant in the whaling crews. But, already in the eighteenth century, Portuguese islanders were making their way as part of whaling crews. The American whaling grounds during this initial stage were concentrated in the Atlantic and, thus, it was only a matter of time before the Portuguese islanders were pulled into the industry. The region of New England can be considered the first great hub of the whaling industry. The Portuguese were first drawn into the hubs of New England, because it was here that the first great wave of whaling began, with a clear focus on the Atlantic grounds. The whales were abundant then and there, making it (relatively) easier to spot prey and turn a profit. As we will see ahead, as the whaling grounds shifted towards the Pacific or the Arctic, so did the Portuguese, becoming familiar with new islands. The whalers' mobilities shifted according to the abundance and movements of the whales themselves.

We shall return to this further ahead, but for now another important point must be made: the key dates here, for the sake of the argument developed, are not the ones on whaling, but rather those on the mills' industry. It is curious, and symptomatic, to note that Portuguese engagement in the New England textile industry occurred precisely as the whaling industry was declining. Beginning in the 1920s, many more Portuguese arrived in the region to work in textile mills. Marylin Halter explained that "during this same period, cheap sources of labour were being sought for the expanding textile mills, on the cranberry bogs, and in the maritime-related occupations of southern coastal New England. Increasing numbers, including women and children, were arriving to fulfil the demand, as they fled their land of continual hunger" (Halter 2008, 36).

One of the migrant groups that filled this demand for labor was the Portuguese, who had already established local networks in the region via the whaling industry. Caroline Brettell has confirmed this trajectory in her essays on the transnationalism, ethnicity, and identity of Portuguese migration:

> The roots of the Portuguese immigrant communities in south-eastern New England can be traced to the early nineteenth century. Whaling boats picked up crews in the Cape Verde and Azoreans Islands and deposited them in the vicinity of New Bedford, MA, for short periods of time as they reoutfitted for a new voyage. Many of these mariners remained in New England after the decline of the whaling industry, settling in Providence and New Bedford and sending for family members. Later in the nineteenth century it was the textile mills that attracted Portuguese immigrants as they attracted other immigrants (Brettell 2003, xii)

The New Bedford Whaling Museum corroborates this trajectory. Its research shows "three waves of Portuguese immigration to the city." The first wave occurred between 1800 and 1870, mostly comprised of Azoreans engaged in the whaling industry, but also of Cabo Verdeans (after the 1850s), both of whom were "eager to find economic opportunities or to escape conscription into the Portuguese army." The second wave, between 1870 and 1924, is comprised of residents of the Azores, as well as some from Madeira and mainland Portugal, who were "looking for opportunities in emerging industries, particularly the textile mills, of New Bedford" (https://www.whalingmuseum.org; also see Bastos 2018a, who analyzes the Portuguese communities of New England during this period). The third wave occurred in the second half of the twentieth century, following a devastating volcanic eruption in the Azores. This genealogy, as constructed or represented in this way, clearly provides a linkage between the original whalers of the Azores who first came to America, with the later migration to the textile mills. As Memory Holloway points out, at a certain period "it was more profitable to work in the textile mills than to take one's chances at sea" (Holloway 2008, 118).

In this event, whalers *became* mill workers, became the antecedents of a busy migratory path that remained active until the late twentieth century. New England became a hub for Portugueseness, an entry point of Portuguese migration, after the movements of whalers had paved the way.

Hawai'i and Jason Perry

Whales have always been significant in Hawaiian cultures. Whale parts and bones were made into amulets; men ate sacralized whale meat (women were prohibited from doing so at a certain point); whale beings were deified, idolized, and rhetorized in myths and cosmogenesis (Creutz 1981). Surrounded and isolated by the sea, Hawaiian communities saw the *kohola*, the great sea creatures, as manifestations of Kanaloa, god of the oceans and its denizens (even though, squid or octopi were the most typical associations) (Beckwith 1970).

But it was not until the 1830s that the whaling industry kicked off in Hawai'i. The first native Hawaiian seamen who shipped off on a modern whaling vessel did so in 1819. According to the captains who brought them aboard, the men were renamed Joe Bal and Jack Ena to "prevent" misfortunes and hardships at sea. From that point on, and until the last quarter of the nineteenth century, whaling became increasingly important in the Hawaiian economy, until the last quarter of the nineteenth century, when it went into decline (Lebo 2010). Indeed, the industry turned Hawai'i into a strategic geopolitical location for western business—a hundred years before the onset of World War I, and fifty years after James Cook

Figure 4. Watercolor of the port of Honolulu. from the logbook of the *Frances* (KWM 602). Captained by Edward Gardner, the ship set sail from New Bedford on November 13, 1843, and returned on July 20, 1847. Its crew list mentions John Domingo and Antone Manuel. Courtesy of the New Bedford Whaling Museum. KWM 602).

first moored there. Whaling was entering its heyday and, with it, Hawai'i was inserted into part of the global network of whaling politics and economics.[5]

As soon as the first whaling ships began to operate off the so-called Sandwich Islands, the first Portuguese sailors appeared on site. A curious newspaper item, published by Sherman Peck, lists all the ships that moored in Lahaina (Maui) between March and June 1843. The count is just over one hundred. The list was presumably an advertisement for his up and coming business, given Mr. Peck's position as the local supplier of ship chandlery, provisions, and "all kinds of Merchandize usually required by ships touching at this Port for recruits."[6] Sherman Peck would later become responsible for C. Brewer & Co., Ltd, a company that made its way into the sugar plantation business in the 1860s. The majority of these ships were, naturally, whaling vessels, judging by the grounds they were bound to, also listed in the document, which recurrently included the northwestern coast of the United States and Japan, two important newly discovered whaling grounds.

If cross-referenced with the crew lists archived at the New Bedford Whaling Museum resources,[7] Portuguese names and surnames start to pop up in almost all of the vessels. For instance, the ship Montpelier, which sailed from New

Bedford in 1842 and arrived in Lahaina on May 14, 1843, had one Manuel Lopes and one Antone Degrace (probably Antonio da Graça). The ship *Acushnet* departed from Fairhaven, under the captaincy of Valentine Pease, and was crewed by one Joseph Luis. The ship L.C. Richmond, sailing from New Bedford, had a Manuel Sylvia, a Josa Sylvia, a John Sylvia, a Josa D. Silva and a Joseph Antone on board. The crew lists for the whaler *America*, which reached the Sandwich Islands on May 11, 1843, appear even more detailed, showing the birthplaces of its sailors, which included a John Christy, Anthony Marks, and Anthony Brown from Flores, Western Islands, as well as a Joseph Domingo, Frank Vearn, and a John Manace from Pico, and one Manuel Sage from Fayal. The list goes on and on.

More evidence could be unearthed so as to give a satisfying account of the presence of the Portuguese in Hawai'i during the prime of the whaling industry in the region (roughly extending between 1830-1870). In *The whaleman's adventure in the Sandwich Islands and California*, a first-hand account of whaling voyages by William Henry Thomes, a man who worked on the hides trade and then relocated to California during the Gold Rush, tells of a Portuguese dark-skinned green-hand being beaten up aboard a ship close to Hawai'i.

"The captain did not wait for the man to finish. He gave a jump, and caught the Portuguese by the neck, and shook him for a moment, and then, finding that such work was fatiguing, knocked him down and jumped upon him, landing heavily upon the man's breast; and I thought had crushed his bones in" (64). This was in the early 1870s. Roughly at the same time frame, some Portuguese finally settled on the islands and made them their home. Historian Donald Warrin attests to this, showing how several Azoreans (Portuguese islanders) appear as preeminent figures in Hawai'i during the years that followed. These included, for instance, Manuel Pico (Pico is one of the islands in the Azorean archipelago), who rapidly started to be referred to as Paiko (the same phonetic value but with Hawaiian spelling), who served as superintendent of roads on Maui. Also, Jason Perry (Jacinto Pereira, in Portuguese), who, in 1876, would become the first Portuguese consul to the Hawaiian King. Together, they bought a schooner, which they outfitted as the whaler *William H. Allen*. Its captain, A. Vera, sailed to Peru and returned "with one hundred barrels of sperm oil and two hundred of whale-oil" (Warrin 2010, 183).

Legend has it that it was Jason Perry who convinced the king of Hawai'i to bring Madeirans into the kingdom (Bastos 2018b), due to their favorable acclimatization and potentially swift-adjustment to the environments of the archipelago, given its similar traits to their tropical homeland. Whether fabled or not, references to Perry appear in a number of sources, including *The Hawaiian Almanac and Annual*, an ongoing record of myths, dialects, sites of interest, politics, and other information about the Sandwich Islands, compiled by the antiquarian and folklorist Thomas George Thrum (who was born in Australia, but relocated to and died in Hawai'i). In the 1887 volume, the following reference appears, signed by one Augustus Marques[8]

> A Portuguese subject here, Snr J. Pereira [Jason Perry], who had established in Honolulu the first dry goods store of that nationality, and who was considered as consular agent for Portugal, insisted that a scheme of immigration from Madeira seemed perfectly practicable and advantageous.... To this gentleman, who was officially named agent of immigration, we owe the first load of these people, which however were not procured without extreme difficulty, owing principally to the fact of the Hawaiian Government not being able to offer very liberal terms, and especially no grants of land, to the immigrants (Thrum 1887, 75).

Perry's name also surfaces in Katharine Coman's (1903) *The History of Contract Labor in the Hawaiian Islands*. Coman was an activist and historian at Wellesley College, who became interested in the Sandwich Islands as a result of her on-going examination of the American West—her writings on Hawai'i coincide with the dates of U.S. annexation. In her book, she noted that "the Portuguese consul at Honolulu, Mr. Perry, supervised the signing of their [the Madeirans'] contracts, allowing them full liberty to choose their employers."[9]. By the late 1870s, the first contingents of Portuguese, mostly from Madeira, were docking in the islands after brutal four-month voyages at sea. They began as plantation workers, eventually moving up the social ladder into shopkeeping—the same strategy that Mary Noel Menezes (1986) has vividly portrayed for the Madeirans in British Guyana, also in the 1800s. These processes have been extensively analyzed by the Colour of Labour project team. Cristiana Bastos examined the social, political, and cultural tensions that the Portuguese faced in Hawai'i (Bastos 2018b, 2019), Nicholas B. Miller researched the politics of immigration in Hawai'i, highlighting the Portuguese case (Miller 2019), and Marcelo Moura Mello has paid attention to similar dynamics in British Guyana[10].

Clearly, there was a link between the wandering Portuguese whalers and the indentured laborers who came after them. To an extent, it would not be too far off to consider that it was the whalers themselves who opened up these channels of migration. Whether they did so or not with direct intervention, as seems to be the case with the influence of Jason Perry, himself the owner of a whaling vessel, the truth is that, when the first contingents of Madeirans arrived to work as plantation laborers, the Portuguese had been docking in and out of Lahaina and Honolulu for more than thirty years. They knew the region and the people; some had already given up whaling and turned to land-based ventures. The migrants followed their trail.

California

The same could be said for the Portuguese of the American West Coast. Much has been written about Portuguese migration to California, which peaked in the first years of the twentieth century (Bastos 2018a) and rose again in the 1960s and 1970s due to a number of socio-economic factors, including the Portuguese Colonial War (1961-1974) and the eruption of the Capelinhos volcano in the Azores in 1957-58, which forced many people to leave the island of Faial (and many other Azoreans followed their trail, benefiting from the Azorean Refugee Act). For instance, Frederick Bohme talks about how "the mainland Portuguese were not numerous until after 1910" (1956: 233). Indeed, literature on the topic has it that the waves of migrants from Portugal, particularly from the Azores, settled either in rural areas to live off of farming and cattle raising or close to the coast to practice fishing activities—which included shore whaling.

What is less evident—but still accounted for—is how these communities were supplied by the movements, the comings and goings of high-seas whaling ships that ventured into the Pacific during the latter half of the nineteenth century. The first Portuguese who wandered into California were sailors, most of them crew members on New England vessels that were exploring the newly discovered whaling grounds of the Pacific. When ships needed fresh supplies and larger crews, captains would berth on the California coast, where the ship chandlery industry was booming. From there, the Portuguese found find their way inland. This happened in the second half of the nineteenth century and, later, throughout the twentieth century. But, what drew them into the region in the first place?

The short answer is: gold. Many of the Portuguese whalers that wandered out and about the Hawaiian shores, and the Pacific seas in general, found themselves lured by the tales of sparkle and glitter during the famed California Gold Rush of mid-nineteenth century. As some of the ships moored on Californian shores to replenish supplies, desertions increased. As Jones, Swartz, and Leatherwood argue, "many crewmen"[had] signed on in New England simply to secure passage to California and its promise of instant prosperity.... Desertion by whalemen when their boats called in at California was a well-documented phenomenon" (Jones, Swartz, and Leatherwood 1984, 122). These were the first Portuguese that made it into the Californian mainland: gold-seeking whaling deserters. The discovery of gold at Sutter's Mill drew even more deserters into the territory. News of gold rapidly spread amongst seafarers and their communities, attracting yet more men. According to Robert Santos (1995), between 1850 and 1860, the number of Portuguese in California rose from about 100 to more than 1,500, of whom 800 can be traced to the goldmines spread out across the county (Santos 1995: 42). Desertion from whaling ships is documented, for instance, in a curious account of a Portuguese man called Joe Silvey, who had joined a whale crew at the age of twelve, and, after reaching the shores of British Columbia in about 1860, decided to try his luck at gold mining in California (Barman 2004).

In 1850, records tell of the existence of a mining community near Redding, California (north of San Francisco), suggestively called the Portuguese Flat. By 1885, the town was gone. A small reference to it appears in a survey of the etymology of place names in California: "locally pronounced *por-tu-gee*, was named for Portuguese settlers in the mining days" (Gudde 1969, 54). Even more interestingly, a logbook for the ship *Ocmulgee*, penned by a man named Joseph Dias, certainly of Portuguese origin, recounts episodes of the Gold Rush of 1848, accounting for how mines were stuck in the back of everyone's heads: "So good bye California and the Gold mines. You can see by this that we had some notion of going to California but something was dropped by some of the crew which made the captain abandon it and perhaps it is all for the best but it is rather hard to think so" (Dias 1848). Apparently, the captain had decided to turn the ship around and return to Hawai'i after just nine days at sea. Given Dias's entry, we might suspect he knew that mass desertions were in the offing.

As gold fever cooled, the Portuguese turned to cattle, fishing, and shore whaling, forming a network of coastal, hybridized communities that sustained themselves by selling dairy products and the spoils of whale hunts. Many of the Portuguese who had deserted the whaling vessels in search of gold had now returned to what they knew best. It is in this timeframe—roughly the second half of the 1800s—that a significant number of whaling stations along the California coast were founded or operated by Portuguese (see fig. 6). According

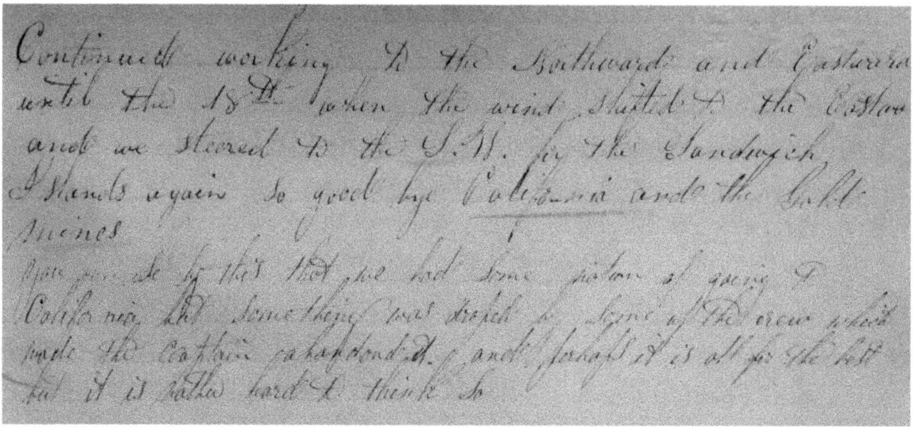

Continued working to the Northward and Eastward until the 18th when the wind shifted to the Eastward and we steered to the S.W. for the Sandwich Islands again so good bye California and the Gold Mines

You can see by this that we had some notion of going to California but something was dreaded by some of the crew which made the Captain abandon it and perhaps it is all for the best but it is rather hard to think so

Figure 5. Joseph Dias's logbook entry for the *Ocmulgee*, November 18, 1848. Courtesy of the New Bedford Whaling Museum.

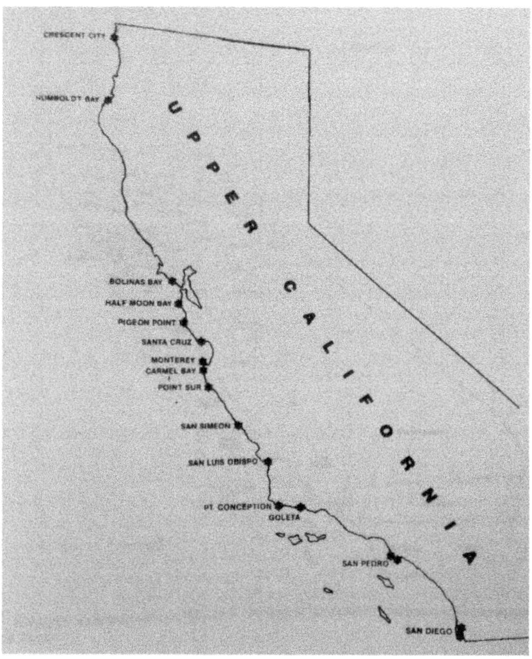

Figure 6. Map of California whaling stations, nineteenth century. Out of a total of fifteen harbors and ports, nine had strong Portuguese ties (Dickens 1998, 6).

to Robert Dickens, most of the whaling stations of California (1850-1900) were in fact of Portuguese origin or, at the very least, had established Portuguese connections. There were at least nine of them: Monterey, Camel, Point Sur, Half Moon Bay, Pigeon Point, San Simeon, San Luis Obispo, Point Conception, and

Portuguese Bend. All of the above had solid and established Portuguese connections, with records of crewmen wandering about, Portuguese captains operating from within and companies being formed (Dickens 1998). From there on, these stations became gateways through which more Portuguese entered California, joining the network of farming and fishing communities across the land.

The figure below depicts the known whaling stations of the American West Coast. Out of a total of 15 harbors and ports, 9 of them reportedly had strong Portuguese ties, according to Robert Dickens (1998).

It is, thus, with a lack of surprise that communities like San Leandro have a historical record of a Portuguese presence. As Meg Rogers suggests, by 1910, nearly two thirds of the population was Portuguese (2008). This population was comprised of remnants of the gold-seeking whalers, along with fresh migrants who had traveled the whaling paths in search of new lives and better conditions. Many had picked up old habits and were now shore-whaling once again. Also, many came from post-annexation Sandwich Islands, or Hawai'i, which, as we saw above, were already formed out of the comings and goings of whalers and the influence these had in those societies. The already-established Portuguese of San Leandro called these migrants *kanakas* (Rogers 2008).

Even the celebrated Jack London acknowledged the presence of Portuguese in San Leandro in his influential novel *Valley of the Moon* (1913): "Forty years ago old Silva came from the Azores. When sheep-herdin' in the mountains a couple of years, then below into San Leandro. These five acres was the first land he leased. That was the beginnin'. Then he began leasin' by hundreds of acres, an' by the hundred-an sixties. An' his sisters an' his uncles an' his aunts begun pourin' in from the Azores—they're all related there, you know; an' pretty soon San Leandro was a regular Porchugeeze settlement"[11]. Old Silva may well have started out as a Pacific whaler.

San Francisco, too, began to see a lot of Portuguese activity during these years. David Bertão explains how, in the city, it was possible to find a significant number of boarding-houses for whalers owned by the Portuguese and/or with Portuguese names, such as the Lusitania House (1871-77), the Lisbon House (1872–90), the New Portuguese Exchange (1868–80), the Azores Hotel (1880–90), and the Bello and Costa (1890) (Bertão 2006, 23). Captains of Portuguese origin also frequented the city. One of them, known as John Rogers (originally da Rosa), was born in Faial in 1837 and by the 1880s was in charge of two whaling vessels out of San Francisco: the *Mary and Susan* and the *Tamerlane* (Warrin 2010, 218). By 1890, "a whaling fleet operated out of San Francisco, many of the ships being owned by New Bedford interests. The masters were, in general, Americans, but the lower-grade officers (boat steerers and boat headers) were nearly all colored men or Portuguese from the Cape Verde Islands. Out of a total of 645 men comprising the whalers' crews in 1892, the Portuguese were second with 93, about 15%" (Bohme 1956, 23). Once again, as in New Bedford and Hawai'i, the channels of migration to California were very much opened by the pioneering movements of whalers and sailors—movements which were depended on the shifting of whaling grounds and the mobilities of the whales themselves. First enticed by the prospects of instantaneous wealth during the Sutter's Mill gold rush of 1848-1855, the Portuguese would eventually settle in the region and become farmers and fishers, including shore-whalers. Many of these men were, indeed, the remnants of the gold-seeking whaling deserters that, once the gold fever cooled down, picked up their farming tools and their old fishing boats, and initiated a network of communities that was used in the twentieth century by the more recent migratory waves.

Conclusion

It is my hope that the data discussed in this article helps to reinforce the importance of mobility, over territory, in defining the circulation of people (namely its causes and consequences) in the nineteenth century. Migratory paths are not solely defined by the pull and push factors of *territories*, but by erratic *mobilities*, often circumstantial and motivated by factors that do not fall within the "normal" scope of analysis. As we saw, the fact that Portuguese islanders (Madeirans, Azoreans, and Cabo Verdeans) were drawn into certain parts of North America may be the result of "mobile happenstances." While it is true that the geographical positioning of the islands was quite important to the process, for these were the only archipelagos located so far out into the Atlantic, making them perfect berthing spots for ships in needs of replenishing (particularly the ones coming from New England, where the bulk of the industry was based), it is also true that the movements of the whales themselves played a decisive role. The movements of whalers were very much tied to the travels of whales, which they could only predict, but not control. As whaling grounds moved into the Pacific, so did the Portuguese, into Hawai'i and California, amongst other places.

It is interesting to see how the mobility of whalers, in creating their own circuits, often evading the regular circuits of transport and freight of Empires, for they gave chase to an animal that they could not control, was responsible for opening channels of labor migration. The movements of the whalers, as they moved through the migratory canals of another species, could be seen as forerunners of sorts, as pioneers of a migration that followed. It is no coincidence that the majority of the Portuguese population in North America in the nineteenth and twentieth centuries was located precisely where the whalers used to operate. The erratic and always-elusive movements of whalers and whales were responsible for a network of harbors and ports in which the Portuguese became a natural and familiar presence. In time, they created the cement for more consistent migratory paths of migrant laborers. This is the case in New England, where there was a shift from whaling to the textile mills, but also in California, where the gold rush attracted many whalers and then saw them return to fishing activities when the fever cooled down, and Hawai'i, where the mythical figure of Jason Perry (Jacinto Pereira), a whaler, is thought to have influenced the King's decision bring in Madeiran labor to work on plantations.

This reinforces the importance of mobility, of erratic and circumstantial mobility even in the flows of migratory movements. The mobilities of the whalers under analysis could well be seen as pioneers of later (Portuguese) migrations into North America, but their agency should not be (exclusively) inscribed into the logics of Imperialism, territorial domination or the like. Instead, their own flows, dictated sometimes by nature itself, by the beasts and beats of the sea, were a major influence.

NOTES

1. This article results from research conducted within the project "The Colour of Labour- The Racialized Lives of Migrants", funded by the European Research Council (ERC) under the European Union's Horizon 2020 Research and Innovation programme (Advanced Grant No 695573 - PI Cristiana Bastos), hosted by the University of Lisbon/Universidade de Lisboa, Instituto de Ciências Sociais. The fieldwork and archival research has been sponsored by the project and the findings are in direct dialogue with its main agenda. I also hereby acknowledge that the idea to explore the mobilities of whalers in the context of this project came from Cristiana Bastos, who pointed me in this direction and provided sources for its study.

2. The term "Portuguese" is not addressed in depth in this article. It should be read/understood as a reference to communities of Portuguese people coming from the insular territories of Portugal.

3. This descriptor, popular during the period, is now the title of the National Park Service's orientation movie at the New Bedford Whaling National Historical Park.

4. It is possible that the migrants from Cabo Verde and those from Madeira or the Azores may have undergone different experiences of racialization in North America due to perceived differences regarding the Africanness of their background, as noted by a reviewer of this paper, but so far that is a matter of speculation beyond the scope of this article.

5. I would like to thank Nic Miller for his suggestions on this section of the paper.

6. Found in a board with lists of ships at the New Bedford Whaling Museum.

7. https://whalinghistory.org/av/crew/

8. Nicholas B. Miller made a valuable presentation on the links between Augustus Marques and the Portuguese in Hawai'i at the international conference "Labour, sugar and long-distance migration: Madeirans and Azoreans in Guyana, the Caribbean and Hawai'I", November 14-15th, 2019, CEHA, Funchal, Madeira. The presentation was titled "Auguste J.B. Marques (1841-1929) and the politics of Portuguese settlement in Hawai'i".

9. Katharine Coman (1903) *The history of contract labor in the Hawaiian Islands*. New York: MacMillan Company.

10. Marcelo Moura Mello made a presentation on this topic at the international conference "Labour, sugar and long-distance migration: Madeirans and Azoreans in Guyana, the Caribbean and Hawai'i", November 14-15th, 2019, CEHA, Funchal, Madeira. The presentation was titled "Madeirans and creoles labourers: thinking through race and labour in post-emancipation British Guiana".

11. Jack London (1913) *Valley of the Moon*. Taken from Rogers 2008.

REFERENCES

Arch, Jakobina. 2018. "Building Empires on the Backs of Whales: 19th Century Japanese Whaling and Territorial Expansion." Presentation at the 132nd annual meeting of the American Historical Association Annual Meeting.

Barman, Jean. 2004. *The Remarkable Adventures of Portuguese Joe Silvey*. Vancouver: Harbour.

Bastos, Cristiana. 2018a. "Migrants, Inequalities and Social Research in the 1920s: The Story of *Two Portuguese Communities in New England*." *History and Anthropology* 29 (2), 163–183.

______. 2018b. "Portuguese in the Cane: The Racialization of Labour in Hawaiian Plantations." In Sofia Aboim, Paulo Granjo, and Alice Ramos (eds.), *Changing Societies: Legacies and Challenges*. Vol. 1, *Ambiguous Inclusions: Inside Out, Outside In*. Lisbon: Imprensa de Ciências Sociais, 65–96.

______. 2019. "Açúcar, ananases e ilhéus portugueses no Hawaii: dinâmicas de migração, etnicidade e racialização no terreno e no arquivo." *Etnográfica* 23 (3), 777–798.

Beckwith, Martha. 1970. *Hawaiian Mythology*. Honolulu: University of Hawaii Press.

Bertão, David. 2006. *The Portuguese Shore Whalers of California, 1854–1904*. San Jose: Portuguese Heritage Publications of California.

Bohme, Frederick. 1956. "The Portuguese in California." *California Historical Society Quarterly*, 35 (3), 233–252.

Brettell, Caroline. 2003. *Anthropology and Migration: Essays on Transnationalism, Ethnicity, and Identity*. Oxford: AltaMira.

Clifford, James. 1997. *Routes: Travel and Translation in the Late Twentieth Century*. Cambridge: Cambridge University Press.

Coman, Katharine (1903) *The history of contract labor in the Hawaiian Islands. Cambridge: Cambridge University Press.*

Cresswell, Tim. 2006. *On the Move: Mobility in the Modern Western World*. New York: Routledge.

Creutz, Elisabeth. 1981. *The Influence of Whales on Ancient Hawaiian Culture*. Honolulu: Bishop Museum.

de Certeau, Michel. 1984. *The Practice of Everyday Life*. Berkeley: University of California Press.

Deleuze, Gilles, and Felix Guattari. 1987. *A Thousand Plateaus: Capitalism and Schizophrenia*. Minneapolis: University of Minnesota Press.

Dickens, Robert. 1998. "Portuguese Shore Whalers in Nineteenth Century California." Master's thesis, East Carolina University.

Dolin, Eric J. 2007. *Leviathan: The History of Whaling in America*. New York: Norton.

Frank, Stuart M. 2012. *Ingenious Contrivances, Curiously Carved: Scrimshaw in the New Bedford Whaling Museum*. Boston: Godine.

Gudde, Erwin G. 1969. *California Place Names: The Origin and Etymology of Current Geographical Names*. Berkeley: University of California Press.

Halter, Marilyn. 2008. "Cape Verdeans in the U.S.: In Luis Batalha and Jorgen Carling (eds.), *Transnational Archipelago: Perspectives on Cape Verdean Migration and Diaspora*. Amsterdam: Amsterdam University Press. 35-46.

Hannerz, Ulf. 1992. *Cultural Complexity: Studies in the Social Organization of Meaning*. New York: Columbia University Press.

Holloway, Memory. 2008. "Making Waves: Cape Verdeans, Whaling, and the Uses of Photography." In Luis Batalha and Jorgen Carling (eds.), *Transnational Archipelago: Perspectives on Cape Verdean Migration and Diaspora*. Amsterdam: Amsterdam University Press. 113-130.

Jones, Mary Lou, and Steven L. Swartz, and Stephen Leatherwood. 1984. The Gray Whale. Orlando: Academic Press, Inc.

Latour, Bruno. 2005. *Reassembling the Social: An Introduction to Actor-Network Theory*. Oxford: Oxford University Press.

Lebo, Susan. 2010. "Hawaii's 19th Century Whaling Economy: Whale Traditions and Government Regulation of Hawaii's Native Seamen and Whale Fishery." In Jan Erik Ringstad (ed.), *Whaling and History III*. Sandefjorg, Norway: Vestfold Museum.

London, Jack. (1913) *Valley of the Moon. Whatever edition is fine.*

Menezes, Mary Noel. 1986. *Scenes from the History of the Portuguese in Guyana*. Self-published.

Miller, Nic. 2019. "Trading Sovereignty and Labour: The Consular Network of Nineteenth-Century Hawai'i." *International History Review*.

Rogers, Meg. 2008. *The Portuguese in San Leandro*. California: Arcadia.

Santos, Robert. 1995. *Azoreans to California: A History of Migration and Settlement*. Denair, CA: Alley-Cass.

Sheller, Mimi. 2013. "Sociology after the Mobilities Turn." In Peter Adey, David Bissell, Kevin Hannam, Pete Merriman, and Mimi Sheller (eds.), *The Routledge Handbook of Mobilities*. New York: Routledge. 45-54.

Sheller, Mimi, and John Urry. 2006. "Editorial: The New Mobilities Paradigm." *Environment and Planning A* 38, 207–226.

Thrum, Thomas. 1887. Hawaiian almanac and annual. PLEASE HELP FILL IN. https://evols.library.manoa.hawaii.edu/handle/10524/659

Virilio, Paul. 1986. *Speed and Politics: An Essay on Dromology*. New York: Columbia University Press.

Warrin, Donald. 2010. *So Ends This Day: The Portuguese in American Whaling, 1765–1927*. Dartmouth: University of Massachusetts Dartmouth, Center for Portuguese Studies and Culture.

ANDRÉ NÓVOA (PhD, Royal Holloway, 2014) is a geographer who previously trained as an historian and anthropologist. He was a researcher at Northeastern University (USA) and an assistant editor of *HAU Magazine: Journal of Ethnographic Theory*. His work has been published in journals such as *Mobilities* and *Environment & Planning*. In "The Colour of Labour" project, he is directly involved with the study of mobilities, addressing the movements of whalers, the journeys of indentured migrants, and the entanglements of labor and mobility.

NICHOLAS B. MILLER[1]

Crossing Seas and Labels: Hawaiian Contracts, British Passenger Vessels, and Portuguese Labor Migrants, 1878–1911

ABSTRACT: During the last quarter of the nineteenth century, over 13,000 European men, women, and children, predominantly from Madeira and the Açores, emigrated to the Kingdom of Hawai'i on contracts of government indenture. Their modality of migration was a contemporary anomaly, as it was restricted in other global contexts at this time to peoples racialized as non-European. This atypical conjuncture of white bonded labor and a government headed by a Polynesian monarch not only upset the contemporary racial geo-politics of the age of New Imperialism, but likewise has long complicated attempts to locate this migration trajectory in comparative histories of migration and indenture. Through a close study of the vessels used to transport European indentured laborers to Hawai'i and the conditions of transhipment they endured aboard, this article probes a boundary case between the two commonly identified global historical migration patterns of the late nineteenth century: (i) European "voluntary" migration to the Americas and Australia and (ii) Asian "indentured" immigration to Euro-American dominated plantation colonies in Asia, Africa, the Caribbean, the Mascarene Islands, and the South Pacific. By tracking the diverse passages made by the same ship, sail and steam, in-between different migrant commissions, this article suggests that a strict delineation of the onboard experience between indentured and voluntary migration is untenable. Further, this article considers the potential and limits of the study of the onboard passenger experience to study racialization processes in migration history, including for the complex context of pre-annexation Hawai'i.

KEYWORDS: Migration, Transportation, Indenture, Hawai'i, Crossing

RESUMO: No último quarto do século XIX, mais de 13.000 homens, mulheres e crianças Europeias, predominantemente da Madeira e dos Açores, emigraram para o Reino do Hawai'i sob contratos de servidão por escritura. A sua modalidade de migração foi uma total anomalia para a época, visto que esta estava normalmente restrita a povos racializados como não-brancos. Esta conjuntura atípica de trabalho "branco" junto com um governo liderado por um monarca polinésio não só perturbou a geopolítica racial contemporânea da era do Novo Imperialismo, como também complexificou as tentativas de localizar essa trajetória de migração na História comparativa da migração e servidão por contrato. Através de um estudo das embarcações usadas para transportar trabalhadores europeus contratados para o Hawai'i e as condições de transbordo que encontraram, este artigo investiga um caso que se situa na fronteira dos dois padrões de migração global mais comuns do final do século XIX: (i) a migração "voluntária" Europeia para as Américas e Austrália e (ii) a imigração asiática "contratada" para as plantações na Ásia, África, Caribe, Ilhas Mascarenhas e Pacífico Sul. Ao rastrear as várias viagens feitas pelo mesmo navio, entre as diferentes comissões de migrantes, este artigo sugere que um delineamento estrito da experiência a bordo entre a migração contratada e voluntária é insustentável. Este artigo demonstra o potencial e os limites do estudo da experiência do passageiro a bordo para estudar os processos de racialização na história da migração, inclusive para o contexto complexo de pré-anexação do Hawai'i.

PALAVRAS-CHAVE: Migração, Transportação, Trabalhadores contratados, Havai, Travessia marítimo

---

Disembarking around the World

On April 14, 1911, the *Hawaiian Gazette* printed a cover story about the arrival of the "British immigrant steamer *Orteric*" with "many laborers aboard" from Portugal and Spain. "Death [had] stalked among the fifteen hundred Spanish and Portuguese immigrants," with fifty-eight deaths recorded, all children, mainly due to measles.[2] Grateful to be off the ship, the migrants ran down the pier to the immigration depot at Kaka'ako. A Spanish man reportedly exclaimed, "Vive le Republique!" A Portuguese migrant shouted, "Away from that jail—away from that jail," looking back with disgust at the steamer, perhaps unaware of what lay ahead. After U.S. officers discovered scarlet fever among the new arrivals, the migrants were promptly interned on Sand Island, which had served as a quarantine site for arriving passenger ships since the mid-nineteenth century.[3]

Contracted to Hawai'i's Territorial Board of Immigration, the migrants represented what Edward P. Irwin called, in a 1910 piece titled "Importing a Population," a continuity and a conclusion. Hawai'i's "assisted immigration" program, he contended, began with the arrival of the *Priscilla* in Honolulu on

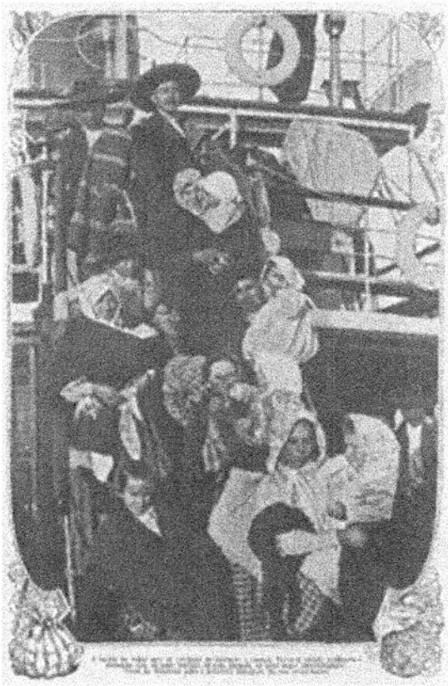

Figure 1 (left). "A bordo do vapor que os conduzio do Barreiro a Lisboa...," *Illustração Portugueza*, March 6, 1911, 315.

Figure 2 (right). "Portuguese Immigrants Landing Yesterday," *Hawaiian Gazette*, April 14, 1911, p. 1.

September 30, 1878, "with 180 Portuguese contract laborers." Their presence was designed to satisfy labor gaps created by the decline of the Native Hawaiian population and the rise of the sugar industry following the 1875 signing of a free trade agreement between the Kingdom of Hawai'i and the United States. Irwin noted that the system had "in some form or other" persisted "up to the present time," bringing more than 100,000 workers to Hawai'i over the course of three decades and across shifting governing formations of kingdom, republic, and U.S. territory. Fortunately, from Irwin's post-annexation perspective, it was finally due to end: "For while there have been some good results from the system, the evil effects are today a curse to the country." The identified problems lay not in the system's punitive characteristics but in the unwelcome demographic changes induced by the most recent arrivals. The latest migrants from Portugal were "poorer mentally, physically and morally than those who came earlier." There had also been the "serious mistake" of "the importation of Russians" and the "blunder that was hardly less than a crime" of the "bringing into the country of about 5,000 Porto Ricans."[4]

"Portuguese Immigrants Landing Yesterday," the *Gazette*'s caption for its striking image of disembarkation, did not quite fit the general tenor of the cover story. Why were Portuguese migrants specifically mentioned, given the article's claim that the majority of the "fourteen hundred are Spaniards"? Why did the reporter state that "the Spanish were easily distinguished from the Portuguese, because of their headgear and corduroy clothing," when the so-called "Portuguese" passengers depicted in the image wore the same items? The reason for these perplexities lies in the origin of the image itself. Although the paper never mentions the fact, the scene did not take place in Honolulu's harbor. More than a month earlier, the picture had been printed alongside a cover story in the *Illustração Portugueza*, the photo-rich weekly edition of the Portuguese newspaper *O Século*.[5] The Jewish Portuguese photojournalist Joshua Benoliel had captured the scene from the docks of Lisbon as these migrants were on the early stages of their voyage from the Iberian Peninsula to Hawai'i.

At this point the migrants had traveled barely seven kilometers by sea. Recruited from Portugal's Alentejo region, they had traveled over land to the port of Barreiro, just across the Tejo River from Lisbon. Now they were disembarking in Lisbon to wait for paperwork. The article spoke harshly of the *Orteric*, the British passenger steamer chartered for the voyage to Hawai'i. Dr. Victor Clark of Hawai'i's Board of Immigration may have contended that it was "a new ship, everything spick and span, and probably in general presented a far better appearance than many irregular lines carrying immigrants,"[6] but the *Illustração* depicted a dungeon, accusing the Hawaiian Board of Immigration of misleading the Alentejano migrants. In the cover article, titled "Os que a fome escorraça" (Those Chased Away by Hunger), the reporter accused the board's special agent, Alexander J. Campbell, of deceptive tactics. Labeling him an *engajador* (a labor recruiter), the writer claimed that the ship was barely capable of transporting its passengers safely and predicted their disillusionment on arrival: "the rest they shall see there on the ground, under the blazing sun, working on the plantation, at the summit of the smoking volcanoes."[7] The article employed a charged term to define the plight of the passengers aboard: *escravatura branca* (white slavery).[8]

How did these migrants fit into the oft-posited trichotomy among the deportation of enslaved Africans, the indentured immigration of Asians to plantation colonies, and the "voluntary" migration of Europeans to North America and Australasia?[9] In general, the 20,000 European contract laborers, mostly Portuguese, who came to Hawai'i between 1878 and 1911 straddled the latter two categories.[10] The *Illustração*'s suggestion of slavery reflected the rhetoric of contemporary labor politics rather than the actual plight of these migrants. The contested local and international politics inherent in Hawai'i's contract labor system persisted throughout its thirty-three-year history, beginning during the kingdom and persisting after annexation. This contest likewise applied to the terms used to describe the migrants and the modality of their passage. In this piece, my goal is to reflect on the riddle of labels used historically and historiographically to refer to the same migrant or the same ship, as in this case of the photograph in the *Hawaiian Gazette* and the *Illustração Portugueza*. The essay considers the labels for the migrants themselves: free migrants, assisted immigrants, indentured laborers, white coolies, and white slaves. It also examines the labels used to describe the ships that carried them, interrogating an often implicit and underconsidered distinction in the literature on nineteenth-century long-distance passenger ships: that between "emigrant ships" associated with European "free migrants" and "coolie ships" associated with Asian indentured laborers. Finally, like other contributions to this collection, it considers the life of labels during the onboard experience of Portuguese migrants to Hawai'i and the extent to which ocean passage was preparation for the world of national and ethnic distinction and difference that defined plantation life.

Labels of Passage

Free migrants or white coolies? This question was posed persistently between 1878 and 1888 by consuls, newspaper columnists, foreign ministers, and port authorities in Lisbon, London, Berlin, Copenhagen, Honolulu, San Francisco, and Funchal. During this decade, more than 13,000 European men, women, and children from Norway, Germany, and, above all, Portugal, traveled by sail and steam to the Kingdom of Hawai'i on contracts of government indenture. The period marked the intensification of Hawai'i's contract labor system, the only time in which Europeans constituted a major component of total Hawai'i-bound labor migrants.[11] The framing of the issue belied the central conceits and dissonances of the contemporary liberal notion of indentured labor as a form of voluntary migration premised on the autonomous individual's contract-making capacities.[12] It also spoke to the implicit racialization of indenture in the figure of the Asian coolie, whether Chinese or South Asian.[13]

From a formal perspective, these European migrants were no doubt indentured. In exchange for free passage, each putatively agreed to bind him or herself for a set period of time, usually three years, to labor on a plantation, assigned after arrival by the Kingdom's Board of Immigration. The penalty for breaking the contract was imprisonment.[14] This provision was routinely enforced, to the fury of the migrants' home governments.[15] In defending the system, Walter Murray Gibson, an American adventurer turned Hawaiian foreign minister, used the term *assisted immigrants*.[16] He and other government officials argued that bonded labor contracts were the only way in which the kingdom could meet the high costs of transoceanic passenger transport; its modest coffers could not cover full subsidization. They further justified the government's approach to immigration using King Kalākaua's populationist discourse of Ho'oulu Lāhui: to raise a nation. That is, they argued that the migrants were intended to amalgamate with the Native Hawaiian population and thus ensure the long-term survival of an independent kingdom.[17]

The use of Ho'oulu Lāhui to justify a rendition of nineteenth-century contract labor migration was both creative and strategic—an attempt to appease a broad spectrum of interests in Hawai'i's small local polity (native elite voters, Sinophobic tradesmen, and Euro-American planters), while remaining consistent with the prevailing passenger shipping and anti-human-trafficking regulations of the major powers, particularly Great Britain, as well as the migrants' origin countries.[18]

In 1881, the *Pacific Commercial Advertiser*, then a government organ, declared, "The 'Suffolk' from the Azores, brings a welcome addition to the population of the Kingdom. The assisted Portuguese immigrants may have been more costly, man for man, than those which the Government, or private individuals, have induced to come here from other parts of the world, but they have assuredly proved more valuable, as laborers and settlers, in a still greater proportion."[19] Targeting its assertions at the kingdom's English-reading public, it presented Portuguese indentured laborers as simultaneously "assisted" immigrants, laborers, and settlers. Yet critics, including newspaper columnists across North America and Europe as well as local abolitionists concerned about the humanitarian abuses of the system, dismissed such explanations as a mask for white servitude or slavery.[20] Discussion was fierce in government assemblies across Europe during the 1880s.[21] Legislators from the sending countries were livid about the insult to national status posed by citizens who were migrating to serve as laborers in a setting ruled by an indigenous monarch. This upset them far more than the possibility that their poorest citizens might find the terms of passage preferable to their present status at home.[22] These reactions, which often revealed racialized notions about the unsuitability of white labor for plantation work in the tropics, continued to define the discussion well after U.S. annexation, when populationist goals were explicitly linked to increasing the white population in the island territory.

Labels of Vessels

Hawai'i occupies a curious place in global accounts of the history of colonialism and labor migration, and perhaps no group is as anomalous as the more than 10,000 Portuguese who ventured there as contract laborers in the decade before U.S. annexation of the islands. There has been no shortage of commemorative work by members of this community, and the importance of it for scholarship on the contextually- and temporally-specific nature of racial categorization has long been of prime interest.[23] Scholars have long been intrigued by the way in which these migrants straddled the distinctive ethnic and racial labels of plantation Hawai'i: as Caucasian but not haole (Anglo-Saxon), as local but not Polynesian or Asian.[24] Yet the onboard story of their migration to Hawai'i has yet to receive extended attention.[25] This is curious, given the importance of these ships in the local structuring of Portuguese heritage: the names of each vessel are well known and appear in nearly every article, book, and documentary about the Portuguese community of Hawai'i.[26] But despite their importance in local identity formation, we know little about the broader history of the vessels themselves. Who owned them? What were their onboard conditions like? How should we label them?

In the controversy over European migration that erupted in the transatlantic press and the international diplomatic system, the passenger ship loomed large. Critics widely shared complaints about onboard conditions, including abysmal food, unsanitary conditions, and deficient medical attention, to frame them as coolie rather than emigrant ships. Gibson's term of choice, *assisted immigrants*, was not accidental; it was typically used to describe the subsidized transport of hundreds of thousands of poor Britons to Australia during this same period.[27] However, scholarship on labor migration to Hawai'i ignores the fact that more than mere labels connected these migrations. Seven of the ships that brought Portuguese indentured immigrants to Hawai'i had previously sailed to Australia with assisted migrants aboard; this was more than half of the ships used on the route from Madeira and the Azores before the fall of the Hawaiian monarchy. These seven ships were the *High Flyer* (a bark), the *Earl Dalhousie* (a bark),[28] the *Dacca* (a steamship), the *Monarch* (a steamship), the *Abergeldie* (a steamship), the *Stirlingshire* (a clipper), and the *Victoria* (a steamship). In most cases, the ship's owner did not change between the passages. In other words, the same ship, at different times, transported passengers who were labeled consecutively as *assisted migrants* or *indentured immigrants*. If we use *migrant ship* as a term to describe a nineteenth-century ship whose passengers were mainly migrants and *coolie ship* as a subcategory to describe a vessel whose passengers were mainly indentured laborers, do we have sufficient grounds to say that these ships morphed between the status of coolie ships and emigrant ships?

The plot thickens even if we restrict the definition of *coolie ship* to apply only to non-European migrants. Ironically, the relevant ships here were those that traveled from Portugal and Spain to Hawai'i *after* U.S. annexation, when the kingdom's British Empire–style indentured labor system (the one featuring an imprisonment clause) was formally abolished. Between 1906 and 1911, several thousand migrants were brought to Hawai'i from the two countries, and the only ships used were large steamships owned by the Bank Line and Century Shipping Company. The *Swanley*, which arrived in Honolulu in 1909, had transported thousands of indentured Chinese mine workers to South Africa in 1904.[29] The *Kumeric*, after landing 1,000 Portuguese migrants in Honolulu in 1907, then took on 1,177 Japanese migrants who were on a temporary layover in Hawai'i. It brought them to Vancouver, British Columbia, where they faced some of the most violent anti-Asian riots in Canadian history.[30]

Was the onboard experience materially different during the different passages of these label-crossing vessels? Limited evidence suggests it was not. Death rates during the passages varied widely, but no significant difference can be discerned in the small sample size provided by ships that made both Queensland and Hawai'i passages. In his magisterial study of British-registered long-distance passenger ships during the nineteenth century, Kevin Brown emphasizes that journey length and mortality rates were subject to great variation due to the quality of crew, the misfortune of disease, and the vagaries of wind, particularly before the steamship came into general use. "The stories of those emigrants who sailed from Europe to the Americas, Australia and New Zealand, and on the coolie ships from India and China to the West Indies, Mauritius and South America, are all diverse." Differences may depend more on the era in which the ship sailed rather than on its putative type.[31]

Let us consider three ships that made both Australian and Hawaiian passages from Europe. The British bark *Earl Dalhousie*, which landed in Honolulu from the Azores on March 27, 1882, had previously made at least half a dozen voyages between Britain and Australia carrying government-assisted migrants, including one immediately before sailing from the Azores. Sailing times between Plymouth and Adelaide (South Australian emigration in 1874 and 1875) or Brisbane (Queensland emigration between 1879 and 1881) ranged between eighty-one and ninety days. The total number of migrant passengers on each voyage ranged from 303 to 381.[32] While the Hawai'i-bound trip from the Azores took somewhat longer (113 days), the number of passengers aboard (322) was within the range of the Australia-bound sailings.[33] Similar conditions also prevailed in the British-registered *High Flyer*, the only one of these ships to have sailed to Hawai'i twice (in 1880–81). On a passenger crossing between London and Marlborough, Queensland, in 1878, it had a total travel time of 122 days and landed 340 passengers, about half of whom were government-assisted, with five deaths on board.[34] The two sailings between the Azores to Hawai'i ranged between 99 and 130 days and landed 337–52 men, women and children.[35]

The first steamship to be used between the Azores and Hawai'i, the British-registered and Orient Company–owned *Abergeldie*, was later used several times to bring assisted migrants from Britain to Australia. The Hawai'i-bound voyage (1883) took sixty-two days, and the ship carried 945 passengers, nine of whom died. There was an outbreak of measles aboard, but supposedly no one died from it.[36] The *Abergeldie* was likewise proclaimed as the "first immigrant steamship to enter Port Jackson [Sydney]" after having returned to Britain and collected assisted migrants at Plymouth.[37] The total number of passengers it carried on its voyages between Britain and New South Wales was fewer than those it brought to Hawai'i, ranging from 595 to 612.[38] Deaths per voyage ranged between two and ten, mainly among children (as was usually the case). In July 1884, the *Sydney Morning Herald* declared that there had been no "material alterations in the fittings of the *Abergeldie* since her first voyage here."[39] Given the short turnaround time between the ship's return from Honolulu and its voyage to Sydney from Plymouth, it is likely that these Australia-bound migrants experienced the same ship conditions that the Hawai'i-bound passengers from Portugal had, except that each individual had somewhat more space.

The journey of Portuguese migrants to Hawai'i was formidable, lasting in many cases well over a hundred days, featuring the double-crossing of the equator, and the rounding of Patagonia.[40] Those aboard steamships made the passage faster, though more than half of the voyages were done by sail. None of the ships on which the Portuguese emigrants sailed were registered in Hawai'i or Portugal. The first, the *Priscilla*, was a German ship charted via the agency of the powerful Hawai'i-based German firm Hackfeld and Company, which had its European headquarters in Bremen.[41] Hackfeld was awarded the concession in 1877-78 by the German medic, botanist, and immigration commissioner Wilhelm Hillebrand, who had moved to Madeira after leaving Hawai'i and was empowered to initiate contract labor migration from Portugal.[42] After Hillebrand's initial work, the business passed the following year to the management of John Hutchison, an Irish-born merchant who served as a Hawaiian consul. With the approval of Honolulu, the concession was next awarded to Abraham Hoffnung in 1878, a Polish-born businessman of Jewish descent and British upbringing, who later served as Hawaiian consul in Britain from 1884 until the overthrow of the monarchy.[43]

Hoffnung was not a shipowner but a well-placed business intermediary specializing in antipodal shipping and migration. His brother, Sigmund, was a successful businessman in Brisbane.[44] Sponsored European migration to Queensland dwarfed that to Hawai'i: roughly 250,000 Europeans arrived in Queensland between 1860 and 1900, 150,000 of whom were sponsored.[45] Hoffnung's familial network placed the Portuguese migration to Hawai'i within the similarly antipodal assisted emigration of poor British and Irish migrants to Queensland.[46] The embedding of the business of shipping migrants from Portugal to Hawai'i within British-focused trading networks was hardly unique; it reflected the semi-dependent character of both sites to a British-dominated global maritime marine during the period. For instance, most of the hundreds of thousands of Portuguese emigrated to Brazil at the end of the nineteenth century traveled aboard foreign, mostly British, ships.[47] While the Hoffnung nexus is hazy to track, given the absence of relevant archives for his firm or its successors, it likely explains the overlap between Hawai'i- and Queensland-bound ships. In contrast, none of the New Zealand–bound emigrant ships were used for Europe-to-Hawai'i indentured passenger shipping.[48]

Hoffnung's role was consistent but controversial.[49] He was seen with contempt by many Hawai'i-born Americans active in the 1888 coup d'etat that forced King Kalākaua to sign the Bayonet Constitution stripping him of most of his effective power and forcing the resignation of Walter Murray Gibson, and which presaged the 1893 coup d'etat that overthrew the Hawaiian monarchy.[50] Controversies about shipboard conditions mingled with criticism of his management; dissatisfaction with the high cost of his brokerage services was linked to political critiques of the patrimonial nature of Kalākaua-era governance.[51] As these issues spread through the global press, European governments resolved to study the situation themselves.[52] In September 1882, for instance, Antonio de Souza Canavarro, the newly appointed Portuguese consul in Hawai'i, was commissioned to examine the passenger ships that were transporting thousands of emigrants from the Azores and Madeira.[53] After visiting the recently arrived *Hansa* in Honolulu's harbor, he noted conditions on board and drew up a set of recommendations for their improvement.[54] Canavarro met and became friendly with Hoffnung, who had come to Hawai'i to lobby for the establishment of a regular shipping line between London and the islands that would also stop at the Azores and Madeira. Even in 1884, a year in which there was a staggering number of fatalities among child passengers, the consul stressed that Hoffnung, his firm, and their Hawai'i-based partners were trying to create the best-possible onboard environment.[55] Given our limited sources, it is difficult to untangle how politics, careerism, and reality affected the behavior of these elites, each of whom had something to gain from claims of abuse or improvement.

The two steamships that arrived in 1884, the *City of Paris* and the *Bordeaux*, had unusually high mortality rates, particularly among children, and both also had unusual ownership characteristics.[56] Hoffnung had purchased the *City of Paris* earlier that year, apparently as part of his ultimately unsuccessful attempt to secure government subsidies for a regular shipping line between Britain and Hawai'i.[57] The *Bordeaux* was a British-built ship that had been recently acquired by a French firm and carried a French crew.[58] Canavarro commissioned a series of interviews with the parents of the deceased, putatively to determine the cause of death and recommend improvements.[59] In fact, the resulting reports largely blamed the parents, particularly the mothers.[60] Yet the controversies did have a substantive effect on the management of Portuguese migration to Hawai'i. Hoffnung sold the *City of Paris* to a French company, and the ship sank the following year off the coast of Marseille, en route to Bắc Kỳ (Tonkin) with French troops aboard.[61] No other French-registered vessel was ever used for shipping Portuguese to Hawai'i.

The onboard reality on migration ships was more complicated than their dominant passenger population might suggest. For instance, most of the vessels also carried commercial goods. With the exception of the *Priscilla*, management of the cargo on most of the ships bringing Portuguese laborers to Hawai'i before 1893 was consigned to George Walter Hunter Macfarlane (1849–1921). Macfarlane had been born in Honolulu to parents of Scottish and English descent, three years after their migration to Hawai'i from New Zealand.[62] He was a close confidant of King Kalākaua, served on his military staff, traveled with him on his 1881 world tour, and served as his chamberlain. Macfarlane's proximity to power enabled him to craft business ties with Hoffnung. In Honolulu newspapers, the arrival of Portuguese migrant ships tended to be announced alongside Macfarlane's advertisements for newly arrived goods.[63] Some migrant ships also transported import symbolic cargo. In 1883, the bark *Earl Dalhousie*, which had sailed at least six times between Britain and Australia as an emigrant ship, carried more than 320 Portuguese indentured laborers along with the famous Kamehameha statue presently located in front of Ali'iolani Hale in Honolulu.[64] Even as passenger transport, these ships were not just vessels of indenture. With limited transportation options between Europe and the Pacific, they afforded a smaller set of higher-status individuals the opportunity to travel to the islands. On later voyages, relatives of successful earlier migrants arrived with their passage fully paid, which allowed them to forego contracts of indenture. This was the case for seventeen of the passengers aboard the *Stirlingshire* (1886).[65] Aboard the same ship was Hugo Kawelo, a young Hawaiian ali'i, who had studied iron working with Mirrlees, Wattson, and Company in Glasgow as part of the kingdom's program to educate select Hawaiian youths abroad.[66] He had boarded the ship upon its initial departure from Liverpool.

Labels of Difference

Much recent literature about the onboard experiences of contract laborers has focused on the crossing of the kalapani, or black waters, by South Asian emigrants en route to European colonies in the Mascarene Islands, the Caribbean, Fiji, and elsewhere.[67] Martin Dusinberre has extended this analysis to the Hawaiian context in his study of the scattered archive relating to ships transporting Japanese contract laborers in the late 1880s and the 1890s.[68] Indentured passengers' own words about the experience are rare, but in the case of the Portuguese migration to Hawai'i we have access to a voyage diary kept in 1887–88 by João Baptista d'Oliveira and Vicente d'Ornellas on their 156-day sail from Madeira to Honolulu aboard the *Thomas Bell*—the longest journey time of any passenger ship bringing Portuguese migrants to Hawai'i.[69] The *Thomas Bell* was the last ship to make the passage between Portugal and Hawai'i for over a decade; it was also the last time a sailing ship was used for the route. It is unclear if it had ever served as a passenger ship to Australia, but the *Pacific Commercial Advertiser* noted it "has been trading mostly in the Colonies and East Indies and is a pretty good sailer [*sic*]."[70] The ship's owner was John Swanson of Liverpool, its captain was James Low, and its medical officer was J. M. Campbell.[71]

The diary left by d'Oliveira and d'Ornellas is typical of the genre, reflecting the writers' gradual adaptation to late-nineteenth-century shipboard life, including their desensitization to the brutal realities of passage. During the first few days, they recorded minutiae about their daily meals; after a few weeks, only particularly terrible instances received mention. This was also the case with child mortality.[72] The first death aboard occurred a week and a half out, when a young boy passed away after having fallen seriously ill. At 6:15 a.m. on the morning of November 25, 1887, his mother mourned his passing, and the ship crew arranged a funeral.

> The body was placed in a shroud, which was merely a sack, with some pieces of coal to weigh it down. Around the shroud, the flag of the Sandwich Islands had been wrapped. At 9 a.m., the captain ordered all persons to come up to the poop deck. As we went up, we noticed the English flag at half-mast, and the flag-covered shroud now was placed on a heavy plank at the edge of the ship.[73]

In d'Oliveira and d'Ornellas's description of this ocean funeral, the symbols of sovereignty, nationality, and power loomed large. The child was wrapped in the flag of the state to which his family was bound on a contract of indenture, though disease had denied him the opportunity of developing any personal feeling of nationality toward that symbol. The ceremony was conducted by a British captain, reading from his English-language Bible, with the symbol of the ship's nationality of registration lowered to half-mast in recognition of the personal loss of one of its passengers. Between the Portuguese jurisdiction of departure and the Hawaiian jurisdiction of arrival sailed a legally and symbolically British space of migration.

As the voyage continued and the discomfort of the long passage intensified, the passengers devised new ways for mocking a crew they described, in national terms, as "the Englishmen."[74] When a plague of bedbugs struck in mid-March, while the ship was crossing the long stretch of ocean between Chile and Hawai'i, d'Oliveira and d'Ornellas made repeated mention of the passengers' nicknames for the pests: "English soldiers" and "red-coats."[75] If this indicated a feeling of solidarity among the passengers versus a crew they perceived as ethnically or nationally different, it was a solidarity that could be ruptured, at least from the perspective of the diarists, by intercultural communication differences. On January 15, 1888, while rounding Patagonia, one of the diarists noted the tension that existed between him and the Portuguese nurse aboard, a woman named Isabel. He claimed she did "not care for me because I know a little English and the officers always send for me when they want information from the passengers. Truly she is a very jealous woman, and has been the cause of many unpleasant experiences."[76]

The social order aboard the migrant ships were clearly distinguished by nationality: the crews were mainly British, and the passengers were mainly Portuguese. The national origins of the crew manning the few non-British-registered ships were less consistent. The Hillebrand- and Hackfeld-brokered German bark *Priscilla* (1878) had a British captain, whereas the *Braunfels* (1895) had a largely German crew.[77] As I have discussed, the *Bordeaux* (1884), a British-built steamship owned by a French firm, had a mainly French crew, who were subject to extensive inquiries on arrival in Hawai'i due to an unusually high volume of deaths in transit.[78] The nationalities aboard remained largely unchanged as governments shifted in Hawai'i. After U.S. annexation, all ships were registered in Britain, with the exception of two small New Zealand ships, the *Warrimoo* (1900) and the *Aorangi* (1901), which sailed from the West Coast of the United States, bringing only about a hundred migrants to the islands, most of whom had previously settled in New England.

A curious reoccurring phenomenon on these ships before the twentieth century was the gig nature of the contracted ship's surgeon. Most were British, and most seem not to have been ordinarily employed in the role. At least one German and two British doctors migrated to Hawai'i between 1880 and 1900 by serving as ships' surgeons aboard migrant ships from Portugal. Dr. St. David Gynlais Walters, formerly a house surgeon at Stanelo Hospital in Liverpool, reached Hawai'i in 1882 after serving as ship's surgeon aboard the *Monarch* (1882). He subsequently served as a government physician at Lihue, Kaua'i in 1882–97; as medical superintendent of the O'ahu Insane Asylum beginning in 1902; and as president of Honolulu's Pacific Club, formerly the British Club, in 1917.[79] Three years later, Dr. S. Ernest Craddock crossed as ship's surgeon aboard the *Dacca* (1885). The eldest surviving son of William Craddock of the Indian Medical Service, he set up shop at 104 Fort Street in Honolulu, advertising his Portuguese-speaking abilities in local newspapers.[80] A German doctor named Dr. E. C. Surmann also established a practice on Fort Street after arriving in Hawai'i as ship's surgeon aboard the only German-registered ship to make the journey after 1878, the *Braunfels* (1895), advertising his services in Hawaiian- and English-language newspapers as a "Kahuna lapa'au Geremania" (German medical practitioner).[81] In some cases, the role of ship's surgeon was simply a means to cover the costs of antipodal transit. In 1886, Dr. Joseph Wardale served as ship's surgeon aboard the *Amana* on his return home from Scotland to New Zealand, where he worked as a physician in Invercargill, Otago, at the Southland District Hospital. Remarkably, due to adverse weather, the steamer took 147 days to reach Hawai'i from Madeira, a longer time than most sailing ships had taken, though still shorter than the *Thomas Bell*'s.[82]

Alcohol played a central role in d'Oliveira and d'Ornellas's narration of their long passage. Port wine and liquor were used to celebrate and relax; their excess consumption threw individuals into rages and sickness. Here a telling gap emerges between what the institutional and personal archives can tell us. British crew lists for Hawai'i-bound vessels, such as the *Abergeldie* (arrived in 1883) and *Amana* (arrived in 1886), reveal an explicit alcohol ban in crew contracts.[83] Even if alcohol was not formally proscribed aboard the *Thomas Bell*, the migrants managed to subvert official regulations at various stages. Despite strict laws in Hawai'i banning the import of alcohol by individual migrants, the diarists reported in one of their final entries that this rule was widely broken. When port officials went to inspect migrants' trunks, "we know of many passengers who passed the guards with their liquor securely tucked away in their clothes."[84]

Arrival

As I have discussed, the emigration of Portuguese nationals to Hawai'i as indentured laborers occurred mainly aboard British passenger vessels, a substantial portion of which had previously brought government-assisted migrants to Australia from Britain. The major difference between these passengers lay neither in their onboard experiences nor in the hoped-for permanence of their settlement. Rather, it lay in the modality of the sponsorship of their passage. In the case of nineteenth-century Portuguese migrants to Hawai'i, mobility costs were sponsored via contracts of indenture with the government's Board of Immigration, adapted from British practice usually associated with Asian labor in plantation colonies. This led to a paradox in their contemporary setting born from a crossing of typologies: these were indentured laborers travelling aboard ships that were also used in the Australian context for assisted immigration. Those typologies became inverted after annexation. Migrants continued to travel on British passenger vessels (now solely steamers), but some of those steamers were also used to transport Asian laborers to South Africa and British Columbia. Despite the formal abolition of the kingdom-era contract labor system after annexation, these "free" laborers were traveling aboard vessels that were also decried as coolie ships.

The mobility of indentured Europeans to Hawai'i in the final decades of the nineteenth century complicated not merely the labels used to describe migration modes or types of passenger vessels but also the implicitly racialized character of these distinctions in present comparative scholarship. This type of logic also framed actor experience. On April 13, 1888, while their ship was being towed into the harbor at Honolulu, the diarists d'Oliveira and d'Ornellas noted a "house" at the center of the port, "which, we are told, is a hospital for the Chinese and Japanese immigrants." To their apparent surprise, this was precisely where they were going. The following morning, at 11 a.m., they were given individual numbers during a roll call. At 3 p.m., they were unloaded to walk down a long pontoon leading them to the Quarantine Depot, the destination of the Portuguese man mentioned at the beginning of this essay, the one who exclaimed joyously on April 13, 1911, about finally being away from "that jail" of a ship, the *Orteric*. Once d'Oliveira and d'Ornellas had entered the depot, they got their first glimpse of Native Hawaiians, whom they termed "Canecas," and settled in at the depot, which featured "four rows of wooden houses, a large kitchen, and a place where we could wash our clothes, a bathroom, a park, and a magnificent house where we registered." The hospital for Chinese and Japanese immigrants had become their next station. D'Oliveira and d'Ornellas did not reflect on the apparent change in their own station, merely noting that the depot was "an interesting place," surrounded by "beautiful shade trees whose names we do not know."[85]

What changed for indentured passengers during the months' long journey from Macronesia to Polynesia? At least as relayed by d'Oliveira and d'Ornellas, it was an introduction to a world of opportunities channeled aboard British passenger vessels. The onboard experience was an introduction to a realm of international mobility increasingly defined by national characteristics—not merely in terms of the politics of the destination country but also in the dominance of global passenger shipping by a small network of British and occasionally German businessmen. Nationality as a means of distinction, twinned with power status, emerged as a social reality. And not incidentally, the passengers would soon be working on plantations owned mainly by families who spoke the captain's language.

NOTES

1. I gratefully acknowledge that this article results from research conducted within the project "The Colour of Labour- The Racialized Lives of Migrants", funded by the European Research Council (ERC) under the European Union's Horizon 2020 Research and Innovation programme (Advanced Grant No 695573 - PI Cristiana Bastos), hosted by the University of Lisbon/Universidade de Lisboa, Instituto de Ciências Sociais.

2. This ship's name is sometimes alternately rendered as the *Osteric* due to unclear handwriting in manuscript ship logs and port documents.

3. "Orteric Arrives with Many Laborers", *Hawaiian Gazette*, Apr. 14, 1911, p. 1.

4. Edward P. Irwin, "Importing a Population", *The Democrat*, Nov. 1, 1910, p. 3.

5. I thank Marta Macedo for first bringing this image to my attention.

6. "Conditions of Departure of the Orteric", *Hawaiian Star*, Apr. 22, 1911, p. 1.

7. *Illustração Portugueza*, Mar. 6, 1911, p. 315. "Aquillo era o começo; o resto elles o veriam lá em baixo, na ardencia do sol, fazendo o trabalho na plantação, no vertice das serranias onde os vulcões fumegam."

8. Ibid., p. 316.

9. Christopher A. Bayly, *Birth of the Modern World, 1780-1914* (Oxford: Oxford University Press, 2004). Jürgen Osterhammel, *Die Verwandlung der Welt: eine Geschichte des 19. Jahrhunderts* (Munich: CH Beck, 2011), 221-52 [English translation by Princeton University Press, 2018]. Adam McKeown, "Global Migration, 1846-1940", *Journal of World History* 15:2 (2004): 155-89.

10. For a review of the concept of "white slavery" in the 19th century British public sphere see: Laura Lammasniemi, "Anti-White Slavery Legislation and its Legacies in England", *Anti-Trafficking Review* 9 (2017): 64-76. On the "white slave" as a historical construction tied to race, colonialism and gender see for instance: Brian Donovan, *White Slave Crusades: Race, Gender and Anti-Vice Activism, 1887-1917* (Urbana, IL: University of Illinois Press, 2010).

11. Edward D. Beechert, *Working in Hawai'i: A Labor History* (Honolulu: University of Hawai'i Press, 1985), 85-88.

12. On contract labor as a component of liberal theory see: David Schwan, "J.S. Mill on Coolie Labor and Voluntary Slavery", *British Journal for the History of Philosophy* 21:4 (2013): 754-66.

13. Compare: Lisa Lowe, *The Intimacies of the Four Continents* (Durham, NC: Duke University Press, 2015), 21-28. David Northrup, *Indentured Labor in the Age of Imperialism* (Cambridge: Cambridge University Press, 1995), 1-15.

14. Cristiana Bastos, "Portuguese in the Cane: The Racialization of Labour in Hawaiian Plantations", in *Changing Societies: Legacies and Challenges*, vol. 1, *Ambiguous Inclusions: Inside Out, Inside In*, eds. Sofia Aboim, Paulo Granjo and Alice Ramos (Lisbon, Imprensa

de Ciências Sociais, 2018), 77. Susana C.O. Castro Caldeira, *Da Madeira para o Hawaii: A emigração e o contributo cultural madeirense* (Funchal: Centro de Estudos de História do Atlântico, 2010), 169-79. For a draft contract see: João Baptista d'Oliveira and Vicente d'Ornellas, "Destination: Sandwich Islands, being the Journal of the 156 Days' Trip from the Island of Madeira to the Archipelago of Sandwich, on the English Vessel *Thomas Bell*", *Hawaiian Journal of History* 4 (1970): 49-50.

15. See the cases analyzed in: Sally Engle Merry, *Colonizing Hawai'i: The Cultural Power of Law* (Princeton: Princeton University Press, 2000), 208-20.

16. See for instance: *Pacific Commercial Advertiser*, Jun. 21, 1884, p. 2. *Hawaiian Gazette*, Nov. 5, 1884, p. 6. Daily *Bulletin*, Nov. 8, 1887, p. 2. Also see the use, in translation from Hawaiian, in the critical take on the purposes of migration by: Mamalamoa, "Some Enlightenment", *Saturday Press*, Dec. 25, 1880, p. 3. On Gibson see: Jacob Adler and Robert M. Kamins, *The Fantastic Life of Walter Murray Gibson, Hawai'i's Minister of Everything* (Honolulu: University of Hawai'i Press, 1986). Also see: Seth Archer, "Hawaiian Health and the Filibuster of Walter Murray Gibson", *American Nineteenth-Century History* 20:2 (2019): 95-113.

17. Jonathan Osorio, *Dismembering Lāhui: A History of Hawaiian Nationhood to 1887* (Honolulu: University of Hawai'i Press, 2002), 173-92.

18. Nicholas B. Miller, "Trading Sovereignty and Labour: The Consular Network of Nineteenth-Century Hawai'i", *The International History Review* (2019), 8-14.

19. *Pacific Commercial Advertiser*, Aug. 27, 1881, p. 2.

20. Beechert, *Working in Hawai'i*, 87.

21. The case of liberal politician and former US resident Friedrich Kapp and his concern about "German coolies" in Hawai'i is exemplary. Uwe Spiekermann has described Kapp's discourse in 1883 in his online blog. For the transcripts of Kapp's speech see: "46. Sitzung am 5. Februar 1883", *Verhandlungen des Reichstages* 69 (Berlin, 1883), 1297-1303 and "53. Sitzung am 14. Februar 1883", *Verhandlungen des Reichstages* 69 (Berlin, 1883), 1496-1501.

22. See the documents relating to controversies over Portuguese, German and Norwegian indentured emigration to Hawai'i collected by the German Auswärtiges Amt in 1883: Berlin Bundesarchiv, BArch R 901/30723.

23. Bastos, "Portuguese in the Cane", 86-92.

24. James A. Geschwender, Rita Carroll-Seguin and Howard Brill, "The Portuguese and Haoles of Hawaii: Implications for the Origin of Ethnicity", *American Sociological Review* 53:4 (1988): 515-27. Moon-Kie Jung, *Reworking Race: The Making of Hawai'i's Interracial Labor Movement* (New York: Columbia University Press, 2006), 77. Boaventura de Sousa Santos, "Between Prospero and Caliban", in *Revisiting the Colonial Question in Latin America*, eds. Mabel Moraña and Carlos A. Jáuregui (Madrid: Iberoamericana, 2008), 166.

25. Addressing this lacunae been a collaborative research venture undertaken by Cristiana Bastos and other members of her ERC project The Colour of Labour (695573), including

myself. See for instance: Cristiana Bastos, "Febre a bordo: migrantes, epidemias, quarentenas", paper at international seminar "Mapeando Controvérsias Contemporâneas: Ecologia, Saúde e Biossegurança", Universidade Federal do Rio Grande do Sul, Jul. 12, 2018.

26. See: John Henry Felix, Peter F. Senecal and Elmer F. Cravalho, *The Portuguese in Hawaii* (Honolulu: published by the authors, 1978). Edgar C. Knowlton, Jr., "Portuguese in Hawai'i", *Kentucky Foreign Language Quarterly* 7:4 (1960). 212-18. A comprehensive list of the ships can be seen in: Ana Isabel Spranger, "Havai, emigração para o", *Dicionário Enciclopédico da Madeira*, http://aprenderamadeira.net/, accessed online on Oct. 2, 2019.

27. For an instance of its use in a Hawaiian newspaper relating to Australia see: "Foreign News", *Pacific Commercial Advertiser*, Jan. 24, 1880, p. 5, and *Daily Bulletin*, May 18, 1883, p. 2. On assisted migration as a common concept in British imperial contexts see: Janice Cavell, "The Imperial Race and the Immigration Sieve: The Canadian Debate on Assisted British Migration and Empire Settlement, 1900-30", *The Journal of Imperial and Commonwealth History* 34:3 (2006): 345-67.

28. A surviving ship newspaper even exists for one of the Australia-bound trips taken by the *Earl Dalhousie*. See: *The Earl Dalhousie Gazette, and New South Wales Intelligencer* (Happy Valley, Marriageton: FB Treatt, 1877).

29. Peter R. Richardson, *Chinese Mine Labour in the Transvaal* (London: Macmillan, 1976), 156-8.

30. Yukari Takai, "Via Hawai'i: The Transmigration of Japanese", in *Digital Meijis: Revisualizing Modern Japanese History at 150*, eds. Tristan R. Grunow and Naoko Kato (Vancouver: University of British Columbia, 2019), 133-38.

31. Kevin Brown, *Passage to the World: The Emigrant Experience, 1807-1904* (Barnsley: Seaforth Publishing, 2013), p. ix.

32. *South Australian Advertiser*, Jan. 13, 1874, p. 2. *South Australia Register*, Feb. 24, 1875, p. 4. Queensland State Archives, Immigration Department, Register of Immigrants, Earl Dalhousie, 1880-1881, Digital Image ID 38374.

33. Augustus Marques, "Portuguese Immigration to the Hawaiian Islands", *Hawaiian Almanac and Annual for 1887* (Honolulu: Press Publishing Company, 1886), 76. *Daily Bulletin*, Mar. 27, 1882, p. 1.

34. Queensland State Archives, Immigration Department, Register of Immigrants, Highflyer, 1878, Digital Image ID 38582.

35. Marques, "Portuguese Immigration", 75-76.

36. *Pacific Commercial Advertiser*, May 5, 1883, p. 2, p. 5.

37. "The Immigrant Steamship Abergeldie", *Sydney Morning Herald*, Feb. 5, 1884, p. 5.

38. *Sydney Morning Herald*, Jul. 8, 1884, p. 6; Aug. 25, 1885, p. 6.

39. Ibid., p. 6.

40. Bastos, "Portuguese in the Cane", 81-84.

41. Jung, *Reworking Race*, 19.

42. Miller, "Trading Sovereignty and Labour."

43. Ibid.

44. Simon Mollan, "S. Hoffnung and Co. 1851–1980: The Case of a Market Intermediary in Australia", *Consumption Markets & Culture* 13:1 (2010): 7-29.

45. Gary B. Magee and Andrew S. Thompson, *Empire and Globalisation: Networks of People, Goods and Capital in the British World, c. 1850-1914* (Cambridge: Cambridge University Press, 2010), 74-75. Helen R. Woolcock, *Rights of Passage: Emigration to Australia in the Nineteenth Century* (London and New York: Tavistock Publications, 1986), 23.

46. Eric Richards, "How Did Poor People Emigrate from the British Isles to Australia in the Nineteenth Century?", *Journal of British Studies* 32:3 (1993): 250-79.

47. Yvette Santos, "Portuguese Emigration, Shipping Companies and the State: The Business of Migrant Transport after the *Belle Époque*", *International Journal of Maritime History* 30:1 (2018): 74-88. Malyn Newitt, *Emigration and the Sea: An Alternative History of Portugal and the Portuguese* (Oxford: Oxford University Press, 2015), 124-45.

48. David Hastings, *Over the Mountains of the Sea: Life on the Migrant Ships, 1870-1885* (Auckland: Auckland University Press, 2006).

49

50. Noenoe K. Silva, *Aloha Betrayed: Native Hawaiian Resistance to American Colonialism* (Durham, NC: Duke University Press, 2004), 123-63. Osorio, *Dismembering Lāhui*, 193-249. Tom Coffman, *Nation Within. The History of the American Occupation of Hawai'i*, 3rd ed. (Durham, NC: Duke University Press, 2016), chs. 9-15.

51. *Saturday Press* (Honolulu), Jul 14, 1883, p. 3. Colin Newbury, *Patrons, Clients and Empire: Chieftaincy and Over-rule in Asia, Africa and the Pacific* (Oxford: Oxford University Press, 2003), 183-215.

52. Berlin Bundesarchiv, BArch R 901/30723. Beechert, *Working in Hawai'i*, 87. Eleanor H. Davis, "The Norse Migration: Norwegian Labor in Hawai'i", *71st Annual Report of the Hawaiian Historical Society* (Honolulu: Honolulu Advertiser, 1963), 28-35.

53. Arquivo Histórico do Ministério dos Negócios Estrangeiros (MNE), Legações de Portugal, EUA/Consulados/Honolulu, Box 623, Sep. 6, 1883, Canavarro to MNE. Luís Mendoça and José Avila, *Emigração açoriana (sécs. XVIII a XX)* (Lisbon: s.n., 2002), 198.

54. *Documentos apresentados ás cortes na sessão legislativa de 1885, pelo ministro e secretário d'estado dos negócios estrangeiros, negócios consulares e comerciais, secção VI, emigração portuguesa para as ilhas havaianas* (Lisbon: Imprensa Nacional, 1885), 5-10.

55. Ibid., 32-35, 54-56.

56. Ibid., 45.

57. *Pacific Commercial Advertiser*, Jul. 1, 1884, p. 7.

58. Ibid., Oct. 7, 1884, p. 6.

59. *Documentos apresentados ás cortes na sessão legislativa de 1885*, 45-47, 54-57.

60. Hawai'i State Archives, FO&Ex 31, 1884, Immigration, Jan-Jun (Chronological Files): "Evidence taken June 17th and subsequently at the Enquiry into the Causes of the Great Mortality among Children during the Voyage of the SS City of Paris."

61. "Fatal Collision at Sea", *Manchester Times*, 7 Mar. 7, 1885. p. 5.

62. Ralph S. Kuykendall, *The Hawaiian Kingdom, Vol. 3: 1874-1893, The Kalākaua Dynasty* (Honolulu: University of Hawai'i Press, 1967), 295-96. See Peter T. Young's online biography of the Macfarlane family. The Macfarlanes, *Images of Old Hawai'i*, http://imagesofoldhawaii.com/the-macfarlanes/, dated Mar. 27, 2015, retrieved Oct. 2, 2019.

63. *Pacific Commercial Advertiser*, Apr. 15, 1882, p. 3; May 12, 1883, pp. 2-3; Apr. 14, 1888, p. 2. *Daily Bulletin*, Mar 11, 1886, p. 7

64. Albert Pierce Taylor, *A Narrative of the Kingdom of Hawai'i* (Honolulu: Advertiser, 1927), 54-58. *Daily Bulletin*, Mar. 27, 1882, p. 1.

65. *Daily Bulletin*, Mar 11, 1886, p. 7.

66. Ibid. Also see: Agnes Quigg, 'Kalākaua's Hawaiian Studies Abroad Program', *The Hawaiian Journal of History* 22 (1988): 170-208.

67. Ashutosh Kumar, *Coolies of the Empire: Indentured Indians in the Sugar Colonies, 1830-1920* (Cambridge: Cambridge University Press, 2017), ch. 4.

68. Martin Dusinberre, "Writing the On-Board: Meiji Japan in Transit and Transition", *Journal of Global History* 11 (2016): 271-94.

69. I thank Cristiana Bastos for first bringing this case to my attention. Cristiana Bastos, "Plantation Islanders: Madeiran Trajectories across Empires", paper at session "Moving and Moving Again: Embodied Identifications along Multiple Trajectories", CASCA/IUAES Annual Meeting 2017, Ottawa, May 5, 2017. d'Oliveira and d'Ornellas, "Destination: Sandwich Islands", 3-52.

70.

71. *Hawaiian Gazette*, Apr. 17, 1888, p. 4.

72. Bastos, "Febre a bordo: migrantes, epidemias, quarentenas." Also see the overview of the voyage of the *Thomas Bell* in: Bastos, "Portuguese in the Cane", 82-83.

73. d'Oliveira and d'Ornellas, "Destination: Sandwich Islands", p. 13.

74. Ibid., pp. 19-20.

75. Ibid., pp. 39-40.

76. Ibid., p. 28.

77. "Arrival of the Portuguese Immigrants", *Pacific Commercial Advertiser*, Oct. 5, 1878, p. 2.

78. *Pacific Commercial Advertiser*, Oct. 7, 1884, p. 6.

79. "In Memoriam, Doctors of Hawai'i, VI", *Hawaii Medical Journal and Inter-Island Nurses' Bulletin* 14:1 (1956): 286.

80. *Daily Bulletin*, Jan. 29, 1885, p. 3 and Mar. 17, 1885, p. 1. *Pacific Commercial Advertiser*, May 4, 1887, p. 3.

81. *Ka Leo o ka Lahui*, Dec. 31, 1895, p. 4 and Apr. 20, 1896, p. 3. *Pacific Commercial Advertiser*, Apr. 20, 1895, p. 7.

82. *Pacific Commercial Advertiser*, Sep. 24, 1886, p. 4.

83. National Maritime Museum, Greenwich. Crews List for *Amana*, no. 71750, 1884; Crews List for Abergeldie, no. 60693, 1884.

84. d'Oliveira and d'Ornellas, "Destination: Sandwich Islands", pp. 47-48.

85. Ibid., pp. 47-48.

BIBLIOGRAPHY

I. Manuscript Sources

Arquivo Histórico do Ministério dos Negócios Estrangeiros (MNE), Legações de Portugal, EUA/Consulados/Honolulu, Box 623, Sep. 6, 1883, Canavarro to MNE.

Berlin Bundesarchiv, BArch R 901/30723.

Hawai'i State Archives, FO&Ex 31, 1884, Immigration, Jan-Jun (Chronological Files).

National Maritime Museum, Greenwich. Crews List for *Amana*, no. 71750, 1884; Crews List for Abergeldie, no. 60693, 1884.

Queensland State Archives, Immigration Department, Register of Immigrants, Earl Dalhousie, 1880-1881, Digital Image ID 38374.

II. Newspapers

Australia

The Earl Dalhousie Gazette, and New South Wales Intelligencer (1877)
South Australian Advertiser (1858-)
South Australia Register (1837-1931)
Sydney Morning Herald (1831-)

Hawai'i

Daily Bulletin (1882-1895)
Democrat, The (1910)
Hawaiian Gazette (1865-1918)
Hawaiian Star (1894-1912)
Ka Leo o ka Lahui (1889-1896)
Pacific Commercial Advertiser (1856-1921)
Saturday Press (1880-1885)

Great Britain
Manchester Times (1828-1922)

Portugal
Illustração Portugueza (1903-1924)

III. Secondary Sources

Adler, Jacob and Robert M. Kamins. *The Fantastic Life of Walter Murray Gibson, Hawai'i's Minister of Everything*. Honolulu: University of Hawai'i Press, 1986.

Archer, Seth. "Hawaiian Health and the Filibuster of Walter Murray Gibson". *American Nineteenth-Century History* 20:2 (2019): 95-113.

Bastos, Cristiana. "Febre a bordo: migrantes, epidemias, quarentenas". Paper at international seminar "Mapeando Controvérsias Contemporâneas: Ecologia, Saúde e Biossegurança", Universidade Federal do Rio Grande do Sul, Jul. 12, 2018.

Bastos, Cristiana. "Plantation Islanders: Madeiran Trajectories across Empires". Paper at session "Moving and Moving Again: Embodied Identifications along Multiple Trajectories". CASCA/IUAES Annual Meeting 2017, Ottawa, May 5, 2017.

Bastos, Cristiana. "Portuguese in the Cane: The Racialization of Labour in Hawaiian Plantations". In *Changing Societies: Legacies and Challenges*, vol. 1, *Ambiguous Inclusions: Inside Out, Inside In*, pp. 65-96. Edited by Sofia Aboim, Paulo Granjo and Alice Ramos. Lisbon, Imprensa de Ciências Sociais, 2018.

Bayly, Christopher A. *Birth of the Modern World, 1780-1914*. Oxford: Oxford University Press, 2004.

Beechert, Edward D. *Working in Hawai'i: A Labor History*. Honolulu: University of Hawai'i Press, 1985.

Brown, Kevin. *Passage to the World: The Emigrant Experience, 1807-1904*. Barnsley: Seaforth Publishing, 2013.

Caldeira, Susana C.O. Castro. *Da Madeira para o Hawaii: A emigração e o contributo cultural madeirense*. Funchal: Centro de Estudos de História do Atlântico, 2010.

Cavell, Janice. "The Imperial Race and the Immigration Sieve: The Canadian Debate on Assisted British Migration and Empire Settlement, 1900-30". *The Journal of Imperial and Commonwealth History* 34:3 (2006): 345-67.

Coffman, Tom. *Nation Within. The History of the American Occupation of Hawai'i*. 3rd edition. Durham, NC: Duke University Press, 2016.

d'Oliveira, João Baptista and Vicente d'Ornellas. "Destination: Sandwich Islands, being the Journal of the 156 Days' Trip from the Island of Madeira to the Archipelago of Sandwich, on the English Vessel *Thomas Bell*". *Hawaiian Journal of History* 4 (1970): 3-52.

Davis, Eleanor H and Carl D. Davis. *Norwegian Labor in Hawaii: The Norse Immigrants.* Honolulu: Industrial Relations Center of the University of Hawai'i, 1962.

Documentos apresentados ás cortes na sessão legislativa de 1885, pelo ministro e secretário d'estado dos negócios estrangeiros, negócios consulares e comerciais, secção VI, emigração portuguesa para as ilhas havaianas. Lisbon: Imprensa Nacional, 1885.

Donovan, Brian. *White Slave Crusades: Race, Gender and Anti-Vice Activism, 1887-1917.* Urbana, IL: University of Illinois Press, 2010.

Dusinberre, Martin. "Writing the On-Board: Meiji Japan in Transit and Transition". *Journal of Global History* 11 (2016): 271-94.

Felix, John Henry, Peter F. Senecal and Elmer F. Cravalho. *The Portuguese in Hawaii.* Honolulu: published by the authors, 1978.

Geschwender, James A., Rita Carroll-Seguin and Howard Brill. "The Portuguese and Haoles of Hawaii: Implications for the Origin of Ethnicity". *American Sociological Review* 53:4 (1988): 515-27.

Hastings, David. *Over the Mountains of the Sea: Life on the Migrant Ships, 1870-1885.* Auckland: Auckland University Press, 2006.

Jung, Moon-Kie. *Reworking Race: The Making of Hawai'i's Interracial Labor Movement.* New York: Columbia University Press, 2006.

Katsuki, Robert Y. "In Memoriam, Doctors of Hawai'i, VI". *Hawaii Medical Journal and Inter-Island Nurses' Bulletin* 14:1 (1956): 286.

Knowlton, Edgar C., Jr., "Portuguese in Hawai'i". *Kentucky Foreign Language Quarterly* 7:4 (1960): 212-18.

Kumar, Ashutosh. *Coolies of the Empire: Indentured Indians in the Sugar Colonies, 1830-1920.* Cambridge: Cambridge University Press, 2017.

Kuykendall, Ralph S. *The Hawaiian Kingdom, Vol. 3: 1874-1893, The Kalākaua Dynasty.* Honolulu: University of Hawai'i Press, 1967.

Lammasniemi, Laura. "Anti-White Slavery Legislation and its Legacies in England". *Anti-Trafficking Review* 9 (2017): 64-76.

Lowe, Lisa. *The Intimacies of the Four Continents.* Durham, NC: Duke University Press, 2015.

Magee, Gary B. and Andrew S. Thompson. *Empire and Globalisation: Networks of People, Goods and Capital in the British World, c. 1850-1914.* Cambridge: Cambridge University Press, 2010.

Marques, Augustus. "Portuguese Immigration to the Hawaiian Islands". In *Hawaiian Almanac and Annual for 1887*, pp. 74-78. Edited by Thomas G. Thrum. Honolulu: Press Publishing Company, 1886.

McKeown, Adam. "Global Migration, 1846-1940". *Journal of World History* 15:2 (2004): 155-89.

Mendoça, Luís and José Avila. *Emigração açoriana (sécs. XVIII a XX).* Lisbon: s.n., 2002.

Merry, Sally Engle. *Colonizing Hawai'i: The Cultural Power of Law*. Princeton: Princeton University Press, 2000.

Miller, Nicholas B. "Trading Sovereignty and Labour: The Consular Network of Nineteenth-Century Hawai'i". *International History Review* 42:2 (2020): 260-77.

Mollan, Simon. "S. Hoffnung and Co. 1851–1980: The Case of a Market Intermediary in Australia". *Consumption Markets & Culture* 13:1 (2010): 7-29.

Newbury, Colin. *Patrons, Clients and Empire: Chieftaincy and Over-rule in Asia, Africa and the Pacific*. Oxford: Oxford University Press, 2003.

Newitt, Malyn. *Emigration and the Sea: An Alternative History of Portugal and the Portuguese*. Oxford: Oxford University Press, 2015.

Northrup, David. *Indentured Labor in the Age of Imperialism* (Cambridge: Cambridge University Press, 1995), 1-15.

Osorio, Jonathan. *Dismembering Lāhui: A History of Hawaiian Nationhood to 1887*. Honolulu: University of Hawai'i Press, 2002.

Osterhammel, Jürgen. *Die Verwandlung der Welt: eine Geschichte des 19. Jahrhunderts*. Munich: CH Beck, 2011.

Quigg, Agnes. "Kalākaua's Hawaiian Studies Abroad Program", *The Hawaiian Journal of History* 22 (1988): 170-208.

Richards, Eric. "How Did Poor People Emigrate from the British Isles to Australia in the Nineteenth Century?" *Journal of British Studies* 32:3 (1993): 250-79.

Richardson, Peter R. *Chinese Mine Labour in the Transvaal*. London: Macmillan, 1976.

Santos, Boaventura de Sousa. "Between Prospero and Caliban: Colonialism, Postcolonialism, and Inter-Identity". In *Revisiting the Colonial Question in Latin America*, pp. 139-84. Edited by Mabel Moraña and Carlos A. Jáuregui. Madrid: Iberoamericana, 2008.

Santos, Yvette. "Portuguese Emigration, Shipping Companies and the State: The Business of Migrant Transport after the *Belle Époque*". *International Journal of Maritime History* 30:1 (2018): 74-88.

Schwan, David. "J.S. Mill on Coolie Labor and Voluntary Slavery". *British Journal for the History of Philosophy* 21:4 (2013): 754-66.

Silva, Noenoe K. *Aloha Betrayed: Native Hawaiian Resistance to American Colonialism*. Durham, NC: Duke University Press, 2004.

Spranger, Ana Isabel. "Havai, emigração para o". *Dicionário Enciclopédico da Madeira*. http://aprenderamadeira.net/. Accessed online on Oct. 2, 2019.

Takai, Yukari. "Via Hawai'i: The Transmigration of Japanese". In *Digital Meijis: Revisualizing Modern Japanese History at 150*, pp. 133-38. Edited by Tristan R. Grunow and Naoko Kato. Vancouver: University of British Columbia, 2019.

Taylor, Albert Pierce. *A Narrative of the Kingdom of Hawai'i*. Honolulu: Advertiser, 1927.

Verhandlungen des Reichstages, Vol. 69. Berlin: Deutscher Reichstag, 1883.
Woolcock, Helen R. *Rights of Passage: Emigration to Australia in the Nineteenth Century*. London and New York: Tavistock Publications, 1986.
Young, Peter T. "The Macfarlanes". *Images of Old Hawai'i*. http://imagesofoldhawaii.com/the-macfarlanes/. Dated Mar. 27, 2015.

NICHOLAS B. MILLER is Assistant Professor of History at Flagler College. He is a global and intellectual historian of Europe's interactions with other world regions, 1750-1900. His current research probes labor migration, scientific careering, and transitions of sovereignty across global sites of colonial intrusion during the eighteenth and nineteenth centuries, with a focus on plantations in Hawai'i and the Malay world. He is author of *John Millar and the Scottish Enlightenment: Family Life and World History* (Oxford: Voltaire Foundation, 2017) and co-editor, with Ere Nokkala, of *Cameralism and the Enlightenment: Happiness, Governance, and Reform in Transnational Perspective* (London and New York: Routledge, 2020). His most recent publications include the article "Trading Sovereignty and Labour: The Consular System of Nineteenth-Century Hawai'I," *International History Review* 42:2 (2020): 260-77. Prior to coming to Flagler, he was a Research Fellow at the University of Lisbon, Institute of Social Sciences, as part of the ERC project The Colour of Labour, PI Cristiana Bastos (ERC-AdG-695573-Colour). nbmiller@flagler.edu. ORCiD: https://orcid.org/0000-0002-4037-642X

MIGUEL MONIZ

The Day of Portugal and Portuguese Heritage, Social Exclusion, and Imagined Mobilities: Legacies of Racialized Migrant Industrial Labor in Contemporary New England

ABSTRACT: Commemorations and monument dedications have been part of Portuguese-speaking migrant place-making and as responses to social exclusion in New England since these arrivals settled in and built industrial and agricultural worker communities beginning in the late nineteenth century. The racialization of migrant laborer identities imposed by discourse and law and supported by scientific studies relying upon genetic data, assisted politicians and elites during the second Industrial Revolution to limit the civic and labor organization rights of workers. This study examines the complex history of Portuguese worker strategies to confront their civic, social, and racial assimilability through civic associations that organized migrant participation in U.S. national celebrations (Fourth of July, Pilgrim ceremonies, war veterans' memorials) and migrant community commemorations (including Portuguese heritage days and monument dedications like Dighton Rock). Contemporary Day of Portugal celebrations and other heritage dedications that shape social participation in multi-cultural democracy are examined in light of the legacies of white nationalist strategies advocating for Portuguese social mobility. The study examines how some of the ritual elements of today's celebrations yet promote discourses of racialized laborer hierarchies.

KEYWORDS: monuments and commemorations, "black" and "white" Portuguese, associations and associativism

RESUMO: Comemorações e dedicatórias de monumentos têm feito parte da construção de "place making" de migrantes lusófonas e como respostas à exclusão social na Nova Inglaterra desde que estes migrantes se estabeleceram em comunidades de trabalhadores industriais e agrícolas a partir do final do século XIX. Durante a segunda Revolução Industrial, a racialização das identidades dos trabalhadores migrantes foi imposta por discursos e leis que foram apoiadas por estudos científicos que se baseavam em dados genéticos. Estes processos de poder racializados ajudaram os políticos e as elites a limitar os direitos cívicos e de organização laboral dos trabalhadores. Este estudo examina a complexa história das estratégias dos trabalhadores portugueses para enfrentar a sua assimilabilidade cívica, social e racial através de associações cívicas que organizaram a participação dos migrantes nas celebrações nacionais dos EUA (4 de Julho, cerimónias dos "Pilgrims", memoriais dos veteranos de guerra) e comemorações da comunidade migrante (incluindo dias do património português e dedicatórias de monumentos como a pedra "Dighton Rock"). As celebrações actuais do Dia de Portugal e outras dedicatórias do património, que moldam a participação social na democracia multicultural, são examinadas à luz do legado histórico das estratégias nacionalistas brancas utilizadas para promover a mobilidade social dos migrantes de Portugal. O estudo examina como alguns dos elementos rituais das celebrações de hoje ainda promovem discursos de hierarquias de trabalhadores racializados.

PALAVRAS-CHAVE: monumentos e comemorações, "black" e "white" Portuguese, associações e associativismo

---

In New England, annual celebrations of Portugal and Portuguese migrant communities known as the Day of Portugal are an important place making ritual, and form part of longitudinal responses to the racialization of migrant labor and attempts among these settler communities to achieve socioeconomic mobility, earn civic rights, and secure safe and fair work conditions.[1] National day and heritage celebrations in Portugal date back to the nineteenth-century industrial era, with a forerunner of today's commemorations taking place in Rhode Island during the debates around and passage of the 1958 Azorean Refugee Act, which presaged the 1965 Immigration and Nationality Act (also known as the Hart-Celler Immigration Act). The legislation dramatically transformed political and racial classifications of migrants, creating space for multicultural, ethnic group as interest group democratic participation. In Massachusetts and Rhode Island, a key political bloc has emerged among communities of Portuguese-speaking migrants with origins and mobilities across continental Portugal, Macaronesia, Portuguese colonial and ex-colonial Africa, and Brazil. Beginning in the early 1980s, during Portugal's post-dictatorship transition to democracy, Portuguese heritage commemorations became popular annual events in southeastern New England, and they are key public place making rituals for migrant communities to participate in local power discourses, and municipal and state electoral politics.

Transoceanic mobile migrant labor from Portugal settled in New England, first arriving from the Azores, Madeira, continental Portugal, and Cabo Verde in the late nineteenth century, following whaling, shipping and trade routes. Although popular historical narratives tend to highlight whaling as an impetus for migration, this obscures the fact that around 90 percent of the migrants from insular and continental Portugal living in the United States between 1820 and 1930 arrived after 1870,[2] coinciding with the recruitment of industrial workers in manufacturing and textile mills, on farms, and as domestic labor. Early twentieth-century industrial interests controlled these migrant workers through an aggregated system of racialized exclusion[3] that empowered white nationalist political coalitions at the federal, state, and local level. To maintain these hierarchies,[4] social degradation and violence against these migrant workers were normalized and codified through discourse[5] and the law and naturalized their status as unassimilable[6]—that is, as culturally, mentally, and genetically inferior and thus inadequately conditioned for and deserving of citizenship, civic participation, and constitutional protections.[7]

This model of labor-class exploitation was also embodied in arguments against women's rights (including suffrage), justifying legal prohibitions on civic participation by likewise naturalizing female identities to negate their presumed genetic assimilability. The identities of industrial migrant laborers from Portugal were racialized and naturalized as unassimilable through a process in "which the material disparities generated by imperialism were read in a different idiom, as expressions of essential difference."[8] These differences were articulated through a political program that legitimized migrant workers' exploitation and thwarted their efforts to redress the terms of their poorly remunerated, dangerous, and arduous position in labor-hierarchies. How these workers negotiated the terms of this difference and their assimilability has been a key structuring feature of migrant mobility efforts to the present.

Industrial mill and farm owners and white nativist skilled labor unions in manufacturing promoted policies and laws to deny civic rights to migrant workers at the bottom of labor and economic hierarchies.[9] These interest groups relied upon scientific writing[10] to support public debates and the passage of legislation that racialized migrant workers' identities to justify violence, incarceration, civic exclusion, punishment, and disregard for workers' bodily well-being.

By naturalizing migrant workers' low status in mill hierarchies, these interests exerted control over efforts to raise wages and improve dangerous work conditions.[11] This included issues of work and personal safety, as well as how labor law can effect access to healthcare and its effectiveness and quality.

Early in the twentieth century, discourses helping to codify migrant industrial workers' assimilability were reflected in the recommendations of the Dillingham Commission and led to the passage of laws such as the 1917 Burnett Act, which presumed that literacy was linked to inherent intelligence. A group of social scientists, intellectual elites,[12] and politicians would confront these tactics by promoting an alternative explanation of the presumed genetic inferiority of migrant laborers. Organizations such as the National American Civic League (NACL) and city-based immigration protection and civic associations were founded nationally, working with partner civic associations in local migrant labor communities. In New England, this included extensive collaboration with the Portuguese Fraternity, a beneficial insurance society with chapters in over 30 industrial mill and agricultural community worker settlements in the first decades of the 1900s. In partnership with state governmental commissions, these migrant associations formed the organizational and intellectual core of the Americanization movement.[13] Proponents promoted upward mobility for industrial migrant workers from conditions of poverty, critically poor health, and residential blight, through access to literacy programs, English language education, and training in civics as a preparation for political participation. The question of migrant "assimilability" was answered not by arguments over their presumed genetic disposition to do certain kinds of work, as was the countervailing position; the cause of their deficiencies was perceived not as inherent, but as due to their lack of cultural knowledge, a shortcoming that could be solved through proper education, a pathway to civic access.[14] Yet, assimilation as evaluated through political participation and economic improvement alone does not consider how the racialization of migrant labor also depended upon the discourses and actions of migrant workers themselves in efforts to transform their position in social mobility hierarchies. While there was a progressive intent in arguments favoring an educational program to counter anti-immigrant narratives based on presumed genetic or natural deficiencies, the Americanization model nonetheless required participation in an Anglo-conformity[15] system. Structured by white nationalist categories of exclusion, the material improvements of migrant low-level workers—including gaining civic rights and political legitimacy—were influenced by their own resistance and negotiations over their position in racialized labor hierarchies.

Studies of U.S. labor organization have produced histories, monographs, and biographies that chronicle politically and culturally relevant voices that drove migration debates and labor activism; however, low-level racialized migrant laborers' voices and organizational agency have been less frequently examined.[16] The direct participation of the many chapters of the Portuguese Fraternity in the Americanization initiatives of national civic leagues is one historical example, but communities settled by these industrial mobile migrant workers from Portugal continue to rely on formal socio-religious, cultural, and economic associations[17] as vehicles for political activism and to promote narratives of civic belonging.[18]

"O Dia de Portugal": Conjuring a National Holiday[19]

The Day of Portugal, held each year on June 10, is an amalgam of loosely connected commemorations of Portugal and expressions of Portuguese nationalism. Celebrated by Portugal's post-dictatorship socialist democracy as the "*Dia de Portugal, Dia de Camões, e Dia das Comunidades Portuguesas*" (The Day of Portugal, Camões, and the Portuguese Communities), the new official post-dictatorship title emphasized a purposeful break with the nationalist propaganda promoted by the Estado Novo regime. The cumbrous name also reflects the composite nature of diverse national commemorations that evolved in dialogue with, but separately from the regime, that are now incorporated into the federal holiday. The day celebrates culture, language, and history; and by explicit reference to Portuguese migrant communities, it also underlines the legal citizenship rights of those living outside national territory. Celebrations in these communities convey nationalist sentiments as "ethnic" identities frequently publicly expressed through symbols of the nation and attachment to one's place of origin, or even to previous migrant generations. The celebrations held in communities outside of Portugal—including those in southeastern New England—support these de-territorialized and transnational notions of citizenship and in-group belonging. The Day of Portugal may celebrate migrant origins, but in New England the celebrations are just as much a public place making ritual of belonging and civic access in America.

In Portugal, the evolution of Portuguese national day celebrations was slow and circuitous, with multiple organizers and proponents. It has been celebrated in different historical contexts under different economic and political systems, by monarchists and republicans and under dictatorship and democracy. The event also gained prominence as a Lisbon municipal celebration that was outside of religious festivals and the control of the Church, even as national commemorations gained public popularity when the day was syncretized with the tradition of popular saints feasts.[20] Portugal's Dom Luis I decreed June 10, 1880, as a "dia de festa nacional" in honor of Camões, the author of the *Lusíadas*, the Portuguese-language epic seafaring poem about Vasco da Gama's arrival in India.[21] The choice of this day memorialized the date that historians had fixed for Camões's death in Lisbon in 1580 (despite not much evidence for their assertion).[22] As a celebration undertaken by multiple and sometimes antagonistic shareholders, public ceremonies around Camões were also used to contest Dom Luis, through "three days of public holiday, [through which]...the commemorative movement grew, transforming the 40,000-strong 'civic' processions into protests against the liberal monarchy, and forming the basis for the republican movement."[23]

In part, the Camões fetes of the late nineteenth century were elements of an ongoing cycle of nostalgia for the tropes and glories of the Portuguese maritime empire within colonial national identity narratives.[24] The *Lusíadas* themes reflected the aspirational ends of political and economic elites, and linked their geo-political endeavors in the creation of a national hero. Promoted by the state, the development of this national celebration has as a counterpart a similar nineteenth-century phenomenon in the UK, which repurposed seafaring chronicles from the early modern period[25] promoting nationalism in the context of overseas colonial labor and resource exploitation. Reprints of original editions, excavations of unpublished narratives, and renewed attention to the glories of English ocean voyages in the sixteenth century promoted white nationalist colonial endeavors in the later 1800s, as the narratives glorified national greatness and justified ongoing state actions that exploited transoceanic colonial labor. Public, state-sanctioned rituals using the tropes of Portuguese navigators and the "voyages of discovery" are still a part of nationalist iconographic representation and shape political and economic action in Portugal.[26] K. David Jackson writes that these tropes illustrated narratives in which "the mariner is husband and lord, awaited savior, a quasi-mythical entity emanating from the sea, whose purpose is teleological, national and existential."[27]

After 1910, the First Portuguese Republic dismantled symbols of the monarchy's rule, changing both the flag and the national anthem as part of a propaganda program that "had at its heart the 'cultural construction of the nation.'"[28] The national day celebrations of June 10, however, continued to thrive in Lisbon during the First Republic, and in ensuing decades would be nationalized under the organization of the Estado Novo. The dictatorship co-opted and controlled popular cultural practices and social rituals, while also restoring older symbols of power.[29] In 1952, the dictatorship adopted June 10 as a state-sanctioned holiday, *Dia de Portugal*, with public commemorations touting the nation, the military, the sovereign, and the *povo* (the people) under the common symbolism of the flag. This iteration of the national day continued to appropriate Camões-related tropes, and the censored press acclaimed the poet as a "symbol of civic virtue." As a swashbuckling figure celebrated both for his own adventures and for his tales of Portuguese conquest, Camões was a useful figure for Estado Novo propaganda purposes. By glorifying Portuguese expansion and exploration as part of a longitudinal grand historical narrative, the Estado Novo was able to obscure the militarized exploitation of labor and resources under which the authoritarian colonial regime operated.[30]

The dictatorship sponsored multiple national commemorations on June 10, including military parades and troop assemblies as part of a *Dia da Bandeira* (Flag Day) and as an official holiday in honor of the Portuguese armed forces. From 1933 until the end of the dictatorship in 1974, the Estado Novo officially referred to the June 10 celebrations as the *Dia da Raça* (Race Day). The press and state also referred to the day as the *Festa da Raça* (Race Festival)[31] as well as the *Dia de Camões, e Portugal, e a Raça*. In this context "*Raça*" is a presumed social category expressing biology, nationalism, and family. The dictatorship promoted the *raça portuguesa* as a Portuguese language version of *Blut und Boden*, romanticizing national identity as an expression of the popular will in the service of colonial aims and maintenance of their control over transoceanic power and labor hierarchies.[32] Estado Novo authoritarian ruler António de Oliveira Salazar's adoption of the multiracial premise embedded in his reading of Gilberto Freyre's luso-tropicalism[33] propagandized the "Portuguese race" within colonial discourses of political repression and economic exclusion.[34] As the Estado Novo military fought an overseas war of colonial subjugation, commemorations of the *Dia da Raça* were part of racializing discourses through which the regime, the army, and the oligarchy rallied the public in efforts to maintain their control and exploitation of colonial labor.

After the 1974 revolution, as the post-dictatorship government stabilized, Estado Novo symbols of power were transformed. The *Ponte Salazar* (Lisbon's signature bridge) was renamed the *Ponte 25 de Abril*, the popular cognomen for the revolution. Reconfiguring symbols of the dictatorship, the new democratic government also embraced state affiliation with the June 10 celebrations. The synthesis of ritual days that encompasses the current iteration of the national holiday reflects a liberalizing spirit and recognizes the geo-strategic importance of migrant settler communities, and other configurations of Portuguese identities among those living outside the national territory of Portugal.

Public Identities and Racialized Labor-Class Exclusion

The Day of Portugal is celebrated within a context of migrant community political mobility since elected politicians in Massachusetts and Rhode Island are primary organizers of the commemoration. In New England, U.S. and Portuguese government officials collaborate to stage the events with migrant sociocultural "associations" (state chartered *associações* or fraternal societies). Formalized Portuguese associations have organized migrant community festivals since the 1800s. They have also been a conduit through which migrants have joined public commemorations of American civic holidays in the U.S. Formal Portuguese involvement in such events and the migrant workers' beneficial societies that organized their participation were described in a book about James Garfield's 1881 funeral cortege and begin appearing in reports from the *Lowell Sun* about the annual municipal Fourth of July Parade as early as 1896. In Portugal, the associations have been a central institution of local community and civic participation and were re-created by migrants upon their arrival in the U.S. The associations support migrant communities' social, economic, and intellectual welfare [35] and were vehicles of migrant agency to challenge racialized labor exploitation. In New England, the first associations were founded in the later third of the nineteenth century. The Lusitanian Benevolent Association in New Orleans, however, is likely the earliest recorded incorporation of an association by migrants from Portugal in the U.S. Founded in 1848, the workers' insurance and health benefit scheme was incorporated in 1851. Another Portuguese organization in the city, the New Lusitanos Benevolent Association, was first convened in 1858.[36] Some associations founded in New England in the nineteenth century are still in existence. For instance, the Luso-American Financial and Fraternal Branches in RI (which names 1868 as its founding date) participated in the 2018 Providence Day of Portugal parade and multiple Espírito Santo associations have been in continuous operation for over 100 years.[37] By the turn of the century, these kinds of organizations, including socio-religious and mutual benefit insurance schemes, were widely established by migrants from Portugal working as industrial and agricultural laborers. The state-incorporated social organizations provided migrants with a statutory vehicle to collectively participate in local politics, pursue economic ends, and engage in the broader civic life of their communities.

The racialization of migrant labor through the early nineteenth-century industrial period constituted "Portuguese" identity as non-white or as contested-white defining these workers as unassimilable and as un-American. Portuguese racial identity was a topic in mid-eighteenth century ethnological writings and became a popular subject of scientific study during the industrial period among progressivist scientists, who increasingly analyzed the Portuguese case. These scientists based their arguments on assumptions that certain genetic data could be used to determine migrant racial classification. These arguments were then repeated in public statements by local, state, and national officials. Debates about the non-white racialized identities of Portuguese migrant workers were part of public discourses in print as well, including local community newspapers. Portuguese themselves participated in these exchanges to contest belonging to and the definition of "white" and "black" Portuguese categories as well as broader Portuguese non-white identities.[38] Communist and socialist organizations, whose activities were often coordinated with migrant fraternal and cultural organizations, offered a viable alternative for industrial laborers to collectively mobilize. However, anti-communist laws supported the positions of mill owners and skilled tradesmen's unions, facilitating efforts to curb and criminalize industrial migrant labor organization.[39] Portuguese migrant workers who joined or took leadership roles in the labor movement were thus vilified by politicians, mill owners, and tradespeople for endangering the "American" way of life.[40] The costs of confronting their position in labor hierarchies and gaining a voice in labor negotiations could be extortionate. Portuguese who joined the socialist- and communist-organized migrant unions lost their jobs, were barred from future employment, were imprisoned, and were targeted by police.[41] Migrant labor organizers were arrested and deported.[42] Migrant workers' political and civic exclusion was advanced through laws that legitimized authoritarian measures ostensibly against "communists," but used ultimately to thwart labor movement organization.[43] These discourses around labor and communism controlled the workers' civic participation, collapsing notions of labor class into presumptions about the political unsuitability of categories of racialized migrant workers. By representing the political activity of a racialized labor class as dangerous and un-American, they reinforced constraints on migrants' civic participation and fed arguments against their presumed genetic, cultural, and political predisposition against assimilability.

Migrant industrial workers' associations participated in the Americanization goals and events of national organizations, such as the NACL.[44] Between 1909 and 1959, in the state of Rhode Island alone, migrants from Portugal incorporated some 150 associations that were dedicated (primarily or in part) to providing members with access to civic participation through classes in citizenship and naturalization, English language proficiency, and political mobilization.[45] Portuguese migrant associations sought to "better understand our civic and political duties as American Citizens in order to better serve our city, state and nation," which they hoped would "elevate the standing of Portuguese-American Citizens," especially "Portuguese American youth striving for better education, better civic and social interests, better recognition, to which full citizenship entitles [them]."[46] One association promoted the assimilability of the "Portuguese-American Race" by celebrating Portuguese culture and history while also instilling "American" civic ideals.[47]

Through the associations, migrant industrial workers participated in patriotic American national celebration days, including the Fourth of July, commemorations of the Pilgrims' arrival in Massachusetts, and civic events, such as fundraisers for World War I bond drives.[48] The public citywide municipal events were pageants for recursive expressions of presumed patriotism, civic virtue, and hardworking industriousness[49]—characteristics written up in the press in positive commentaries about the migrants and their participation in celebrations of America. Through these demonstrations the associations were able to shape public narratives of belonging that could rebut the anti-immigrant and white-nationalist political arguments about the migrants' presumed lack of assimilability.[50]

Assimilability and the social mobility (social well-being and civic participation)[51] program of the Americanization movement were embedded in discourses and laws codifying racialized hierarchies, with success, in part, predicated on the ability of the program to transform the racial identities of low-level migrant laborers. Historical efforts to pass more inclusive and overturn restrictive legislation and activities that shaped public debates have challenged structural inequalities, as has migrant participation in the industrial labor and social justice movement. Throughout the century, however, other efforts undertaken by many associations and individuals to improve migrant social mobility have taken a more conciliatory approach to the existence of racialized mobility hierarchies.[52]

The "black" and "white" Portuguese categories that appeared in census[53] and immigration data were considered relevant as units of scientific analysis[54] and were terms used in public debate, shaping social relations and limiting civic rights to control migrant labor. These categories, however, were also used by migrants who were themselves from Portugal in second-order[55] adoption of exclusionary discourses that marginalized and racialized other low-wage industrial workers, creating a binary opposition with the black Portuguese category to support their own mobility in the white category.[56] As a result, analyses of labor racialization are incomplete without understanding the role of migrant workers from diverse Portuguese geographies who were themselves responsible for promoting and participating in white nationalist discourses in negotiations for their own assimilability and racial mobility.[57]

In *The Old World in the New* (1914), the sociologist Edward Ross relies on the "black" and "white" Portuguese categories to argue that among migrant laborers, low "social rank" "somewhat corresponds within the grades of natural ability existing within a people." He contrasts the Portuguese with the superior "race traits...defining the American people."[58] Denigration of the "natural abilities" of "multitudes of 'black Portuguese'" from the Cabo Verdean Islands[59] was consistent with his descriptions of the failed morals and physical and cultural shortcomings of the "'white Portuguese'"[60] category. Although presented as separate but interconnected groups, Ross's hairsplitting of racialized difference placed both white and black Portuguese at the bottom of assimilability hierarchies.

Portuguese themselves used the existence of a "white Portuguese" category as part of strategies of mobility through the broader Americanization movement. In their responses, some sought to reject marginalization not by challenging underlying racialized structures of worker exploitation, but by exploiting them to promulgate their own civic inclusion and social mobility.[61] In the decades after the 1920s, constructions of the "white Portuguese" category facilitated such negotiations over assimilability. Many associations changed their original Portuguese names (including some of the oldest in New England) to English names in state filings, often rewriting charters and bylaws as they did so. Some of these associations sought to codify white Portuguese identities into their re-incorporation. For instance, in 1952, when two of the oldest Portuguese migrant associations in Newport, Rhode Island, merged, previous Portuguese names were anglicized to create the Vasco Da Gama Holy Ghost Society. The new organization's bylaws were rewritten to limit membership to Portuguese of the "white race."[62] Americanization mobilities were facilitated by adopting these oppressive, racialized categories of difference to reconstruct industrial migrant Portuguese identities as white, American, assimilable, and deserving of civic participation. These discourses and public arguments over assimilability were also repeated among older migrant generations to marginalize post-1960s cohorts with similar racialized discourses favoring their own assimilable identities at the expense of the more recent group.[63]

New England Celebrations of Portugal and Longitudinal Civic Advocacy

During the first forty years of its post-revolution existence, the Day of Portugal, Camões, and the Communities was always held in Portuguese national territory, in cities and towns on the continent and in the islands. Despite the celebration's stated purpose, no host cities had been named outside the country until 2016. In that year, state ceremonies convened in Lisbon and Paris. In 2017, the president of Portugal selected Porto, Rio de Janeiro, and São Paulo. In 2019, the host communities were Porto Alegre, Brazil, and Cabo Verde. Prior to cancellation from public health measures against the SARS-CoV-2 Corona virus pandemic, the host cities for the 2020 celebration were to be in Madeira and South Africa.

In 2018, the Azores and the Portuguese communities in New England were chosen by Portugal's president, Marcelo Rebelo de Sousa, to hold the celebrations, selecting host cities Ponta Delgada (São Miguel), Providence (Rhode Island), and Boston (Massachusetts), along with a side visit to New Bedford (Massachusetts). After attending the New England festivities, Portugal's prime minister, António Costa, traveled to Azorean-Portuguese communities in California. Returning to Portugal after the commemorations, the president flew to Washington DC some weeks later to attend bilateral meetings with the U.S. president. As was the case in the geopolitically important cities of Rio and Paris, the Portuguese delegation used the local migrant celebrations in New England as an opportunity for state-level diplomacy; meetings with local, regional, and federal officials; and the signing of educational exchange protocols. Throughout his public appearances, Portugal's president advocated a pro-migration, pro-environment, pro–European Union/NATO platform, weaving the story of the "Portuguese Communities" in North America into political speeches about the "special relationship" between Portugal and the United States. Couching his criticisms in language favoring multicultural diversity, he rebuked the Trump administration for its rhetoric against NATO and its revitalization of white nationalist identity politics.

Underlining the selection of the Azores and New England, the president appointed Onésimo T. Almeida as the event's grand marshal and *presidente* of the *comissão* (national organizing committee). Almeida, a long-time chair and professor of Brown University's Portuguese and Brazilian Studies Department, was born in the Azores but has lived in New England most of his life. He is a celebrated international public scholar who has had a critical political impact among local Portuguese migrant communities. The delegation also included the chief of the General Staff of Portugal's armed forces, Portugal's ambassador to the United States, and various members of parliament. Presidents of Portuguese universities also attended some official events with their counterparts from several U.S. universities. Congressional, state, and local policy makers rubbed elbows with VIPs, educators, transnational business executives, well-connected Americans in Portugal, prominent Portuguese in America, ambassadors, governmental and consular diplomats, and steady streams of Portuguese migrants and their families coming together for the festivities.

Although the president certainly amplified the excitement around the 2018 edition of the Day of Portugal, annual celebrations in Massachusetts and Rhode Island date back to the 1980s, shortly after the Portuguese 1974 Revolution, and "Portuguese Heritage Day" events had been organized by state officials even earlier. Events are also coordinated by the Consulate of Portugal, which supports Day of Portugal celebrations financially, through advertising, and with assistance arranging logistics. The organizational rubric of the celebrations still runs through local Portuguese migrant associations in cooperation with Portuguese migrant elites in business, politics, and education, who take on responsibilities for planning content.[64]

Like other Portuguese *festas*, Day of Portugal events in New England have a carnivalesque and communal atmosphere. Material culture displays draw on longitudinal representations of Portuguese public identities and practices and provide a space for more recent and creative forms[65] of public collective representation. In Providence, for example, throngs of paradegoers watched the 2018 Day of Portugal *parada* (from "parade," as the *cortejo ethnográfico* is locally called) while dressed in national-team *futebol* jerseys and draped in Portuguese flags. The parade featured wild and highly entertaining thematic floats, including a cardboard sculpture of the *Padrão dos Descobrimentos*; a live-action, eyepatch-clad, *gorgeira* (ruff) collared Camões; a wooden replica of a Graciosa windmill; and a crudely mechanized larger-than-life panorama of Mozambique-born Portuguese national team soccer God Eusébio, depicted scoring a goal for Lisbon's Benfica. Sports clubs and Portuguese language schools marched, and *ranchos folclóricos*, *filarmónica* bands, and *fado* singers performed in the parade and at separate public events. A comparison with social media videos from Day of Portugal parades in New England, California, and Canada reveals the widespread participation of Portuguese associations with similar celebrations and ritual elements.

Through staged public events the day mobilizes the instruments and ornaments of Portuguese migrant community material culture to evoke ethnic/national/in-group identity—signifying the distinctness of the group while also signaling its suitability to participate in local power hierarchies necessary to access social, economic, and political rights. Among contemporary associations, interest group politics expressed in multicultural democratic practices are one legacy of the racialization of migrant labor. Migrant groups themselves have constructed social, racial, and class categories through which they negotiate political power and advocate for social mobility.

Politicians, Flag Day, and Recursive Expressions of Identity

During the 2018 celebration, the governors of Massachusetts and Rhode Island met the presidential delegation, and the event displayed the heightened pomp one would expect during a foreign head-of-state visit. State politicians have participated in (and helped to organize) New England's Portuguese heritage celebrations in collaborative efforts that have assisted the Portuguese government to connect to constituents in local Portuguese migrant communities and have helped the state to advance its own diplomatic and geo-strategic aims. The Day of Portugal pageants in New England unfold with remarkable continuity, despite their organization by separate (but sometimes overlapping) associations and individuals. They include parades, homages, elegies, and exhibitions of Portuguese material culture; scholarships are awarded, and dinners are held in collaboration with Portuguese associations in ceremonies attended by local elected officials. Along with parades and public events, such as *arraials* (large festive gatherings) or communal dinners, a key ritual element is the deliverance of prepared and impromptu speeches by policy makers, association officers, and special guests. Typical speeches discuss Portuguese place making and group building efforts, invoke migrant community origin mythologies, and extoll the virtues of the hardworking and industrious communities of patriotic immigrant Americans.

Current Day of Portugal celebrations reflect the arrival of a newer (post-1958) wave of mobile labor migration. Estado Novo diplomacy was undertaken in collaborations with community associations that used Portuguese maritime iconography, monument dedications, and commemorations as a means to influence U.S. support for Portugal's colonial endeavors. Post-dictatorship democratic Portugal still relies on a transnational nation building project in which de-territorialized migrant communities help to promote the state's diplomatic goals. Earlier, Estado Novo-era precedents of the Day of Portugal in New England include Portuguese heritage events, as well as other forms of memorialization that have taken place since at least the late 1920s. In June 1958, a Portuguese heritage commemoration was proclaimed by Dennis Roberts, Rhode Island's governor, that honored the Portuguese voyages of exploration by hosting two of the Estado Novo's war frigates in the port of Providence. The event was supported by the Estado Novo consular office. Organization and celebration of the 1958 holiday took place during the debate and passage of Rhode Island senator John O. Pastore's proposed Azorean Refugee Act, designed to assist the recent victims of a volcanic eruption on the islands. Passage of the act required superseding 1920s immigration laws, which had restricted migration from Portugal and other nations that had provided early twentieth-century migrant labor for U.S. industry and were part of broader white nationalist codification of racialized labor hierarchies. The importance of Portugal-U.S. geopolitical relations, dominated by the U.S military's use of Lajes Air Force Base on the Azores in the post-World War II period, was one part of the argument for passage, and public speech-making worked to justify the vote by emphasizing Azoreans' (American) patriotism and industriousness. The Azorean Refugee Act presaged changes to the 1965 Hart-Celler Act[66] (a political companion to the 1964 Civil Rights Act), which opened migration but required re-engagement with the assimilability question as it challenged the basis of exclusion of racialized categories of mobile labor communities. It also presaged other Estado Novo efforts to promote positive images of Portugal as part of cultural diplomacy to help influence U.S. support for Portuguese colonial wars in the 1960s and 1970s—a period that coincided with dramatic transformations in how racialized hierarchies (including those implicating migrants) in the U.S. would be structured under the law.

Multicultural political organizations in the U.S. emerged through migrant agencies in longitudinal negotiations over their racialized identities. Alongside the 1964 Civil Rights Act, the new migration laws empowered those from the "unassimilable" industrial labor categories to gain a legal status of equality, a necessary step to advocate for effective civic equality. U.S. political parties would re-align after the passage of this legislation. Over the subsequent decades Southern Democrats gradually left the party to join the Republican Party, as newer political blocs of racialized industrial migrant workers and union members were integrated into the Democratic coalition. Local association drives for civic involvement activated the constituencies that supported the politicians who changed the laws. The polemics linked to the legislation's passage brought migrant assimilability and efforts to shape their own racialized identities to the fore, and they would presage debates around post-1960s power configurations, including debates around Portuguese minority status.[67]

Migrants from Portugal who arrived in New England after these legal changes continued as domestic, manual, and industrial factory labor;[68] and their socioeconomic mobility and political participation have been an ongoing challenge.[69] Similarities in objectives between the Day of Portugal and earlier Americanization-movement efforts to remake assimilable identities have made these celebrations key public rituals in the construction of the "Portuguese" political category within contemporary multicultural power-sharing arrangements. In the legislative districts of former mill cities, constituency bases of electoral power depend on support from ethnic-group-as-interest-group coalitions. The ambiguity and fluidity of racial identities of communities of migrant mobile laborers from Portugal are evident in the celebration. Ritual elements promote the group as a unique migrant culture linked to other migrant minority groups, while simultaneously using twentieth-century heritage narratives, that, intentionally or not, continue to negotiate Portuguese white racial identity.[70]

Speechmakers at Day of Portugal celebrations in New England speak frequently about Portuguese communities in highly affirmative if not hagiographic platitudes that rarely mention the social or economic challenges faced by the group. They describe "the Portuguese" as hardworking[71] immigrants[72] who were embraced warmly by American institutions, never complained or protested, and became (through their work ethic, religiosity, and so forth) contributors to their states and communities. When hardships are mentioned, they are used to illustrate an obstacle that has since been successfully overcome—an act that itself confers a special status upon the "successfully integrated" Portuguese (in this sense, *integrated* serves as a gloss for *assimilable*). Conflicts and issues that stem from unequal power access, historical discrimination, poverty, and the racialized marginalization of migrant labor hierarchies are not a part of the rhetoric or symbolic representation of the Day of Portugal and other Portuguese heritage commemorations.

Speeches and public events during these celebrations also incorporate Portuguese Flag Day tributes that take place in various public political spaces, association halls, Veterans of Foreign Wars halls, town and city halls, and in the legislative chambers and ceremonial spaces of the Massachusetts and Rhode Island state houses, which have all hosted Day of Portugal related ceremonies attended by local, state, and national politicians. In 2018, the president and prime minister of Portugal presided at a Portuguese flag-raising ceremony at Boston's city hall in their first public event in the United States. As much as Day of Portugal celebrations in New England have been used by local politicians to connect with key electoral blocs, the emergence and staying power of the commemorations are also linked to the Portuguese migrant and Portuguese-descended state and municipal officials who are increasingly elected to represent districts among Portuguese migrant communities or appointed to other state positions. Dozens of these state senators, representatives, mayors, and town selectmen serve on the organizing committees for various Day of Portugal events, and the legislators in Massachusetts and Rhode Island belong to Portuguese American caucus delegations—advocating for and voting collectively on issues affecting the communities of their many Portuguese American constituents.

In New England, these issues mostly coalesce around working-class Democratic Party politics. The necessity of Portuguese community constituent support, however, makes such caucuses and the Day of Portugal equally important to Republican elected officials in those districts.[73] For Portuguese migrant politicians of either party, celebrations provide opportunities for them to speak Portuguese in the state house chambers and broadcast or stream such speeches across the state. Aside from the many policymakers who have close connections to Portugal, the events also bring out public officials who may have distant familial connections to the country, but who do not otherwise participate in contemporary migrant community activities. For them, the Day of Portugal is a chance to signify, to creatively pronounce Portuguese words while staking the right to claim the day as a celebration of "us." It is a chance for self-described Hispanic and Italian American officials to pay homage and talk about the similarities between the experiences of their own families and communities and those of the "hardworking Portuguese."

The migrant place making experience is portrayed through Portuguese exemplars of success, through mythic imaginings of Camões and other heroes. For speechmakers, the Day of Portugal and Portuguese heritage celebrations are not an opportunity to reflect critically about Portuguese migrants' place in contemporary and historical local labor hierarchies, nor about how they fit into broader anti-migrant discourses and laws, nor about how they continue to confront the structural challenges necessary to overcome the economically troubled urban areas that they inherited and where they still live, long after the decline of the textile industry. Policy makers may recognize and work to address these challenges through legislation, collaboration with community organizations, and sponsored programs; but on the Day of Portugal their rhetoric sticks to platitudes of aspirational optimism and uses the event as an occasion to invoke the shibboleths of national and ethnic communalism. Among the most frequently evoked narratives during Day of Portugal festivities are references to mythic maritime icons and tangential connections to U.S. history. Migrant community origins in the U.S. are linked to the so-called "voyages of exploration and discovery," through readings of history that place the Portuguese in America before the Pilgrims and obscure the communities industrial labor mobility roots.

Dighton Rock and Other Arguments about Portuguese Racial Identities

The rhetorical flourishes of political speechmaking reflect longitudinal counter-narratives against racialized political discourses and exist in the context of legislation and statutes that have shaped Portuguese public identities. In 2018, even the Portuguese president Marcelo Rebelo de Sousa used a key symbol of negotiations over migrant racialized identities in North America when he mentioned Dighton Rock during a speech at the Massachusetts State House.[74] Dighton Rock is a three-meter-long boulder—originally found partially submerged under water on the bank of the Taunton River. The face of the boulder is etched with a palimpsest of petroglyphs, many of them weathered beyond recognition and altered or obscured by more recent renderings. Since the rock art was first depicted in 1680[75] it has been a popular object of curiosity and scientific study. Historical writing on the petroglyphs' origins have yielded divergent interpretations that can reveal more about the biases of an author than about the rock itself. Despite manifest evidence of an indigenous origin, the rock art has been attributed by some of these writers to Vikings and other Europeans.

Brown University psychology professor Edmund Burke Delabarre (1863-1945) analyzed many of the studies about the origins of Dighton Rock. In an uncritically connected synthesis of historical evidence, he conjectured that the rock had been etched by the Portuguese North Atlantic seafaring expedition captain and cartographer Miguel Corte-Real in 1511.[76] Delabarre concluded that Miguel Corte-Real (who had disappeared in 1502 after sailing from Portugal to Newfoundland) was not actually lost, but rather had sailed south to Narragansett Bay and then up the Taunton River where he encountered a group of indigenous inhabitants. Delabarre asserted that Corte-Real, through a combination of conciliation and force, was able to supplant the Sachem as leader of the Wampanoag inhabitants.[77] The historical analysis treated Corte-Real as a civilized "white savior" archetype, who Delabarre names the "first European dweller in New England."[78]

The speculative account relied on Delabarre's creative discernment of a Portuguese heraldic symbol and lines of Latin text including the etching "V. DEI hIC DVX IND" (an alleged abbreviation of "Voluntate Dei hic Dux Indorum").[79] Delabarre extrapolates the entire inscription to read "Miguel Cortereal. 1511. By the will of God, leader of the natives of India in this place."[80] Delabarre's writing and other historical scientific studies since the mid-nineteenth century about the origins of Dighton Rock are discussed by Hunter in the context of racist American eugenics and migrant community place making that have resulted in the erasure of indigenous authorship. Dighton Rock, Hunter writes, is a pareidolia upon which "theorists turned Indigenous peoples in whom they detected intellectual and cultural capabilities into whites, or [were people] improved in the past by the superior cultures, technologies, and blood of Europeans."[81]

Rejected by scholars in Portugal, the Corte-Real myth was first linked to assimilability narratives of Portuguese whiteness in the 1920s by a group of educated, well-off, and politically connected elites, who were supported over subsequent decades by Estado Novo consular officials to promote the rock's Portuguese provenance. Since the 1960s, no individual did more to promote the myth (and argue for Portuguese whiteness) than Dr. Luciano da Silva. Da Silva was a Portuguese-trained medical doctor who had migrated to Rhode Island as a teenager. Controversial among academics and others for his analysis,[82] the abundantly confident da Silva was a popular figure among the local communities and at association events. He delivered throughout his life over 500 public presentations (primarily at migrant association events) and wrote articles and two books promoting the notion of the Portuguese "discovery" of North America, which occurred, by his estimation, more than 100 years before the Pilgrims had landed in New England. Da Silva's version of indigenous erasure and promotion of the

Corte-Real origin story provided a public narrative reconfiguring non-white racialized Portuguese identities as white.

In Portuguese communities, promotion of the Corte-Real myth and legends of early sixteenth-century Portuguese settlement in New England began shortly after Delabarre's first publication on the topic. In 1926, the New Bedford daily Portuguese-language newspaper *A Alvorado* met with Delabarre to visit Dighton Rock and published articles and translations promoting his theory as a serious scientific study. Delabarre himself noted that "his Portuguese friends" had taken a keen interest in promoting and preserving the rock as early as 1927.[83] Early efforts were undertaken by the Portuguese American Civic League and Abílio de Oliveira Águas, the Portuguese Consul in New Bedford, who translated Delabarre's 1923 article for a Portuguese scientific publication.[84] Joseph Damaso Fragoso, a language professor at New York University, added to Delabarre's theories,[85] promoted the myth, and raised money for preservation efforts through the Miguel Corte-Real Memorial Society (MCRMS), a Portuguese association he chartered in New York in 1951.[86]

The Corte-Real narrative celebrating a white Portuguese leader of natives creates an inversion trope that reimagines the reasons for New England's Portuguese settlement. Migrant origins in the myth are linked to the great maritime explorers of the "*Descobrimentos*" period, a quite different narrative from the reality of the community's position as a non-white and politically marginalized group of migrant mill and farm laborers. Da Silva would recall in public lectures that he had heard about Dighton Rock as a teenager in Portugal; and while studying for an undergraduate degree in biology at New York University, he joined the MCRMS and served as the organization's secretary.[87] In 1959, the *Fall River Herald* published a photograph of Dighton Rock in which da Silva had traced his interpretation of what he perceived as Corte-Real's engravings. The photo was widely circulated in newspapers and shown at public lectures throughout the Portuguese communities.

Da Silva also self-published the book *Portuguese Pilgrims and Dighton Rock: The First Chapter in American History* (1971),[88] in which he argued that the Portuguese were the first Europeans to settle in what is now the United States and attempted to racialize Portuguese migrant identities as white. Da Silva's text provides a bookend of sorts to the bibliographical genealogy of twentieth-century scientific writing and elite discourse promoting white and non-white racialized Portuguese identities. *Portuguese Pilgrims and Dighton Rock* was published in the context of congressional debates over Portuguese minority status taking place at the time and of growing anti-Estado Novo and anti-colonial activism among U.S. migrants. Proposals over minority status split the communities, with much of the pushback coming from elites who feared the classification would codify their non-white identity and as a result hinder their social mobility.

The Corte-Real reading was not taken seriously by historians and scholars of Portugal or New England. Nonetheless, da Silva's tireless public lecturing on the theory[89] and work on preserving Dighton Rock ensured that the myth has remained popular among some in the region's Portuguese migrant communities and it was used as part of broader Diaspora nation building discourses by the President of the Portuguese Republic during his Day of Portugal visit. Da Silva's book, lectures, and activities are examples of efforts by some elites working through Portuguese civic and cultural associations to seek social mobility through racial hierarchy mobility by transforming Portuguese non-white identities. In the chapter "White American Indians" da Silva constructs a narrative about "the genetics" of the "Wampanoag Tribe" complete with charts of eugenic data.[90] The book is filled with specious explanations, over-generalizations, and suspect evidence. Couched in a hagiography of Portugal's glorious early modern seafaring conquests—the "first modern nation to have an empire in which the sun never set"[91]—Da Silva gives examples of "promiscuity" and "interbreeding" that mixed the "pure white" and "white genes" of the Portuguese with non-white races around the world.[92] Like Salazar, Da Silva drew on Gilberto Freyre's theories of luso-tropicalism to argue that native populations in areas of Portuguese mercantile trade contact in the Atlantic, Indian, and Pacific Oceans had been improved by "genetic and cultural intercourse with [Portuguese] white men."[93] Da Silva applies the argument to North America and effectively credits Portuguese luso-tropicalism as a pivotal variable in the English settlement of New England and the U.S. Beginning his argument with the claim that Wampanoag means "white men" rather than "easterners," "people of the dawn," or "early light," as it is defined in Wampanoag usage, da Silva then cites a few selective quotes from historical writing (including the Pilgrims). These "descriptions of 'white and friendly (Wampanoag) Indians,'" in da Silva's estimation, "constitute enough anthropological evidence" to conclude that the narratives of friendly and cooperative relations between the English and the Wampanoag were the result of luso-tropicalist "genetic" improvement. The "friendly" Wampanoag were only that way, in da Silva's rendering, through "interbreeding" with the "genes" of Corte-Real's "pure white" men, which imbued the barbaric inhabitants with the "Portuguese manner of civilization."[94] Tellingly, da Silva did not use luso-tropicalism to say that the Wampanoag were Portuguese, but rather that they—an otherwise implicitly inferior group—were improved by the genes of Portuguese white men.

Da Silva, like many other mid-twentieth-century Portuguese migrants, sought to improve migrant social standing in racialized hierarchies by embracing shibboleths of American patriotism and attempting to interweave the story of the Portuguese with that of the United States. His arguments also attempted to challenge the Pilgrims elevated position in regional and national culture and supplant them with the Portuguese. Plymouth Plantation (located ˜20 miles from Dighton Rock) was the first permanent English settlement in New England. The anniversary of their arrival has been celebrated with monuments and parades,[95] and it has been annually memorialized during the U.S. national socio-religious holiday of Thanksgiving. For Da Silva and others who believed the myth, the real Pilgrims were not English, but Portuguese.

Touting the legend of early sixteenth-century Portuguese settlement in New England as part of place making activities[96] can be compared to efforts among Italian Americans to nationalize the celebration of Columbus Day in response to their own position in racialized industrial labor hierarchies. Declared a national holiday in 1934 by President Roosevelt, Columbus Day was made a federal holiday in 1971, the same year that *Portuguese Pilgrims and Dighton Rock* was published. Da Silva argued not only that the Portuguese were the true Pilgrims, but also that Corte-Real had "discovered America"—not Christopher Columbus. Federal recognition of Columbus had helped narratives of Italian-American assimilability in white supremacist and white nationalist power configurations. Unable to gain much of an audience for his theories outside of the Portuguese migrant enclaves of New England, national acceptance of the Corte-Real legend was never realized. As his efforts to promote Corte-Real as the "discoverer" of America gained little traction, Da Silva tried another tack, and attempted to appropriate Columbus for his cause, self-publishing a co-authored book titled *Christopher Columbus was Portuguese!*[97] In his two books, Da Silva claimed for the Portuguese ownership of Thanksgiving and Columbus Day[98]—or two of the four U.S. federal holidays commemorating the nation's founding.

The collaboration of Portuguese civic and cultural associations was fundamental to the promotion of the legend. The associations sponsored lectures, fundraised, and provided organizational leadership to conserve Dighton Rock and purchase land to build a museum in which they could tell their version of its origins.[99] The Portuguese American Civic League was among the first associations to begin work on a museum. The civic association had collaborated with national Americanization movement organizations, which promised social and racial mobility. Efforts to preserve the rock and build a museum began in the 1920s, shortly after Delabarre's publication of his theories. Portuguese migrant associations would take a leading role. The rock was removed from the bank of the Taunton River in 1963 and a design from the 1950s proposed that the museum be constructed in the Manueline architectural style.[100] Although current descriptive signage in the museum building housing the rock relates multiple origin theories (including "American Indian"), the curation overtly suggests the Corte-Real myth. The only other large physical objects aside from the rock on display are a replica of a Portuguese *padrão* (stone pillars left by Portuguese seafaring expeditions expressing territorial possession) and two scale models of Portuguese caravels. The ship models are exhibited so that they sail at the entrance of the display and are aligned in a triangle with the *padrão*, centered in the back of the room and immediately to the right of the entrance to the rock.

Among communities of migrants from Portugal in New England there existed both support for and criticism of Salazar. Those opposed to the dictatorship included migrants of diverse political persuasions. Political factions in Portugal were reflected in the transnational politics of the migrant communities, but reactions to the fascist dictatorship in New England were also part of local political and civic participation discourses. Expression of anti- and pro-Salazarism in the migrant communities can be analyzed against assimilability tensions and mobility strategy choices over different historical periods. The post-1958 wave of migrants arriving from the Azores, Madeira, Portugal, and Cabo Verde came in the midst of debates on and passage of federal immigration and civil rights reform laws. They also arrived during (and as a result of) Portugal's colonial wars. Tensions emerged between older generations with their reliance on Americanization movement and "Anglo-conformity" models and the newer arrivals, who would embrace burgeoning multiculturalism models. Interestingly, among anti-Salazarists, some spoke out as leftist labor organizers and anti-colonialists, while others, as in Da Silva's case, challenged Salazar through twentieth-century anti-fascist expressions of American patriotism.[101] Yet, as the museum curation demonstrates, Da Silva (who served as volunteer director) and other migrants, continued to celebrate maritime tropes of Estado Novo propaganda that glorify Portuguese seafaring prowess while erasing the exploitation and abuse of an underclasses of laborers in the service of elite trade, historical mercantile capitalist expansion, and colonial exploitation. In the process, they also erase the difficult history of the mobile migrant laborers who did settle New England.

In a testament to the power that the Corte-Real myth continues to have among migrant Portuguese communities, the Azorean Regional Government (working with Portuguese associations, Luciano da Silva, and the museum) sponsored a 2011 commemoration at Dighton Rock State Park celebrating "500 years of Azorean presence in North America," as the headlines were written in articles published by the *Herald News* (Fall River) and the *Portuguese American Journal*.[102] That the event was a celebration of the "Azorean presence" rather than a Portuguese one is due to the fact that the Azores are the point of origin for the majority of Portuguese-speaking migrants in New England. It also suggests more contemporary twists in the narrative among the post-Azorean Refugee Act wave of mobile labor migration. These migrants celebrate the Corte-Real myth by emphasizing his links to the islands. For instance, his father, João Vaz Corte-Real, was named Capitão of S. Jorge and after expeditions to Newfoundland in 1474 he was named Capitão of Angra by the king. The Azorean cooption of the Corte-Real myth also suggests that more recent migrant arrivals from the Azores continue to position themselves in racialized assimilability hierarchies.[103] In this context, Luciano da Silva's continental identity and status as a medical professional set him apart from the low-level mobile laborers from the Azores who arrived after passage of the Azorean Refugee act in 1958.[104] The myth persists as a ritual of assimilability among multiple mobile migrant laborer cohorts and shows how these migrants have adapted common iconography to accomplish goals over several historic periods.

Memorialization and monument dedications also point to the collaboration between associations and governments in place-making and public cultural and political programs. The padrão and the model replicas of caravels, for example, were likewise funded with contributions from the Azorean Regional Government. Associations have led efforts to raise funds and erect other monuments to seafaring explorers[105] in place making efforts promoting the visibility of the Portuguese. Some of these efforts, intentionally or not, circulate narratives of Portuguese social and racial assimilability consistent with the Dighton Rock polemics. One of these memorialization efforts is the Portuguese Discovery Monument in Newport, which was initiated by two Portuguese migrant associations and paid for with funds from the state of Rhode Island and the Portuguese government. The monument was built in 1988 and, after falling into disrepair, was redesigned and rededicated in 2014. It is a paean to Sagres, a town in the Atlantic corner of Portugal and the clifftop site of Dom Infante Henrique (Prince Henry the Navigator)'s so-called "nautical school" and a point of embarkation for expeditions patronized by the Prince. The location of the monument in Newport, the same town as the U.S. Naval War College, underlines U.S.-Portugal naval and military cooperation through NATO and bilateral agreements.

Situated on a rolling palisade overlooking the ocean, the Portuguese Discovery Monument evokes in miniature form Sagres' dramatic cliffs. There are several explicit references to Sagres and Portuguese maritime navigation, including a semicircle of sixteen bollards suggesting a compass rose, a representation of an *esfera armilar* (the navigation instrument on the Portuguese flag), and a twenty-foot sandstone obelisk dedicated with a stone plaque engraved with the names of famous Portuguese maritime explorers (including Miguel Corte-Real).[106] Dedicated "In memory of the Navigators Mapmakers, Explorers, Fleet Commanders and those others who enabled the discoveries of sea routes by the Portuguese of two-thirds of the world," the monument is another representation of the voyages of exploration that reimagine and memorialize Portuguese industrial worker settlement communities through the mythologies of maritime empire. Although the Portuguese Discovery Monument in Newport and Dighton Rock museum were created using Estado Novo era propaganda iconography, both were supported with governmental funds during Portugal's post-dictatorship period.

The Portuguese "explorers" and "navigators" making glorious "discoveries" on these expeditions were military merchants who also "enabled" the abduction and purchase of captured humans and transported these individuals under the threat of violence and death on "sea-routes," forcing them to labor across "two thirds of the world." Although racialized coerced laborers are certainly included among the "others" etched into the monument's dedication, it is unlikely that memorializing their contributions was the intention. In fact, these brutal realities are absent and erased from the mariners' representation as icons of celebration and veneration. Da Silva, for example, denied Corte-Real's role in the transatlantic slave trade, and celebrations touting Portuguese maritime prowess erase the centrality of slave and other coerced laborers in Portugal's transoceanic expansion efforts, both as a commodity to be sold and as a forced and violently brutalized labor force that made military mercantilism and resource extraction (also known as "exploration" and "the discoveries") possible.

The twentieth-century Corte-Real legend combines narratives featuring the Portuguese "*Heróis do Mar*" (heroes of the sea) from a decidedly local perspective. Portuguese heritage celebrations (such as Day of Portugal) in New England likewise incorporate narratives connecting Portugal and Portuguese migrants to historical events in the United States founding myths as well. One of these narratives celebrates Peter Francisco, who served under George Washington, as a Portuguese hero of the American Revolution.[107] Francisco was the ward of a wealthy and politically well-connected magistrate in Virginia, but what his alleged Portuguese origins might have meant during his life[108] is separate from how his figure has been appropriated for contemporary purposes. In this scenario, a once homeless Portuguese immigrant turned hero had an important role in the foundational history of America. He is linked to today's Portuguese migrant settlers, whose own patriotic values are publicly expressed via references to him. The same can be said of the frequent invocations during the Day of Portugal to other American origin-myth moments, such as narratives in which the founding fathers used Madeira wine[109] to toast important events in early U.S. history.

Many of these imaginings—Dighton Rock etchings, museum displays, monuments, statues, plaques, conflations among nationality, blood, first claims to land, and belonging—are based on squishy archaeology or rely on speculative reconstructions. But that is largely beside the point. They are all used to narrate a Portuguese migrant community origin myth[110] unbound by racialized labor-class power inequalities. History is used not as social critique but as a means through which to idealize an aspirational relationship between Portugal and America forged at foundational moments of the United States' creation. Expressed in a language of heroism and common purpose, the narratives support origin myth discourses of Portuguese whiteness and assimilable identities. In truth, of course, the racialization processes of Portuguese migrant communities in New England have less to do with Portugal's celebrity appearances in the footnotes of U.S. history than they do with the far more relevant chapter about physical, economic, and political labor-class exploitation.[111]

The 2018 Rhode Island Day of Portugal Lusophone Calendar Art Contest also served to help re-imagine these identities. Youth artists submitted illustrations, which judges evaluated to create a bilingual calendar of Portuguese holidays that serves as a pedagogic tool for Portuguese-language students studying in area schools. The calendar codified representations of Portuguese identity based on a broader language group, expressed visually through drawings of national flags and material-culture items from places in the world where Portuguese is spoken. The contest attracted 450 entries, and the winning artists and their illustrations were featured during the Portuguese heritage celebrations at the Rhode Island State House. Children ages five through seven were asked to illustrate a popular Portuguese children's story (*Galinha Ruiva*), and those ages eight through ten were asked to depict food from the lusophone world. The three winning drawings in this second category all depicted classic food items representing Portugal: *vinho de porto*, *caldo verde* soup, Sagres beer, and the more recently ubiquitous *pastel de nata*. Students ages eleven through thirteen were asked to illustrate the islands of the lusophone world; these winners depicted an alligator against the backdrop of the Angolan flag, the iconic *Portas da Cidade* of São Miguel (and its replica in Fall River), and a map of Madeira.

The oldest group of illustrators (ages fourteen to eighteen) were assigned to portray aspects of the "Age of Exploration." All three winning images depicted a vignette of a Portuguese caravel, but one entry stood out as an example of how Estado Novo colonial discourses repeat in contemporary representations of Portuguese cultural identity in New England, where mythologies around the "discoveries" are embedded in racialized migrant identity constructions. The illustration is drawn from the perspective of a Portuguese captain who is standing behind his pilot at the wheel. The viewer looks down from the deck of the caravel as it approaches the shore, gazing through the rigging of the ship and its prow down onto a beach with grass huts and several nondescript, darkly pigmented, loincloth-clad figures. The title of the entry, "Portuguese Exploration Ship Discovers Tribe," clarifies the artist's intention. (With a few tweaks, the entry might well have illustrated Delabarre's and Da Silva's vision of Miguel Corte-Real landing at Dighton Rock.)

Here again, the economic and political history of racialized Portuguese migrant workers in industrial New England has been transformed through association with images of the "discoveries," casting the Portuguese in opposition to the encountered and racialized other—including those who were forcibly transported and violently coerced to work in a slave labor system. Like the previous examples, it points out that one's position of power in situations of assimilability—as viewed from the beach or the deck of the ship—is ultimately relative. The fact that the image was declared a winner in the contest and appeared on thousands of calendars given to local students and the public speaks to how these identities are reproduced and how racialized colonial discourses about the Portuguese and idealized narratives celebrating 500 year-old transoceanic exploits continue to structure contemporary migrant mobility contexts.

Awards and Honorifics

Day of Portugal celebrations in New England often include the public awarding of scholarships to college-bound Portuguese heritage students. Indeed, galas and annual dinners of the region's Portuguese associations are held as fundraisers and award ceremonies for student scholarships. Eligibility is based on candidates' identification as "Portuguese" (which is construed differently in different sponsoring organizations) and their academic record. Having family members who are active in the sponsoring association also helps. These largely American-born scholarship recipients are publicly recognized at key moments, and they often take on a prominent ceremonial role in the heritage celebrations, such as raising the Portuguese flag.

Other Day of Portugal ceremonies recognize figures who have made "contributions" to the "Portuguese community." For instance, in one 2018 event held on the Portuguese navy's tall ship *Sagres* (anchored in Boston during the celebration), the Portuguese president presided over an award ceremony attended by the organizing commission and political and educational elites, which conferred membership in the chivalric Order of Dom Infante Henrique on five recipients from Massachusetts and Rhode Island. The award, according to the presidential website, recognizes "distinguished contributions to Portugal both in the country and abroad," including "the development of Portuguese culture; and knowledge of Portugal, its history, and its values."[112] *Values* is a term frequently invoked by politicians in national contexts, although defining the specifics of a national value and how it is shared by a nation's citizens remains elusive. In this case, however, the honorees were recognized more for their actions than their values. Two were Portuguese-American philanthropists who had donated money to two Portuguese studies centers at universities and to a university library's Portuguese migrant studies archive. A third was a former Rhode Island state representative and chair of the House finance committee. He was praised by the Portuguese president for having spearheaded funding efforts to refurbish the

Portuguese Discovery Monument of Newport[113]. In an earlier ceremony at the Massachusetts State House, the Portuguese-American Legislative Caucus conferred the Portuguese Heritage Award, recognizing the prominent contributions to "their community" by individuals who "excelled in their lives and who serve as role models for others to emulate." On behalf of the caucus, the Portuguese president handed out fifteen awards, split evenly among Portuguese migrants and the children and grandchildren of migrants. Recipients included elected officials, bank officers, businesspeople, association officers, and a chief of police. All were lauded for their "strong" "Portuguese-American work ethic."

The story told through these awards depicts a community that has risen to the height of political, economic, and public success. Emphasizing the continued importance of Americanization movement discourses, one recipient was nominated for assisting "hundreds of Portuguese immigrants in obtaining their U. S. Naturalization" and for teaching English language and civics classes. One could have easily swapped the recipients at the shipboard and state house ceremonies; their biographies were similar. Indeed, several of the honorees had already received the other award. As upwardly mobile professional categories, the work of politicians, businesspeople, philanthropists, artists, and those dedicated to Portuguese culture, history, language, and the arts contrasts with the low-level labor hierarchies of historical and contemporary classes of Portuguese migrant workers. In the Day of Portugal pageant, these presidents, prime ministers, honorees, and cultural and political elites are joined to mythic historical figures, national heroes, God, the nation, flags, "the communities," and symbolic trappings of the celebrations. In 2018, the ceremonies took yet another meta-turn when the Portuguese president conferred the Prince Henry the Navigator Order of Merit on the organizer of both the Boston and Provincetown Portuguese heritage days.

Like other aspects of the Day of Portugal pageant, the glories of the communities' most "successful" and important members—including scholarship recipients—are used to represent the character of all Portuguese migrants, providing an inversion narrative that, instead of amplifying the bad actions of a few to condemn a group, amplifies the positive contributions of a few as emblematic of the whole. To be certain, the individuals recognized in the ceremonies contributed to the material and civic improvement of their communities. Recognition at the ceremony for individual achievements that promoted public welfare, social justice, equality and civic participation were deserved. Further, the awards recognize the hard work that is required to achieve these goals. In practical terms, providing immigrant services, advocating for civic rights, and supporting education (including scholarships) and other charitable activities are important ways to promote social equality. The awards also publicly recognize that those living in Portuguese migrant communities take a far more active role in civic activism than is generally indicated solely by data from surveys about economic mobility and electoral participation.

As part of a public ceremony, however, acknowledgement does more than highlight the recipients' important contributions to the well-being of their communities. In a public and publicized event, these professionally accomplished honorees are presented as exemplars of the migrant community. There is a similar logic to associations awarding scholarships to college-bound students, whose educational goals are aided while their achievements as Portuguese honorees reflect upon the community as a whole. These representations are perhaps nowhere more prevalent than at memorial dedications to Portuguese migrant and Portuguese American war dead. Day of Portugal commemorations and other dedications will solemnly intone Portuguese who died to protect and defend the values of America. The memorial allows a broader community to argue for assimilability and inclusion through the reflected achievements of some of its members, who, in the case of the war dead, are apotheosized through their sacred sacrifice for America, proving incontrovertibly that they (and theirs) belong.

Multicultural Power Sharing, Mobility, and Assimilability

Despite ongoing participation in Americanization movement goals, the social organizations have remained hubs for the production of material culture, Portuguese language learning, community economic assistance and development, and Portuguese migrant worker political and civic engagement. These activities have directly assisted migrant agencies to gain social and economic mobility. Migrant associations in operation since the late nineteenth century were reinvigorated by the post-1958 generation, who founded new organizations and brought new energy, cultural knowledge, and organizational expertise to older associations with dwindling membership lists. The diverse activities of these members critique characterizations of the Portuguese as a so-called "invisible minority,"[114] a description that delegitimizes the social and political role that migrant community centered institutions play in organizing social welfare and public civic engagement activities. Portuguese cultural events sponsored by the organizations structured migrant personal support networks and served as an organizing fulcrum of collective representation. Rather than diminishing practices supporting Portuguese material culture, the associations' collaborative participation in Americanization activities allowed them to continue Portuguese cultural programming without having the practices politicized as disqualifying. Americanization is in this regard less about making the "Portuguese" into "Americans" than about mediating the boundaries of social exclusion and civic inclusion. Stated another way, social mobility is examined not as an outcome of generational, cultural, or economic "assimilation," but rather as a collective negotiation for power that is rooted in ongoing arguments over Portuguese assimilability.

The Day of Portugal in New England is a key ritual in Portuguese ethnic-group-as-interest-group politics, assisting migrant communities to participate in contemporary multicultural power configurations. As is the case in Massachusetts, contemporary interest groups and political factionalism in Rhode Island reflect legacies of migrant communities settled by industrial workers from Ireland, then French-Canada, and later in the nineteenth century Italy, Syria, Armenia, Poland, and Portugal. (Providence already had an Irish mayor in the first decade of the 1900s as the Portuguese were arriving.) Concessions have been won since the darker periods of industrial manufacturing's exploitation of migrant workers. Nonetheless, industrial labor practices and labor laws still favor the capital class in its negotiation for low-wage workers whose bodies are subjected to the most punishing and debilitating tasks. Labor representation and securing the right to organize are ongoing political issues.

Historical narratives of twentieth-century socioeconomic mobilities suggest that the Portuguese were the last large-scale industrial migrant group to work in mill cities in Massachusetts and Rhode Island and that there were not significant migrants from other groups to replace them in these lower-level jobs after labor movement gains and the decline of the industry sent textile manufacturing to the south (as they themselves had previously supplanted French-Canadian workers in some urban mill contexts).[115] As migration from the original southern European labor cohorts arriving to work in industrial mills at the turn of the century was restricted after the 1920s, the renewal of Portuguese migration in the 1960s (which increased by 80 percent in the twenty years after the Capelinhos volcano eruption) meant that there was indeed a group replacing Portuguese migrant industrial workers in New England; however, it was composed of a newer group of migrant labor from Portugal. Those migrating to work in these settlements confronted the legacy of more than a half-century of migrant labor-class racialization of earlier cohorts and their descendants as they struggled themselves to gain civic and political access.

Avenues to political inclusion, however, were recast in the post-1960s civil and civic rights era as electoral coalitions formed in New England democratic power-sharing arrangements among multicultural, ethnic-interest-groups. In this political environment, earlier arrived migrant labor groups from Portugal working in factories, manufacturing, agriculture, and the service economy have been joined by more recently arrived migrant laborers from Mexico, the Caribbean, Central America, and Southeast Asia. Local mayors, state representatives, and state executive branch officers from migrant communities, including the Portuguese, have won office on the strength of electoral blocs expanded from the contemporary in-group identities of former industrial worker communities. Elections also reflect the multicultural power-sharing configurations of newer migrants, who serve in state and municipal elected positions including recent Providence mayors whose parents were from the Dominican Republic and Guatemala.

Public displays of in-group identities are a part of negotiations for civic legitimacy and electoral power among groups in multicultural power-sharing configurations. The tension between older industrial workers' racial mobilities, civic inclusion, and white national politics with newer configurations of multicultural identities is reflected in the Day of Portugal pageant, which highlights the uniqueness of the Portuguese among multiple ethnic-groups-as-interest-groups. In Rhode Island, for example, the 2018 Portuguese commemorations were just one part of a much larger citywide festival, the fourth annual PVD Fest,[116] a public block party in Providence held on the closed-off downtown streets around Kennedy Plaza and Waterplace Park. Sponsored by the city's Department of Art, Culture, and Tourism jointly with FirstWorks (a cultural and arts association), the PVD Fest features multicultural music, arts, and food.

In 2018 there were lectures and art exhibits, as well as Pakistani food trucks, Latin dance performances, Australian acrobats, a bachata Guinness World Record attempt, a Laotian youth group, and the Portuguese custard sweets *pastéis de nata*. The format of the festival draws on other previous celebrations in the city including the Providence Pride festival which has roots in the 1970s and annual parades since the 1980s. Day of Portugal Rhode Island and the PVD fest also coincide with the broadly celebrated Pride Month in Providence. In effect, the PVD fest promotes public visibility and society-wide celebration of diverse and less visible migrants comprising Providence's civic community. In 2018, the Day of Portugal Rhode Island parade, Presidential speech and other public events were part of the PVD fest program and were also the featured theme of the June 10 staging of Providence's renowned public arts exhibit, WaterFire, commenced by the Portuguese president and attended by the *comité*, Rhode Island's governor and congressional delegation, and the Mayor of Providence. Both on its own and as part of the broader festival and public activities, the Day of Portugal's parade and performances—*fado* and *filarmónicas*, mythic heroes from literature and sports, dramatic ballgowns and folk costumes—gave the Portuguese the material-cultural wherewithal with which to claim their corner of the festival as they literally paraded around the block and through the heart of the city. Yet, despite the prominence of public events taking place under temporarily hanging Portuguese flags, the celebration was merely one part of a larger showcase for the multicultural city and an ongoing part of negotiations over state codification and narratives defining belonging and civic access in New England.

Contemporary narratives of Portuguese and other migrant communities' socioeconomic mobilities—bolstered by well-designed research and collected data sets—often seek to examine levels of integration, adaptation, and assimilation as measured through a rubric of socioeconomic or educational success and political participation. The discourses, laws, and social actions that arbitrate and conciliate power inequalities and civic participation of a racialized labor class, however, are a related factor in these determinations, as subsequent migrant generations and descendants have continued to resist (and promote) labor-class inequalities through discourses of racialized assimilability. This includes ongoing racialization processes around whiteness and blackness for diverse groups of migrants from Portugal and its former colonies. Migrants from these geographies have been aware of their position in racial hierarchies and have contributed to activities that have both resisted and maintained racial inequality. Along with racialized industrial workers from various origins, the Portuguese share similar structural trajectories confronting power inequalities and navigate white nationalist discourses of inclusion and exclusion by negotiating racial identity as a precondition of civic participation.

In the case under study, the existence of legally and scientifically codified white and black Portuguese categories, including various competing definitions of how people from different geographies fit into the groups, points to a fluidity in Portuguese identities and demonstrates how discourses of assimilability and racial mobility are embedded in Portuguese-speaking migrant communities' social mobility efforts. Scholarship from the 1990s examining structures and mechanisms of racialized inequality rightly concludes that constructions of upwardly mobile white identities are a key variable supporting the maintenance of racial hierarchies.[117] In this regard, one of the interesting characteristics of Portuguese migrant laborer racialization is how, despite the "white" and "black" categories, Portuguese racial identity remains unsettled. This fact is underlined by racial mobilities that not only move toward whiteness, but also in certain contexts depend on maintaining their ambiguity.

Discourses promoting multiculturalism as a model of Portuguese civic participation have further complicated older assimilability narratives. Efforts to gain civic rights and social mobility have come through conscious and willful engagement with racialized marginalization over a century and have not been monolithic. Labor movement organization and other civic engagement activities (including their support for candidates for public office), indicate that the migrant associations were a highly active and essential form of social organization structuring Portuguese efforts to gain civic inclusion in multiple historical periods of North American settlement. These organizations provide a key unit of analysis to understand longitudinal settlement and place making strategies as a response to the exploitation of transoceanic mobile labor. Migrant associations, as we have seen, were important to the Estado Novo and to post-dictatorship democratic governments, which have advanced diplomatic goals by collaborating with the civic organizations, mounting public heritage projects that use Portuguese maritime and cultural iconography. Migrant workers negotiate with local power hierarchies mediated by global capitalist economies, but categories of racialized marginalization have also been influenced by related transatlantic geostrategic maneuvering and nation building projects.

Many of the representations of Portuguese cultural patrimony at Day of Portugal and other Portuguese heritage celebrations are still drawn from Estado Novo symbols of maritime glory. For contemporary organizers and participants, these symbols are part of place making efforts coalescing around in-group identities and are not used by most to promote white nationalist discourses of belonging, unconsciously or overtly, but rather, as a celebration of a unique ethnic group. Nonetheless, elevating the icons of a glorious transoceanic empire while erasing the humans who were brutalized to make that empire possible perpetuates narratives of racial and social marginalization. Finding solutions to structural power inequalities requires honesty to recognize how these categories of exclusion are created and maintained. A constant feature of the Day of Camões and iterations of the Day of Portugal in nearly 150 years of annual celebrations, is that the commemoration has been used to promulgate multiple and polysemous representations of identities used to express often contradictory political principles. The ritual in New England is no different in this regard.

The challenges of migrant place making have not yet been overcome; they are not a remnant of history but an ongoing challenge. Portuguese migrant communities have collectively created a political voice through civic participation in multicultural democracy. Democracy is strengthened for all by re-thinking Portuguese identity narratives that would perpetuate racialized inequalities. This is a conclusion about migrants in a-social-justice-oriented, multi-cultural North America that was suggested by the President of Portugal in his speeches in Providence and the Massachusetts State House. In his official June 10 Day of Portugal, Camões and the Communities speech, the president admonished: "Nobody lives alone in the world.... I cannot understand how one can have their own people migrating and not accept other people migrating." Heritage events that represent the lived histories of this community, that discuss challenges honestly, and that link the story of Portuguese migrants in New England to the struggles of other migrant communities can shape these celebrations to more directly support contemporary social and racial justice movements and help all migrant laborer communities to navigate toward social equity and civic inclusion.

NOTES

1. This paper was submitted as a Research Fellow of the ERC Advanced Grant Project Colour of Labour: the racialized lives of migrants-PI Cristiana Bastos (Universidade de Lisboa, ICS) [ERC-2015-AdG-695573, 2016-2021]; http://colour.ics.ulisboa.pt. Framed and supported by the Colour project, the research included broad archival work on the civic engagement and political and economic marginalization of migrant labor in New England, examining racialization processes among Portuguese industrial and agricultural workers. Participant-observation research at the 2018 Day of Portugal celebrations in New England was also part of the project mission. I have attended and conducted research on Day of Portugal celebrations for decades in Providence, Boston, Falmouth, Fall River, New Bedford, Ponta Delgada, Angra, and Lisbon as well as other heritage celebrations in Portugal and Portuguese migrant contexts. Longitudinal participant observation in New England on Portuguese migrant racialization and marginalization includes a paper presented at the *Race, Culture, Nation* conference (April 6-8, 2001. University of Massachusetts Dartmouth & Brown University) that was developed for publication

through the FCT Post-Doc grant, A Critical Interrogation of the Nation and the Power of the State to Define Belonging [SFRH/BPD/20473/2004]. Field and archival research on the formation and role of migrant associations in racialization processes was also supported through the FCT project Ritual, Etnicidade, Transnacionalismo-PI João Leal, CRIA-Universidade Nova de Lisboa [PTDC/CS-ANT/100037/2008], an in-depth field research project studying New England socio-religious associations (FES). I am grateful for the financial and intellectual support of the Portuguese studies units at the University of Massachusetts Dartmouth: the Center for Portuguese Studies and Culture, Ferreira-Mendes Portuguese American Archives, and Tagus Press; at UMass Lowell: the Saab Center for Portuguese Studies and the Lowell Center for History; as well as Lowell's Boott Cotton Mills Museum (U.S. National Park Service); Meg Costello at the Falmouth Historical Society Archive; Portuguese and Brazilian Studies, Brown University; and the Luso-American Foundation (FLAD). I would like to acknowledge Daniel Georgianna (UMass Dartmouth), Prof. Robert Forrant (UMass Lowell), and Prof. Philip T. Silvia (Bridgewater State) for their influential research and personal insights assembling the story of migrant industrial labor in New England to which this paper is indebted. I am especially grateful to Onésimo T. Almeida, who made research for this paper possible as a result of a generous invitation to accompany him in his role as Grand Marshall of the Day of Portugal and to participate in events with the Portuguese President and the official delegation.

2. Extrapolating from Jerry Williams, *And Yet They Come. Portuguese Immigration from the Azores to the United States* (New York: Center for Migration Studies, 1982). Examining how history is told in New Bedford and its implications for local migrant communities in the city, Kingston Heath argues that the histories of the industrial workers are underrepresented in favor of the whaling period. Kingston W. Heath, "From Whalers to Weavers: New Bedford's Urban Transformation and Contested Identities," *IA: Journal of the Society for Industrial Archaeology* 40, 1/2 (2014): 7-32. Romanticized narratives of Portuguese whaler origins also typically mask the difficult lives faced by racialized workers on whale boats as well as merchant ships.

3. Carter, Green, and Halpern provide a historical synthesis of the construction of labor class racial identities examining power hierarchies in the 1900-1925 U.S. industrial period. They examine governmental actions and the passage of laws constructing the racial status of labor classes, with the "racialization of migrant labor" working "to naturalize differences and normalize exclusions." Bob Carter, Marcie Green and Rick Halpern, "Immigration Policy and the Racialization of Migrant Labour: The Construction of National Identities in the USA and Britain," *Ethnic and Racial Studies* 19, 1 (January 1996): 135-157.

4. Shimazu discusses the assimilability question regarding civic rights and arguments over whiteness in the racialization of Japanese migrant workers in the U.S. during

the period. Naoko Shimazu, *Japan, Race and Equality: The Racial Equality Proposal of 1919* (New York: Routledge, Nissan Institute Japanese Studies Series, 1998), 77-78.

5. Analytically separate from laws, and other state-codified categories (that both drive discourses and that discourses participate in constructing), discourse is used here in two senses: 1. migrant agencies and activism through issue organization and control of public displays of material culture, and 2. challenges to migrant civic participation and the racialization of migrant labor in popular, scientific, and political debates.

6. These exclusions are embedded in the "policing and refurbishment" of racialized labor classes that limit mobility by controlling "assimilability...[T]he reconstitution of national identities...articulated through concepts of 'race' in which, amongst other things, colour, country of origin and religion, came to operate as key signifiers of difference. Through immigration and nationality laws, governments and administrations ranked human populations into hierarchies of assimilability." Carter, Green and Halpern, "Immigration Policy and the Racialization of Migrant Labour," 136. See also Robert Miles, *Racism and Migrant Labour* (London: Routledge, 1982); *Capitalism and Unfree Labour* (London: Tavistock, 1987); *Racism after 'Race Relations'* (London: Routledge, 1993).

7. The notion that laborers were genetically inferior and unequipped for citizenship also structured power hierarchies in slave labor systems. See, for example, the ethnologist arguments featured in E. N. Elliot, ed., *Cotton is King, and Pro-Slavery Arguments: Comprising the Writings of Hammond, Harper, Christy, Stringfellow, Hodge, Bledsoe, and Cartwright, on this Important Subject* (Augusta GA: Pritchard, Abbott & Loomis, 1860). Caroline Karcher discusses the ethnologists' presumptions about the racialization of forced laborers, low-share whale ship sailors, and other wage earners in her reading of Melville's "The 'Gees'." Carolyn L. Karcher, "Melville's 'The 'Gees': A Forgotten Satire on Scientific Racism," *American Quarterly* 27, 4 (Oct 1975): 421-442; Herman Melville, "The 'Gees," *Harpers New Monthly*, (March 1856): 507-09. Stanley 1998 examines how contract and wage labor were used to structure social relations based in the slave system, Amy Dru Stanley, *From Bondage to Contract: Wage Labor, Marriage, and the Market in the Age of Slave Emancipation* (Cambridge; New York: Cambridge University Press, 1998). See also Carter, Green and Halpern, "Immigration Policy and the Racialization of Migrant Labour," 135-157; and Ariela Julie Gross. *What Blood won't Tell: a History of Race on Trial in America* (Cambridge, Massachusetts: Harvard University Press, 2008). The *Reports of the Immigration Commission [Dillingham Commission Reports]* (U.S. Congress, 1911), especially vols. 5, 10, 21, and 41, which provide various examples. Benton-Cohen examines the nebulous formation of racial categories of migrants. Katherine Benton-Cohen, *Inventing the Immigration Problem: The Dillingham Commission and Its Legacy* (Cambridge: Harvard University Press, 2018).

8. Carter, Green and Halpern, "Immigration Policy and the Racialization of Migrant Labour," 143. In this study, as a result of industrial capitalism.

9. Beckert discusses how merchants gained control over labor and wages. Sven Beckert, "Building War Capitalism," 29-55, *Empire of Cotton: a Global History* (New York: Alfred A Knopf, 2014).

10. See, for example, sections on Portuguese industrial laborers in Bushee (1903) and Ross (1914) where they discuss the migrants' capacities for civic participation and socio-economic advancement in reference to racial classifications of low-hierarchy workers. Frederick A. Bushee, *Ethnic Factors in the Population of Boston* (New York: The Macmillan Company for the American Economic Association, 1903). Reprint by American Immigration Experience Series. (New York: Arno Press and New York Times, 1970); Edward A. Ross, *The Old World in the New: The Significance of Past and Present Immigration to the American People* (New York: The Century Co., 1914).

11. Portuguese laborers organized unions, participated in strikes, and faced criminal conviction and deportation as a result of political affiliations and protest activities. See oral history interviews with communist labor organizer Eula Mendes, New Bedford Textile Worker's Strike of 1928 Oral History Interviews and Research Collection, University of Massachusetts, Dartmouth, Archives and Special Collections: Interview by Daniel Georgianna, 1985, MC9 Box 8, Tape 56, 57, 58; Interview by Penn Reeve, MC9 Box 1, 16. Oral history interview with Joseph Figueredo, Tamiment Library & Robert F. Wagner Labor Archives, https://wp.nyu.edu/tamimentcpusa/joe-figueredo/, 2017. Implicit intersections of racial categories and political organization are referenced in Philip T. Silvia, Jr., "The Position of 'New' Immigrants in the Fall River Textile Industry," *The International Migration Review* (Summer 1976) 10, 2: 221-232; Daniel Georgianna with Roberta Hazen Aaronson, *The Strike of 1928* (New Bedford, Massachusetts: Spinner Publications, Inc., 1993); and Penn Reeve, "Portuguese Labor Activism in Southeastern Massachusetts," in *Community, Culture and the Makings of Identity*, ed. Andrea Klimt and Kim Holton (North Dartmouth, Massachusetts: Tagus Press, University of Massachusetts, Dartmouth, 2009), 337-56. An implicit examination of these processes is found in Marcia Walker-McWilliams, *Reverend Addie Wyatt Faith and the Fight for Labor, Gender and Racial Equality* (University of Illinois Press, 2016). See also John Higham, *Strangers in the Land: Patterns of American Nativism 1860-1925* (New Brunswick: Rutgers University Press, 1994); Alexander Keyssar, "Unemployment and the Labor Movement in Massachusetts, 1870-1916," 233-250, in *The New England Working Class and the New Labor History*, ed. Herbert G. Gutman and Donald H Bell (Chicago: University of Illinois Press, 1987); Nancy Zaroulis, "Daughters of Freemen: The Female Operatives and the Beginning of the Labor Movement," 141-158, in *Cotton was King: a History of Lowell, Massachusetts*, ed. Arthur L. Eno, Jr, (New Hampshire Publishing Co, 1976).

12. In notes and public talks from 1916-1924, Brown University President William Faunce lectured throughout the industrial northeast about core tenets of Americanization

principles as a remedy to social problems in industrial worker neighborhoods. (Special Collections, John Hay Library, Brown University, Providence, Rhode Island.)

13. Edward George Hartmann, *The Movement to Americanize the Immigrant* (New York: AMS Press Inc, 1967 [1948]). See also Sara Errington, "The Language Question: Nativism, Politics, and Ethnicity in Rhode Island, 1919-1925," in *New England Disharmony: the Consequences of the Industrial Revolution*, ed. Douglas Reynolds and Katheryn Viens (Kingston: Rhode Island Labor History Society and the Labor Research Center, URI, 1993), 92-111.

14. Franz Boas made a complementary argument against genetic disposition theories in volume 38 of the *Dillingham Commission Reports*, challenging the fixed categories of Folkmar and Folkmar's *Dictionary of Races or Peoples* (vol. 5) whose collected genetic data was used to define inherent abilities and genetic constraints on assimilability.

15. "The Anglo-conformity theory demanded complete renunciation of... ancestral culture in favor of the behavior and values of the Anglo-Saxon core;... the melting-pot idea envisaged a biological merger... and blending of respective cultures into a new indigenous type; and cultural pluralism postulated the preservation of...significant portions of culture... within the context of American citizenship and political and economic integration into American society." Milton M. Gordon, *Assimilation in American Life: the Role of Race, Religion, and National Origins* (New York: Oxford University Press, 1964), 85. See also Nathan Glazer and Daniel Moynihan, *Beyond the Melting Pot. The Negroes, Puerto Ricans, Jews, Italians and Irish of New York City* (Cambridge, Massachusetts: The M.I.T. Press, 1963). George L. Hicks, *Experimental Americans: Celo and Utopian Community in the Twentieth Century* (Champaign-Urbana: University of Illinois Press, 2001.)

16. Labor conditions of migrants from Portugal working in industrial mills in New England are described by Silvia, Jr., "The Position of 'New' Immigrants," 221-232; Georgianna, *The Strike of 1928*; Reeve, "Portuguese Labor Activism," 337-56; Daniel Georgiana, Penn Reeve, and others who collected the Strike of 1928 oral history archives (Claire T. Carney Library, University of Massachusetts, Dartmouth). See also Jett W. Lauck, *Cotton Goods Manufacturing in the North Atlantic States; Woolen and Worsted Goods Manufacturing. Vol. 10 Reports of the Immigration Commission [Dillingham Commission Reports]* U.S. Congress, 1911; Jett W. Lauck, "The Cotton Mill Operatives of New England," *Atlantic Monthly*, 109 (May 1912): 706-13; George, Kenngott, *The Record of a City: a Social Survey of Lowell, Massachusetts* (New York: The MacMillan Company, 1912). Other oral history and community archives including the UMass Lowell Center for History, Falmouth Historical Society, the Woods Hole Historical Museum, and the Cape Cod Cape Verdean Museum also have historical documents related to the racialization of Portuguese migrant labor.

17. Henry Radecki, *Ethnic Organizational Dynamics: The Polish Group in Canada* (Waterloo, Ontario: Wilfrid Laurier University Press, 1979); João Sardinha, *Immigrant Associations, Integration and Identity: Angolan, Brazilian and Eastern European Communities in Portugal* (Amsterdam:

University Press, 2009); Daniel Melo and Eduardo Caetano da Silva, eds., *Construção da Nação e Associativismo na Emigração Portuguesa* (Lisboa: Imprensa de Ciências Sociais, 2009); Joseph Bradley, *Voluntary Associations in Tsarist Russia* (Cambridge, Massachusetts: Harvard University Press, 2009); João Leal, *Azorean Identity in Brazil and the United States: Arguments about History, Culture and Transnational Connections* (North Dartmouth Massachusetts: Tagus Press, University of Massachusetts, Dartmouth, 2011); João Leal, "Festivals, Group Making, Remaking and Unmaking," *Ethnos* 81 4 (2016): 584-599. Leal also examines how the associations have used the rituals in adaptive and creative migrant cosmopolitan contexts. João Leal, "Migrant Cosmopolitanism: Ritual and Cultural Innovation among Azorean Immigrants in the USA," in *Cosmopolitanism in the Portuguese-Speaking World (European Expansion and Indigenous Response, 27)* ed. Francisco Bethencourt (Leiden, The Netherlands: Brill. doi: https://doi.org/10.1163/9789004353435, 2017), 233–249.

18. Hartmann, *The Movement to Americanize the Immigrant.*

19. Isabel provides an historical bibliography and analysis on the origins and evolution of the Day of Portugal: Maria Isabel João, "The Invention of the Dia de Portugal," 66, *Portuguese Studies*, 31, 1 (2015): 64-84. See also Fernando Catroga, "Ritualizações da História," in *História da História em Portugal Secs. XIX–XX*, ed. Luís Reis Torgal, José Amado Mendes and Fernando Catroga (Lisbon: Círculo de Leitores, 1996), 551–55.

20. João, *The Invention of the Dia de Portugal*, 66.

21. The Camões link also serves contemporary Day of Portugal and other heritage celebrations as a tie-in to help promote Portuguese language and culture, including several prominent events in New England that receive support from universities and the Consulate of Portugal.

22. See João, *The Invention of the Dia de Portugal*, 64-65; citing Jordão de Freitas, "Morte e Enterramento de Camões," *4º Centenário do Nascimento de Camões, 1524—1924*, ed. Pedro de Moura e Sá (Lisboa: Comissão das Festas Camonianas, 1924), 14.

23. Nuno Monteiro and Antonio Costa Pinto, "Cultural Myths and Portuguese National Identity," in *Contemporary Portugal. Politics, Society, Culture*, ed. Antonio Costa Pinto (New York: SSM Columbia University Press, 2011), 62; citing Alexandre Cabral, *Notas Oitocentistas II. Luís de Camões, Poeta do Povo e da Pátria* (Lisboa: Livros Horizonte, 1980.)

24. Monteiro and Costa Pinto, "Cultural Myths and Portuguese National Identity," 62. See also David Corkill and José Carlos Pina Almeida, "Commemoration and Propaganda in Salazar's Portugal: The 'Mundo Português' Exposition of 1940," *Journal of Contemporary History*, Vol. 44, No. 3 (July 2009): 381-399. Camões was himself on a nostalgia trip, not finishing the poem until toward the end of his life; and Camões may have written about Vasco da Gama, but the publication date of the *Lusíadas* in 1572 was about as close on the timeline to the birth of the Marques de Pombal (1699) as it was the birth of the first Portuguese seafaring captain to reach India (1469).

25. For example, reprints of English texts, including Edward Arber, *The Last Flight of the Revenge at Sea* (London: English Reprints, 1871) and Edmund Goldsmid's annotated republication of Richard Hakluyt's: *Principall Navigations* (Edinburgh: 1884 [1589;1598-1600]).

26. Monteiro and Costa Pinto, "Cultural Myths and Portuguese National Identity," 62.

27. K. David Jackson, *Adverse Genres in Fernando Pessoa* (New York: Oxford University Press, 2010).

28. Monteiro and Costa Pinto, "Cultural Myths and Portuguese National Identity," 1-54, citing Teófilo Braga, *Os Centenários como Síntese Afectiva nas Sociedades Modernas* (Oporto: A. J. da Silva Teixeira, 1884), 227. See essays examining uses of national symbols and state power in Eric Hobsbawm and Terrence Ranger, eds. *The Invention of Tradition* (Cambridge University Press, 2000) and David I. Kertzer, *Ritual, Politics and Power* (New Haven: Yale University Press, 1988).

29. The dictatorship instituted forms of social control on fado singers, *ranchos folclóricos*, and *filarmónica* bands through restrictions on repertoire, costumes, and venues of performance. Holton examines how communities, through the *ranchos* and cultural associations, contested Estado Novo authoritarian control. Her analysis of Salazar-era propaganda programs included negotiations over the freedom of association itself. Kimberly Holton, *Performing Folklore: Ranchos Folclóricos from Lisbon to Newark* (Bloomington: University of Indiana Press, 2005).

30. Corkill and Pina Almeida, "Commemoration and Propaganda," 381-399.

31. João, *The Invention of the Dia de Portugal*, 67;70.

32. This included assuming control of and restoring dilapidated architectural heritage from the medieval period and earlier, elevating controlled displays of popular culture in programs romanticizing national Portuguese identity, and entrenching a state patriarchy that was supported by an oppressive church and the state's national and colonial military regime.

33. Gilberto Freyre, *Casa-grande & Senzala: Formação da Familia Brasleira sob o Regimen de Economia Patriarchal* (Rio de Janeiro, Maia & Schmidt, 1933).

34. Patricia Ferraz de Matos, *The Colours of the Empire: Racialized Representations during Portuguese Colonialism* (New York, Oxford: Berghahn, 2013); Monteiro and Costa Pinto, "Cultural Myths and Portuguese National Identity," 1-54.

35. Leal, *Azorean Identity*; Leal "Festivals, 584-599;" Melo and da Silva, *Construção da Nação e Associativismo*.

36. According to an annotated chronology of Azorean history (with numerous documented historical inaccuracies, including the Corte-Real Dighton Rock myth, *op cit.*), the first of the two associations was founded by Azoreans recruited as field workers in Louisiana sugar cane plantations. Manoel da Silveira Cardozo, *The Portuguese in America 590 BC-1974* (Dobbs Ferry, NY: Oceana, 1976). If accurate, this would open a number of

interesting research questions. Did they arrive directly from the Azores, or perhaps, as is more likely, through a secondary migration from Caribbean sugar cane plantations? What kinds of work were the migrants doing and where were the laborers from Portugal situated on racial and assimilability hierarchies? How did these migrants fit into categories used to maintain white supremacist control of forced black labor in Louisiana cane fields? What was the relationship between the membership of the two organizations and the workers they represented? By 1881, the organizations had around 500 active members between them, but the original Portuguese founders had given way to lists of non-Portuguese executive officers. A description of the Lusitanian Benevolent Association, likely written by the organization itself, makes the following statement: "Formerly, none but Portuguese were admitted to membership; but that rule has of late years been changed; and now we find all nationalities represented among the members, the majority, of course, belonging to the Latin race." The "of course" part of the description requires deeper analysis, but speaks to Portuguese assimilability, suggesting how the New Orleans organizations were a part of negotiations over racialized identity hierarchies among "Latins" as a presumed genetic category, as well as the "Little Races" discussed by Gross, "Citizenship of the 'Little Races,'" 111-39. See brief descriptions of the organizations in Edward C. Wharton, *A History of the Proceedings in the City of New Orleans on the Occasion of the Funeral Ceremonies in Honor of James Garfield* (New Orleans: A.W. Hyatt, 1881).

37. See collective data of the multi researcher FCT grant project *Ritual, Etnicidade, Transnacionalismo: as Festas do Espírito Santo na América do Norte* (PI-João Leal, Center for Research in Anthropology, Universidade Nova, Lisboa); João Leal et al, Festas do Espírito Santo, "Ritual, Etnicidade, Transnacionalismo: as Festas do Espírito Santo na América do Norte" (PCDT/CS/-ANT/100037/2008). http://festasdoespiritosanto.pt/

38. Portuguese as a non-white or contested white group is an implicit and explicit topic of newspaper discourses in New England in references to Portuguese as early as 1894, in an article in which they are called "half-whites" (*Lowell Sun*, February 17, 1894). The use of "Portuguese" as a legal status that is neither white nor black is examined by Gross, *What Blood won't Tell*, in the southern U.S. See also literature reviews and arguments that point out contestations or negotiations over Portuguese racial identities in Gerald Estep, "Portuguese Assimilation in Hawaii and California," *Sociology and Social Research*, 26, 1 (September 1941): 61-69; Robert F. Harney, "'Portygees and Other Caucasians': Portuguese Migrants and the Racialism of the English Speaking World," in *Portuguese Migration in Global Perspective*, ed. David Higgs (Toronto: The Multicultural History Society of Ontario, 1990): 113-35; Jean E. Barker, "Cape Verdean-Americans: A Historical Perspective of Ethnicity and Race," *Trotter Review* 10: 1 (1996): 17-20; Miguel Moniz, "The Shadow Minority," 409-30, in *Community, Culture and the Makings of Identity*, ed. Andrea Klimt and Kim Holton (North Dartmouth: Tagus Press, University of Massachusetts, Dartmouth,

2009); Ana Yolanda Ramos-Zayas, "Stereotypes of the Tropics in 'Portuguese Newark: Brazilian Women, Urban Erotics and the Phantom of Blackness," 431-460, in *Community, Culture and the Makings of Identity*, ed. Andrea Klimt and Kim Holton (North Dartmouth: Tagus Press, University of Massachusetts, Dartmouth, 2009); Rui Vitorino Azevedo, "Not Quite White: The Ethno-Racial Identity of a Portagee," *Op. Cit.* 12 (2010): 19-34; Cristiana Bastos, "Migrants, Inequalities and Social Research in the 1920s: the story of 'Two Portuguese Communities in New England,'" *History and Anthropology* 29: 2 (2018): 163-183.

39. Racialized migrant laborers were barred from joining the (white) trade unions as the inclusion of migrants would diminish the power of the craftsmen's bargaining units.

40. See interviews with Eula Mendes 1985, 1987; and Joe Figueredo 2017.

41. *Falmouth Enterprise* (Massachusetts), Saturday, May 31, 1924, 3; New Bedford Strike of 1928, oral history file Claire T. Carney Library Special Collections, University of Massachusetts, Dartmouth.

42. As was the case with labor organizer Eula Mendes and other Portuguese leaders during both the late 1920s and 1950s Red Scare authoritarian political movement.

43. Eula Mendes interviews (1985, 1987) and Joe Figueredo (2017).

44. Hartmann, *The Movement to Americanize*.

45. Rhode Island Secretary of State Archives, Charter Documents, (Non-Business Associations).

46. Charter documents of Portuguese American Political Club of Pawtucket and Portuguese American Civic League, Rhode Island Secretary of State Archives, Charter Documents, (Non-Business Associations).

47. Charter documents of União Portuguesa Beneficiente (Cumberland), 1928 and The Gremial Daughters of Portugal (Bristol), 1937, Rhode Island Secretary of State Archives, Charter Documents, (Non-Business Associations).

48. Hartmann, *The Movement to Americanize*. This included the work of other beneficial, religious, and cultural associations. The economic, political, and civic engagement activities of the Portuguese Fraternity (especially related to World War I bond drives) were the subject of reports in English-language newspapers. Begun as an insurance scheme, there were more than 30 Portuguese Fraternity branches spread throughout industrial and rural Portuguese migrant communities, promoting citizenship and naturalization drives to create a voting bloc. Portuguese migrant association public participation in American civic celebrations pre-date the early twentieth-century Americanization movement. For example, Portuguese industrial migrant worker associations were lauded in the *Lowell Sun* for joining the city's Fourth of July Parades in 1896, 1898, and 1904, in contrast to other migrant associations, which did not. Interestingly, in *The Record of a City* (1912) Kenngott describes the Azoreans of Lowell as largely white, even as contemporaneous writing about them in Boston and Cape Cod characterize them as non-white.

49. Philip E. Leis, "Ethnicity and the *Fourth of July* Committee," in *Ethnic Encounters: Identities and Contexts* ed. George L. Hicks, Philip E. Leis (North Scituate, Massachusetts: Duxbury Press, 1977), 239-58.

50. As seen in *Dillingham Commission Reports* vols. 5, 10, 21 41 and in cited newspaper archives (op. cit.); for protest, unionization and public civic actions see Silvia, Jr., "The Position of 'New' Immigrants," 226; Pap, *The Portuguese-Americans* (Boston: Twayne Publishers, 1981), 160; Harney, "'Portygees' and other Caucasians," 113-35; Georgianna 1993: 77; Moniz "The Shadow Minority," 409-30; Azevedo, "Not Quite White," 19-34; Bastos, "Migrants, Inequalities and Social Research," 163-183. Racialization processes among broader classes of industrial worker organization are examined by Wertheimer, *We Were There: the Story of Working Women in America* (New York: Pantheon Books, 1977), 199; Buhle, *Marxism in the USA: from 1870 to the Present Day* (London: Verso, 1987), 271; Theodore Kornweibel, *'Seeing Red.' Federal Campaigns against Black Militancy 1919-1925* (Bloomington: Indiana University Press, 1998); Regin Schmidt, *Red Scare, FBI and the Origins of Anti-Communism in the United States, 1919-1943* (Copenhagen: Museum Tusculanem Press, University of Copenhagen, 2000); Brauer, *Nellie Stone Johnson, The Life of an Activist* (St. Paul MN: Ruminator Books, 2001).

51. Faunce, "Papers," 1916-1924; Errington, "The Language Question."

52. Public displays and arguments over Portuguese racial categorizations were used to construct (and contest) white identities in various contexts: Pap, *The Portuguese Americans*, 161 describes different Portuguese associations banning members based on presumed racial identity. Harney, "'Portygees and Other Caucasians,'" 113-35, has collected various examples. Moniz, "The Shadow Minority," 409-430, examines racialization of the white category around minority status debates in the post-1960s civil rights period. Bastos, "Migrants, Inequalities and Social Research," 163-183, examination of Donald Taft, *Two Portuguese Communities in New England. Studies in History, Economics and Public Law* (New York: Longman's, Green & Co, 1923) provides an example of Portuguese migrant efforts to construct white identities through protests among Portuguese migrant industrial worker communities mobilized against Taft's descriptions.

53. Gina Sánchez Gibau, "Contested Identities: Narratives of Race and Ethnicity in the Cape Verdean Diaspora," *Identities* 12:3 (2005): 405-38.

54. Ross, *The Old World in the New*, 179.

55. To borrow a concept from Edward W. Said, "Orientalism Now," 160-258, *Orientalism* (London: Routledge and Keegan, 1978), 253.

56. Examples of the racialization of migrant Portuguese labor as well as Portuguese attempts to argue for their own whiteness and assimilability are encapsulated in one example from a community that saw a rapid expansion of seasonal fruit pickers from Portugal living and settling on Cape Cod, Massachusetts. Fred K. Swift, a member of one the largest regional cranberry bog families and employers of Portuguese seasonal

agricultural workers, used racialized categories to describe and disdain his employees as well as the new Portuguese residents. Writing in his journal he refers to his employees as "darkies" and used dehumanizing language in letters to the editor of a local newspaper, likening the Portuguese to dirty animals, and lamenting these "odiferous" "coloured people" who live near his house. The sentiment was seconded by Winfield S. Baker who called for Portuguese children to be placed into a segregated school. Several Portuguese residents wrote letters to the paper defending the community by pointing to tensions in the town over racial and socio-economic mobility at a time when many of them had left seasonal work as pickers in the bogs to purchase cheap land in the town and cultivate their own strawberry farms. In a clear example of racialization discourses negotiating "white" and "black" Portuguese categories, one letter from a Portuguese writer addressed the discrimination in these terms, making distinctions between white and non-white migrants from different Portuguese geographies. One of the first Portuguese commercial strawberry farmers in the town, however, had the last word on the debate in the paper. John Emerald (João Amaral) wrote an eloquent defense of all of the migrants from Portugal in the town, condemning local and U.S. national systems of racialized migrant-labor hierarchies in and of themselves: "Kansas draws the color line and Mr. Swift draws the line between the Yankee and the Portuguese," which, he adds, "is a race issue fit for Mississippi." See letters to the editor of the *Falmouth Enterprise* from the winter of 1905. In correspondence to the newspaper fifteen years later (1921), a Portuguese-community resident, Thomas Ferreira (who would become a Portuguese Fraternity officer), defends the migrant community by pointing to racial discrimination and socio-economic mobility efforts, indicating the persistence of this problem as the migrant settlement grew.

57. Williams, *And Yet They Come*, for example shows data on "white Portuguese" in the U.S. in 1930 separated from data on "Portuguese" in earlier decades.

58. Ross, *The Old World in the New*, 282.

59. Cape Verdeans also self-identified in the white Portuguese category. See published examples in Marilyn Halter, "Identity Matters," 163-178, *Between Race and Ethnicity: Cape Verdean Immigrants 1860-1965*, (University of Illinois Press, 1993).

60. Ross, *The Old World in the New*, 179.

61. See David Theo Goldberg, *Racist Culture: Philosophy and the Politics of Meaning* (London and Massachusetts: Blackwell, 1993; David R. Roediger, *Towards the Abolition of Whiteness: Essays on Race Politics and Working Class History* (London, New York: Verso, 1994); David R. Roediger, *Working Toward Whiteness; How America's Immigrants Became White*, (London, New York: Basic Books, 2018 [2005]). Theodore W. Allen, *The Invention of the White Race. Volume 1: Racial Oppression and Social Control and Volume 2 The Origin of Racial Oppression in Anglo-America* (London, New York: Verso, 1994); Noel Ignatiev, *How the Irish Became White* (New York: Routledge, 1995); Carter, Green and Halpern, "Immigration Policy"; Pap,

The Portuguese-Americans, 161, describes different Portuguese associations banning members based on presumed racial identity. Halter, "Identity Matters," 163-178, points out that Cabo Verdean migrant workers were aware of the implications of racial mobilities and the power of inclusion in the white category. How Portuguese migrant communities reproduced racial hierarchies to argue for their own assimilability is evident in efforts for and against their status as a federal minority group in the EEOC debates of the 1970s in Moniz, "The Shadow Minority," 409-30; and in court cases defining racial identities and civic rights in Gross, *What Blood won't Tell*.

62. Bylaws, "Vasco da Gama Holy Ghost Society," 1952. University of Massachusetts Dartmouth Archives and Special Collections, Ferreira-Mendes Portuguese American Archives: MC 95/PAA.

63. See Almeida's discussion of responses to the violent rape of a woman at a New Bedford bar and the later criminal trial of her attackers around what were racialized media discourses that set older migrant generations against newer arrivals. Onésimo T. Almeida, "Media Made Events, Revisiting the Case of Big Dans," 247-262, in *Community, Culture and the Makings of Identity*, ed. Andrea Klimt and Kimberly Holton (North Dartmouth: Tagus Press, University of Massachusetts, Dartmouth). One example is the use of the disparaging term "Greenhorn" by U.S.-born generations and other discourses that racialize the labor of newer generations of Portuguese workers.

64. Day of Portugal commemorations or Portuguese heritage celebrations take place throughout Southeastern New England in cities and towns including Providence, East Providence, Pawtucket, Cumberland and Bristol in Rhode Island; Boston, New Bedford, Fall River, Taunton, Cambridge, Lowell, Falmouth, and Provincetown in Massachusetts; and Hartford and Danbury in Connecticut. Day of Portugal Rhode Island depends on the collaboration of multiple associations and members spread throughout the state.

65. Leal, "Migrant Cosmopolitanism," 233-249; João Leal, "What's (not) in a Parade? Nationhood, Ethnicity and Regionalism in a Diasporic Context," *Nations and Nationalism* 20, 2 (2014): 200-217.

66. The Azorean Refugee Act was used by policy makers in 1958 to argue for opening restrictions on former industrial labor migrant groups. Daniel Marcos, *The Capelinhos Eruption. Window of Opportunity for Azorean Emigration* (Providence: Gávea-Brown Press, 2008).

67. Choldin discusses the emergence of and changes to the Hispanic category over several censuses. Harvey M. Choldin, "Statistics and Politics: The 'Hispanic Issue' in the 1980 Census," *Demography* 23, 3 (August 1986): 403-418. How the census constructs and racializes identity categories is examined by David I. Kertzer and Dominique Arel, "Census, Identity Formation and the Struggle for Political Power," in *Census and Identity: the Politics of Race, Ethnicity and Language in National Censuses*, ed. David I. Kertzer and Domnique Arel, (Cambridge University Press, 2002), 1-42; and Melissa Nobles, "Racial

Categorizations and Censuses," in *Census and Identity: the Politics of Race, Ethnicity and Language in National Censuses*, ed. David I. Kertzer and Domnique Arel, (Cambridge University Press, 2002), 43-70. In reference to statutory codifications of the Portuguese legal minority category in New England see Moniz "The Shadow Minority," 409-30; and in the U.S. south see Gross, *What Blood Won't Tell.*

68. American-born residents of communities founded by older migrant cohorts used language to racialize the identities of more recently arrived migrants, such as the ubiquitous term "greenhorns" or "Manny Labor" (the latter example a pun on the common Portuguese migrant name Manuel with the manual work of low hierarchy labor). The older generation used the (manual) labor of the newer migrants to mark difference, promoting their own mobilities at the expense of others by absorbing and re-articulating discourses of racialized assimilability hierarchies.

69. Clyde Barrow, *Portuguese-Americans and Contemporary Civic Culture in Massachusetts* (North Dartmouth: University of Massachusetts, Dartmouth, Center for Portuguese Studies and Culture and the Center for Policy Analysis, 2002); Miguel Moniz, "Confronting the Migrant Challenge," in *Capelinhos: a Volcano of Synergies*, Tony Goulart, ed. (San Jose, California: Portuguese Heritage Publications, 2008), 121-30.

70. Codification of the Portuguese category in Massachusetts and Rhode Island statutes continues to reflect this ambiguity. For example, current Massachusetts state regulations on the founding of non-profit organizations (the statute under which many current migrant cultural associations are chartered) require that "at least 51% of the organization's Board of Directors and Voting Membership must be women and/or members of a minority group or of Portuguese descent." After naming "Qualified minority groups" derived from federal law, the statute notes "that Portuguese is a separate group for the purpose of NPO certification, and includes persons having Portuguese origin." In fact, for the purposes of the state law, the Portuguese are not a separate group at all since they fall under the same legal protections as historically underrepresented non-white groups. The fact that the statute's language pointedly removes the Portuguese from this group makes clear the political implications of ongoing racial assimilability efforts that would promote the Portuguese as a minority, but without the group losing status as white.

71. These discourses around the "nature" of hard-working and accommodating Portuguese labor have resulted in continued exploitation of migrant labor.

72. Among the Portuguese communities the term most often used is "immigration," rather than "migration." The distinction is perhaps less about defining well-parsed descriptive categories and mechanisms of transnational labor mobility than it is about promoting assimilability distinctions between *immigration*, as a European (and white) mobility phenomenon and more recent *migration*, which can be used to describe non-white and less assimilable mobile labor groups.

73. Given longitudinal anti-migrant rhetoric in U.S. political discourse, it is ironic that genuine bipartisan political agreement would be fostered by a foreign national flag day.

74. The president's speeches were diverse in their tenor and content. His remarks at City Hall, shortly after his arrival in Boston, relied heavily upon transnational Diaspora-building metaphors of Portuguese commonality and jingoistic descriptions of global greatness. His remarks in Providence at Kennedy Plaza and at the Massachusetts State House were more reflective about the place and role of the Portuguese migrant communities in the U.S. and were presented against a backdrop of criticism in diplomacy engaging contentious areas of Portugal's transatlantic relations with the U.S. during the Trump administration.

75. Hunter, *The Place of Stone: Dighton Rock and the Erasure of America's Indigenous Past* (Chapel Hill: University of North Carolina Press, 2017), 20; 200; citing Garrick Mallery, "Pictographs of the North American Indians," *Fourth Annual Report of the Bureau of Ethnology to the Secretary of the Smithsonian Institution*, ed. J. W. Powell (Washington D.C.: Government Printing Office, 1882-83).

76. First presented by Edmund Burke Delabarre, "Dighton Rock: the Earliest and most Puzzling of New England Antiquities," *Old Time New England* 14, 2 (October 1923): 51-72, the theory was expanded upon in a book: presented primarily in the chapter "A New Interpretation of the Records," 165-186, *Dighton Rock: a Study of the Written Rocks of New England* (New York: Walter Neale, 1928).

77. Delabarre, *Dighton Rock: a Study*, 177-180.

78. Delabarre, *Dighton Rock: a Study*, dedication page.

79. Delabarre, *Dighton Rock: a Study*, 173. The highly speculative nature of this assertion was parodied by 2018 Day of Portugal Grand Marshall Onésimo T. Almeida, in the 1978 satirical comedic play *Ah! Monim dum Corisco (Porto: Salamandra, 1998)* Almeida also points out that Corte-Real was unlikely to have known Latin: Onésimo T. Almeida, *O Peso do Hifen: Ensaios Sobre a Experiencia Luso-Americana* (Lisboa: ICS. Imprensa de Ciencias Sociais, 2010), 97-105. *After the president's remarks mentioning the rock,* Almeida cautioned Presidential speechwriters and administrative staff from repeating the fantastic as fact.

80. Delabarre, *Dighton Rock: a Study*, 181.

81. Hunter, "A Lost Portuguese Explorer's American Boulder," *The Place of Stone*, 10.

82. In the 1990s I spoke with Luciano Da Silva on occasion, and once followed him as a talk show guest on a cable television show on which he frequently discussed Dighton Rock, the southeastern New England cable access program: *The Portuguese Around Us* (Syndicated, Rhode Island Portuguese Channel, Bristol, RI). Teresa Labonte, interviewer, episode first broadcast, January 31, 1998, 30 minutes.

83. Hunter, relying on published and unpublished research from Gilberto Fernandes, provides a detailed history of efforts in the Portuguese communities over the twentieth

century to promote the Corte-Real myth. Hunter "American Place-Making: Dighton Rock as a Portuguese Relic," *The Place of Stone*, 215-239; See Gilberto Fernandes, "Of Outcasts and Ambassadors: the Making of Portuguese Diaspora in the Postwar North" (PhD diss., York University, 2014); Gilberto Fernandes, "'Oh Famous Race!' Imperial Heritage and Diasporic Memory in the Portuguese American Narrative of North America," *The Public Historian*, 38, 1 (February 2016): 18-47.

84. "A Rocha de Dighton e Miguel Côrte Real," *Boletim da Agência Geral das Colónias*, 3, 30 (December 1927): 44-58.

85. José Dâmasa Fragoso, "O Emblema da Ordem de Cristo Gravado na Pedra de Dighton," *O Mundo Lusíada* 1, 9 (1951): 207-208.

86. José Dâmasa Fragoso, *A Historical Report of Twenty-Eight Years of Patriotic and Dramatic Efforts to Save Dighton Rock*, (New Bedford, Massachusetts: Miguel Corte-Real Memorial Society, 1954).

87. Hunter, "American Place Making," *The Place of Stone*, 227-228.

88. Manuel Luciano da Silva, *Portuguese Pilgrims and Dighton Rock: the First Chapter in American History* (Bristol, RI: Manuel Luciano da Silva, 1971).

89. He continued to lecture on the topic up until weeks before his death in 2012.

90. Da Silva, *Portuguese Pilgrims and Dighton Rock*, 68.

91. Da Silva, *Portuguese Pilgrims and Dighton Rock*, 70.

92. Da Silva, *Portuguese Pilgrims and Dighton Rock*, 67-69.

93. Da Silva, *Portuguese Pilgrims and Dighton Rock*, 68.

94. Da Silva, *Portuguese Pilgrims and Dighton Rock*, 67.

95. The 1920 tricentenary featured a number of pilgrim commemorations (such as Provincetown on Cape Cod) in which Portuguese migrant associations participated, in part, through Americanization movement activities. For historical material on uses of pilgrim celebrations to promote white nationalist and anti-migrant labor class discourses, see Christine Arnold-Lourie, "Baby Pilgrims, Sturdy Forefathers, and One Hundred Percent Americanism: The Mayflower Tercentenary of 1920," *Massachusetts Historical Review*, 17 (2015): 35-66.

96. See studies of migrant Portuguese place making in New England relative to public rituals and the groups that organize them in Leal, *Azorean Identity in Brazil and the United States; and* Leal, "Festivals, Group Making, Remaking and Unmaking," 584-599.

97. Manuel Luciano da Silva and Sílvia Jorge da Silva, *Christopher Columbus was Portuguese!* (Authors edition: 2008).

98. This remains the name of the official federal holiday, even as many municipalities and some states have begun to change the commemoration from a celebration of Columbus to one that appropriately acknowledges the indigenous populations who were killed and enslaved as a result of seafaring expeditions and European settlement in the Americas.

99. See Gilberto Fernandes, "'Oh Famous Race!'" 18-47.

100. Hunter, "American Place Making," *The Place of Stone*, 227. He also provides a detailed discussion of the history of the museum, its curation and its founding.

101. Whatever the multiplicity of opinions about the dictatorship that existed during the twentieth century in New England, by the 1970s a vocal anti-Estado Novo and anti-colonial sentiment had emerged in communities of migrants from Portuguese speaking geographies in New England.

102. "500 Years of Azorean Presence in North America Celebration," *Portuguese American Journal*, September 18, 2011, https://portuguese-american-journal.com/500-years-of-azorean-presence-in-north-america-celebration/; "Celebrating Azorean history at Dighton Rock:...500 years of Azorean presence in North America," Marc Larocque, *Herald News* (Fall River), September 23, 2011. https://www.heraldnews.com/x387123367/Celebrating-Azorean-history-at-Dighton-Rock.

103. Historical precedents include categories in Bushee, *Ethnic Factors*; Ross, *The Old World in the New*; Taft, *Two Portuguese Communities*; Pap, *The Portuguese-Americans.*

104. In Toronto, transnational nation building in "Portugal Day" celebrations is complicated because Azoreans do not participate in events as a result of tensions with continental Portuguese organizers. See João Leal, "What's (not) in a Parade?" 200-217.

105. Fernandes, "'O Famous Race!'" 18-47.

106. See "Portuguese Discovery Monument," Cultural Landscape Foundation, https://tclf.org/landscapes/portuguese-discovery-monument.

107. Despite the lack of conclusive proof about his actual birthplace: George Monteiro, "The Unhistorical Uses of Peter Francisco," *Southern Folklore Quarterly* 27 (June 1963): 139-59; George Monteiro, "Peter Francisco, Revolutionary War Hero," *The Parade of Heroes: Legendary Figures in American Lore*, ed. Tristam Potter Coffin and Henning Cohen (Garden City, NY: Anchor Press/Doubleday, 1978), 194-97.

108. Monteiro, "Peter Francisco," 194-197.

109. An initiative by the Portuguese Ambassador to the U.S. in conjunction with the Bristol Sports Club (Rhode Island), a Portuguese migrant association, promoted this narrative in a 2017 program centered on Madeira wine and the signing of the Declaration of Independence. Madeira wine (often shipped through the Azores) was a staple libation in colonial America, in part because it enjoyed favorable tax status in the English colonies. The point of the Madeira wine narrative, however, was not to discuss the early history of transatlantic commerce, but to conduct commercial diplomacy connecting a "typical" Portuguese product (which is a contemporary export commodity) in a clever, even kitschy, way to the migrant communities through the U.S. founding myth. See Nova Inglaterra TV, "Toast to America by the Portuguese Government in RI," uploaded July 3, 2017, video, 20: 24. https://www.youtube.com/watch?v=WHyvHsaHhKI.

110. Almeida, *O Peso do Hifen.*

111. Aspirational mobility narratives at these events likewise promote racial and social mobility through romanticizing the otherwise arduous and exploited low-hierarchy labor of Azorean and Cape Verdean whale men, largely ignoring the industrial worker period, Heath, "From Whalers to Weavers," 7-32. Harney, "'Portygees' and other Caucasians," 113-35, makes note of the non-white categorization of Portuguese on whale ships; and Melville's satire on racism and mid-1800s ethnologist science uses "Gee" (a derivation of Portagee) as an explanatory racial category. Melville, "The 'Gees,'" 507-09. In the satire, the 'Gees' are used as a gloss collapsing various geographic origins including Cabo Verde and Portugal, and is itself a stand-in for broader forms of racialized slave and wage labor (Karcher, "Melville's 'The 'Gees,' 421-42). The text even addresses assimilability, as the non-white narrator (according to Karcher) wonders if the Gees, like Chinese or Native Americans, may also overcome their genetic shortcomings to study at Dartmouth or be "taken merely for an eccentric Georgia planter" on the docks.

112. "...distinguir os que houverem prestado serviços relevantes a Portugal no País e no estrangeiro [...] serviços na expansão da cultura portuguesa ou para conhecimento de Portugal, sua história e seus valores..." Presidente da República, "Historia da Ordem do Infante D. Henrique," http://www.ordens.presidencia.pt/?idc=128

113. Interestingly, in 1968, Luciano da Silva was awarded membership in the order by the Estado Novo (his rank was then raised in 2012). Membership in another Portuguese chivalric order (St. James of the Sword) was conferred upon Edmund Burke Delabarre by the Estado Novo in 1933.

114. Estellie M. Smith, "Portuguese Enclaves: The Invisible Minority," paper presented at the Southern Anthropological Society Meeting, Wrightsville Beach, North Carolina, March 1973.

115. Silvia, Jr., "The Position of 'New' Immigrants," 221-232.

116. "About PVD Fest," Providence, RI, PVD Fest website, © 2015-2019, http://pvdfest.com/about-us/

117. Miles, *Racism after 'Race Relations'*; Goldberg, *Racist Culture*; Roediger, *Towards the Abolition of Whiteness*; Roediger, *Working Toward Whiteness*; Allen, *The Invention of the White Race. Volume 1 and 2*; Ignatiev, *How the Irish Became White*; Carter, Green and Halpern, "Immigration Policy;" and Gross, *What Blood won't Tell.*

ARCHIVES

Boott Cotton Mill, U.S. National Park Service, Lowell, MA

Cape Cod Cape Verdean Museum

Claire T. Carney Library, New Bedford Strike of 1928 archive, Special Collections archives University of Massachusetts, Dartmouth

Falmouth Enterprise, Falmouth Public Library Archive (Massachusetts)
Falmouth Historical Society Archives
Ferreira-Mendes Portuguese American Archives, University of Massachusetts, Dartmouth
Hay Library, Special Collections, Brown University
Lowell History Center, University of Massachusetts, Lowell
Lowell Sun, Lowell Public Library Archive (Massachusetts)
Massachusetts Secretary of State Archives
New Bedford Whaling Museum Special Collections, Portuguese Consul file
Rhode Island Secretary of State Archives
Woods Hole Historical Museum

BIBLIOGRAPHY

"500 Years of Azorean Presence in North America Celebration." *Portuguese American Journal*. September 18, 2011. https://portuguese-american-journal.com/500-years-of-azorean-presence-in-north-america-celebration/

"A Rocha de Dighton e Miguel Côrte Real." *Boletim da Agência Geral das Colónias*, 3, 30 (December 1927): 44-58.

"About PVD Fest," Providence, RI. PVD Fest website. © 2015-2019, http://pvdfest.com/about-us/

Allen, Theodore W. *The Invention of the White Race. Volume 1: Racial Oppression and Social Control; Volume 2 The Origin of Racial Oppression in Anglo-America*. London, New York: Verso, 1994.

Almeida, Onésimo T. *Ah! Mónim dum Corisco*. Lisbon: Edições Salamandra, 1978 (1998).

Almeida, Onésimo T. "Media Made Events, Revisiting the Case of Big Dans." In *Community, Culture and the Makings of Identity*, edited by Andrea Klimt and Kimberly Holton, 247-262. North Dartmouth, MA: Tagus Press, University of Massachusetts, Dartmouth.

Almeida, Onésimo T. *O Peso do Hifen: Ensaios Sobre a Experiencia Luso-Americana*. Lisboa: ICS. Imprensa de Ciencias Sociais, 2010.

Arber, Edward. *The Last Fight of the Revenge at Sea*. London: English Reprints, 1871.

Arnold-Lourie, Christine. "Baby Pilgrims, Sturdy Forefathers, and One Hundred Percent Americanism: The Mayflower Tercentenary of 1920." *Massachusetts Historical Review* 17 (2015), 35-66.

Azevedo, Rui Vitorino. "Not Quite White: The Ethno-Racial Identity of a Portagee." *Op. Cit.* 12 (2010): 19-34.

Barrow, Clyde. *Portuguese-Americans and Contemporary Civic Culture in Massachusetts*. North Dartmouth: University of Massachusetts, Dartmouth, Center for Portuguese Studies and Culture and the Center for Policy Analysis, 2002.

Barker, Jean E. "Cape Verdean-Americans: A Historical Perspective of Ethnicity and Race." *Trotter Review* 10: 1 (1996): 17-20.

Bastos, Cristiana. "Migrants, Inequalities and Social Research in the 1920s: the story of 'Two Portuguese Communities in New England.'" *History and Anthropology* 29, 2 (2018): 163-183.

Beckert, Sven. *Empire of Cotton.* Alfred A. Knopf, 2014.

Benton-Cohen, Katherine. *Inventing the Immigration Problem: The Dillingham Commission and Its Legacy.* Boston: Harvard University Press, 2018.

Braga, Teófilo. *Os Centenários como Síntese Afectiva nas Sociedades Modernas.* Oporto: A. J. da Silva Teixeira, 1884.

Bradley, Joseph. *Voluntary Associations in Tsarist Russia.* Cambridge, MA: Harvard University Press, 2009.

Brauer, David. *Nellie Stone Johnson. The Life of an Activist.* St. Paul MN: Ruminator Books, 2001.

Boas, Franz. *Changes in Bodily Form of Descendants of Immigrants.* Vol. 38. *Reports of the Immigration Commission [Dillingham Commission Reports]* U.S. Congress, 1911.

Buhle, Paul, *Marxism in the USA: from 1870 to the Present Day.* London: Verso, 1987.

Bushee, Frederick A. *Ethnic Factors in the Population of Boston.* New York: The Macmillan Company for the American Economic Association, 1903. Reprint by American Immigration Experience Series. New York Arno Press and New York Times, 1970.

Cabral, Alexandre. *Notas Oitocentistas II. Luís de Camões, Poeta do Povo e da Pátria.* Lisboa: Livros Horizonte, 1980.

Cance, Alexander. *Recent Immigrants in Agriculture.* Vol. 24. *Reports of the Immigration Commission [Dillingham Commission Reports]* U.S. Congress, 1911.

Carter, Bob; Green, Marcie; and Rick Halpern. "Immigration Policy and the Racialization of Migrant Labour: the Construction of National Identities in the USA and Britain." *Ethnic and Racial Studies* 19, 1 (January 1996): 135-157.

Cardozo, Manoel da Silveira. *The Portuguese in America 590 BC-1974.* Dobbs Ferry, NY: Oceana, 1976.

Catroga, Fernando. "Ritualizações da História." In *História da História em Portugal Secs. XIX–XX*, edited by Luís Reis Torgal, José Amado Mendes and Fernando Catroga, 547-671 (Lisbon: Círculo de Leitores, 1996).

"Celebrating Azorean History at Dighton Rock:...500 years of Azorean Presence in North America," Marc Larocque, *Herald News* (Fall River), September 23, 2011. https://www.heraldnews.com/x387123367/Celebrating-Azorean-history-at-Dighton-Rock.

Choldin, Harvey M. "Statistics and Politics: The 'Hispanic Issue' in the 1980 Census." *Demography* 23, 3 (August 1986): 403-418.

Corkill, David and José Carlos Pina Almeida. "Commemoration and Propaganda in Salazar's Portugal: The 'Mundo Português' Exposition of 1940." *Journal of Contemporary History* 44, 3 (July 2009): 381-399.

Delabarre, Edmund Burke. "Dighton Rock: the Earliest and most Puzzling of New England Antiquities." *Old Time New England* 14, 2 (October 1923): 51-72

Delabarre, Edmund Burke. *Dighton Rock. A Study of the Written Rocks of New England.* New York: Walter Neale, 1928.

[Dillingham Commission Reports] Reports of the Immigration Commission, Vols. 1-41, U.S. Congress, 1911.

Elliot, E. N., ed. *Cotton is King, and Pro-Slavery Arguments: Comprising the Writings of Hammond, Harper, Christy, Stringfellow, Hodge, Bledsoe, and Cartwright, on this Important Subject.* Augusta GA: Pritchard, Abbott & Loomis, 1860.

Eno, Arthur L. Jr., editor. *Cotton was King: a History of Lowell, Massachusetts.* New Hampshire Publishing Company, 1976.

Errington, Sara. "The Language Question: Nativism, Politics, and Ethnicity in Rhode Island, 1919-1925." In *New England Disharmony: the Consequences of the Industrial Revolution*, edited by Douglas Reynolds and Katheryn Viens, 92-111. Kingston: Rhode Island Labor History Society and the Labor Research Center, URI, 1993.

Estep, Gerald A. "Portuguese Assimilation in Hawaii and California." *Sociology and Social Research* 26, 1 (September 1941): 61-69.

Faunce, William. 1916-1924. The Spirit of America or Teaching Democracy; The Meaning of America. (five versions) Box 6, Folder II.A108

Fernandes, Gilberto. "Of Outcasts and Ambassadors: the Making of Portuguese Diaspora in the Postwar North." PhD diss., York University, 2014.

Fernandes, Gilberto. "'Oh Famous Race!' Imperial Heritage and Diasporic Memory in the Portuguese American Narrative of North America." *The Public Historian* 38, 1 (February 2016), 18-47.

Ferraz de Matos, Patricia. *The Colours of the Empire: Racialized Representations during Portuguese Colonialism.* New York, Oxford: Berghahn, 2013.

Figueredo, Joseph. Oral History Interview at Tamiment Library & Robert F. Wagner Labor Archives. https://wp.nyu.edu/tamimentcpusa/joe-figueredo/, 2017.

Folkmar Daniel assisted by Elnora Folkmar. *Dictionary of Races or People.* Vol. 5, *Reports of the Immigration Commission [Dillingham Commission Reports]* U.S. Congress, 1911.

Fragoso, José Dâmasa. "O Emblema da Ordem de Cristo Gravado na Pedra de Dighton." *O Mundo Lusíada* 1, 9 (1951): 207-208.

Fragoso, José Dâmasa. *A Historical Report of Twenty-Eight Years of Patriotic and Dramatic Efforts to Save Dighton Rock.* New Bedford, MA: Miguel Corte-Real Memorial Society, 1954.

de Freitas, Jordão. "Morte e Enterramento de Camões." In 4º *Centenário do Nascimento de Camões, 1524—1924*, edited by Pedro de Moura e Sá (Lisboa: Comissão das Festas Camonianas, 1924).

Freyre, Gilberto. *Casa-grande & Senzala: Formação da Familia Brasleira sob o Regimen de Economia Patriarchal*. Rio de Janeiro, Maia & Schmidt, 1933.

Georgianna, Daniel with Roberta Hazen Aaronson. 1993. *The Strike of 1928*. New Bedford, Massachusetts: Spinner Publications, Inc.

Goldberg, David Theo. *Racist Culture: Philosophy and the Politics of Meaning*. London and Massachusetts: Blackwell, 1993.

Goldsmid, Edmund, ed. *Principal; Navigations, edited by Richard Hakluyt*. Re-edition edited and annotated by by Edmund Goldsmid, 16 volumes. Edinburgh: 1884 [1589;1598-1600].

Gross, Ariela Julie. *What Blood won't Tell: a History of Race on Trial in America*. Cambridge, MA: Harvard University Press, 2008.

Halter, Marilyn. *Between Race and Ethnicity: Cape Verdean Immigrants 1860-1965*. University of Illinois Press, 1993.

Harney, Robert F. "'Portygees and Other Caucasians': Portuguese Migrants and the Racialism of the English Speaking World." In *Portuguese Migration in Global Perspective*, edited by David Higgs, 113-35. Toronto: The Multicultural History Society of Ontario, 1990.

Hartmann, Edward George. *The Movement to Americanize the Immigrant* (Studies in History, Economics and Public Law Series), edited by Faculty of Political Science of Columbia University No. 545). New York: AMS Press Inc, 1967 [1948].

Heath, Kingston William. "From Whalers to Weavers: New Bedford's Urban Transformation and Contested Identities." *IA: Journal of the Society for Industrial Archaeology* 40, 1/2 (2014): 7-32.

Hicks, George L. *Experimental Americans: Celo and Utopian Community in the Twentieth Century*. Champaign-Urbana: University of Illinois Press, 2001.

Higgs, David, ed. *Portuguese Migration in Global Perspective*. Toronto: The Multicultural History Society of Ontario, 1990.

Higham, John. *Strangers in the Land: Patterns of American Nativism 1860-1925*. New Brunswick: Rutgers University Press, 1994.

Hobsbawm, Eric and Terrence Ranger, eds. *The Invention of Tradition*. Cambridge University Press, 2000.

Holton, Kimberly. *Performing Folklore: Ranchos Folclóricos from Lisbon to Newark*. Bloomington: University of Indiana Press, 2005.

Hunter, Douglas. *The Place of Stone: Dighton Rock and the Erasure of America's Indigenous Past*. Chapel Hill: University of North Carolina Press, 2017.

Ignatiev, Noel. *How the Irish Became White*. New York: Routledge, 1995.

Jackson, K. David. *Adverse Genres in Fernando Pessoa*. New York: Oxford University Press, 2010.

João, Maria Isabel. "*The Invention of the Dia de Portugal*." *Portuguese Studies* 31, 1 (2015): 64-84.

Karcher, Carolyn L. "Melville's 'The 'Gees': A Forgotten Satire on Scientific Racism." *American Quarterly* 27, 4 (Oct 1975): 421-442.

Kenngott, George, *The Record of a City: a Social Survey of Lowell, Massachusetts*. New York: The MacMillan Company, 1912.

Kertzer, David I. *Comrades and Christians: Religion and Political Struggle in Communist Italy*. New York: Cambridge University Press, 1980.

Kertzer, David I. *Ritual, Politics and Power*. New Haven: Yale University Press, 1988.

Kertzer, David I. and Dominique Arel. 2002. "Census, Identity Formation and the Struggle for Political Power." In *Census and Identity: the Politics of Race, Ethnicity and Language in National Censuses*, edited by David I. Kertzer and Domnique Arel, 1-42. Cambridge University Press, 2002.

Keyssar, Alexander. "Unemployment and the Labor Movement in Massachusetts, 1870-1916." In *The New England Working Class and the New Labor History*, edited by Herbert G. Gutman and Donald H Bell, 233-250. Chicago: University of Illinois Press, 1987.

Kornweibel, Theodore. *'Seeing Red.' Federal Campaigns against Black Militancy 1919-1925*. Bloomington: Indiana University Press, 1998.

Lauck, W. Jett. *Cotton Goods Manufacturing in the North Atlantic States; Woolen and Worsted Goods Manufacturing*. Vol. 10 *Reports of the Immigration Commission [Dillingham Commission Reports]* U.S. Congress, 1911.

Lauck, W. Jett. "The Cotton Mill Operatives of New England." *Atlantic Monthly* 109 (May 1912): 706-13.

Leal, João. *Azorean Identity in Brazil and the United States: Arguments about History, Culture and Transnational Connections*. North Dartmouth: Tagus Press, University of Massachusetts, Dartmouth, 2011.

Leal, João. "What's (not) in a Parade? Nationhood, Ethnicity and Regionalism in a Diasporic Context." *Nations and Nationalism* 20, 2 (2014): 200-217.

Leal, João. "Festivals, Group Making, Remaking and Unmaking." *Ethnos* 81 4 (2016): 584-599.

Leal, João. "Migrant Cosmopolitanism: Ritual and Cultural Innovation among Azorean Immigrants in the USA." In *Cosmopolitanism in the Portuguese-Speaking World (European Expansion and Indigenous Response, 27)*, edited by Francisco Bethencourt Leiden, The Netherlands: Brill. doi: https://doi.org/10.1163/9789004353435, 2017.

Leal, João, et al. Festas do Espírito Santo. "Ritual, Etnicidade, Transnacionalismo: as Festas do Espírito Santo na América do Norte" (PCDT/CS/-ANT/100037/2008). http://festasdoespiritosanto.pt/

Leis, Philip E. "Ethnicity and the *Fourth of July* Committee." In *Ethnic Encounters: Identities and Contexts*, edited by George L. Hicks, Philip E. Leis, 239-58. North Scituate, Massachusetts: Duxbury Press, 1977.

Mallery, Garrick. "Pictographs of the North American Indians." *Fourth Annual Report of the Bureau of Ethnology to the Secretary of the Smithsonian Institution*, edited by J. W. Powell. Washington D.C.: Government Printing Office, 1882-83.

Marcos, Daniel. *The Capelinhos Eruption. Window of Opportunity for Azorean Emigration.* Providence: Gávea-Brown Press, 2008.

Melo, Daniel and Eduardo Caetano da Silva, eds. *Construção da Nação e Associativismo na Emigração Portuguesa*. Lisboa: Imprensa de Ciências Sociais, 2009.

Melville, Herman. "The 'Gees." *Harpers New Monthly* (March 1856): 507-09.

Mendes, Eula. Oral History Interviews: Eula Mendes, Eula Mendes, New Bedford Textile Worker's Strike of 1928 Oral History Interviews and Research Collection, University of Massachusetts, Dartmouth, Archives and Special Collections: Interviews by Daniel Georgianna, 1985, MC9 Box 8, Tape 56, 57, 58; Interviews by Penn Reeve, 1987, MC9 Box 1, 16.

Miles, Robert. *Racism and Migrant Labour.* London: Routledge, 1982.

Miles, Robert. *Capitalism and Unfree Labour.* London: Tavistock, 1987.

Miles, Robert. *Racism after 'Race Relations'*. London: Routledge, 1993.

Moniz, Miguel. "Confronting the Migrant Challenge." In *Capelinhos: a Volcano of Synergies*, edited by Tony Goulart, 121-30. San Jose, California: Portuguese Heritage Publications, (2006) 2008.

Moniz, Miguel. "The Shadow Minority." In *Community, Culture and the Makings of Identity*, edited by Andrea Klimt and Kim Holton, 409-30. North Dartmouth: Tagus Press, University of Massachusetts, Dartmouth, 2009.

Monteiro, George. "The Unhistorical uses of Peter Francisco." *Southern Folklore Quarterly* 27, (June 1963): 139-59.

Monteiro, George. "Peter Francisco, Revolutionary War Hero." *The Parade of Heroes: Legendary Figures in American Lore*, edited by Tristam Potter Coffin and Henning Cohen, 194-97. Garden City, NY: Anchor Press/Doubleday, 1978.

Monteiro, Nuno and Antonio Costa Pinto. "Cultural Myths and Portuguese National Identity." In *Contemporary Portugal. Politics, Society, Culture*, edited by Antonio Costa Pinto, 55-72. New York: SSM Columbia University Press.

Nobles, Melissa. "Racial Categorizations and Censuses." In *Census and Identity: the Politics of Race, Ethnicity and Language in National Censuses*, edited by David I. Kertzer and Domnique Arel, 43-70. Cambridge University Press, 2002.

Nova Inglaterra TV. "Toast to America by the Portuguese Government in RI," Uploaded July 3, 2017, Bristol Sports Club, Bristol RI. Video 20:24. https://www.youtube.com/watch?v=WHyvHsaHhKI.

Pap, Leo, *The Portuguese-Americans.* Boston: Twayne Publishers, 1981.

The Portuguese Around Us. (Syndicated, Rhode Island Portuguese Channel, Bristol, RI). Teresa Labonte, interviewer. Episode first broadcast, January 31, 1998. Video 30:00. Ferreira-Mendes Portuguese American Archives, Claire T. Carney Library, UMass, Dartmouth.

"Portuguese Discovery Monument." Cultural Landscape Foundation. https://tclf.org/landscapes/portuguese-discovery-monument

Radecki, Henry. *Ethnic Organizational Dynamics: The Polish Group in Canada.* Waterloo, Ontario: Wilfrid Laurier University Press, 1979.

Ramos-Zayas, Ana Yolanda. "Stereotypes of the Tropics in 'Portuguese Newark: Brazilian Women, Urban Erotics and the Phantom of Blackness." In *Community, Culture and the Makings of Identity*, edited by Andrea Klimt and Kim Holton, 431-460. (North Dartmouth, MA: Tagus Press, University of Massachusetts, Dartmouth, 2009).

Reeve, Penn. "Portuguese Labor Activism in Southeastern Massachusetts." In *Community, Culture and the Makings of Identity*, edited by Andrea Klimt and Kim Holton, 337-56. North Dartmouth: Tagus Press, University of Massachusetts, Dartmouth, 2009.

Roediger, David R. *Towards the Abolition of Whiteness: Essays on Race Politics and Working-Class History.* London, New York: Verso, 1994.

Roediger, David R. *Working Toward Whiteness; How America's Immigrants Became White.* London, New York: Basic Books, 2018 [2005].

Ross. Edward A. *The Old World in the New: The Significance of Past and Present Immigration to the American People.* New York: The Century Co., 1914.

Said, Edward W. *Orientalism.* London: Routledge and Keegan, 1978.

Sánchez Gibau, Gina. "Contested Identities: Narratives of Race and Ethnicity in the Cape Verdean Diaspora." *Identities* 12:3 (2005): 405-38.

Sardinha, João. *Immigrant Associations, Integration and Identity: Angolan, Brazilian and Eastern European Communities in Portugal.* Amsterdam: University Press, 2009.

Schmidt, Regin. *Red Scare: FBI and the Origins of Anti-Communism in the United States, 1919-1943.* Copenhagen: Museum Tusculanem Press, University of Copenhagen, 2000.

Shimazu, Naoko. *Japan, Race and Equality: The Racial Equality Proposal of 1919.* New York: Routledge, Nissan Institute Japanese Studies Series, 1998.

da Silva, Manuel Luciano. *Portuguese Pilgrims and Dighton Rock: the First Chapter in American History*. Bristol, RI: Published by Manuel Luciano da Silva, 1971.

da Silva, Manuel Luciano and Sílvia Jorge da Silva. *Christopher Columbus was Portuguese!* Authors edition: 2008.

Silvia, Philip T. Jr. "The Position of 'New' Immigrants in the Fall River Textile Industry." *The International Migration Review*. (Summer 1976) 10, 2: 221-232.

Smith, Estellie M. "Portuguese Enclaves: The Invisible Minority," paper presented at the Southern Anthropological Society Meeting. Wrightsville Beach, North Carolina. March 1973.

Stanley, Amy Dru. *From Bondage to Contract: Wage Labor, Marriage, and the Market in the Age of Slave Emancipation*. Cambridge; New York: Cambridge University Press, 1998.

Statements and Recommendations Submitted by Societies and Organizations Interested in the Subject of Immigration. Vol 41, *Reports of the Immigration Commission [Dillingham Commission Reports]* U.S. Congress, 1911.

Taft, Donald. *Two Portuguese Communities in New England. Studies in History, Economics and Public Law*, edited by Columbia University Political Science Faculty. New York: Longman's, Green & Co, 1923.

Walker-McWilliams, Marcia. *Reverend Addie Wyatt Faith and the Fight for Labor, Gender and Racial Equality*. University of Illinois Press, 2016.

Wertheimer, Barbara Mayer. *We Were There: the Story of Working Women in America*. New York: Pantheon Books, 1977.

Wharton, Edward C., compiler. *A History of the Proceedings of the City of New Orleans on the Occasion of the Funeral Ceremonies in Honor of James Garfield*. New Orleans: A.W. Hyatt, 1881.

Williams, Jerry. *And Yet They Come. Portuguese Immigration from the Azores to the United States*. New York: Center for Migration Studies, 1982.

Zaroulis, Nancy. "Daughters of Freemen: The Female Operatives and the Beginning of the Labor Movement." In *Cotton was King: a History of Lowell, Massachusetts*, edited by Arthur L. Eno, Jr, 141-58. New Hampshire Publishing Co., 1976.

MIGUEL MONIZ is a Senior Researcher at the Center for Research in Anthropology (CRIA-ISCTE/IUL) and a Visiting Scholar at the Department of Portuguese and Brazilian Studies at Brown University. From a rural migrant Azorean and Cape Verdean community on Cape Cod, Moniz lives in Lisbon and spends as much time as possible between Portugal and New England.

DIANA SIMÕES

A Diáspora como Base da Identidade Cabo-Verdiana em *Ilhéu dos Pássaros*, de Orlanda Amarílis, e *Chiquinho*, de Baltasar Lopes

RESUMO: As agrestes condições ambientais das ilhas do arquipélago de Cabo Verde dão o mote para a temática da emigração, justificada como escape a uma vida miserável de trabalho árduo, ameaçada pela fome. A identidade cabo-verdiana passa pela vivência dessa realidade, sem, no entanto, estar restrita aos limites geográficos do arquipélago. De acordo com a interpretação de Bradley Smith, ser cabo-verdiano é assumir uma identidade fundacionalmente diaspórica, caracterizada pelo hibridismo da mestiçagem e por uma condição de dupla consciência em reverso (subversão da tese de Paul Gilroy). Baltasar Lopes, em *Chiquinho*, e Orlanda Amarílis, em *Ilhéu dos Pássaros*, usam com mestria o mote da emigração, abrangendo diversas fases de desenvolvimento do país e consequentes mudanças de mentalidade, pelo que apresentam visões distintas das possibilidades diaspóricas para lá das ilhas. Será igualmente dado destaque à importância da língua na formação da identidade nacional, através da competição do crioulo cabo-verdiano não só com o português-padrão, em contexto de ascensão social nos regimes colonial e pós-colonial, mas também com outras línguas estrangeiras de utilidade em contexto diaspórico, como o inglês ou o francês.

PALAVRAS-CHAVE: Identidade, Emigração, Diáspora Cabo-Verdiana, Crioulo

ABSRTACT: The harsh environmental conditions of the Cape Verde islands introduce the theme of emigration as a justifiable escape from a miserable life of hard work, threatened by starvation. Cape-Verdean identity is built upon the experience of that reality, without being confined to the geographical borders of the archipelago. According to Bradley Smith's definition, being Cape-Verdean means assuming a foundationally diasporic identity, characterized by hybrid miscegenation and by a feeling of double consciousness in reverse (subverting Paul Gilroy's thesis). Baltasar Lopes, in *Chiquinho*, and Orlanda Amarílis, in *Ilhéu dos Pássaros*, skillfully use the motto of emigration in a broad sense, which encompasses different phases of country development and the mentality changes that follow, thus presenting distinct views of the diasporic possibilities beyond the islands. This article will also highlight the importance of language in the formation of national identity, through competition faced by creole against standard Portuguese (in the context of social mobility in colonial and post-colonial regimes) and other foreign languages, like English or French (useful in the diaspora).

KEYWORDS: Identity, Emigration, Cape-Verdean Diaspora, Creole

---

1. Introdução: *Claridade*, Baltasar Lopes e *Chiquinho*; *Certeza*, Orlanda Amarílis e *Ilhéu dos Pássaros*

Baltasar Lopes (1907-1989) e Orlanda Amarílis (1924-2014) são dois dos nomes mais proeminentes na literatura cabo-verdiana. Partindo da análise crítica do romance *Chiquinho* (1947) de Lopes, e do volume de contos *Ilhéu dos Pássaros* (1982), de Amarílis, será explorada neste artigo a temática da emigração como fator da construção identitária cabo-verdiana. A fundamentação teórica terá por base a noção de Bradley Smith, desenvolvida na sua análise de *Chiquinho*, de uma identidade de dupla não-pertença, fundacionalmente diaspórica, e a originalidade da experiência diaspórica da comunidade cabo-verdiana nos Estados Unidos, defendida por Marilyn Halter. A descrição histórica do percurso de Cabo Verde de colónia portuguesa a território independente e a relação de Lopes e Amarílis com os movimentos das revistas *Claridade* e *Certeza* serão relevantes para perceber o contexto histórico, político e ideológico das duas obras literárias e as relações estabelecidas neste artigo entre elas.

As revistas *Claridade* (nove números entre 1936 e 1960) e *Certeza* (três edições entre 1944 e 1945) informam a produção literária de Lopes e Amarílis, respetivamente. A revista *Claridade* foi a primeira tentativa real da procura de uma voz crítica que se insurgia contra a condição social e política da colónia portuguesa, apesar de estar fortemente limitada pela censura do regime ditatorial em vigor na metrópole (Brookshaw 182). Fundada em 1936 por Jorge Barbosa, Baltasar Lopes e Manuel Lopes, *Claridade* iniciou um movimento literário que considerava as referências da seca e da emigração como fundacionais na formação da identidade cabo-verdiana. Advogavam o orgulho na mestiçagem e promoviam o crioulo como língua da cultura, ainda que o considerassem como um dialeto do português-padrão. Alguns dos capítulos de *Chiquinho* apareceram em números da revista antes da sua publicação em forma de romance, em 1947. São visíveis as influências autobiográficas de Baltasar Lopes na personagem que dá título à obra que, tal como o autor, é natural da povoação de Caleijão, na ilha de S. Nicolau. Neste *bildungsroman* (romance de aprendizagem) acompanhamos, pela voz do próprio, o percurso de Chiquinho desde Caleijão, onde nasceu, passando por São Vicente, para continuar os seus estudos, de volta a São Nicolau, onde se torna professor, e, por fim, rumo aos Estados Unidos, para fugir à crise social e económica da seca e da fome e reunir-se com o pai, emigrante em New Bedford.[1]

O romance de Lopes, fundacional na literatura e constituição identitária cabo-verdianas, foi pela primeira vez, em 2019, traduzido para inglês, e publicado simbolicamente no espaço americano que se tornou o destino migratório de gerações de ilhéus, Nova Inglaterra, com o título *Chiquinho: A Novel of Cabo Verde*. Este esforço académico ilustra a crescente visibilidade de uma comunidade que, durante décadas, viveu na margem da sociedade estado-unidense, como demonstrarei de seguida. Ao contrário de *Chiquinho*, vários contos de Amarílis estão, desde a década de 1980, traduzidos para alemão e para inglês, em antologias de contos (*Frauen in der Dritten Welt*, 1986, e *Across the Atlantic: An Anthology of Cape Verdean Literature*, 1986, respetivamente). De acordo com a "Nota Bibliográfica" em *Cais-do-Sodré Té Salamansa*, redigida por Manuel Ferreira, vários contos de Amarílis estão traduzidos para holandês, húngaro, italiano e russo (Ferreira 7-8). A abrangência dos espaços linguísticos das traduções ilustra o facto de a obra da autora ter tido, desde cedo, uma maior exposição internacional que Lopes.

O escritor português Manuel Ferreira, futuro marido de Orlanda Amarílis, e um dos maiores especialistas nas literaturas africanas de expressão portuguesa, funda, com um grupo de intelectuais cabo-verdianos, a revista *Certeza*, em 1944. Inspirada no pensamento marxista e no movimento literário neorrealista português, vai continuar o percurso da caboverdianidade já iniciado na revista *Claridade*. Tal como os claridosos, defende a singularidade da cultura cabo-verdiana e o uso do crioulo como língua da cultura; contudo, faz uma crítica à anterior atitude eurocentrista e à recusa das influências africanas na língua crioula e no folclore das ilhas. De acordo com um dos intelectuais do movimento *Certeza*, Onésimo Silveira, é preciso "tornar o homem comum cabo-verdiano consciente do seu destino africano" (Laranjeira 221). É a consciência do destino africano que Amarílis problematiza na sua escrita, em particular na coletânea de contos *Ilhéu dos Pássaros*, em que se torna evidente a ligação entre as ilhas e o território continental.

Apesar da maior parte das suas obras ser publicada depois da independência (*Ilhéu dos Pássaros* é de 1982), Amarílis é uma autora associada à revista *Certeza* – foi a única mulher a fazer parte do movimento. Ao contrário dos escritores de *Claridade*, em que a experiência da mulher era secundária, as obras de Amarílis oferecem uma perspetiva feminina da situação social cabo-verdiana e da diáspora europeia, na linguagem das "mulheres contidas, a caminho de libertarem-se do código de manifestações que a sociedade masculina ao longo dos tempos lhes impôs" (Abdala Junior 215). Para Gregory McNab, que também escreveu sobre Amarílis, a vitimização de uma mulher transforma-se no paradigma de vitimização e exploração da população cabo-verdiana em geral; assim, a identidade feminina e a identidade nacional sobrepõem-se (67). Amarílis aborda o tema da diáspora e o sentimento de desadequação social com a legitimidade de alguém que, à semelhança de algumas das suas personagens, viveu uma vida de itinerância, escrevendo fora das fronteiras físicas de Cabo Verde. Nos seus contos explora a oralidade, numa escrita que cruza o português-padrão com versões do crioulo das diferentes ilhas, assumindo orgulhosamente a africanidade da cultura cabo-verdiana. Para Amarílis, o escritor tem um dever para com a sua terra: o de preservar, através do registo escrito, as tradições culturais do país. Diz a autora, em entrevista a Laban, que "[q]uando surge um país novo e se esse país é o nosso, há deveres aos quais não podemos negar o nosso contributo. Além de que esses registos podem vir a contribuir para o espólio cultural do futuro" (Laban 278).

2. Cabo Verde e os Movimentos Migratórios

O arquipélago de Cabo Verde, espaço privilegiado das duas obras aqui em análise, é formado por um conjunto de dez ilhas e dezasseis ilhéus – um dos quais será alvo de análise, o dos Pássaros. De constituição maioritariamente vulcânica, o solo das ilhas é árido e de difícil cultivo, pelo que a exploração agrícola nunca foi um dos fatores económicos relevantes para o desenvolvimento do país. A isso se junta uma escassa e irregular época de chuva, de agosto a outubro, com períodos extensos de seca. A situação económica precária reflete-se no limitado acesso a meios de subsistência, com consequências devastadoras para a população, já debilitada. *The Cape Verde Islands: From Slavery to Modern Times*, de Elisa Andrade (1973), ou *Historic Dictionary of the Republic of Cape Verde*, de Richard A. Lobban Jr. e Paul Khalil Saucier (2007), são duas referências relevantes que estabelecem a ligação entre a história do país e a pobreza e exploração das suas gentes, bem como a preocupação com o desenvolvimento socioeconómico das ilhas. Será essa pobreza o fator impulsionador dos movimentos migratórios para os Estados Unidos e para a Europa, retratados nos textos de Lopes e Amarílis – as experiências diaspóricas e um constante estado de desadequação informam a identidade cabo-verdiana nas duas obras.

Desabitado aquando da sua descoberta pelos navegadores portugueses no século XV, Cabo Verde tornou-se no mais importante entreposto comercial para o crescente tráfico dos navios negreiros entre África e Portugal ou Brasil, trazendo prosperidade às ilhas. O estabelecimento de uma colónia foi motivado pela sua localização estratégica nas rotas comerciais portuguesas (Challinor 88). Com o declínio da escravatura, no século XIX, os seus portos passaram a ser paragem obrigatória nas rotas dos baleeiros americanos a caminho dos mares do sul, cuja navegação é explorada largamente em *Chiquinho*. A emigração surge, desde cedo, como derradeiro recurso para escapar de um país sem futuro. Durante o século XIX e primeiras décadas do século XX, retratadas por Baltasar Lopes, o destino preferencial fora os Estados Unidos, principalmente a zona de Nova Inglaterra. Fazer parte da tripulação de um navio baleeiro ou trabalhar nas fábricas de algodão eram destinos comuns para os emigrantes cabo-verdianos. Décadas depois, algumas das personagens de *Ilhéu dos Pássaros* ilustram uma nova tendência: com o decréscimo da procura de mão-de-obra e as restrições impostas pelas leis migratórias, as atenções voltaram-se para a Europa, com países como França, Suíça ou Portugal atraindo as massas migrantes.

Para a população cabo-verdiana, "a migração é estrutural enquanto estratégia de sobrevivência" (Challinor 84). Sob dominação portuguesa durante séculos, Cabo Verde tornou-se independente a 5 de julho de 1975 – ano seguinte ao da revolução de 25 de abril, que pôs fim à ditadura salazarista em Portugal. A falta de recursos e a má gestão colonial trouxeram resultados desencorajadores para o território, economicamente fraco: a distribuição severamente desigual de terras aliou-se a vários anos de seca, para revelar níveis extremamente baixos de subsistência e uma elevada taxa de mortalidade. A isso se junta um modelo de governação colonial que omitiu a necessidade de fazer esforços em prol do desenvolvimento do país ou de enviar ajuda, pelo que a situação política, social e económica ficou insustentável (Andrade 264-290). A emigração surge novamente como recurso da população carenciada, que sai das ilhas em busca de melhorias.

Quer Lopes quer Amarílis exaltam a miscigenação e crioulização da cultura das ilhas, dando-lhe grande destaque na sua produção literária. Elizabeth Challinor descreve a sociedade cabo-verdiana como uma mistura entre africanos escravizados, trazidos do continente africano, e os seus donos portugueses, sendo que estas relações íntimas (quer no que toca à proximidade vivencial quer no que concerne a miscigenação) entre colonizadores e colonizados acabaram por diluir as fronteiras sociais e as rígidas divisões entre brancos e negros (88). A população das ilhas, que se define como crioula, foi o resultado da colonização portuguesa; é maioritariamente miscigenada, com características europeias e africanas presentes no mestiço, ou mulato. A cultura do país apresenta-se igualmente como uma mistura de tradições europeias e africanas, discerníveis ao nível da comida, da música e da língua comum a todas as ilhas do arquipélago, o crioulo (com variantes regionais), falada e compreendida nas várias classes sociais.

3. Consciência Diaspórica e Identidade

Between Race and Ethnicity: Cape Verdean American Immigrants, 1860-1965, de Marilyn Halter (1993), visa a realidade da diáspora cabo-verdiana nos Estados Unidos, focando-se no conceito de "dupla invisibilidade" como fundacional na construção da identidade cabo-verdiana. No estudo de Halter, destaca-se o facto de Cabo Verde ter sido local de recrutamento de mão-de-obra barata: a eficiência dos trabalhadores, tanto nos navios como nas fábricas têxteis americanas, não lhes garantia pagamentos adequados; apesar de se saberem explorados, o desespero de fugir à crise impelia-os à deslocação para destinos mais prósperos. Halter defende que a comunidade de "Cape-Verdean Americans" é a única com peso significativo no conjunto das comunidades americanas de descendência africana a ter feito voluntariamente a viagem transatlântica, ao contrário de todas as outras, relocadas no âmbito do tráfico de escravos. Devido às condições históricas que o tornaram possível, o empreendedorismo da comunidade cabo-verdiana nos Estados Unidos, no que toca ao controlo dos meios de passagem e entrada no país, apresenta-se como um outro aspeto da sua singularidade: no final do século XIX, com o declínio da indústria baleeira, os navios de pesca tornaram-se obsoletos e ficaram disponíveis a baixo custo. Alguns dos primeiros emigrantes cabo-verdianos tiraram partido dessa oportunidade e converteram os navios de pesca em navios de transporte de mercadorias e de passageiros, conhecidos como paquetes ou vapores, passando a fazer viagens regulares entre os portos de New Bedford e Providence e as ilhas de Cabo Verde.[2]

Apesar da longa história da imigração cabo-verdiana para os Estados Unidos, a obscuridade da comunidade cabo-verdiana nesse país encontrava apenas paralelo na histórica falta de reconhecimento dentro do império colonial português, pelo que a antropóloga Deidre Meintel a descreve como duplamente invisível (Halter 6). Bradley Smith enfatiza a manifestação do poder colonial através da ausência, uma vez que funciona através do abandono da colónia aos caprichos atmosféricos e da economia global (250). Ser cabo-verdiano equivalia a estar à margem do império português – que nunca priorizou o investimento económico na colónia – e, simultaneamente, ser parte de uma diáspora duplamente marginalizada (quer nos Estados Unidos, destino migratório das personagens do romance de Lopes, quer nos territórios europeus como Portugal ou França, retratados nos contos de Amarílis). Enquanto sujeitos coloniais de cidadania portuguesa, os imigrantes cabo-verdianos procuravam, nos Estados Unidos, o reconhecimento enquanto "Portuguese Americans"; no entanto, acabaram afastados tanto da comunidade portuguesa branca (de origem madeirense ou açoriana), como da sociedade americana, simplisticamente estratificada entre brancos e negros, que os identificava como "Black Americans" (a quem direitos civis básicos eram negados). Podemos afirmar que a comunidade cabo-verdiana vivia um dilema entre, por um lado, a exclusão destas duas classes que se identificavam como brancas (a americana e a dos imigrantes portugueses) e, por outro, uma dupla pertença representada pela mestiçagem crioula, através de uma cultura de base simbiótica afro-europeia. Estima-se que a diáspora cabo-verdiana seja o dobro da população das ilhas (Rodrigues, "Cape Verde"), pelo que a ligação entre quem parte e quem fica seja uma parte significativa da constituição identitária cabo-verdiana, à qual se pode atribuir o que James Clifford designa por "consciência diaspórica." Esta consciência diaspórica é formada por aspetos positivos e negativos: constitui-se positivamente através da identificação das comunidades imigradas com forças culturais e políticas histórico-mundiais; contudo, tem de negativo as experiências de discriminação e exclusão, reforçadas por restrições socioeconómicas e limitadas oportunidades de progresso (256). A busca por melhores condições de vida de quem emigra liga-se à esperança no progresso e prosperidade de Cabo Verde, possíveis em grande parte devido às remessas (em géneros e capital) enviadas pelos emigrantes aos familiares que permanecem nas ilhas. A consciência diaspórica de origem híbrida ou mestiça, desenvolvida por Bradley Smith em "Other Atlantics: Cape Verde, *Chiquinho* and the Black Atlantic World," será pertinente para a análise comparativa das obras de Lopes e de Amarílis, abaixo. Os textos literários deste autor e desta autora ilustram o dilema da emigração como única forma de proporcionar o sustento da família, apesar das limitações encontradas nos países de acolhimento – principalmente no que diz respeito à discriminação e exclusão, como refere Clifford.

Na esteira da interpretação histórica da comunidade imigrante cabo-verdiana nos Estados Unidos por Halter, Bradley Smith, na sua leitura de *Chiquinho*, aproveita o conceito de "double consciousness," originalmente cunhado por W. E. B. Du Bois e trabalhado por Paul Gilroy em *The Black Atlantic* (1993), atualizando-o, no entanto, numa dupla consciência em reverso, de não pertença nem à comunidade europeia/americana nem à comunidade negra como Gilroy a entendia – a mestiçagem cabo-verdiana não se encaixa, segundo Smith, no conceito fechado de "blackness" de Gilroy. Partindo da premissa de Smith de que mais cabo-verdianos vivam fora das ilhas do que no arquipélago, a diáspora tem de ser obrigatoriamente tida em consideração na construção da identidade nacional.[3] Smith destaca dois conceitos fundamentais na obra de Gilroy: "dupla consciência" e "diáspora." Fazer parte do Atlântico Negro é, para Gilroy, estar dividido entre duas realidades: o Eu encontra-se fragmentado entre os polos africano e europeu/americano; a identidade diaspórica configura-se assim como um modo transnacional de comunidade, de dupla pertença. Contudo, segundo Smith, o carácter singular da diáspora cabo-verdiana faz com que o sentimento de dupla pertença se inverta numa consciência de dupla não-pertença, fugindo, dessa forma, ao influente paradigma formulado por Gilroy: no romance de Lopes, a negligência portuguesa em relação ao território cabo-verdiano não permite considerar o arquipélago como parte significativa do estado português (europeu), do mesmo modo que a aparente distância das origens europeias não permite a afirmação de uma extensiva africanidade (Smith 251). Na sua análise de *Chiquinho*, romance em que a personagem principal com o mesmo nome convive de perto com a realidade diaspórica (o pai e vários outros homens partiram das ilhas em busca de uma vida melhor), Smith destaca o facto de os emigrantes cabo-verdianos serem conhecidos nos Estados Unidos como "Black Portuguese," negligenciados tanto pela comunidade portuguesa, por serem originários de um território colonial, quanto pela sociedade americana branca, que os classificava como negros. Apesar de referir-se apenas à realidade da diáspora cabo-verdiana nos Estados Unidos, o argumento de Smith é também pertinente no contexto da diáspora presente em territórios europeus, sobretudo Portugal e França, dois dos destinos para onde emigram as personagens dos contos de Amarílis. Para Smith, a fundação da identidade cabo-verdiana assenta na consciência diaspórica de origem híbrida ou mestiça: a diversidade étnica, consubstanciada na crioulidade, terá um papel de maior destaque por oposição à solidariedade racial transnacional assente na negritude, como defende Gilroy. A isso se junta o tropo da ausência do pai, uma constante na literatura portuguesa, passível de ser observado nas figuras do avô e do pai de Chiquinho, ausentes da vida do protagonista do romance (Smith 249-51). Os contos de Amarílis evidenciam igualmente uma ausência masculina; as protagonistas são, na sua maioria, mulheres que, num primeiro momento, estão confinadas às ilhas, e que depois vão em busca de novas oportunidades fora do arquipélago. Em Cabo Verde, é notória a ausência de adultos do sexo masculino nos núcleos familiares.[4]

O pai ausente a que Smith se refere não se limita à figura paterna apartada da família; é também o colonizador português que negligencia o território cabo-verdiano com a sua ausência de investimentos no país. Nas palavras de Alfredo Margarido, Portugal visto a partir de Cabo Verde é o "lugar distante e vazio, que envia autoridades incompetentes e incapazes" (cit. em Sapega 165). Este colonizador ausente é representado, em *Chiquinho*, na figura do Ministro das Colónias, a quem Andrézinho envia um telegrama para pedir ajuda para resolver a crise de fome e que fica, contudo, sem resposta, revelando a incompetência e incapacidade (aliada à falta de vontade) da metrópole de solucionar os problemas da então colónia portuguesa. Apesar de ausente, o pai colonial deixa marcas profundas nas ilhas e nos seus habitantes, marcas essas que se tornam constitutivas da identidade cabo-verdiana que, apesar dos muitos traços de originalidade, não está assim tão distante daquela do colonizador – um dos exemplos será o generalizado orgulho cabo-verdiano nas suas raízes europeias, que os diferencia dos africanos continentais. Challinor refere que o caboverdianismo defendido pela revista *Claridade*, criada ainda no período colonial, deu mais ênfase às raízes europeias do que às africanas na construção da identidade crioula (87). Pelo contrário, a defesa das raízes africanas será mais enfatizada na *Certeza* e, por conseguinte, está mais visível na coletânea de Amarílis, contribuidora da revista. De certa forma, *Ilhéu dos Pássaros* pode ser lido como uma reinterpretação de *Chiquinho*. As principais dicotomias presentes nos dois textos serão exploradas de seguida.

4. Visão Utópica e Distópica dos Destinos da Diáspora Cabo-Verdiana

As obras *Chiquinho* e *Ilhéu dos Pássaros* ambas se debruçam sobre a realidade da diáspora, oferecendo visões opostas, uma utópica, a outra distópica, sobre os destinos de emigração – Estados Unidos e Europa, respetivamente. De forma abrangente, podemos dizer que, em *Chiquinho*, a América é a terra das oportunidades e da prosperidade; já nos contos de *Ilhéu dos Pássaros*, a Europa é palco de tragédias. No entanto, não é possível fazer uma divisão maniqueísta ligando utopia somente a *Chiquinho* e remetendo a distopia apenas para *Ilhéu dos Pássaros*: nem sempre a América de Chiquinho é retratada de forma otimista, e nos contos de Amarílis podemos encontrar também (raras) perspetivas positivas sobre o que é ser emigrante na Europa.

Chiquinho, o protagonista e narrador da obra de Lopes, mantém uma visão consistentemente idílica da América. Inspirado pelas cartas do pai, tem também conhecimento da realidade diaspórica de vários outros filhos das ilhas, pois é o porta-voz das mensagens de além-mar. Grande parte da população cabo-verdiana tem baixos níveis de literacia, pelo que é Chiquinho quem lê as cartas dos patrícios aos seus parentes iletrados. A inocência do seu olhar de criança sobre a imigração – uma realidade que lhe é distante, mas, ao mesmo tempo, tão próxima –, impregna a visão desse mundo imaginado. Para ele, a América apresenta-se como uma versão fértil de Cabo Verde, onde projeta a realidade rural de São Nicolau, com bonitas ribeiras e hortas fartas, com chuva suficiente para boas colheitas, diferente do que sabemos ter sido a realidade industrial de New Bedford, onde o pai trabalha. O jovem Chiquinho é apresentado pelo narrador (o mesmo Chiquinho já adulto) como uma personificação da alma sonhadora das gentes das ilhas, que mantêm a esperança mesmo em tempos de crise e que têm no sonho de destinos desconhecidos prósperos uma forma de escape à realidade cruel. Diz ele que "[l]á não havia a face negra da fome rondando casa de pobre. Lá fora não devia haver pobre... O mar tinha tanta água que dava comida para todo o mundo" (Lopes 248). Nesta perspetiva, tudo na América é idílico e bom.

Porém, outras personagens nos mostram que nem sempre há finais felizes para a diáspora. Como leitor oficial das cartas dos patrícios, Chiquinho não pode deixar de transmitir igualmente más notícias. Um desses momentos acontece quando é chamado para ler a carta em que António João Duarte tem o triste dever de comunicar a morte do filho de Nhá Tudinha, Manuel, num terrível acidente com uma máquina na fábrica onde trabalhava. A revolução industrial trouxe a automatização dos processos de fabrico, com máquinas sofisticadas que permitiam uma maior eficiência e produtividade, mas condições de trabalho precárias. A eficiência era, muitas vezes, feita à custa de vidas humanas, pois a falta de mecanismos de segurança levava a frequentes acidentes de consequências trágicas. Por José Lima, um ex-emigrante nos Estados Unidos que regressara a Cabo

Verde para passar a velhice, tomamos conhecimento de que a aceitação de imigrantes nos Estados Unidos estava dependente de um humilhante exame físico a que os cabo-verdianos tinham obrigatoriamente de se submeter na Casa da Emigração de New Bedford, onde eram alvo de chacota. Para ele, um emigrante toma necessariamente consciência de quão relativa a posição social que tinha em Cabo Verde pode ser, concluindo que "a todos as fábricas nivelaram, reduzindo a nada a sua aristocracia intelectual com que saíram das ilhas" (259). Trabalhar anos a fio numa fábrica têxtil, sem equipamento de proteção, causa doenças crónicas, como a tosse seca que nunca o largava. Apesar de tudo, consegue ver o lado positivo da experiência: ir para a América foi uma aventura, o ponto alto da sua vida, saindo enriquecido enquanto ser humano e cabo-verdiano. O final em aberto do romance, com Chiquinho num navio rumo à América, permite-nos pensar na possibilidade de uma vida de novas oportunidades para a diáspora cabo-verdiana; predomina a esperança num futuro mais próspero.

A carta onde se comunica a morte de Manuel, em *Chiquinho*, encontra paralelo no conto de *Ilhéu dos Pássaros*, "Thonon-Les-Bains," através da carta que Gabriel envia à madrasta, nh'Ana, transmitindo a dolorosa notícia do assassinato da sua filha Piedade. Destino frequente de emigração, a cidade francesa de Thonon-Les-Bains (parte oriental perto da fronteira com a Suíça) representa o cenário distópico por excelência nesta coletânea de contos de Amarílis. Sabemos que Gabriel conseguira convencer nh'Ana a enviar a filha Piedade para França, com a promessa de que em breve ela e mais dois filhos se lhes juntariam. Assim, tenta sempre mostrar o lado positivo da experiência diaspórica, descrevendo nas escassas cartas o quanto gosta do trabalho na fábrica de esquis, que o patrão de Piedade os deixa dormir no *caveau* da escada no corredor do hotel onde esta faz limpeza, e como é bom ter a possibilidade de comprar uma televisão a cores com controlo remoto. Mas inferimos que o trabalho é duro e que as condições de vida são precárias. Nh'Ana sonha com o dia em que pudesse começar o seu próprio negócio na ilha com o dinheiro que Piedade lhe enviaria de França; mantém a esperança numa vida melhor, providenciada pela filha emigrante.[5] Nas cartas, Gabriel comunica que Piedade tem um noivo francês, Jean, mais velho que ela, com quem espera casar-se em breve. É Jean o responsável pela morte de Piedade, degolando-a na casa de banho da casa de uns amigos de Gabriel. O acontecimento trágico tem consequências não menos funestas: Gabriel e os amigos são expulsos da casa onde vivem e ninguém lhes aluga quarto, o que os obriga a sair da cidade e a começar a vida do zero. Ele sabe ser Jean o culpado, mas acusá-lo às autoridades teria sido em vão: "Eles sabiam mãe Ana, sabiam, isto é, desconfiavam, mas eu sou emigrante. Emigrante é lixo, mãe Ana, emigrante não é mais nada" (Amarílis 25). Na análise ao conto, McNab caracteriza este acontecimento macabro como a primazia do nativo europeu sobre o estrangeiro não-europeu, mas também como a supremacia racial do branco sobre o não-branco e, de forma mais abrangente, do primeiro mundo sobre o terceiro; o sexismo, a xenofobia e o racismo são as razões ocultas de Jean para assassinar Piedade (65-66).

Distópico é também o destino de Xanda, a personagem feminina do conto do *Ilhéu dos Pássaros* com o mesmo nome. Menina atrevida, é levada ao gabinete das autoridades por ter chamado "piducas" a dois polícias.[6] As idas frequentes à administração fazem com que a família suspeite de um caso amoroso com o administrador. Pouco depois, anuncia a sua ida para Lisboa por ter lá emprego garantido (um favor do amante, talvez). Por ser jovem, tem uma visão otimista da vida: quer trabalhar e continuar a estudar, sonha tirar um curso. Mas, já em Lisboa, um encontro inesperado com um seu conterrâneo, Ildo, mostra como a realidade é bem diferente do que Xanda tinha imaginado. Sabemos, por ele, que se transformou em *persona non grata* pela sua ligação à PIDE: "Ninguém te pode salvar agora. Segue o teu caminho. Pidoca! Bufona!" (Amarílis 117). Acaba em Dakar, fugida. Desde *Chiquinho*, Dakar (capital do Senegal) é por excelência a cidade associada à prostituição, a única alternativa migratória para as mulheres; não há razões para pensarmos que a sorte de Xanda tenha sido diferente da de tantas outras.

A realidade distópica que temos vindo a tratar pode ser resumida pela mãe de Mandinha, no conto "Canal Gelado": "Vida é vida. Vida não é romance" (Amarílis 75). A realidade crua é o oposto da ficção, onde tudo é belo e feliz. Contudo, apesar de ficcional, esta obra não é um romance e muito menos feliz: a coletânea começa com uma tragédia e termina em tom de lamento, o que não traz bons augúrios para o futuro da diáspora cabo-verdiana. O último conto, "Requiem," narra a história de Bina, uma aspirante a escritora que se sente frustrada por não conseguir escrever. *Requiem* é o nome dado à missa por alma dos defuntos, designando também as composições musicais associadas à morte e ao luto. Vindos de uma escritora de inspiração neorrealista, acreditamos que os retratos que Amarílis nos oferece nestes contos são relativamente fiéis ao universo das ilhas. A possibilidade de resolução dos conflitos sociais pela escrita combativa também não será solução: Bina acaba por deitar os papéis da história que estava a escrever no lixo, num gesto de desalento que reflete o desânimo de Cabo Verde nos anos da pós-independência (que chegou em 1975). A esperança num futuro melhor, que *Chiquinho* oferece ao deixar a narração da sua história em aberto, é deitada fora em *Ilhéu dos Pássaros*; o *requiem* anuncia o fim: não há uma perspetiva otimista do que está para vir.

5. Força Centrífuga e Força Centrípeta – Dispersão e Convergência

As forças em ação nas narrativas aqui analisadas merecem, igualmente, reflexão. Se, por um lado, há um movimento de dispersão a que podemos chamar de força centrífuga, com um ponto de partida que impulsiona para o exterior, existe um movimento contrário de convergência, o da força centrípeta, em que vários pontos dispersos são projetados numa única direção. As epígrafes de *Chiquinho* e *Ilhéu dos Pássaros* são bons pontos de partida para essa reflexão, uma vez que dão o mote para a leitura das histórias. Referi acima que um dos objetivos das revistas *Claridade* e *Certeza* era a defesa do crioulo como língua literária. Ao escolher um excerto de morna em crioulo (com tradução em português), Lopes assume essa posição de orgulho da língua e cultura que caracterizam a caboverdianidade. Diz a epígrafe: "O corpo, que é escravo, vai; / O coração, que é livre, fica..." (9). A abundância de ideias paradoxais nestes pequenos versos demonstra a riqueza da música cabo-verdiana. A morna é geralmente um género cantado em tom de lamento, de cadência lenta, em que os temas da partida, do mar e da saudade são dominantes, refletindo a realidade diaspórica que informa a identidade cabo-verdiana.[7] Corpo e coração dividem-se: o primeiro é o objeto material obrigado a sair de Cabo Verde em busca de destinos mais promissores, escravo das duras circunstâncias climatéricas; o segundo é etéreo e imaterial: apesar de ir com o corpo, permanece ligado à terra-mãe por um sentimento que supera a distância física da ausência. Wilson Trajano Filho salienta que a difícil escolha entre partir e ficar é um dilema experimentado pelos migrantes através da noção de saudade. Este fator de tensão social e sofrimento transformou-se num dos tropos das manifestações culturais do arquipélago, presente na poesia, na música popular e na literatura, levando à cristalização da imagem dos cabo-verdianos enquanto povo profundamente dividido entre o impulso de partir e o de ficar (525). Essa divisão anímica é basilar às obras aqui analisadas.

Todas figuras migrantes que Lopes nos apresenta em *Chiquinho* são versões do corpo que vai e ilustram o movimento centrífugo de dispersão, como "pontos lançados ao acaso no meio do Atlântico. As ilhas eram a nossa base para partirmos" (236). Alguns eram antigos homens do mar, como o avô de Chiquinho (que desapareceu quando regressava a casa), Nhô Chic'Ana (marinheiro), Chico

Zepa (trancador do baleeiro *Wanderer*), Nhô João (cujas soldadas ganhas no mar lhe permitiram comprar tudo o que tinha), Nhô Loca (que saiu ainda novo para a pesca da baleia nos mares do sul), ou Nhô Maninho Bento (antigo capitão de um navio negreiro). Outros sonhavam com o mar, como o jovem Tói Mulato, que queria ser capitão de um navio e tinha no pai, morto tragicamente a bordo de um carvoeiro onde era *donkeyman*, um modelo a seguir. Outros, ainda, estabeleceram-se em Nova Inglaterra, como o pai de Chiquinho ou José Lima, operários fabris na indústria têxtil. O corpo vai, mas o coração fica, cria amarras às ilhas, quais sereias que chamam docemente pelos marinheiros, com um canto eterno que magnetiza e atrai. José Lima destaca a "saudade crioula que puxa irresistivelmente para o arquipélago o filho das ilhas mais inveterado no ritmo da vida americana" (Lopes 259). O velho sábio Totone Menga Menga sintetiza bem esse sentimento: "desembarque é que matou embarque" (Lopes 31). Uma vez em terra, já não há como escapar ao apelo irresistível das ilhas. O senhor Euclides dá, por isso, um sábio conselho a Chiquinho: "Não te deixes prender, Chiquinho. Esta terra de Cabo Verde, com a sua pobreza, não sei o que tem que puxa, atrai e pega como que grude" (Lopes 236); ficar não pode ser opção para o jovem.

Apesar de a dispersão ser a força motriz de *Chiquinho*, é possível estabelecer uma ponte de ligação com a coletânea de contos de Amarílis no sentido da convergência: Chiquinho menciona "o farol do ilhéu que deflagra o seu tríplice espasmo vermelho" (Lopes 188), tal como Bina, em "Requiem," pensa no farol do Ilhéu dos Pássaros. O farol existe para guiar os barcos em segurança para o porto, fazendo com que elementos dispersos se reúnam num único ponto, atraídos pela força centrípeta. O Ilhéu dos Pássaros é central para ler os contos da obra com o mesmo nome: é o ponto de convergência do olhar e do pensamento. Não é por acaso que dá título à coletânea: aí se reúnem sete histórias independentes, sem ligação aparente entre si, forçadas a conviver num mesmo espaço material – o livro – que é, ele mesmo, o Ilhéu de que Amarílis se serve para ancorar as personagens dispersas à sua identidade cabo-verdiana. Por mais diferenciados que sejam os percursos dos protagonistas, uma coisa têm em comum: a ligação às origens.

O Ilhéu dos Pássaros aparece em todas as epígrafes dos contos e adquire diversos significados, pertinentes para entender a ligação da diáspora à terra-mãe. Em "Thonon-Les-Bains," é o local onde a vista descansa, o ponto isolado que oferece tranquilidade de espírito a Gabriel depois de este tomar a resolução de vingar a morte da irmã. Porém, pelo contrário, pode ser o local agreste, escarpado, onde o mar revolto se bate com as rochas, representando o estado mental demente de Luísa. Em "Luna Cohen," é a sentinela que guarda os portões de entrada no arquipélago ao qual nem todos têm acesso; é o sítio seguro que precisa de senha – Luna tem essa senha e ambiciona voltar à pátria dos avós, dos pais e da infância, à qual pertence. Quando tudo o resto nas ilhas muda, é o espaço que representa a estabilidade, imponente apesar da sua pequenez. O Ilhéu também é o espaço do luto que recebe as flores atiradas ao mar em gesto de saudade: quando alguém morria a bordo de um navio, como no caso de Bibinha, o seu corpo era lançado ao mar. É símbolo do desejo de regresso às origens daqueles que se encontram distantes e que têm saudades da terra-mãe. No último conto da coletânea, "Requiem," é a memória que emerge do inconsciente, a lembrança embutida na mente de Bina que aflora quando o filtro do consciente deixa de funcionar: a imagem do farol surge como uma espécie de guia que a conduzirá a casa em segurança. Afastado da terra e rodeado de mar, o Ilhéu é a materialização do sentimento de não-pertença de que fala Smith.

Challinor explora a dicotomia entre o partir e o ficar, afirmando que o senso de identidade social cabo-verdiana é formado pela interpenetração e interdependência do "aqui" e do "lá," ligados através da circulação transnacional de bens, dinheiro e pessoas (88). A autora serve-se da simbologia atribuída a Jano, deus romano dos inícios e transições, como a metáfora mais apropriada para examinar as manifestações cabo-verdianas de identidades sociais em que passado, presente e futuro estão em constante negociação nos limites entre a fronteira de herança africana e a de herança europeia. Jano é retratado com duas caras, em lados opostos da cabeça, o que lhe dá a habilidade de olhar simultaneamente para o passado e para o futuro. Challinor atribui à identidade cabo-verdiana uma configuração jânica, pois é marcada pelo olhar coletivo de duplo sentido: em direção ao futuro, o das novas localizações geográficas da diáspora, onde família e amigos se estabeleceram; e em direção ao passado, em que família e amigos ficaram no espaço do arquipélago, que se transforma numa pátria imaginada e desejada (84). A dicotomia entre o partir e o ficar, manifestada na oposição entre a ação centrípeta e a centrífuga presente em *Chiquinho* e *Ilhéu dos Pássaros*, é uma das principais forças motrizes das manifestações culturais cabo-verdianas em geral, e destas duas obras em particular.

6. A Emigração no Masculino e no Feminino

As experiências diaspóricas são sempre marcadas do ponto de vista de género (Clifford 258). No que toca à diáspora cabo-verdiana, homens e mulheres têm destinos diferentes, e as suas experiências migratórias têm peso desigual nas duas narrativas, consoante se trate de uma visão masculina (*Chiquinho*) ou feminina (*Ilhéu dos Pássaros*) das suas vivências. Em *Chiquinho*, as possibilidades migratórias são muito mais diversificadas para os homens, com a opção de deslocar-se para fora do espaço das ilhas, do que para as mulheres, ancoradas a terra. Clifford destaca a tendência para ignorar a marcação de género nas experiências diaspóricas, facto que normaliza as experiências masculinas e apaga as femininas (258). Escrito nas primeiras décadas do século XX (excertos publicados na revista *Claridade*, nos anos 30), o romance não problematiza a condição feminina de estagnação territorial; o fenómeno é naturalizado e aceite como parte da vida no arquipélago. As mulheres ficam nas ilhas, amarradas aos deveres de esposa, mãe e dona de casa, e são os homens que emigram para sustentar a família. A exceção à regra é descrita no final da história, com Chiquinho já a bordo do navio que há-de levá-lo à América: lá, observa uma mulher e o seu filho, que vão provavelmente encontrar-se com o marido, fazendo pensar que há esperança na mudança de paradigmas. Os destinos mais comuns da diáspora são os navios baleeiros e as fábricas têxteis de Nova Inglaterra; contudo, há no romance referência a patrícios emigrados na Argentina, como Amâncio (marido da Tia Alzira), Eusébio (marido de Nhá Cidália), ou o tio de Tói Mulato.

A casa construída com o dinheiro ganho pelo avô "de riba da água do mar" (Lopes 79) é governada pela mãe e pela avó de Chiquinho, as esposas em terra dos homens que partiram, com os dólares que o pai envia da América. A geração seguinte, a de Chiquinho e Nuninha, tem aspirações mais arrojadas: ele quer estudar numa universidade americana e ela quer fugir com ele, chegando a propor-lhe irem para Dakar ou para o Brasil. Chiquinho quer que ela se junte a ele na América, mas não para trabalhar fora de casa ou para estudar; o seu destino passaria por ser a "operária da casa... a dona da casa de um trabalhador" (Lopes 196). Numa sociedade patriarcal, a situação feminina estaria sempre ligada ao espaço doméstico, privado, da família, mesmo no território distante da diáspora.

A única alternativa para as mulheres que procuram mudar de vida passa pela cidade senegalesa de Dakar. Enquanto cidade portuária, é destino para os homens que querem fazer negócio e embarcar rumo ao estrangeiro. Porém, para as mulheres, Dakar é sinónimo de prostituição; tornar-se mocrata era o derradeiro sacrifício para fugir à miséria. Dakar rouba a inocência dessas meninas que vão para a cidade para serem exploradas, trabalhando a troco de comida e teto, e vendendo a virgindade na devassidão dos cabarés para pagar dívidas da família.

Algumas fazem bom dinheiro e conseguem arranjar parceiros que as sustentem; no entanto, têm uma vida dura e degradante. Décadas depois, através dos contos de *Ilhéu dos Pássaros*, percebemos que a situação se alterou: as mulheres já não são imóveis, têm a mesma liberdade que os homens para sair das ilhas e tentar a sorte noutros países, apesar de nem sempre serem bem-sucedidas. É o caso de Piedade, que acaba assassinada, ou de Xanda, renegada por ser uma espia da PIDE, e que foge de Lisboa para Dakar, cidade que, muitas décadas depois de *Chiquinho*, continua ligada ao estigma da prostituição feminina. No extremo oposto, temos Luna Cohen, uma investigadora que se desloca à Nigéria para trabalhar na tese de doutoramento, ou Bina, assistente do Poeta e intérprete em Dakar, onde trabalhava com os fugitivos da Guiné.

Clifford tenta reverter o silêncio a que são votadas as experiências diaspóricas femininas, ao atribuir-lhes uma significativa importância: a migração feminina, muitas vezes em situações-limite de desespero social e económico, quando os homens estão ausentes do seu papel tradicional de chefes de família, permite a essas mulheres uma relativa independência e controlo através de um rendimento próprio (ainda que conseguido a custo da sua exploração laboral). A vida das mulheres na diáspora não está ausente de sofrimento, devido às inseguranças materiais e espirituais de uma terra desconhecida (259). Clifford questiona se as experiências diaspóricas reforçam ou atenuam a subordinação de género (259). Em *Chiquinho*, o narrador em primeira pessoa tem a intenção de reforçar as estruturas patriarcais cabo-verdianas em solo americano, mantendo Nuninha como dona de casa. Em *Ilhéu dos Pássaros*, assistimos a uma mudança de mentalidades e de perspetiva narrativa, pois observamos o lado feminino das experiências migratórias. Apesar do reforço da ligação entre Dakar e prostituição, as mulheres dos contos de Amarílis têm acesso a vidas que as de Lopes nem sonham: estudam, têm profissões liberais e deslocam-se entre os vários espaços, independentes dos seus contrapontos masculinos.

Curiosamente, verifica-se, na coletânea de Amarílis, um intercâmbio entre a Inglaterra e a Nigéria enquanto espaços de diáspora. No aeroporto de Ikeja, Luna (personagem principal do conto com o mesmo nome) conversa com um homem inglês, engenheiro, que lhe diz estar na Nigéria como emigrante em busca de melhores oportunidades: "Sou engenheiro, mas lá [Inglaterra] o trabalho não garante o sustento de uma casa" (51). Inglaterra tem baixa procura de mão-de--obra qualificada, em alta demanda na Nigéria; pelo contrário, as camadas mais baixas da população nigeriana encontram em Londres o espaço onde montar o seu pequeno comércio, como descreve o conto "Requiem": "os da Nigéria, dos Barbados, da Jamaica, quiseram o espaço debaixo da ponte para mercado" (Amarílis 130). O trânsito entre um ex-território colonial e a metrópole que o controlou durante décadas ou séculos não se restringe à realidade portuguesa; verificamos, com a referência à dicotomia Inglaterra/Nigéria, que os diferentes tipos de mão-de-obra têm pesos e influências distintos: os trabalhadores não qualificados, oriundos dos países africanos, têm somente à sua disposição trabalhos mal remunerados nas metrópoles que outrora os governavam; por outro lado, os trabalhadores qualificados, como o engenheiro britânico, encontram nos países africanos o potencial de desenvolvimento económico que lhes permite tentar uma nova forma de controlo (colonial) através da superioridade intelectual que não é valorizada no seu país de origem.

A miséria, a falta de infraestruturas e o limitado sector da educação levam a que grande parte da população cabo-verdiana se encontre fora dos limites geográficos do arquipélago. Em *Chiquinho*, assistimos à emigração do setor mais carenciado da população como êxodo à fome e à seca, para territórios onde apenas os trabalhos mais pesados e mal pagos estavam disponíveis. Em *Ilhéu dos Pássaros*, encontramos não só quem consiga trabalhos que requerem mão-de-obra não qualificada, mas também uma geração diferente de emigrantes, com estudos, que procura no estrangeiro uma forma de valorização pessoal das suas capacidades intelectuais. Diz Pires Laranjeira que emigrar não é desistir, mas insistir na melhoria de vida e a única forma de quebrar o cerco do isolamento e do provincianismo; parte-se com o objetivo de regressar com mais condições do que aquelas com que se foi (209). E, até se regressar, as remessas enviadas aos familiares nas ilhas, quer em géneros quer em capital, são essenciais para a economia do arquipélago.

7. Considerações Finais: Ser Cabo-Verdiano em *Chiquinho* e em *Ilhéu dos Pássaros*

Independentemente da razão que os leve a sair de Cabo Verde, os filhos e filhas das ilhas terão sempre uma ligação afetiva com a terra que os viu nascer. O mar, a saudade, a terra-longe e o regresso são poderosos tropos da cultura popular que mantêm vivo o desejo de aventura numa terra distante (Trajano Filho 524). A identidade cabo-verdiana retratada por Lopes e Amarílis está intimamente ligada ao mar, nos seus sentidos mais ambivalentes. O mar é mulher caprichosa que precisa de afagos, de canções, de carinho, e campo de batalha para conquistas amorosas; o mar é a barreira que separa quem fica de quem parte, e é a ponte de ligação entre o mundo conhecido e o desconhecido, para onde se parte à aventura; o mar é ponto de partida, mas também última morada, onde ficam sepultados os que morrem nos navios. Existe uma ironia nessa ligação identitária cabo-verdiana à água que não passa despercebida a Halter: os emigrantes encontram a prosperidade económica nos laços com o mar, enquanto a terra-mãe definha com a seca e falta de chuva (23). Enquanto nação insular com um clima árido, o país permanece vulnerável às secas e à baixa produtividade agrícola (cerca de 90 porcento da comida é importada), ao que se junta um aumento substancial da população, concentrada agora em áreas urbanas onde o investimento se torna crucial (Rodrigues, "Cape Verde"). A seca, o mar e a diáspora são Cabo Verde. Outro dos fatores fundacionais da identidade cabo-verdiana é o sentimento diaspórico de dupla não-pertença, como Smith bem mostrou. Um emigrante é um navio em trânsito entre dois portos, duas realidades, não pertencendo verdadeiramente a nenhuma: não está fisicamente em Cabo Verde, mas não é aceite pela sociedade onde pretende recomeçar a vida. Nessa linha, a diáspora é também o Ilhéu que permanece no espaço "entre," algo que tem uma aura de mistério, que está longe e, ao mesmo tempo, perto.

A língua é igualmente um fator a ter em conta na construção identitária em Lopes e Amarílis: ambos defendem o crioulo como língua literária e fazem uso da tradição oral para mostrar a sua força expressiva em relação ao português. Apesar de oficial (adotado pelo Estado desde a sua independência), o português é, tal como o inglês ou o francês, aprendido como segunda língua; é útil para quem sai das ilhas em busca de novas oportunidades, mas não é a língua falada no dia-a-dia. O crioulo continua a ser a língua materna de uma grande maioria de cabo-verdianos, ainda que não faça oficialmente parte do programa de ensino público – situação que tem vindo a ser revista, com a introdução de programas-piloto de ensino bilingue em português e crioulo, como o de Ana Josefa Cardoso, tendo por base a pesquisa da sua tese de doutoramento (Almeida, "Ensino Bilingue").[8] Esta situação de diglossia demonstra a ligação entre prestígio social e a língua do antigo colonizador – Rodrigues ("Cape verde") afirma mesmo que esta se pode considerar uma forma de reprodução pós-colonial do colonialismo luso. Um quarto fator identitário é a miscigenação. Ser cabo-verdiano não é sinónimo de ser negro ou africano (designações atribuídas aos cabo-verdianos na sociedade americana): é ser herdeiro de uma mistura de etnias africanas e europeias, sintetizadas na figura do mulato. Num cenário diaspórico, o orgulho crioulo é motivo de exclusão e traz angústia, pois é difícil saber qual o seu lugar na sociedade. No conto "Requiem," Bina é expulsa de um comício de negros de forma insultuosa: "Get out of here. Tu não és da nossa raça, tu és cruzada" (Amarílis 130), situação embaraçosa à qual se vem juntar uma outra, com uma senhora a perguntar-lhe se era brasileira.

A caboverdianidade manifestada nas obras de Lopes e Amarílis está ligada, de forma inequívoca, às experiências diaspóricas. Esta diáspora de que tenho vindo a falar corresponde à definição do termo por William Safran, cujas principais características incluem: um historial de dispersão de um centro para locais periféricos, a manutenção de mitos e memórias da pátria, a alienação do país anfitrião que não aceita as comunidades migrantes, o desejo de um eventual regresso à pátria, o compromisso de apoio e renovação da pátria, e a identidade coletiva e solidariedade de grupo desenvolvida em relação à pátria (Clifford 247). Todas estas características podem ser encontradas nas representações literárias da diáspora cabo-verdiana das duas obras literárias: o centro, Cabo Verde, dispersa-se por vários continentes, sendo a Europa e a América do Norte os principais espaços geográficos da diáspora; as memórias da pátria são mantidas vivas por aqueles que estão longe e se veem impossibilitados de regressar; a não-aceitação das comunidades migrantes nos países anfitriões é explorada por Lopes e Amarílis, com um humilhante exame físico a que os cabo-verdianos tinham obrigatoriamente de se submeter na Casa da Emigração de New Bedford, onde eram alvo de chacota (*Chiquinho*), e o trágico assassinato de Piedade em França, e a expulsão do seu irmão Gabriel da comunidade de Thonon-Les-Bains (*Ilhéu dos Pássaros*). O desejo de regresso à pátria está intrinsecamente ligado ao compromisso de apoio ao país que se deixou para trás, através das remessas de dinheiro que têm por objetivo não só ajudar a sustentar as famílias que ficaram em Cabo Verde, mas também planear um futuro regresso com estabilidade económica e ostentação de bens materiais.

Do ponto de vista das elaborações literárias da condição sociocultural cabo-verdiana partilhada pelas obras de Lopes e Amarílis, ser cabo-verdiano é pertencer a uma comunidade original miscigenada de grande riqueza cultural e linguística onde são visíveis as influências africanas, europeias e americanas, e que não pode ser entendida apenas dentro das fronteiras geográficas do território. A diáspora tem um peso significativo no entendimento da identidade deste povo e a análise comparativa entre *Chiquinho* e *Ilhéu dos Pássaros* aqui apresentada mostra como é possível, ao longo de décadas, fazer uso desse mote de forma fértil em contexto literário. Não é minha pretensão afirmar que tropo da identidade cabo-verdiana enquanto diaspórica se restrinje à análise destas duas obras; este tópico abrangente tem vindo a ser alvo de estudos e debates académicos, tão recentes quanto, por exemplo, a conferência organizada pela Universidade de Cabo Verde a 28 de Abril de 2016, com o premiado poeta José Luís Tavares como principal palestrante, ou o conjunto de ensaios *Diáspora Cabo-Verdiana: Temas em Debate*, organizado por Iolanda Évora, e publicado no mesmo ano. Como prova a recente tradução inglesa de *Chiquinho* e as prolíficas pesquisas de base literária, sociológica, antropológica e histórica, Cabo Verde e as suas comunidades diaspóricas têm vindo a conquistar a merecida visibilidade de que foram privados por décadas de exclusão social, económica e política.

NOTAS

1. Baltasar Lopes tinha um projeto para a continuação de *Chiquinho* que retrataria a sua vida de emigrante já nos Estados Unidos. Chamar-se-ia *Acushnett Street*, mas nunca chegou a ser escrito.

2. António Coelho foi o primeiro cabo-verdiano americano a ser dono de um desses navios, o "Nelly May," que levantou velas para Brava em 1892.

3. De acordo com dados de 2009 do International Center for Migration Policy Development, recolhidos por Iolanda Évora em "Migration or Diaspora? Perceptions of the Cape Verdean Dispersion in the World," o censo de 2000 indicava que 500 mil cidadãos cabo-verdianos viviam no estrangeiro, e 450 mil nas ilhas, confirmando que Cabo Verde mantém uma comunidade diaspórica maior que a residente no arquipélago.

4. Dados sobre a emigração na área rural de Santiago, entre 1979 e 1981, confirmam que por cada 100 migrantes, 92 são homens (Trajano Filho 527).

5. Uma parte substancial do dinheiro que circula localmente em Cabo Verde vem diretamente das remessas dos que vivem no estrangeiro, enviadas para subsistência dos parentes que permanecem na ilha, para a construção da casa em que sonham viver quando regressarem, ou para pagar o arrendamento de hortas de que os familiares tomam conta (Trajano Filho 535).

6. Nome depreciativo para se referir à Polícia Internacional e de Defesa do Estado, comummente conhecida por PIDE, na época da ditadura salazarista.

7. Há mais duas referências importantes às mornas em *Chiquinho*: uma tem o título "Pau Matou o Meu Filho," em que uma mãe conta a história do filho que se afogou na viagem de regresso a casa, da América, depois de ter trabalhado como escravo; a outra morna é a de Chiquinho e Nuninha, que Alcides escreveria. Diz ele que seria diferente das mornas tradicionais de "saudades lancinantes, da tristeza da separação e do desespero das noivas pelo destino dos namorados emigrantes que os navios de vela sepultam no fundo do Golfo quando regressam da América" (134), pois seria uma história de amor com final feliz.

8. A experiência-piloto do Ensino bilingue foi implementada nas escolas de Ponta d'Água, na cidade da Praia, e de Flamengos, em São Miguel (ilha de Santiago), no ano letivo 2013/14. Nos anos letivos seguintes, o projeto foi alargado a mais algumas escolas de São Vicente; no entanto, não houve seguimento por necessidade de implementação de melhorias, segundo declarações da ministra da Educação e Inclusão Social, Maritza Rosabal, ao jornal eletrónico *Muzika* (21 fevereiro de 2019).

OBRAS CITADAS

Abdala Junior, Benjamin. "Globalização, Cultura e Identidade em Orlanda Amarílis." *Portuguese Literary / Cultural Studies 8: Cape Verde – Language, Literature & Music*. Center for Portuguese Studies and Culture, University of Massachusetts Dartmouth, 2003, pp. 213-26.

Almeida, Sara. "Ensino Bilingue: Duas Línguas a Par e Passo." *Expresso das Ilhas*, 27 de fevereiro de 2015, https://expressodasilhas.cv/pais/2015/02/27/ensino-bilingue-duas-linguas-a-par-e-passo/44130. Acesso em 18 de julho de 2019.

Amarílis, Orlanda. *Ilhéu dos Pássaros*. Plátano Editora, 1982.

Andrade, Elisa Silva. "7: Cape Verde. *A History of Postcolonial Lusophone Africa*, edição de Patrick Chabal et al. Indiana UP, 2002, pp. 264-290.

———. *The Cape Verde Islands: From Slavery to Modern Times*. United Nations African Institute for Economic Development and Planning, 1973.

Carvalho, Alberto de. "Lugares Étnicos e Maravilhosos do Imaginário Cabo-Verdiano (em *Chiquinho*, de Baltasar Lopes)." *Portuguese Literary / Cultural Studies 8: Cape Verde – Language, Literature & Music*. Center for Portuguese Studies and Culture, University of Massachusetts Dartmouth, 2003, pp. 171-93.

Challinor, Elizabeth Pilar. "Home and Overseas: The Janus Faces of Cape Verdean Identity." *Diaspora*, vol. 17, nº 1, 2008, pp. 84-104.

Clifford, James. *Routes: Travel and Translation in the Late Twentieth Century*. Harvard University Press, 1997.

David Brookshaw. "Part II: Cape Verde." *The Postcolonial Literature of Lusophone Africa*, edição de Patrick Chabal. Hurst & Company, 1996, pp. 179-233.

Ellen, Maria M., trad. *Across the Atlantic: An Anthology of Cape Verdean Literature*. Center for the Portuguese Speaking World (Southeastern Massachusetts University), 1988.

Évora, Iolanda, org. *Diáspora Cabo-Verdiana: Temas em Debate*. CEsA – Centro de Estudos sobre África, Ásia e América Latina, 2016.

Évora, Iolanda. "Migration or Diaspora? Perceptions of the Cape Verdean Dispersion in the World." *Centro de Estudos sobre África e do Desenvolvimento*, 2013, https://pascal.iseg.utl.pt/~cesa/files/Doc_trabalho/WP115-2.pdf. Acesso em 23 de julho de 2018.

Halter, Marilyn. "Introduction: The Cape Verdeans – All Shades, All Hues." *Between Race and Ethnicity: Cape Verdean American Immigrants, 1860-1965*. University of Illinois Press, 1993, pp. 1-33.

Laban, Michel. *Cabo Verde: Encontro com Escritores*, vol. 1. Fundação Eng. António de Almeida, 1992.

Laranjeira, Pires. "Parte III – Cabo Verde." *Literaturas Africanas de Expressão Portuguesa*. Universidade Aberta, 1995, pp. 177-250.

Lobban Jr., Richard A. e Paul Khalil Saucier. *Historical Dictionary of the Republic of Cape Verde*. Scarecrow, 2007.

Lopes, Baltasar. *Chiquinho*. Prelo, 1961.

———. *Chiquinho: A Novel of Cabo Verde*. Tradução de Isabel Fêo Rodrigues e Carlos Almeida, Tagus Press, 2019.

McNab, Gregory. "Sexual Difference: The Subjection of Women in Two Stories by Orlanda Amarílis." *Luso-Brazilian Review*, vol. 24, nº1, 1987, pp. 59-68.

"Projeto Bilingue: Há um Conjunto de Situações a Resolver para que Seja Implementado de Outra Maneira, Diz Ministra." *Muzika*, 21 de fevereiro de 2019, https://muzika.sapo.cv/eventos/novidades-eventos/artigos/projeto-bilingue-ha-um-conjunto-de-situacoes-a-resolver-para-que-seja-implementado-de-outra-maneira-diz-ministra. Acesso em 18 de julho de 2019.

Rodrigues, Isabel. "Cape Verde." *Oxford Bibliographies – African Studies*, 2014, https://www.oxfordbibliographies.com/view/document/obo-9780199846733/obo-9780199846733-0155.xml. Acesso em 20 de maio de 2019.

Sapega, Ellen W. "Notes on the Historical Context of *Claridade*." *Portuguese Literary / Cultural Studies 8: Cape Verde – Language, Literature & Music*. Center for Portuguese Studies and Culture, University of Massachusetts Dartmouth, 2003, pp. 159-70.

Schreiner, Kay-Michael. *Frauen in der dritten Welt - Reportagen, Erzählungen, Gedichte*. Hammer, 1986.

Smith, Bradley. "Other Atlantics: Cape Verde, *Chiquinho* and the Black Atlantic World." *Comparative Literature Studies*, vol. 49, nº 2, 2012, pp. 246-64.

Trajano Filho, Wilson. "The Conservative Aspects of a Centripetal Diaspora: The Case of the Cape Verdean Tabancas." *Africa*, vol. 79, nº 4, 2009, pp. 520-42.

DIANA SIMÕES é doutorada em Estudos e Teoria Luso-Afro-Brasileiros, pela Universidade de Massachusetts Dartmouth (2019). A sua pesquisa centra-se na narração póstuma de contos e romances dos séculos XX e XXI escritos em português, através da lente da teoria pós-colonial. A autora tem artigos publicados em várias revistas especializadas e está, atualmente, a preparar o seu manuscrito para publicação. Atualmente, desempenha funções de instrutora visitante de língua e culturas portuguesas na Universidade de Massachusetts Lowell.

MAGDALENA EDWARDS

The Maritime Micro-Gestures in Elizabeth Bishop's Brazil Poems and Translations

"too many waterfalls here [...] hurry too rapidly down to the sea"

ABSTRACT: The North American poet Elizabeth Bishop published poems about Brazil as well as translations of the work of some of her Brazilian contemporaries, including Clarice Lispector and Carlos Drummond de Andrade. This essay examines a selection of Bishop's Brazil poems and translations that perform maritime micro-gestures—that is, subtle movements of the sea and connected bodies of water—in order to consider the insights and dangers contained therein. I discuss these gestures in the spirit of the new media theorist Vilém Flusser and argue that Bishop's poems can teach us to better examine our own ways of looking at the world and ourselves and to recognize that things are often not quite what they seem.

KEYWORDS: Vilém Flusser; Clarice Lispector; Carlos Drummond de Andrade; poetry; translation; gesture; micro-gesture; sea; water; ocean; maritime; Brazil

RESUMO: A poeta norteamericana Elizabeth Bishop publicou poemas sobre o Brasil e traduções de alguns dos seus contemporâneos brasileiros, incluindo Clarice Lispector e Carlos Drummond de Andade. Este ensaio examina uma selecção de poemas e traduções de Bishop sobre Brasil que cumprem micro-gestos marítimos —ou seja, movimentos sutis do mar e das aguas ligadas— para considerar os conhecimentos e perigos incluídos. Eu analiso os "gestos" de Bishop pensando no teórico da cultura da mídia Vilém Flusser e argumento que os poemas de Bishop nos podem ensinar como melhorar nosso processo de examinar nosso olhar para o mundo e ao nossos mesmos, para entender que as vezes as coisas não são exatamente o que parecem ser.

PALAVRAS-CHAVE: Vilém Flusser; Clarice Lispector; Carlos Drummond de Andrade; poesia; tradução; gesto; micro-gesto; mar; água; oceano; marítimo; Brasil

---

The Pulitzer Prize–winning poet Elizabeth Bishop (1911–79) was North American, but she lived in Brazil for more than fifteen years and wrote extensively about it in her poems. She also translated into English the work of several contemporaneous Brazilian poets and the prose writings of Clarice Lispector. In 1972, she co-edited (with Emanuel Brasil) the first bilingual twentieth-century Brazilian poetry anthology for Wesleyan University Press. In this essay, I consider how Bishop navigated her position as a traveler, visitor, tourist, and expatriate by looking at the maritime micro-gestures in her Brazil poems and translations. By *maritime micro-gestures* I mean the subtle shifts in her texts that both evoke the sea or other connected bodies of water and show them in movement. My use of the word *gesture* follows the lead of the new media theorist Vilém Flusser (1920–91), who defined it as a physical movement that we read as holding specific meaning.[1] Flusser writes, "To understand [gesture], one must know its 'significance.' That is exactly what we do continually, very quickly and effectively. We 'read' gesture" (*Gestures* 2). He is specifically concerned with human gestures—movements of the human body: his chapters have titles such as "The Gesture of Writing," "The Gesture of Painting," and "The Gesture of Smoking a Pipe."

In many of her poems and translations, Bishop, too, plays with the notion of gesture. She pushes us to read bodies of water and their movements, as well as the movements within movements and the micro-movements belied by stillness. They serve as a portal through which to read the human as a fundamentally dynamic condition or experience while honing in on complex moments of human gesturing—sometimes on the meta-level of the poet, writer, or translator; sometimes through the poetic voice or narrator; sometimes within the texts themselves. Her poems and translations teach us to read her maritime micro-gestures "continually, very quickly and effectively"; she makes the sea and its connected bodies of water move in her work in order to give them meaning. Cumulatively, they create meaning across her oeuvre, revealing a relationship to and reading of Brazil's waters, land, and people. Of course, she also reads herself in and through Brazil and its waters.

Bishop's maritime micro-gestures do not begin with her Brazil poems. "The Map," the first poem in her first book, *North & South* (1946), not only lays out an ars poetica, or blueprint, for reading all of Bishop's oeuvre but also offers a template for the maritime micro-gestures traceable throughout her work, from "The Imaginary Iceberg" to "The Bight" to "At the Fishhouses" to "Cape Breton." "The Map" begins with a confident declaration: "Land lies in water." But quickly the poem questions itself: "Or does the land lean down to lift the sea from under?" And then: "Is the land tugging at the sea from under?" What is the relationship between the land and the sea from the land's perspective—lying, lifting, tugging—and how does the sea conduct itself? In the last stanza, Bishop provides a double promise of more to be revealed: "Mapped waters are more quiet than the land is" and "More delicate than the historians' are the map-makers' colors." She sets the human gesture of writing against the gesture of painting, in which mapmaking is evoked as a kind of painting. Significance deployed through written language (by the historians) is pitted against meaning crafted through visual techniques (by the mapmakers), and the implication of the poem's title is that the poet, in comparison to historians who make "History" with words, is a kind of mapmaker or painter too.

This is, of course, a contradiction, because the poet (and her poetic voice, the speaker), as painterly as she might be, relies on words to make her art. When Bishop's poetic voice describes the sea or a connected body of water, she uses written language; and often what is being described is a visual experience, the process of looking at the reflective surface of water, a kind of mirror in which the image (the self) might look back. In his chapter "The Gesture of Painting," Flusser discusses "specific phases of the gesture, a specific stepping back from the canvas or a specific look," which he calls "autoanalysis": "the gesture is constantly monitoring and reformulating its own meaning" (*Gestures* 65). The mapmaker who paints water or the painterly poet who describes mapped waters, then, engages in an autoanalytical gesture that is continually in movement in regard to its own meaning.

If we look back at the goings-on over the course of "The Map," we see that Bishop's mapmaking speaker is not on clear footing at all, and the maritime gestures she uses to "investigate the sea," while meaningful, are not predictable or coded in ways that are stable or constant. An unexpected and dynamic moment happens between the eleventh and thirteenth lines of the twenty-seven-line poem: "We can stroke those lovely bays, / under a glass as if they were expected to blossom, / or as if to provide a clean cage for invisible fish." Who are we? You and me? Me and the poetic voice, maker of maps with verse? Without question the reader is implicated here in the act of looking and reading. We're on the hook. This is an important moment to remember as we move forward into the rest of Bishop's oeuvre, for in the Brazil poems and translations the poetic voice becomes a traveler, visitor, and tourist steeped in the visual, in the gesture of painting with words and the autoanalytic.

Bishop's poetic voice in "The Map" invokes "we"—you and me, the reader and her—to consider a physical, sensual gesture. The potential action in which "we" might stroke the "lovely bays" is filled with unexpected possibility, as if the mapped inlets and their curves are suddenly three-dimensional and can be petted like a friendly dog, stroked erotically like a lover, or even coaxed into transformation, "as if they [are] expected to blossom" "under a glass" like a houseplant that thrives in a bell jar. Bishop transposes a section of the two-dimensional map, with its "lovely bays," into a possible three-dimensional ecosystem that we might observe under glass. And something may happen as we watch; the bays may "blossom." Now she takes another turn in the same sentence: "We can stroke these lovely bays, / under a glass as if they were expected to blossom, / or as if to provide a clean cage for invisible fish." The "or as if" gives us the most surprising scenario of all: "to provide a clean cage for invisible fish." The cloche, an observable ecosystem for the plantlike bays expected to blossom, suddenly becomes a "clean cage" for fish we cannot see with the naked eye. The poetic voice recalls, as if in a daydream, that the "lovely bays" are indeed comprised of water and that in those waters live sea creatures. The thought experiment that turns the mapped bays from two to three dimensions, so that they might be stroked and blossom like plants under glass, now brings back the water and the invisible fish that were there all along.

Bishop contradicts the possibility of a contained ecosystem—the lovely bay, the cloche, the aquarium—in the next movement, the fourteenth line: "The names of seashore towns run out to sea." The text on the map is here personified as something that moves along the map's surface and spills into the water. If we keep the notion of the poet as a mapmaker in mind, we might note that "The Map," with its twenty-seven lines, is a double sonnet, with the central fourteenth line functioning as an equator shared by both sonnets, north and south. The second sonnet runs from the fourteenth line into the fifteenth to complete the sentence two lines later: "the names of cities cross the neighboring mountains / —the printer here experiencing the same excitement / as when emotion too far exceeds its cause." The excess of letters tumbling across the map's landscape, into the water or across the adjacent mountains but always beyond the bounds of the place those letters are meant to name, is paralleled by the emotional excess or excitement of the printer. It is "too far," it is beyond, and it is a kind of blossoming. The earlier image of the "lovely bays...expected to blossom" also comes to fruition within the structure of the poem as the first sonnet begets (blossoms into) a second sonnet in its fourteenth line. And yet there is a comma at the end of the fourteenth line that creates a pause, a kind of edge: "The names of seashore towns run out to sea, / the names of cities cross the neighboring mountains." Boundaries, mapped edges, and ecosystems, though present, are not tidy; and Bishop demands our participation in her poetic thought experiments. The "lovely bays" have the possibility of blossoming because of human contact through stroking. Similarly, "The Map" has the possibility of blossoming into a meaningful text through the reader's close attention. If Flusser had written a chapter called "The Gesture of Reading," he might also have written a chapter called "The Gesture of Blossoming."

Bishop first docked in Brazil in November 1951. A late November letter to her dear friend and fellow poet Robert Lowell (1917–77) is addressed from the "Merchant Ship *Bowplate*" stationed "Somewhere off the coast of Brazil":

> I sent you a postcard just as I was leaving N.Y. but I had to put so many stamps on it I probably completely covered up my message.... It wasn't until I had decided on this crazy trip and went down to see the Rahvs one evening before sailing (as I then thought—I was held up a couple of weeks by the dock strikes) that I knew where you were. Philip said you intended spending the winter in Amsterdam, which somehow surprised me, but maybe no more than my decision to go through the Straits of Magellan will surprise you. At least I think that's where I'm bound for. At present we're approaching Santos—a couple of days late because of storms—and first I'm going to visit in Rio for a while.... Oh dear—there is so much to talk about. (*One Art* 224)

Many of the observations in this letter found their way into "Arrival at Santos," the first poem in her third collection, *Questions of Travel* (1965), which is divided into two sections: "Brazil" and "Elsewhere." This is a telling dichotomy and an autoanalytical moment, given that Bishop ended up living, accidentally, in Brazil for fifteen years (1951–66) and then on and off until 1971. "Arrival at Santos" conveys a sardonic self-awareness of the speaker's position as a traveler, visitor, and tourist who is never quite at ease in transit, never quite at home anywhere. It sets the tone for the entire book: "Oh, tourist, / is this how this country is going to answer you // and your immodest demands for a different world, / and a better life"? This moment of self-address, the tourist talking herself off a ledge, comes in the seventh line of the poem. What precedes is the setup of the poetic ecosystem, which of course Bishop will ultimately blur, boundaries and all. How she accomplishes this and creates the maritime micro-gestures within the poem provide clues as to how one might answer Bishop's own inquiry set up by the title of her collection *Questions of Travel*.

"Arrival at Santos" begins tidily enough, with the poetic voice painting a quick visual scene for the reader:

> Here is a coast; here is a harbor;
> here, after a meager diet of horizon, is some scenery:
> impractically shaped and—who knows?—self-pitying mountains,
> sad and harsh beneath their frivolous greenery,
>
> with a little church on top of one. And warehouses,
> some of them painted a feeble pink, or blue,
> and some tall, uncertain palms. Oh, tourist,
> is this how this country is going to answer you
>
> and your immodest demands for a different world,
> and a better life, and complete comprehension
> of both at last, and immediately,
> after eighteen days of suspension?
>
> Finish your breakfast. The tender is coming...

The poetic voice is pat, overconfident—here is this and here is that—as if the limit between coast and water, harbor and sea, were entirely obvious; as if we were listening to a real estate agent trying to sell us the property, quick! Here is the kitchen, here is the dining room, and here is the fireplace with architectural accents..."but of course" (to borrow a phrase from the fifth stanza) we know, as readers of Bishop's "The Map," that such confident demarcation only holds—if at all—at first glance. In the third line of the first stanza, the poetic voice's pat absolutes begin to collapse, as the tone shifts from confident clarity to unimpressed, judgmental, and dismissive notes—"who knows?" and "self-pitying mountains" and "frivolous greenery"—until she turns the judgment on herself: "Oh, tourist." How does the tourist look at "this country"—presumably in a list of countries visited, photographed, checked off—and how does the place offer the tourist what she wants, given her "immodest demands for a different world" and "a better life" and "complete comprehension." Is this why the tourist travels? To find herself anew, reframed, understood at last?

The poetic voice then changes the topic, and thus she abandons her awkward and failure-ridden attempt to use travel to understand herself: "Finish your breakfast. The tender is coming." Let's get on with it, shall we? And soon enough it's time: "we climb down the ladder backward" and get off the mother ship and onto the tender, the smaller boat that will take us to land or the dock. Who is the "we" here? Most immediately it's the poetic voice and Miss Breen, who "is about seventy, / a retired police lieutenant, six feet tall." Bishop met a woman named Breen during her travels, as she tells Lowell in her 1951 letter: "[a] lady [...] I like very much [...] a 6 ft. ex-policewoman who has retired after being head of the Women's Jail in Detroit for 26 years. She's about 70; very gentle and polite" (*One Art* 225). Miss Breen's name finds its way into the poem because it rhymes with the "green coffee beans" that are about to be loaded into the "twenty-six freighters." Meanwhile, the use of the pronoun "we" brings us, dear readers, along for the ride. Ultimately, when we arrive, the poetic voice realizes that "Ports are necessities, like postage stamps or soap, // but they never seem to care what impression they make," and neither does the poetic voice: "We leave Santos at once; we are driving to the interior." The fact is that in "Arrival at Santos" the water is only implied, never directly painted, through words like "coast" and "harbor" and "tender" and "freighter" and "port" and the "blue" of the warehouses and Miss Breen's "beautiful bright blue eyes" that may as well reflect the sea. The key is that the arrival at the port of Santos, where the waters mapped by the poem prove to be extremely quiet, is a mere formality, and travel will continue as the poetic voice drives to the interior.

In the next poem in *Questions of Travel*, "Brazil, January 1, 1502," we find ourselves in the interior, no coast in sight, surrounded by lush and abundant "foliage" that is "hell-green" (a variation on the land "shadowed green" in "The Map"), "fresh as if just finished / and taken off the frame." The landscape is compared to a freshly made work of art, and the poem aligns itself with visual art immediately with an epigraph from Sir Kenneth Clark's *Landscape into Art*: "embroidered nature...tapestried landscape." The only blue here appears to be embroidered in the leaves—"big leaves, little leaves, and giant leaves, / blue, blue-green, and olive"—and in the "blue-white sky, a simple web." There are "flowers, too, like giant water lilies / up in the air—up, rather, in the leaves," but no water, no sea. The poem ends with a terrible colonial scene in which the Christians in their armor—"each out to catch an Indian for himself"—pursue their prey, comprised of "those maddening little women who kept calling, / calling to each other (or had the birds waked up?) / and retreating, always retreating." The tone of these final lines is decidedly rapacious. However, Bishop's poetic voice invokes the colonial history of the place more subtly in the poem's opening lines, which focus on the view, noting simply that it is the same one the Christians saw in the early sixteenth century: "Januaries, Nature greets our eyes / exactly as she must have greeted theirs." This turns out to be a gentle warmup for what is to come.

The poem's final line about the maddening women "retreating, always retreating" leaves the reader in suspense, until the Christians, "hard as nails, / tiny as nails, and glinting, / in creaking armor" catch them. The line contains a borrowed phrase from Bishop's translation of Lispector's short story "The Smallest Woman in the World": "The tiny race [of pygmies], retreating, always retreating, has finished hiding away in the heart of Africa, where the lucky explorer discovered it." The explorer in Lispector's story, Marcel Pretre, is a colonial Frenchman in Africa, where slaves were taken and transported to Brazil. The Christian soldiers in their "creaking armor" in Bishop's poem seem to be Portuguese or French (they are "humming perhaps / *L'Homme armé* or some such tune") who are stationed in colonial Brazil. Because of the retreat of the pygmies and the women, both Bishop's Christians and Lispector's explorer go further into the interior of the territories they are plundering. One of the impossibilities of translation is the fact that the word "to explore" in Portuguese —*explorar*— also means "to exploit."

In her translation Bishop adds a detail to Lispector's story that is not in the original. The ambiguous setting "no Congo Central" (which translates as "in the Central Congo") (*Laços de familia* 68) becomes, in Bishop's version, "the Eastern Congo, near Lake Kivu" (*Kenyon Review* 501). Why did Bishop do this? Lake Kivu, one of the African Great Lakes, rests on the border between the Republic of Congo and Rwanda. If you look at a present-day map you will see a boundary line between the two countries that goes through the lake itself. Bishop's choice exemplifies her interest in blurry boundaries and the less-than-tidy nature of limits and containment. Her decision to add a geographic detail to her translation and specifically evoke a lake that contains fish species and endemic crabs and is on the border of two countries is an example of a maritime micro-gesture. How so if Lake Kivu is freshwater? The answer lies in the way in which it is ultimately connected to the Atlantic Ocean, through a system of interconnected bodies of water: Lake Kivu connects to the Ruizi River, which then flows to Lake Taganyika through a delta, and this lake ultimately connects via the Lualaba River to the Congo River (the second-longest in the world, after the Nile), which goes to the Atlantic.

Bishop's reference to Lake Kivu and everything it contains appears once in the story and could very easily go unnoticed, a reminder of the "invisible fish" that appear in the middle of "The Map." But her rendering of Lispector invites us to read carefully: "In the Eastern Congo, near Lake Kivu [Marcel Pretre] really did discover the smallest pygmies in the world. And—like a box within a box within a box—obedient, perhaps, to the necessity nature sometimes feels of outdoing herself—among the smallest pygmies in the world there was the smallest of the smallest pygmies in the world." Lispector personifies nature—"the necessity nature sometimes feels of outdoing herself"—and a similar moment of personifying female nature, Mother Earth, appears in the opening of Bishop's "Brazil, January 1, 1502": "Januaries, Nature greets our eyes / exactly as she must have greeted theirs." How might nature have greeted the explorer and shown the "necessity" "of outdoing herself" if he had visited Lake Kivu and its freshwater ecosystem, like a "box within a box within a box"? There are always more places to look. We are never done looking inside.

For Flusser, "The Gesture of Searching" occurs when "one does not know in advance what one is looking for." He wrote, "This testing gesture known as the 'scientific method,' is the paradigm of all our gestures. It now holds the dominant position that religious ritual gesture did in the Middle Ages" (*Gestures* 147). In "Brazil, January 1, 1502," the confluence of religious ritual gesture ("the Christians" and their "Mass" and ritual songs such as "*L'Homme armé* or some such tune") and the gesture of searching as the discovery of the unknown (they "came and found it all," "wealth, plus a brand-new pleasure," and "they ripped away [...] / each out to catch an Indian for himself") plays out in colonial Brazil while echoing into the present-day moment of Bishop's poem. Five centuries later, the poetic voice is a tourist who finds herself standing in the place of those early sixteenth-century Christians. The "maddening little women" who are "retreating, always retreating" invoke Lispector's Little Flower and how she contests Marcel Pretre in Bishop's translation of "The Smallest Woman in the World," a story that precisely unveils the "crisis" Flusser sees bound to erupt in the gesture of searching and the scientific method upon which it rests. The story investigates how Marcel Pretre "really did discover" and name Little Flower. This is his version of events, as a white European male on a voyage of discovery, described in the story's first line as "the French explorer, Marcel Pretre, hunter and man of the world." Little Flower (with her "flat nose" and "black face" and "splay feet," who "looked like a dog") negates his narrative with a gesture: at the very moment

Pretre names her, "Little Flower scratched herself where no one scratches." Little Flower's tribe of pygmies, the Likoualas, "use few names; they name things by gestures and animal noises," and Pretre chooses to read and respond to her gesture of scratching with a gesture of his own: he "look[s] the other way."

Little Flower and her gesture of scratching remind us that we must always read gesture, even if we struggle as Pretre does. "The Smallest Woman in the World" also pushes us to read ourselves, to engage in the autoanalytic process Flusser identifies with the gesture of painting. It seems no accident that Bishop's "Brazil, January 1, 1502" is ultimately a meditation on visual art, the "embroidered nature...[and] tapestried landscape" referred to in the poem's epigraph. Art, both the making and reading of it, pushes us to be autoanalytic.

During her time in Brazil, Bishop published poetry, prose, journalism, and translations, which included three stories by Lispector and poetry by Manuel Bandeira, João Cabral de Melo Neto, Joaquim Cardozo, Carlos Drummond de Andrade, and Vinicius de Moraes. Her translation of Drummond's "Travelling in the Family" ("Viagem na familia") is of particular interest here because of the poem's relationship to Bishop's *Questions of Travel*, notably the eponymous poem with its "streams and clouds [that] keep travelling, travelling." "Questions of Travel," the third poem in the collection, begins with excess: "There are too many waterfalls here; the crowded streams / hurry too rapidly down to the sea." The poem enacts the movement from interior streams to the ocean in a way that parallels the movement from Lake Kivu to the Atlantic Ocean in Bishop's translation of "The Smallest Woman in the World." The poetic voice watches the waterfalls and the "pressure of so many clouds" that "spill over the sides in soft slow-motion / turning to waterfalls under our very eyes," and the sight leads her to go even further than the sea and think of home in the next stanza.

Bishop's poetic voice commands herself and the reader to "think of the long trip home. / Should we have stayed at home and thought of here? / Where should we be today?" Her inquiry into the ethics of travel and her question about whether she should be home offer the inverse of Drummond's poem, in which the speaker is taken "by the hand" by "the shadow of my father" to visit his father's home and past. Though Drummond did not leave his country in the way Bishop left hers for Brazil, he did move from his home in Itabira, Minas Gerias, in 1934 to live in Rio de Janeiro until his death in 1987. His poem "Travelling in the Family" ends with water—specifically, a "river of blood" in abundance, if not excess. Though this moment is part of a dreamlike apparition in which Drummond's poetic voice embraces his father and addresses him directly, it feels altogether real:

> ...and in this ghostly embrace
> it's as if I were being burned
> completely, with poignant love.
> Only now do we know each other!
> Eye-glasses, memories, portraits
> flow in the river of blood.
> Now the waters won't let me
> make out your distant face,
> distant by seventy years...
>
> I felt that he pardoned me
> but he didn't say anything.
> The waters cover his moustache,
>
> the family, Itabira, all.

The power of the waters and the memories they carry in "Travelling in the Family" recall Bishop's early poem "At the Fishhouses," in which the poetic voice chats with a friend of her grandfather's and in this way enters into a meditation with the past that is facilitated by the sea. Here, the water burns, recalling Drummond's speaker, who says it's "as if I were being burned / completely, with poignant love":

> [...] The water seems suspended
> above the rounded gray and blue-gray stones.
> I have seen it over and over, the same sea, the same,
> slightly, indifferently swinging above the stones,
> icily free above the stones,
> above the stones and then the world.
> If you should dip your hand in,
> your wrist would ache immediately,
> your bones would begin to ache and your hand would burn
> as if the water were a transmutation of fire
> that feeds on stones and burns with a dark gray flame.
> If you tasted it, it would first taste bitter,

then briny, then surely burn your tongue.
It is like what we imagine knowledge to be:
dark, salt, clear, moving, utterly free,
drawn from the cold hard mouth
of the world, derived from the rocky breasts
forever, flowing and drawn, and since
our knowledge is historical, flowing, and flown.

The waters of the "same sea" have a temperature ("your hand would burn") and a taste ("bitter, / then briny, then surely burn your tongue") and a movement ("dark, salt, clear, moving, utterly free" and "flowing and drawn" and "flowing, and flown") that connect to "knowledge" and its "historical" quality. This recalls Bishop's "The Map" and its final line: "More delicate than the historians' are the map-makers' colors." The poet as mapmaker not only contends, in her arguably more delicate way, with history and the historical in her poem-maps, but does so with the help of those "mapped waters" that are "more quiet than the land is," as seen in "At the Fishhouses" and Bishop's translation of Drummond's "Travelling in the Family."

Bishop read her translation of Drummond's poem alongside her own poems during readings she gave in the United States in the late 1960s. In a May 31, 1969, letter to Drummond, she wrote: "During the past year and a half, I have given six or seven public readings of poetry, most of them at universities, including Harvard and the University of California, and at all of them I have read my translation of your poem, 'Viagem na familia,' with a few explanatory remarks of my own. This was [...] received with great interest."[2]

"Travelling in the Family" is a prime example of how the act of translation enriched Bishop's own creative process, and how her translations shed light on her original work. Of particular interest is the connection between Drummond's voyage through family guided by his dead father and her poem "First Death in Nova Scotia," in which her poetic voice, now quite childlike, recounts saying goodbye to her "little cousin Arthur" who is "laid out" in the "cold, cold parlor." The death of a young contemporary is much different, though perhaps no less haunting, than the absence and shadowy presence of the adult speaker's father in Drummond's poem. Bishop lost her father at a young age: William Thomas Bishop died of Bright's disease in 1911, when his daughter was eight months old. Her father's death was, in fact, the "first death" she experienced, but at that time the family lived in Worcester, Massachusetts. For this reason, the poem about "little cousin Arthur" is called "First Death in Nova Scotia," where she later moved to live with her mother's family.

Bishop never wrote the poem that could have been called "First Death in Massachusetts," where she, too, died in 1979. Instead she translated "Travelling in the Family," in which the speaker's walk with "the shadow of my father" leads to a realization that no doubt struck Bishop: "Only now do we know each other!" Her translation, first published in the June 1965 issue of *Poetry*, allowed her to return to "First Death in Nova Scotia," which had appeared in the March 10, 1962, issue of the *New Yorker*, in order to address the even earlier death she had encountered as a child, the loss of her father. While it seems highly unlikely that her translation of "Travelling in the Family" influenced the composition of "First Death in Nova Scotia," especially because Bishop first wrote to Drummond on June 27, 1963 (more than a year after her poem's publication), to ask for his opinion on her translation, the thematic confluence between the two poems is significant.

"First Death in Nova Scotia" appears in the second half of *Questions of Travel*, in the section titled "Elsewhere." The poem contains an interesting double moment that could be considered a maritime micro-gesture. The poetic voice's "little cousin Arthur" is laid out for viewing in the parlor that contains several objects that impress the childlike poetic voice as much, at times even more, than her cousin's body does. The chromographs, or lithographic prints, of two pairs of royals—Prince Edward and Princess Alexandra, and King George and Queen Mary—are neighbors to another item that commands attention:

> Below them on the table
> stood a stuffed loon
> shot and stuffed by Uncle
> Arthur, Arthur's father.
>
> Since Uncle Arthur fired
> a bullet into him,
> he hadn't said a word.
> He kept his own counsel
> on his white, frozen lake,
> the marble-topped table.
> His breast was deep and white,
> cold and caressable;

his eyes were red glass,
much to be desired.

"Come," said my mother,
"come and say good-bye
to your little cousin Arthur."
I was lifted up and given
one lily of the valley
To put in Arthur's hand.
Arthur's coffin was
a little frosted cake,
and the red-eyed loon eyed it
from his white, frozen lake.

This is a strange set of moments, and movements. The stuffed loon, shot by Arthur's father, is an object of fascination: its breast is "deep and white, / cold and caressable"; its red eyes are made of "glass, / much to be desired." It sits atop a "marble-topped table" that the childlike voice describes as "his white, frozen lake." This metaphoric maritime micro-gesture, the loon's frozen lake in the parlor, appears a second time in the poem and rhymes with "little frosted cake" — the metaphor that Bishop's childlike poetic voice uses to describe her cousin's coffin.

The perfect rhyme of "cake" and "lake" is terrible, shocking, even grotesque, yet emotionally complements the moment in which the mother, who has not appeared in any of Bishop's other poems to this point, engages with the child. Without question "First Death in Nova Scotia" is a fundamental starting point for talking about Bishop's later poem "One Art" from her final collection, *Geography III* (1976), and its reference to her mother: "I lost my mother's watch." When Bishop's poetic voice loses her "mother's watch" in "One Art" —and as the poem tells us "the art of losing's not too hard to master / though it may look like (*Write* it!) like disaster"—it is the lost timepiece as well as time with her mother and her mother's gaze (watch) on Bishop as a child that prove disastrous. We see the poetic voice's mother as quite involved in the earlier poem: "I was lifted up and given / one lily of the valley / to put in Arthur's hand." The voice's gesture of saying goodbye to the little boy is impossible without her mother's coordinated cooperation, though once the voice finds herself next to Arthur to deposit the flower, the mother's presence is no longer visible: "Arthur was very small. / He was all white, like a doll / that hadn't been painted yet," white like the "white, frozen lake." The comparison is apt because cousin Arthur's body is an ecosystem, like the lake, now frozen, in the boy's case, "Forever." The frozen lake in "First Death in Nova Scotia," metaphorical or not, contains knowledge, "historical, flowing and flown," and the red-eyed loon, who sits atop the frozen lake and has "kept his own counsel" since being shot by Uncle Arthur, at last can be part of a pairing, like the paired-off royals in the chromographs, at least for a time. The loon is paired with little Arthur as he eyes him, and the loon is paired with the poetic voice, who may turn to him soon enough for counsel regarding her and her family's past.

It is never made clear in "First Death in Nova Scotia" if the poetic voice says the words her mother tells her to speak: "say good-bye / to your little cousin Arthur." One does not have to say the word "good-bye" to complete the gesture of saying good-bye, which is universally understood as the wave of a hand, but can also simply be communicated through the eyes. For Flusser "The Gesture of Speaking" is relational—"the speaker seeks others; his words are tentacles in the direction of others" (*Gestures* 30)—and within the gesture itself is the relationship between silence and language. Flusser addresses "the question of silence": "Silence is, of course, not stillness but the gesture that arrests the word before it comes into the mouth. To grasp the gesture of speaking, one must first observe that of being silent, for in silence the word speaks and glows" (*Gestures* 28). Silence is maintained in the poem by little cousin Arthur, who is dead, and by the loon, who "hadn't said a word" since being killed by Uncle Arthur's bullet. The poetic voice seems to remain silent too, though this is not clear because she speaks to us intimately throughout the poem. It is clear that she manages to follow her mother's instructions to put "one lily of the valley / [...] in Arthur's hand" because in the final stanza she asks the reader: "But how could Arthur go, / clutching his tiny lily, / with his eyes shut up so tight / and the roads deep in snow?" There is no answer other than the silence at the end of the poem. However, we must remember Flusser's assertion that "silence is, of course, not stillness." Silence speaks.

Bishop wrote a trio of poems published in the *New Yorker* between 1978 and 1979, the year she died, and each engages in maritime micro-gestures. Two are set in Brazil, the other in Maine. "Santarém" concerns the meeting of two rivers, the Tapajós and the Amazon, and the poetic voice's memory of seeing it: "Of course I may be remembering it all wrong / after, after—how many years?" The poem begins by instantly questioning itself and interrogating the process of remembering as well as the process of experiencing something: "I liked the place; I liked the idea of the place. / Two rivers. Hadn't two rivers sprung / from the Garden of Eden? No, that was four / and they'd diverged." The poem meditates on the impossibility of "literary interpretations / such as: life/death, right/wrong, male/female" because "such notions would have resolved, dissolved, straight off" in the meeting of the "watery, dazzling dialectic." In many ways we find ourselves back in the territory of "The Map," where we cannot entirely be sure of the relationship between things, whether the land and the sea, the colors used on the map, or the names of cities and how much space they take up. In this late poem, the question of mortality lingers. Bishop quietly slips in a meditation on death at the end, which offers a more specific memory inside the memory of her having visited Santarém "after—how many years?" In the poem's final lines, the voice finds herself in "the blue pharmacy" where she "admired" an unexpected souvenir: "an empty wasps' nest [...] / small, exquisite, clean matte white, / and hard as stucco." The pharmacist gives it to the speaker and then, suddenly, "my ship's whistle blew. I couldn't stay." Once she is back on board, she engages with a "fellow-passenger, Mr. Swan," who "wanted to see the Amazon before he died" and who asks her, "What's that ugly thing?"

Bishop wrote "North Haven," set on an island off the coast of Maine, in memory of Robert Lowell. Here, the relationship between land and sea shifts in the poetic voice's mind because she wants to imagine "that they're free within the blue frontiers of bay":

> The islands haven't shifted since last summer,
> even if I like to pretend they have
> —drifting, in a dreamy sort of way,
> a little north, a little south or sidewise,
> and that they're free within the blue frontiers of bay.

The imagined shifts in the islands are miniscule—"a little north, a little south or sidewise"—and these impossible micro-gestures imply land that is "drifting" and "dreamy," set "free within the blue frontiers of bay." The bay here recalls the "lovely bays" in "The Map" that "we can stroke" and might "blossom." The poetic voice seeks freedom, change, and renewal by using her imagination to "pretend," but she knows that she is wishing for the impossible. The question of death's permanence, the final change, versus what does not change even when a loved one dies looms throughout the poem. In the final lines the poetic voice addresses her "sad friend": "And now—you've left / for good. You can't derange, or re-arrange / your poems again. (But the Sparrows can their song.) / The words won't change again. Sad friend, you cannot change." The voice recalls Lowell telling her a memory he had of North Haven from his childhood: "Years ago, you told me it was here / (in 1932?) you first 'discovered *girls*' / and learned to sail, and learned to kiss." We enter into Lowell's past through Bishop's recollection of what he told her, and sailing in the waters around North Haven is part of that memory, "historical, flowing and flown."

"Pink Dog" shifts to a focus on the deaths of the most vulnerable and invisible members of society. It is one of Bishop's most overtly political poems. (Though she was not a *poet engagé* in the strict sense, politically significant meditations appear throughout her work.) "The Map" and its careful considerations about the role of mapmakers and historians and the implied politicians, military or otherwise, who determine a nation's boundaries, opens her first collection *North & South* (1946), published the year after the end of the World War II. "Pink Dog," first published in the February 26, 1979, issue of the *New Yorker*, is set in late 1970s Rio de Janeiro during Carnival time, at the midpoint of Brazil's long military dictatorship (1964–85). The poem offers the portrait of a dog, and begins innocently enough: "Naked and pink, without a single hair... / Startled, the passersby draw back and stare." The passersby are "mortally afraid of rabies," but the poetic voice knows what the dog is really suffering from: "you have a case of scabies / [...] Where are your babies? // (A nursing mother, by those hanging teats.) / In what slum have you hidden them, poor bitch, / while you go begging, living by your wits?"

The pink dog is a conduit for speaking and thinking about the human slum dwellers and how the government deals with them:

> Didn't you know? It's been in all the papers,
> to solve this problem, how they deal with beggars?
> They take and throw them in the tidal rivers.
>
> Yes, idiots, paralytics, parasites
> go bobbing in the ebbing sewage, nights
> out in the suburbs, where there are no lights.
>
> If they do this to anyone who begs,
> drugged, drunk, or sober, with or without legs,
> what would they do to sick, four-leggèd dogs?

In the cafés and on the sidewalk corners
the joke is going round that all the beggars
who can afford them now wear life preservers.

Rio de Janeiro's beggars are being thrown into the tidal rivers of Guanabara Bay, which empty into the Atlantic Ocean, a quick solution by the powers-that-be to get rid of undesirable people. Of course, the implicit critique is that the poetic voice cares more about the dog than she cares about the human beggars who "go bobbing in the ebbing sewage," especially as the poem goes on and the poetic voice continues her meditation, not on the humans but on how to help this particular dog to evade capture. Because the dog cannot "float, much less [...] dog-paddle," the poetic voice suggests that "the sensible // solution is to wear a *fantasia*," or a Carnival costume, so it won't be detected. Then the voice moves on to more pressing details: "What sambas can you dance? What will you wear?" This line suggests that all will be well, while also folding in a reference to Bishop's translations of four anonymous sambas, first published in 1965 in the *New York Times Magazine* with an accompanying article.[3] Meanwhile "Pink Dog" ends with a kind of grotesque glee: "Carnival is always wonderful! / A depilated dog would not look well. / Dress up! Dress up and dance at Carnival!"

In "Pink Dog" the kind of knowledge, "historical, flowing, and flown," carried by Rio de Janeiro's waters is something we have not seen in Bishop's work before and demands a closer look. The poem tackles the challenges of human society when we do not want to see what is in front of us. It begs the question: what is the difference between ignoring the beggars on the street and throwing them into the river where they will drown? One gesture is intentional, and the other is not. Flusser asks about "The Gesture of Destroying" and its relationship to "the question of evil" (*Gestures* 55): "Disturbance and destruction are not evil, however, as long as they have an intention" (*Gestures* 59). How would he read the gesture of destroying the visible presence of the beggars as eyesores on the streets of Rio de Janeiro by throwing them into rivers, as a matter of intentional government strategy? The poem highlights the intentionality at hand: "Didn't you know? It's been in all the papers, / to solve this problem, how they deal with beggars? / They take and throw them in the tidal rivers." The poetic voice's response to this startling and uncomfortable fact is to echo the response of society in general, to make a "joke" of it so the situation can be (somewhat) palatable. What lingers potently in the backdrop of the poem is a scary human truth: while most of us do not commit intentional gestures of destroying other people, (nearly) all of us traffic in the unintentional destruction of others. The poem is emphatic about the challenges of paying attention because the destruction around us can be covered up, by "sewage" and night and distance and the lack of "lights": "Yes, idiots, paralytics, parasites / go bobbing in the ebbing sewage, nights / out in the suburbs, where there are no lights." We must look at, and struggle to see, our neighbors, strangers, ourselves.

Bishop's maritime-micro gestures span the range of her oeuvre, from North to South America, from Brazil to elsewhere, from the private to the political. The movement of "mapped waters" may be more quiet, delicate, and divergent than the land is, but no less urgent and in need of careful study.

NOTES

1. Flusser's life as a traveler, visitor, and foreigner in Brazil and elsewhere influenced his work as a new media theorist. Born in Prague into a family of Jewish intellectuals, he moved to Brazil in 1940 and stayed there for thirty-one years. In 1963, he published his first book, *Lingua e realidade* (*Language and Reality*), in Portuguese in São Paulo. Over the course of his career he eventually published essays and books in four languages: German, Portuguese, French, and English. Flusser also practiced self-translation (*autotradução*), rewriting his work into those languages and publishing various versions. According to Nancy Ann Roth, the English-language translator of *Gestures*, "he was articulating a theory of translation closely bound up with his own sense of himself as leading a nomadic, '*bodenlos*'—literally, 'foundationless'—life" (vii).

2. Arquivo Carlos Drummond de Andrade, Museu Casa de Rui Barbosa, Rio de Janeiro.

3. Bishop published an article about Carnival in Rio titled "On the Railroad Named Delight" — accompanied by her translations of "Four Sambas"— in *The New York Times Magazine* (March 7, 1965). Her discussion, in many ways, centers on the political climate in Rio, "a city that reflects the uncertainties of the entire nation since an army coup last March and April" (84).

BIBLIOGRAPHY

Elizabeth Bishop. *The Complete Poems, 1927–1979*. New York: Farrar, Straus and Giroux, 1983.

______. "On the Railroad Named Delight." The New York Times Magazine. 1 March 1965: 30, 84–6.

______. *One Art: Letters*. Sel. and ed. Robert Giroux. New York: Farrar, Straus, and Giroux, 1994.

Lispector, Clarice. *Laços de familia*. 1960. Rio de Janeiro: Editora Rocco, 1998.

______. "Three Stories by Clarice Lispector Translated from the Portuguese by Elizabeth Bishop." *The Kenyon Review* 26 (1964): 501–11.

Vilém Flusser. *Gestures*. Translated by Nancy Ann Roth. Minneapolis: University of Minnesota Press, 2014.

MAGDALENA EDWARDS is a writer, actor, and translator from Spanish and Portuguese based in Los Angeles, California. She is a vsiting scholar at UCLA's Latin American Institute and a Contributing Editor at the *Los Angeles Review of Books*. Her translations include the work of Raúl Zurita, Nicanor Parra, Silviano Santiago, Márcia Tiburi, Noemi Jaffe, and Clarice Lispector. She has authored several academic essays on Clarice Lispector, including "The Body Speaks: Clarice Lispector on Screen" in *After Clarice: Reading Lispector's Legacy in the Twenty-First Century* (Cambridge: Legenda, 2021); and "Clarice Lispector e a ética do ator-tradutor" in *El arte de pensar sin riesgos: 100 años de Clarice Lispector* (Buenos Aires: Corregidor, 2021). She holds a PhD in Comparative Literature from UCLA and a BA in Social Studies from Harvard. www.magdalenaedwards.com

Interviews

Uma Entrevista com António Hespanha

1. Como tem visto ser retratado o tema dos mares na cultura Portuguesa? Qual o seu valor e importância?

O tema tem sido um clássico na cultura erudita portuguesa. Tanto mais que "mar" parece rimar bem como outros temas canónicos – "viagem", "aventura", "saudade". Não tenho a certeza de que tenha a mesma centralidade no conjunto da cultura popular, pois, para muitas culturas do interior, o mar é uma referência longínqua. Seja como for, o tópico de que Portugal está plantado à beira-mar fez com que o mar apareça frequentemente como marcando a identidade portuguesa, seja isso o que for. É um mito, produto de reconstruções fantásticas da história, de leituras arbitrárias da nosso espaço geográfico, de efabulações sobre a geometria da nossa alma. Mas a verdade é que carecemos tanto de levantamentos exaustivos das relações dos portugueses com o mar, como abundamos de arroubos poéticos sobre o tema. Transportadas as coisas para as propostas políticas, verifica-se um paradoxo semelhante – a retórica do destino marítimo e atlântico não tem grande tradução em políticas públicas ou privadas correspondentes.

2. E na historiografia? Como tem a historiografia Portuguesa lidado e utilizado o tema dos mares? Os mares aparecerem sempre como um traço umbilical da identidade Portuguesa?

Todos sabemos como a historiografia portuguesa tem sido atraída pela "gesta marítima". A série de crónicos sobre os feitos no mar é mais vasta do que as que contam a história dos portugueses com os pés na terra. Porém, é uma história muto seletiva. Todavia, o papel do mar nas configurações sociais, culturais e económicas do mar na idade média, não tem sido objeto de estudos exaustivos, a despeito de notáveis inícios (por exemplo na obra de Alberto Sampaio, *As Póvoas Marítimas do Norte de Portugal*, 1905). Sabe-se pouco sobre atividades importantes, embora protagonizada por "gente humilde" – a pesca, o comércio de cabotagem, a complementaridade entre agricultura e atividade marítima... Mesmo depois disso, quando se começa a ver os portugueses como "heróis do mar", a historiografia não se tem importado muito com os que não foram "heróis". O quotidiano da marinharia, os processos de recrutamento das armadas, o povoamento das "conquistas" e "feitorias", as relações dos colonos pobres e remediados com as populações locais, tudo isso tem sido proporcionalmente pouco estudado. Na história contemporânea, a história dos portugueses emigrados no ultramar – em África, no Brasil, na Califórnia, na Venezuela, no Havai – não merecei ainda um tratamento conjunto. Por isso, Malyn Newitt pode chamar a esta história uma "história alternativa" (*Emigration and the Sea: An Alternative History of Portugal and the Portuguese*, 2015).

3. Considera que Portugal continua a glorificar os mares como uma espécie de avatar de Portugalidade, uma metonímia de coragem e bravura?

Isso tem dado o tom à nossa cultura erudita. Já em 1925, António Sardinha construía uma genealogia fantástica dos portugueses que radicava nos Atlantes. E assentava sobre isso a identificação dos seus traços mais autênticos e permanentes. Talvez sem este desvario genealógico, muito desta ideia continua incrustada no nosso imaginário. Quanto às virtudes atávicas e a sua relação com o mar. Realmente pode haver muita bravura e tenacidade nas fainas do mar. Quem, como eu, ainda viu, na costa de Aveiro, os grandes barcos da xávega a empinar-se nas ondas ou quem conheceu gente de Ílhavo e das Gafanhas que passava metade das suas vidas nas lonjuras geladas da Gronelândia, pode ter uma ideia de como o mar pode ser um lugar de sofrimento, de coragem e de estoicismo. Mas, normalmente, não é disso que se fala. Os temas com os quais se construíram esses mitos foram os ligados às viagens transcontinentais, cujo quotidiano pouco se estuda e cujos relatos têm de tudo. Têm braveza, persistência, aventura, saber, mas também desleixo, falta de organização, mesquinhez, ganância, crueldade. Já se nota que não gosto muito de mitos épicos e simplificadores...

4. Recentemente, deu-se um grande debate público sobre um presumível Museu dos Descobrimentos (ou das Descobertas). Muitos afiram que tal contribui para uma glorificação arcaica da história de Portugal, uma que nega os impactos da escravatura e colonialismo. Outros consideram que o museu é perfeitamente razoável e "natural". Onde se posiciona?

Já expliquei longamente a minha posição numa entrevista ao Jornal de Letras e em outros lados. Mas volto às suas linhas principais. Conhecer o nosso passado (como conhecer, em geral) é sempre positivo. E, nesse sentido, tudo quanto seja criar oportunidades para informar as pessoas da história de Portugal é bom. Lisboa – mas também, o Porto, Vila do Conde, Aveiro, o Algarve – estão muito ligadas a esta história das viagens dos portugueses. E, a meu ver, faz sentido que haja "centros interpretativos" sobre isso nessas terras para responder à curiosidade natural de visitantes ou indígenas. Com uma condição: que deem uma visão completa, complexa, multifacetada, do que aconteceu. Digo mesmo mais. Dado o enviesamento "heroico" e "autogratificante" da nossa "cultura pública", estes dispositivos culturais devem privilegiar uma visão crítica do senso comum e da história rósea e amável que habitualmente se conta. E isto não por uma qualquer ânsia de "correção política" ou por um doentio espírito de autoflagelação. Mas justamente para problematizar a *correção política estabelecida* e por fim aos contínuos afagos de *ego* coletivo.

5. Considera que Portugal ainda não chegou a termos com o seu passado colonial, com o seu passado esclavagista, que muito deve a tal glorificação dos mares (enquanto metonímia de uma nação valente e de exploração)?

Confesso que durante algum tempo não me dei bem conta de como o tema da escravatura tem estado ausente da nossa historiografia. Não ignoro que, na sociedade metropolitana o impacto dos escravos não tinha a dimensão que teve no espaço colonial "português" – Brasil, África Ocidental e Oriental e Golfo de Bengala. E também me recuso a reduzir toda a história moderna metropolitana e ultramarina a esta questão. Há âmbitos da história – social, económica e cultural – em que o fenómeno esclavagista não tem grande poder explicativo. Porém, também não imaginava a violência polémica com que se tem reagido à proposta de dar mais realce a esta questão na agenda académica, nos programas escolares ou na cultura pública. Ou contra ideia de criar memória "reparadora" que promova um sentimento de auto-consciencialização e de repúdio dessas práticas do passado. Esta atitude de negação e de recusa é tanto mais chocante quanto o que domina o nosso senso comum é uma imagem benévola da relação passada dos portugueses com povos colonizados – como descobridores audazes, como civilizadores exemplares, como missionadores caritativos, como mediadores eficazes, neutros e bondosos.

Interview conducted in 2018.

ANTONIO HESPANHA foi um historiador Português, professor na Faculdade de Direito, Universidade Nova de Lisboa. O seu trabalho influenciou uma geração inteira de académicos, com mais de 150 artigos e 30 livros publicados. É o historiador Português mais citado internacionalmente.

ANDRÉ NÓVOA (PhD, Royal Holloway, 2014) is a geographer who previously trained as an historian and anthropologist. He was a researcher at Northeastern University (USA) and an assistant editor of *HAU Magazine: Journal of Ethnographic Theory*. His work has been published in journals such as *Mobilities* and *Environment & Planning*. In "The Colour of Labour" project, he is directly involved with the study of mobilities, addressing the movements of whalers, the journeys of indentured migrants, and the entanglements of labor and mobility.

ANDRÉ NÓVOA

An Interview with Cristiana Bastos

1. How do you see the theme of the sea in Portuguese culture? What is its value and importance?

The Portuguese are schooled from an early age on that theme through different forms. As geography: the country is presented as the westernmost frontier of Europe, and its people are seen as prone to explore the oceans, move west, move south, connect continents. As history: the fifteenth- and sixteenth-century ocean crossings of Portuguese caravels are presented as central to the transformation of global connectivity, often alongside the trope of Portuguese nautical talent and pioneering qualities. As literature: the nation's major epic poem, *The Lusiads,* is about Vasco da Gama's sea voyage to India, and many other literary expressions also evoke the experience of the sea. As art: the national style, *Manuelino,* is defined by sculpted maritime motifs. As nourishment: an important component of the traditional economy is associated with fishing and fish processing. As religion: some of the most complex *círios* (cycles of itinerant religious festivities) are in coastal regions and include boat processions. As a lifestyle: over time the seaside became a prime choice for leisure—first for elites, later for everyone. As a brand: the landmark and transformative Expo '98 adopted the theme of oceans. As a trend: surfing in Portugal is a a popular sport and also a major international attraction. The list could go on; there is always something to add. Yet there are also many other themes to mix, match, produce, and re-create as individual and collective identifiers. Some people live inland and have no direct exposure to the sea; or do not care for maritime epics; or cannot differentiate Manueline baroque from neoclassical; or do not like fish, or surf, or the seaside. Nationalist regimes are keen to produce collective identifiers, symbols, and narratives that are later naturalized or taken as the cultural core, but we can see beyond the myths.

I am one of those people who adores the ocean and who is not fully happy when too far from the shore. I believe many of us Portuguese feel that way. I also believe that we are not the only people on earth who experience that feeling and who have the ocean as the main identifier of our culture and history. While some groups ignore or avoid the ocean—even when living on the coast—many are experienced navigators and traders. Polynesians have been long-distance explorers for centuries, settling in most islands of the Pacific. Eastern Mediterraneans crossed the waters all the way to the Atlantic. So as critical analysts of our history, we may not want to endorse a metaphysical approach to the centrality of the ocean in our particular culture. Perhaps we should leave that to the ingenuity (*engenho e arte*) of poets, composers, and other artists.

2. How has Portuguese anthropology dealt with the maritime theme?

Nineteenth- and early twentieth-century anthropologists were prone to grand generalizations about the national character and cultural traits of the Portuguese. We no longer work along those lines—which, as I have said, are better left to art. Instead, anthropologists focus on the collective and individual lives that directly depend on the oceans: fishing communities and other shore settlers; sailors and those involved in the sailing infrastructure, from the material production of vessels to the demographic, gendered, and family impact of sailing and sea trading; shore leisure, including seasonal tourism, service industries, beach culture, water sports, surfing, festivals, and so on.

3. Do you believe that Portugal still glorifies the sea as an avatar of Portugueseness, as a metonym of bravery?

We hear that in a few different ways—sometimes as a direct glorification of empire via the idiom of overseas discoveries; at other times as a version of the theme of "bravery when facing the unknown" that has stripped away the conquest component. At still other times, it is morphed into contemporary themes of global connection. More rarely, it is linked with the actual experience of fishing crews that went through the most dire conditions after whales, tuna, cod, and still endure all-around life challenges after sardines, mackerel and other domestic fisheries.

4. Recently, there has been public debate about the possibility of creating a Museum of the Discoveries in Lisbon. Many say that a museum with such a name would further glorify an archaic Portuguese history and negate the impacts of slavery and colonialism. Others see this name as reasonable and natural. Where do you stand on this issue?

I was among those who signed the letter asking the mayor of Lisbon to rethink his proposal for a discoveries museum. Most of us who signed it find the concept archaic, out of tune with contemporary awareness that one doesn't really discover what others already know. Still, many people continue to believe that the discoveries are iconic Portuguese events that should be celebrated, even as others are fully aware of their imperial resonance and argue that discoveries and expansion cannot be addressed without also acknowledging the destructive and devastating aspects of empire. That is why some proposals suggest that a slavery memorial (approved during the *orçamento participativo*, one of Lisbon's community-based competitions for urban projects) should be coupled with the new museum. Having visited the National Museum of African American History in Washington, D.C., and several other memorials to slavery and indentured labor around the world, I believe that there are many ways to capture and curate such complex and painful histories and to provide tools to help address the fractures and wounds that persist in our societies. Related museum projects in Portugal should learn from international examples and seriously engage with the contemporary consequences of imperial histories, including structural racism. It may take time, but we shall get there.

5. Do you think that Portugal is yet to come to terms with its slaver past, which owes much to the glorification of the seas?

We are a still a long way away, but things are happening and we shall get there some day, at least in part. There are academic and community-based events addressing that aspect of collective history. There is growing recognition of the link between the plantation-related traffic in humans and the consolidation of racism and racialism. More literature is available, and less people follow lusotropicalism, a pervasive ideology that softens history by invoking the benign exceptionalism of Portuguese colonial ventures. Change will not be easy, or smooth, or immediate, but we are moving toward more general awareness of colonial violences and their aftermath. But coming to terms with that, doing something about it, promoting justice in a wounded society, rescuing the visibility and citizenship of those excluded in the process...that is a whole other chapter that needs further engagement. Creating awareness is one necessary step along that route.

Interview conducted in 2018.

CRISTIANA BASTOS (PhD, CUNY, 1996) is an anthropologist at the Institute of Social Sciences, University of Lisbon, whose interests combine the disciplines of anthropology, history, and the social study of science, technology, and medicine. She is currently the Principal Investigator (PI) of the European Research Council project The Colour of Labour (ERC AdG 695573), where she is directly involved with the fields of Guyana, Hawai'i, New England, and Angola.

ANDRÉ NÓVOA (PhD, Royal Holloway, 2014) is a geographer who previously trained as an historian and anthropologist. He was a researcher at Northeastern University (USA) and an assistant editor of *HAU Magazine: Journal of Ethnographic Theory*. His work has been published in journals such as *Mobilities* and *Environment & Planning*. In "The Colour of Labour" project, he is directly involved with the study of mobilities, addressing the movements of whalers, the journeys of indentured migrants, and the entanglements of labor and mobility.

Uma Entrevista com Joacine Katar Moreira

1. Como tem visto ser retratado o tema dos mares, na cultura Portuguesa, a partir do ponto de vista dos Estudos Africanos? Serão os mares uma "ponte" ou mais um lugar de sofrimento?

Do ponto de vista colonial e das ramificações da ideologia colonial que persistem até à actualidade, os mares são vistos como pontes e estradas que possibilitaram aquilo a que se denomina insistentemente por "encontros entre os povos", "primeira globalização", "descobrimentos" e "expansão". Neste prisma, os mares foram uma imensidão de possibilidades bem aproveitadas pelos portugueses para o firmamento de um império colonial. Mares, portanto, como unificadores de interesses diversos e de continentes diferentes.

Claro que esta visão parcial da História não é empática com os colonizados, privilegiando a visão do colonizador e os interesses deste. Neste contexto, os mares são vistos como *ponte* para alcançar os feitos históricos de uma nação de pequena dimensão, mas cujos nacionais são dotados de grande coragem e grandeza. Os mares como lugares de oportunidades incalculáveis e da concretização da missão civilizadora lusitana. Tudo isto permitiu que os mares e a sua navegação fossem também motores para a construção de uma identidade nacional baseada na conquista e no poder coloniais, que marcou uma época histórica considerada por muitos como sendo a (única) época áurea portuguesa.

Do ponto de vista de uma africana, que estudou Estudos Africanos, os mares são para mim um tema sobre o qual escrevo sobretudo textos literários, porque as metodologias académicas não me permitem expressar sentimentos que considero importantes para a análise da temática. Os mares foram a estrada que permitiu a existência do período mais violento da história africana, que foi a colonização. Uma estrada que se tornou vermelha do sangue e dos corpos dos filhos de África nele tombados. Os mares aparecem como a separação (e não como *encontro*), as estradas que em vez de unirem separaram povos, famílias, culturas e conhecimentos. Graças aos mares se deu o tráfico de pessoas escravizadas, sendo claramente um lugar de sofrimento e de dores profundas que se fazem sentir até hoje na forma como os filhos e descendentes do continente africano continuam a ser tratados e (sub)entendidos.

2. Considera que Portugal continua a glorificar os mares como uma espécie de avatar de bravura e coragem?

A forma como os mares são retratados na cultura portuguesa pode resumir-se a esta estrofe dos *Lusíadas*, de Luís Vaz de Camões:

As armas e os barões assinalados
Que da Ocidental praia Lusitana,
Por mares nunca dantes navegados
Passaram ainda além da Taprobana,
Em perigos e guerras esforçados
Mais do que prometia a força humana
E entre gente remota edificaram
Novo Reino, que tanto sublimaram;

Aqui, os mares são espaços de engrandecimento e heroicidade. Uma heroicidade baseada na invasão colonial e na exploração dos territórios ocupados a todos os níveis – económico, político, religioso, material, cultural e simbólico. E um engrandecimento que é feito à custa do rasuramento dos africanos e dos indígenas, dos seus corpos, da sua história e das suas experiências. Simultaneamente, a normalização e a aceitação dessa heroicidade colonial portuguesa passa sobretudo pela omissão das violências do colonialismo português e pela transmissão de uma história parcial que tende a suavizar e a mascarar o colonialismo de bondade e de carácter messiânico.

3. Recentemente, houve um grande debate sobre um presumível Museu dos Descobrimentos. Muitos dizem que tal contribuirá para uma glorificação mais ou menos arcaica da história Portuguesa, negando (ou secundarizando) os processos de colonialismo e escravatura. Outros afirmam que tal museu é razoável e apenas "natural". Como vê a polémica?

Fui uma das escritoras, e naturalmente subscritora, da carta "Não a um museu contra nós!"[1] (Público, 22 de Junho de 2018) na qual negras e negros marcaram a sua posição na discussão pública sobre o projecto de um museu denominado "Da Descoberta", alertando para o facto desse museu vir a ser "construído sobre os ombros do silenciamento da nossa História". Subscrevera também a primeira carta dos cientistas sociais "Porque é que um museu dedicado à 'Expansão' portuguesa e aos processos que desencadeou não pode nem deve chamar-se 'Museu das Descobertas'?" (Expresso, 12 de Abril de 2018) e da carta "Agentes culturais contra a designação e missão do "Museu da Descoberta" da Câmara Municipal de Lisboa" (Público, 22 de Maio de 2018).

Uma das primeiras lições que podemos tirar desta proposta socialista da Câmara Municipal de Lisboa, é a de que existe um consenso, em todas as quadrantes políticas, no que à valorização histórica do período colonial português diz respeito. A segunda lição é também a de que a academia tem feito o seu trabalho fechada sobre si própria, para conceitos como "descoberta", "descobertas" e "descobrimentos" continuarem a ser usados pelo estado e autarquias, quando esta discussão já leva décadas na produção historiográfica. Outro aspecto é a enorme resistência na revisão dos preceitos históricos do colonialismo português e a recusa em aceitar que este período heróico foi afinal um período marcado por brutalidade, desumanização e violência a larga escala.

Portugal criou uma imagem de si próprio absolutamente surreal que faz com que haja grande celeuma cada vez que esta visão de si e da sua sociedade é questionada. O mesmo acontece com o racismo, a que muita gente recusa sequer a existência, ignorando todas as vozes que o denunciam, porque reconhecer que o país é estruturalmente racista implica o reconhecimento de privilégios de que ninguém quer abdicar.

Acredito que um museu com esta denominação não avançará, tendo em conta toda a polémica criada à sua volta. Em primeiro lugar importaria saber sobre o porquê de um *museu da descoberta*, sendo que não faltam monumentos e estátuas que evoquem o passado colonial português de forma heroicizada. Em segundo lugar é a sua denominação, que claramente pretende dar seguimento e reforçar as falácias que criadas sobre o colonialismo português. Em terceiro é perceber o conteúdo de um museu desta natureza e para todas estas questões a resposta é claramente negativa, a meu ver.

4. Considera que Portugal ainda não chegou a termos com o seu passado colonial, com o seu passado esclavagista, que muito deve a tal glorificação dos mares (enquanto metonímia de uma nação valente e de exploração)?

Considero que começa só agora uma discussão pública (a académica já tem o seu tempo, embora nem tanto) questionadora do passado colonial português e que esta discussão que toma o seu início há um ano e meio atrás já se encontra mais ou menos controlada pelos conservadores (conservadores da História como tem sido contada, e conservadores no sentido político do termo). Há uma grande resistência em reavaliar e assumir a verdade do colonialismo português e por verdades entendem-se também as violências perpetradas, sobretudo no corpo da mulher negra, objectificado, diminuído, explorado e violado.

Portugal ainda está na fase da recusa da sua história, enquanto noutros países já se discutem os termos da reparação histórica e a devolução de arte africana saqueada na época colonial. Esta recusa é resultado da romantização do colonialismo e da defesa da identidade nacional e da história que a sustenta.

No que diz respeito à Escravatura, um dos primeiros passos passa por escrevê-la com maiúsculas, assim como se faz com o Holocausto, por respeito às suas vítimas e à verdade. Nos livros escolares de História os africanos escravizados continuam a ser retratados, sem qualquer pensamento crítico, como produtos e como peças. E aqui os mares e a sua visão mercantilista têm sem dúvida grande impacto na dificuldade com que Portugal lida com a sua própria História.

Interview conducted in 2018.

NOTE

1. https://www.publico.pt/2018/06/22/culturaipsilon/opiniao/nao-a-um-museu-contra-nos-1835227#gs.Uy7p7JQB

JOACINE KATAR MOREIRA (PhD, ISCTE, 2017) é uma académica, activista e política luso-guineense. Fundadora do Instituto da Mulher Negra em Portugal (INMUNE), ela foi a primeira mulher negra a encabeçar as listas de um partido político em Portugal, nomeadamente nas eleições legislativas de 2019 pelo Livre. Actualmente, é deputada no Parlamento Português.

ANDRÉ NÓVOA (PhD, Royal Holloway, 2014) is a geographer who previously trained as an historian and anthropologist. He was a researcher at Northeastern University (USA) and an assistant editor of *HAU Magazine: Journal of Ethnographic Theory*. His work has been published in journals such as *Mobilities* and *Environment & Planning*. In "The Colour of Labour" project, he is directly involved with the study of mobilities, addressing the movements of whalers, the journeys of indentured migrants, and the entanglements of labor and mobility.

An Interview with Miguel Vale de Almeida

1. How do you see the theme of the sea in Portuguese culture? What is its value and importance?

I think that "the sea" functions as a key-symbol in Portuguese culture. Representations of the sea as a central theme probably started as literary artifacts that were part of the process of constructing a national identity by the cultural elites and the state. The notion then percolated to the popular masses. I doubt that the rural common folk of, say, the nineteenth century, adhered to it but the appropriation of Camões's work as a narrative of the national experience became, in due time, part of the core of the imagined community. The theme of the sea certainly is connected, after the nineteenth century, with the central role of expansion, discoveries, and colonialism in national identity. The fact that the sea as symbol and metaphor can be used romantically to evoke adventure, freedom, self-discovery, voyage, and so on probably facilitated its general appropriation and toned down aggressive nationalistic overtones. I do not have data on that, but probably a young person in 2019 would talk about the sea in a way that bundles meanings, from the discoveries, to beach culture, to surfing, to "you'll find Portuguese anywhere in the world," to notions of Portugal as "Europe's West Coast."

2. How has Portuguese anthropology dealt with the maritime theme?

The strong romantic tradition of studying rural communities and peasant society as the essence of the "folk," which characterized early anthropology (and was refashioned as the study of the popular classes in the post-dictatorial period), did not leave room for "the sea." In addition, Portuguese colonial anthropology (relatively weak when compared to other imperial formations) was mostly concerned with the administration of colonized populations, not with historical processes (a very different story can be told about History). In recent decades, however, with the reconstruction of Portuguese anthropology and its internationalization, including the growth of postcolonial and post-imperial studies, anthropologists have been instrumental in the critique and deconstruction of the prevailing lusotropicalist narrative. This endeavor involved a cultural analysis of the sea symbol and metaphor and of the ways in which it romanticizes aspects that legitimize its nationalist, colonialist, and racist roots.

3. Do you believe that Portugal still glorifies the sea as an avatar of Portugueseness, as a metonym of bravery?

One of the most disturbing aspects of democratic Portugal's society and culture is the survival and adaptation of the lusotropicalist narrative, including the sea symbol. This seems to indicate that it has become a central feature of national identity, cutting across social classes, regions, cultural capitals, and so forth. From tourism branding to history textbooks, it is truly hegemonic and is articulated by "the man on the street" in automatic fashion. Its survival in the democratic period may be part of a phenomenon of compensation: for loss of empire, for high rates of emigration, for European integration, for the homogenizing effects of globalization. The democratic period tried to refashion the lusotropicalist narrative as "universalist" and "intercultural," but this only contributed to its continuation and its whitewashing.

4. Recently, there has been public debate about the possibility of creating a Museum of the Discoveries in Lisbon. Many say that a museum with such a name would further glorify an archaic Portuguese history and negate the impacts of slavery and colonialism. Others see this name as reasonable and natural. Where do you stand on this issue?

Let me resort to sarcasm: the entire country is already a big Museum of the Discoveries, from monuments and street names, to official and commercial iconography, to almost any aspect of collective life. I use *museum* in a vernacular, pejorative sense, meaning something old and stuffy, and *discoveries* in the politically charged tone of the dictatorship. This does not mean that the country has no room - cultural and political - for a museum of "that-which-was-called-the-discoveries". If it were to exist, such a museum should be a space for critical questioning, for conflicting narratives, for the visibility of what has been invisible for so long. The first step should be not using the term *discoveries*. What is the alternative? I do not know. And we should seriously think about what "I do not know" means. Could it mean that such a museum is impossible, not to say undesirable? I tend to think so, in a more radical fashion ("Let's stop this nonsense once and for all, and start imagining ourselves as something else"). But "the sea," "the discoveries," "lusotropicalism," and even the democratic refashionings of "universalism and interculturalism" are entwined and entrenched. This makes these tropes virtually impossible to eliminate from the national narrative and very difficult to resignify.

5. Do you think that Portugal is yet to come to terms with its slaver past, which owes much to the glorification of the seas?

Of course. And the debate on the Museum of the Discoveries is relevant to how we address the memory of slavery and slave traffic and, crucially, how we ignite a renewed anti-racist activism. Recently, a proposal put forward by Djass – Associação de Afrodescendentes for a monument to enslaved people won the competition in Lisbon's *orçamento participativo*. No such monument was ever proposed by official entities, even when in the hands of officials or parties on the Left—the same that seem to lack critical perspective on anything concerning "the discoveries." Simultaneously, there has been a strong debate about Portugal's historical role in slave traffic in the op-ed sections of the major newspapers and in social media. This debate is inseparable from political positions on Portuguese colonialism and the adapted continuation of colonial formations in post-colonial Portugal—namely, in what concerns racism and the critique of the popular (and official) narrative of Portugal as a "non-racist country." Actually, I tend to think that at the center of the emotional maelstrom in the debates around the discoveries and slavery is the denial of racism in Portugal.

Interview conducted in 2018.

MIGUEL VALE DE ALMEIDA (PhD, ISCTE, 1994) is a Portuguese anthropologist, LGBT activist, and professor at the Instituto Superior de Ciências do Trabalho e da Empresa (Iscte – Instituto Universitário de Lisboa). He is the current editor-in-chief of the journal *Etnográfica* and member of CRIA (Centro em Rede de Investigação em Antropologia) and APA (Associação Portuguesa de Antropologia).

ANDRÉ NÓVOA (PhD, Royal Holloway, 2014) is a geographer who previously trained as an historian and anthropologist. He was a researcher at Northeastern University (USA) and an assistant editor of *HAU Magazine: Journal of Ethnographic Theory*. His work has been published in journals such as *Mobilities* and *Environment & Planning*. In "The Colour of Labour" project, he is directly involved with the study of mobilities, addressing the movements of whalers, the journeys of indentured migrants, and the entanglements of labor and mobility.

An Interview with Pedro Schacht Pereira[1]

1. How do you see the theme of the sea in Portuguese culture? What is its value and importance?

I'd say the theme of the sea intersects Portuguese culture from literature to music, architecture to painting, the decorative arts to cinema, but also from water sports to hedonistic beach parties. That line can be traced from the Middle Ages to the present. It is very easy to recognize its presence across multiple genres and periods and, since Expo '98, its role in giving a new impulse to the commemorative drive that has characterized the relationship between the state and the historical memory of the maritime voyages and overseas expansion. But it is perhaps less easy to establish its present cultural relevance, amid the calls to make the oceans *the* country's strategic economic sector and the tentative materializations of such a vision in recent attempts to promote offshore oil prospecting in southern Portugal. Yet even as there is an obsessive nurturing of the theme in celebrations of historical memory, I am struck by its relative absence from significant contemporary cultural production in the new century. It may be that the historical prevalence of the grand narratives has conditioned how we read references to the sea in Portuguese texts. It is undeniable that from Joham Zorro's "Em Lixboa, sobre lo mar, / Barcas novas mandei lavrar" to Ruy Belo's "O meu país é o que o mar não quer," the sea beckons the reader, but it is also incumbent to acknowledge that forty-five years of democracy have not been enough to entirely disrupt the imperial lens through which we engage with this theme or allow us to pay adequate attention to the different storylines that are there to be read, particularly in literature. Finally, some iconic readings of the theme, such as Pessoa's, may still cast their shadow and prevent us from devising newer meanings, but I'm not entirely sure this is the case.

I grew up in a coastal town, where the presence of the sea can be felt miles inland, through *maresia*. The foghorns punctuating the silence of the night and death at sea marked the daily life of the fishing communities that compose a significant portion of the population. These dramas have shaped a certain culture of the sea, and Raul Brandão, the best painter of the sea we have ever had, left a vivid memory of it in *Os Pescadores*. From Camões to António Lobo Antunes, and from

História Trágico-Marítima to *A Costa dos Murmúrios*, the sea is almost literally palpable on page after page. From the sea of conquest to the sea of rejection, from usury to loss, and from mapping to wayward navigation, Portuguese literature has been through it all. The public space in some of our cities has domesticated some of our past worst nightmares: thus, in Lisbon, we can linger on as the sun sets over the Atlantic in the Miradouro de Santa Catarina, under the aegis of Adamastor. Or I should say we could, because since last June the mayor has decided to fence the park off, in an apparent concession to the gentrifying forces that consume Portugal's main cities, where the sunset-loving crowds can now be seen as rejects washed ashore. Nowadays the tides that matter may just be for those who look for thrills in Nazaré, or the throngs of tourists arriving every day by the airships whose traces in Lisbon's skies could be contemplated from Adamastor.

2. How have Portuguese Studies dealt with the maritime theme?

If anything, the record here is more mixed. More than ever, we still need studies that highlight the diversity of themes that I tried to outline in my answer to the previous question. While in the field of History, the curricular offerings are far from accompanying the work that a cadre of new researchers—so many of them entangled in the precarity imposed by the new, neoliberal division of intellectual labor and knowledge production, subject as they are to the whims of national and international grant competitions—is publishing in Portuguese and international venues alike. As regards literary and cultural studies, it is still unclear to me if anything is being done in terms of a sustained inter- and transdisciplinary study of the oceanic theme in Portuguese culture. I can think of specific publications in which the theme of the sea has been studied, I know PLCS published an issue dedicated to the South Atlantic not too long ago, and I also know that there has been a certain buzz about transatlantic and transoceanic studies, but it is not clear to me that it is more than a passing trend, and certainly not that it is more prevalent in Portuguese studies than it is in, say, Hispanic or Anglophone studies.

3. Have these visions evolved from the nineteenth century (when nationalisms were born) until today? Or have they crystallized?

I would venture to say that, in certain corners at least, the emphasis and focus on the study and teaching of Portuguese oceanic expansion and the so-called "discoveries" remains very nationalistic, even if there are several examples of a historiography that has evolved in other directions. It is interesting that the focus on social history is still rare in the Portuguese historiography of fifteenth- and sixteenth-century expansion, and has not made its way from the new studies that have appeared in the last two decades to high school curricula and undergraduate history degrees. So, I would say there has definitely been a crystallization of the way these themes are addressed and studied in school, and even more so in the way they are treated in public debates in Portuguese media, even if that is not necessarily the case with the scientific research that is being carried out in Portuguese as well as foreign universities.

4. Do you believe that Portugal still glorifies the sea as an avatar of Portugueseness, as a metonym of bravery?

I think that is evident from the direction that the public debate about the putative Museum of Discoveries has taken place since last spring and from the ease with which certain metaphors are employed in public discourse (recent examples can be found in the speeches by Lisbon's mayor and Portugal's prime minister at the start of the Web Summit in November 2018). A glance at the history manuals adopted by Portuguese schools illustrates how that view is imparted to the younger generations, an approach that has changed very little since the 1970s.

5. Recently, there has been public debate about the possibility of creating a Museum of the Discoveries in Lisbon. Many say that a museum with such a name would further glorify an archaic Portuguese history and negate the impacts of slavery and colonialism. Others see this name as reasonable and natural. Where do you stand on this issue?

I was a signatory of the open letter that some Portuguese scholars published in the newspaper *Expresso* last April, which detailed why the idea of creating such a museum was ill conceived. I have also published a few opinion articles in Portuguese newspapers in which I attempted to engage critically—within the space and conceptual constraints of the medium—with some of the arguments advanced by defenders of the project. The first thing that needs to be said is that the debate was tainted from the start, as it emerged primarily as a response to the fact that the project to build a memorial to slavery in downtown Lisbon won the participatory budget competition that Lisbon's municipality promotes every year. This bad faith was already apparent in the debates that ensued after the publication, in the spring of 2017, of another open letter, this one denouncing the anachronism in a speech by the president of Portugal during a state visit to Goree

Island in Senegal. In that speech he celebrated Portugal's presumed (and untrue) pioneering role in the abolition of slavery, while doing nothing to acknowledge and atone for its long-standing responsibility and troubling record in the history of the institution. The idea of the Museum of the Discoveries, which was first inscribed as a project in the political slate that Lisbon's mayor ran on in the 2017 local elections, was wielded in opinion articles in the Portuguese press, with bylines by nationalist historians and conservative public figures, as a counterpoint to the slavery memorial. That prompted the publication of the open letter in which signatories pointed out the inadequacy of the proposed terminology, which consecrates a single viewpoint about a historical process whose complexity the museum was supposed to showcase and highlight.

The debate intensified considerably from then on, involving many public figures and sectors in Portuguese society, including a group of one hundred self-identified Afro descendants. A multiplicity of artists from different disciplines detailed their concerns in yet another open letter, but there was also at least one public letter in favor of the museum, promoted by a nationalist platform with a presence in social media. It is not surprising that the proposed museum would attract support from conservative circles; after all, such support confirms the project's conceptual strictures. More troubling is that so many public figures on the left, or at least with a known antiauthoritarian past, have chosen to come forward not so much in favor of the museum but markedly against the public stances taken by the many signatories of the letters that oppose it.

Thus, last spring Eduardo Lourenço complained about the "need to crucify this country," and a former minister of education, Maria de Lourdes Rodrigues, decried those public stances as "an act with perverse consequences." Just last week, the writer Lídia Jorge told an audience at the Guadalajara Book Fair, at which Portugal was featured as the special guest country, that there was "a movement, mainly by university people," that wants "[us to] expiate our [colonial] guilt." I have no idea what she understands by a "movement," but in my understanding an open letter signed by scholars in different countries does not necessarily and automatically constitute one. What these reactions show is that the view of the discoveries as an untouchable subject is consensual across the political spectrum; furthermore, they show that some public figures, whose work as essayists and/or fiction writers had a profound impact upon the cultural landscape of 1960s–1990s Portugal, seem to be incapable of distinguishing civic engagement and critical stances from unpatriotic ruse. It is disconcerting to me that these sacred cows of democratic Portugal are echoing the calls to silence dissent that some of them dared to disobey during harsher times, often at the cost of exile. My response to them is this. It is not for them to have the last word about how Portugal's colonial history is to be understood. I am forever grateful to Lídia Jorge's *A Costa dos Murmúrios*, a momentous book that established a nonconformist legacy in Portuguese culture, but it is time for us to move on. Likewise, I would say to Eduardo Lourenço that *O Colonialismo como nosso impensado* is an enormous contribution to our understanding of Portugal's conundrum on the eve of the end of empire, but it is time for us to acknowledge that the idea of the end of empire as a noiseless, mostly happy return to European shores (as if those who returned were exactly the same as those who left) is a fiction. It may have been tempting to read the return as a frictionless event in 1975, when there was so much uncertainty about the course of the political process following the revolution, but today only those who are willfully blind and deaf to the new voices that have emerged in the past few years can still believe its benevolent charm. If we are to move from hagiography to criticism, we need to start interrogating Lourenço's ideas more forcefully, and that is the best contribution we can make to the success of his legacy.

In sum, I would say that, although in principle I am not against the idea of a museum that could tell the stories of Portugal's travels in the *long durée* in all their complexity and richness, I am doubtful that such an endeavor will be successful in the current environment. If anything, the current debate shows that there is little appetite for complexity, when it is easier for public figures with responsibility for Portugal's democratic experiment to create scarecrows that they vilify rather than to engage with the real arguments that scholars put forward for consideration. It is striking and ironic that the historical prevalence of the grand lusotropical narrative has been coetaneous with the dereliction of the country's archives and research institutions whose collections are directly and indirectly related to the preservation of the memory of the empire. Something in how we've been celebrating empire is detrimental to the constructive transformation of the modes of knowledge production and diffusion. This should give us pause. My hope is that, instead of embarking on a new, necessarily expensive and conceptually questionable museological adventure, resources will be invested so that dying institutions acquire the life they have never had, researchers and staff alike can work in dignifying conditions, and modern editions of so many of the texts that are key to the memory of empire can be accessed by all who want to read them. Until then, the memory of empire will just keep serving the short-term political needs of politicians invested in a social order that is not too different from the one overthrown in 1974.

6. Do you think that Portugal is yet to come to terms with its slaver past, which owes much to the glorification of the seas?

From what I have already said above, we can surmise that yes, a reckoning with Portugal's past as a slave-trading power has yet to happen and is made more difficult by the enduring allure of the lusotropical narrative, which has shown great resilience across different periods of the country's colonial and postcolonial history. This coming to terms should not be seen, as it has been in so many opinion articles and public interventions since the open letter I promoted was published in April of 2017 (against President Marcelo Rebelo de Sousa's statements in Gorée Island, Senegal), as a process of expiation, to use Jorge's terminology, or as a "crucifixion" of the country, as Eduardo Lourenço put it. I reject this Christian lexicon and question its adequacy to the task of understanding what is at stake in a process of coming to terms with one's own past. This process should rather be seen as a necessary stage in the mourning and overcoming of the country's colonialist legacy that was interrupted in 1975, and conveniently "forgotten" upon the country's admission into the European Union. Guilt is only productive in a logic of hypocrisy; coming to terms with the nation's troubling past—and its concomitant colonialist legacy—should mean that we do not recognize guilt, but we do take responsibility for that past by ensuring that the present it made possible is on the way to a future free of the betrayal of the human rights values that society has enshrined. It is only by understanding how we failed them that we can ensure that we understand what those values really mean and can then strive to observe them going forward. This does not mean, as has been said ad nauseam, that we want to judge the past with the eyes of the present or that we want to reject our history. On the contrary, we celebrate that history when we learn from it; and to refuse to face present consequences—such as racism—of past errors is to ensure the perpetuation of a colonialist mentality that cannot serve the truth and welfare of the entire national polity.

There is hardly any difference in the way in which the history of Portugal's overseas expansion is taught in schools today from how it was taught when I was a student in Portugal. And it helps that the history of slavery is simply a marginal subfield in Portuguese historiography, a countercurrent against what is happening in Brazil, the United States, and other European societies, where these issues, although not easier by any means, are nonetheless more present on the political agenda. Was it by chance that 2015 commemorations of the fortieth anniversary of the independence of the former Portuguese colonies in Africa (a struggle in which Africans and Portuguese both paid an immense human price, and which was instrumental to the Portuguese conquest of freedom in 1974–75) were hardly noticeable? Yet what hope is there for forging freer and fairer relationships with those new countries if we insist on ignoring our common history and on perpetuating a colonialist view that promises nothing more than paternalism, bad faith, and mutual disrespect? Much more could be said about this, and I hope the debates will intensify. I will finish with the words of Achille Mbembe, from a recent essay about patrimonial restitutions, because I think they are imbued with the wisdom we need: "In order to weave new ties, [Europe] needs to honor truth, because truth institutes responsibility. This debt to truth is in principle ineffaceable. It will haunt us until the end of Times. To honor truth, we need to engage in remembering together. If we want to share the beauty of the world, we need to learn to be in solidarity with all its suffering, [...] and to heal together the fabric and the face of the world."[2] Portugal may yet choose not to engage in this learning process; it would be a choice for the past over the future, and that would be sad. But a choice can only be made when the stakes are clear to everyone, and we are not there yet. Can we still choose not to choose?

Interview conducted in 2018.

NOTES

1. My thanks to Lisa Voigt and Isabel Ferreira Gould for their reading and editing suggestions.

2. Achille Mbembe, "À propos de la restitution des artefacts africains conservés dans les musées d'Occident," *AOC Media*, October 5, 2018, https://aoc.media. The translation is mine.

PEDRO SCHACHT pereira (PhD, Brown, 2006) is based at Ohio State University, where he has directed the LusoGlobe working group and co-directed the Iberian Studies Working Group of the Humanities Institute. He is a member of the team that created the new PhD program in Studies of the Portuguese-speaking World in 2012 at OSU.

ANDRÉ NÓVOA (PhD, Royal Holloway, 2014) is a geographer who previously trained as an historian and anthropologist. He was a researcher at Northeastern University (USA) and an assistant editor of *HAU Magazine: Journal of Ethnographic Theory*. His work has been published in journals such as *Mobilities* and *Environment & Planning*. In "The Colour of Labour" project, he is directly involved with the study of mobilities, addressing the movements of whalers, the journeys of indentured migrants, and the entanglements of labor and mobility.

Other Essays

PEDRO SEPÚLVEDA

Fragments of the Future: Pessoa's *Orpheu* and the *Athenaeum*

ABSTRACT: Fernando Pessoa understood literary work as a project always to be realized, as a fragment of a pursued but never achieved totality. His publications in the journal *Orpheu*, together with his numerous earlier editorial projects, reveal a particular understanding of the fragment that can be applied to his work as a whole. It links to the concept of the fragment as developed by Friedrich Schlegel and Novalis, particularly in the versions published in the *Athenaeum*, the founding journal of German romanticism, which Pessoa knew through a French edition of Novalis's fragments. This essay analyzes commonalities and differences in the concept of the fragment in these works, distinguishing Pessoa's by showing how the fragment in his writing is not an aesthetic program but the result of a failure.

KEYWORDS: Fernando Pessoa, *Orpheu*, German Romanticism, Fragment, Friedrich Schlegel, Novalis, *Athenaeum*.

RESUMO: Fernando Pessoa entendeu a obra literária como projeto sempre por realizar, enquanto fragmento de uma totalidade almejada mas nunca alcançada. As publicações de Fernando Pessoa na revista *Orpheu*, assim como os inúmeros projetos editoriais que as precedem, revelam um entendimento particular do fragmento, que pode ser aplicado à obra pessoana enquanto todo. Este entendimento relaciona-se com o conceito de fragmento desenvolvido por Friedrich Schlegel e Novalis, particularmente nas versões publicadas no *Athenaeum*, a revista fundadora do Romantismo Alemão, que Pessoa conhecia através de uma edição francesa dos fragmentos de Novalis. Este ensaio procura analisar traços comuns e diferenças do conceito de fragmento nestas obras, distinguindo a conceção pessoana através da demonstração de que o fragmento em Pessoa não é um programa estético mas o resultado de uma falha.

PALAVRAS-CHAVE: Fernando Pessoa, *Orpheu*, Romantismo Alemão, Fragmento, Friedrich Schlegel, Novalis, *Athenaeum*.

Athenaeum.

Eine Zeitschrift

von

August Wilhelm Schlegel

und

Friedrich Schlegel.

Ersten Bandes Erstes Stück.

Berlin, 1798.

bey Friedrich Vieweg dem älteren.

Figure 1. Cover page of the first volume of the *Athenaeum*, Berlin, 1798. Collection of the University of California.

It has become almost a habit among Pessoa's critics to regard him as an author of fragments, as a writer who was incapable of completing or finalizing a work. His incapacity has been associated with an aesthetic program that regards the fragment as a necessary end. This essay, however, analyzes a seldom-noticed link between the concept of the fragment as seen in the writings of Friedrich Schlegel and Novalis in the *Athenaeum* and in Pessoa's work in the journal *Orpheu*. By analyzing the position and meaning of Pessoa's publications in *Orpheu* within the context of his work as a whole, we see that he shares with Schlegel and Novalis the idea of a temporal dynamic of the literary work, perceived in terms of a project that is always to be realized. Much like the German romantics, he recognizes the impossibility of achieving a totality of meaning. Yet, unlike them, he doesn't conceive of the fragment as an aesthetic program, designed to achieve a purpose, but as the result of a failure or as the expression of an unfortunate lack of correspondence between an ideal and its realization.

The *Athenaeum* and the Concept of the Fragment

The *Athenaeum* was a literary journal published in Berlin between 1798 and 1800. Edited by the brothers August Wilhelm Schlegel and Friedrich Schlegel, it is considered the founding publication of German romanticism, gathering contributions from the Schlegel brothers, Novalis, Friedrich Schleiermacher, and others of their generation. According to Philippe Lacoue-Labarthe and Jean-Luc Nancy, in their study *L'Absolu littéraire* [*The Literary Absolute*], they comprised the first avant-garde group in history, and the journal was the birthplace of modern literature (17).[1] To justify this characterization, they point out the writers' use of the fragment as a way to question a full access to truth or totality of meaning (57–80). The volumes of the *Athenaeum* are filled with various genres, not only fragments but also philosophical and critical essays, poems, dialogues, and reviews. I focus here on the gathered fragments, particularly the ones by Friedrich Schlegel and Novalis, and on the implied concept of the fragment.

The first number of the journal includes a well-known collection of fragments by Novalis, entitled *Blütenstaub* [*Grains of Pollen*]. The second presents a collection of anonymously published fragments, the majority later attributed to Friedrich Schlegel. Novalis's first fragment reads as follows: "Wir *suchen* überall das Unbedingte, und *finden* immer nur Dinge." ["We *seek* the absolute everywhere and only ever *find* things"] ((*Fragmente und Studien* 5; *Philosophical Writings* 23).[2] Immediately we are aware of the philosophical background of the romantics' aesthetic program.

When seeking for the absolute, our only possible access is through individual elements that bear a relation to a whole that we cannot fully reach. This is a decisive element of the romantics' ideas about the fragment and fragmentary writing. The fragment under study here is very close to an aphorism: a brief individual piece showing a certain unity and expressing a general truth without being exhaustive about the subject (Susini-Anastopoulos, 14–22). The fragment thus questions the possibility of access to a totality of meaning. It also has an essayistic character that demands further development and often treats a variety of objects simultaneously.

According to Lacoue-Labarthe and Nancy (61), the *Athenaeum* did not offer an exact definition of the fragment, probably because such a boundary would contradict the principles of the undertaking. Therefore, to comprehend the concept, we must analyze the practice of writing in fragments. Nevertheless, different images are linked to the idea. One is Novalis's "literary seedings," which he conceived in the context of his considerations on the art of writing books yet to be invented:

> Die Kunst Bücher zu schreiben ist noch nicht erfunden. Sie ist aber auf dem Punkt erfunden zu werden. Fragmente dieser Art sind literärische Sämereien. Es mag freilich manches taube Körnchen darunter sein – indes wenn nur einiges aufgeht. [The art of writing books has not yet been invented. But it is on the point of being invented. Fragments of this kind are literary seedings. Many among them may indeed be sterile—still if only some grow.] (*Fragmente und Studien* 31; *Philosophical Writings* 42)

"Literary seedings" implies that writing in fragments has the aim of revealing, as Novalis puts it, "das Unbedingte"—the absolute or the unconditional (*Fragmente und Studien* 5). Contrary to a postmodern aesthetic of the fragment, which in some cases denies any relation to a whole, a truth, or a totality of meaning, the fragment here is a tool, a way of achieving at least a partial sense of this whole.

In his monograph *La genèse du romantisme allemand*, Roger Ayrault points out this key component of the romantics' notion of fragment, which "se détache de l'incessante activité de l'esprit comme de l'absolu et, isolé, demeure fidèle à son origine" (136) [comes out of the unceasing spiritual activity, as out of the absolute and, isolated, remains faithful to its origin]. This idea is associated with a fragment by Friedrich Schlegel. He comes close to creating a definition of the fragment but writes in prescriptive terms, stating how it should or must be and using an image; this time the famous metaphor of the hedgehog: "Ein Fragment muss gleich einem kleinen Kunstwerke von der umgebenden Welt ganz abgesondert und in sich selbst vollendet sein wie ein Igel" ["A fragment, like a small work of art, has to be entirely isolated from the surrounding world and be complete in itself like a hedgehog"] (*"Athenaeums"—Fragmente* 99; *Friedrich Schlegel's "Lucinde"* 189, trans. amended). The fragment is seen here as isolated from the surrounding world and in itself complete. The image of a hedgehog, however, indicates that the fragment has a presence within the framework of its surroundings, bearing, in terms of an individual and autonomous work, a relation to the whole. It is therefore a complete work, which relates to an absolute, total work, bearing the full meaning, yet to be conceived but never to be fully apprehended.[3]

Another fragment by Schlegel links the fragment with a *project*, defined here as a fragment *of* or *from* the future. The German concept "Fragmente aus der Zukunft" integrates both meanings. According to this notion, projects have, as fragments, a progressive dimension:

> Ein Projekt ist der subjektive Keim eines werdenden Objekts. Ein vollkomenes Projekt müsste zugleich ganz subjektiv, und ganz objektiv, ein unteilbares und lebendiges Individuum sein. [...] Der Sinn für Projekte, die man Fragmente aus der Zukunft nennen könnte, ist von dem Sinn für Fragmente aus der Vergangenheit nur durch die Richtung verschieden, die bei ihm progressiv, bei jenem aber regressiv ist. Das Wesentliche ist die Fähigkeit, Gegenstände unmittelbar zugleich zu idealisieren, und zu realisieren, zu ergänzen, und teilweise in sich auszuführen. Da nun transzendental eben das ist, was auf die Verbindung oder Trennung des Idealen und des Realen Bezug hat; so könnte man wohl sagen, der Sinn für Fragmente und Projekte sei der transzendentale Bestandteil des historischen Geistes. [A project is the subjective germ of a developing object. A perfect project should be at once completely subjective and completely objective, should be an indivisible and living individual. [...] The sense for projects – which one might call fragments of the future – is distinguishable from the feeling for fragments of the past only by its direction: progressive in the former, regressive in the latter. What is essential is to be able to idealize and realize objects immediately and simultaneously: to complete them and in part carry them out within oneself. Since transcendental is precisely whatever relates to the joining or separating of the ideal and the real, one might very well say that the sense for fragments and projects is the transcendental element of the historical spirit. [*"Athenaeums"-Fragmente* 78; *Friedrich Schlegel's "Lucinde"* 164, trans. amended]

Projects are fragments *of* the future, as they relate to something that should take place in the future, and also fragments *from* the future, as they originate in an anticipated meaning of future achievements. Described in dialectical terms, a project is seen as an "indivisible and living individual" (such as the fragment understood as a "hedgehog") and "at once completely subjective and completely objective"; it is therefore a subjective creation, including also an objective element, as it refers to a specific object. Through projects, one has the ability to idealize and realize things simultaneously, as projects are not seen as empty ideas or mere unfulfilled projections but bear in themselves a certain substance by connecting the ideal and the real. In this connection, Schlegel conceives of the "transcendental element of the historical spirit," described in Hegelian terms.

Pessoa as Reader of Schlegel and Novalis

Before discussing how these ideas relate to Pessoa's work, it is important to point out to what extent Pessoa knew them, and what kind of access he could have had to the fragments of *Athenaeum* and especially to the works by Friedrich Schlegel and Novalis. Nevertheless, I will point out further on that Pessoa's ideas regarding the fragment can be traced back to some of the notions underlying the fragments published in the *Athenaeum*, regardless of his factual knowledge of them.

We cannot be sure how well Pessoa knew the work of Schlegel, but we know he was an attentive reader of Novalis's fragments, including the ones published in the *Athenaeum*. A French edition of a collection of these fragments, together with the prose work "Die Lehrlinge zu Sais" ["The Novices of Sais"], edited and translated by Maurice Maeterlinck and published in 1914, is preserved in Pessoa's private library, profusely underlined and annotated (CFP 8-388).[4]. His library also includes a monograph on Novalis by the French critic Henri Lichtenberger, in an edition dated 1912 (CFP 9-45). This is an extensive study of Novalis's work, including biographical information, chapters on his philosophical and religious doctrine, and writings on his poetry and poetics. Some passages are underlined, particularly those in chapters concerning his philosophical and religious ideas. One underlined passage concerns the Gospels, quoting Novalis's statement that they were only "l'ébauche d'Evangiles futurs et supérieurs" (170) [drafts of future and superior Gospels]. This idea clearly relates to the image of fragments as "literary seedings," with apparently established works regarded here as unfinished fragments and possible sources for future developments.

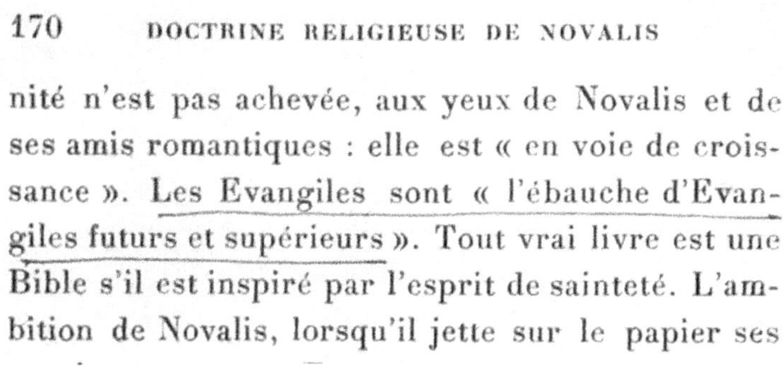

170 DOCTRINE RELIGIEUSE DE NOVALIS

nité n'est pas achevée, aux yeux de Novalis et de ses amis romantiques : elle est « en voie de croissance ». Les Evangiles sont « l'ébauche d'Evangiles futurs et supérieurs ». Tout vrai livre est une Bible s'il est inspiré par l'esprit de sainteté. L'ambition de Novalis, lorsqu'il jette sur le papier ses

Figure 2. Underlined passage in *Novalis*, by Henri Lichtenberger, Paris, 1912. CFP 8-169, p. 170.

Another extensive monograph preserved in the library, John George Robertson's *The Literature of Germany* (1913), travels through every period of German literature, including romanticism (CFP 8-470). Pessoa underlined some passages related to historical and geographical facts and to judgments of the work of various authors. Through this kind of reading, he reflected on the meaning and importance of German romanticism, as he does in a passage attributed to the fictional author António Mora, referring to the Schlegel brothers and Novalis:

> Com o romantismo alemão, propriamente dito, o dos Schlegel, de Tieck e de Novalis, entra com a literatura germânica uma decadência, referindo-nos, por comparação, à precedente literatura de Schiller e de Goethe, se bem que o primeiro pecasse na sua utilização do que admirava no paganismo. (*O Regresso dos Deuses* 145) [With German romanticism, properly speaking, that of Schegel, Tieck, and Novalis, a certain decadence comes to define German literature, if we refer, by comparison, to the precedent literature of Schiller and Goethe, although the first one sinned in his use of what he admired in paganism.]

Considering German romanticism as a whole, and specifically mentioning the Schlegel brothers, Ludwig Tieck and Novalis, Pessoa sees it as a period of decadence in German literature, in comparison to the previous one, represented by Schiller and Goethe.[5] This reaction should be considered within the context of his more general censure of romanticism, as opposed to classicism, a recurrent motif in Pessoa's aesthetic writings. This censure has to do mainly with what he considers to be the romantics' inability to properly construct literary work.[6] Pessoa often mentions the metaphor of the Aristotelian tradition of the poem as an animal, an image for the literary work as an organized whole, the different parts forming an organic totality. Some of these references mention romanticism as the period in which the failure of this aim was particularly evident. In a discussion of the principles of sensationism, his proposal for a new aesthetic movement, Pessoa writes, in a letter to a unidentified English publisher: "I call these three principles 1) that of Sensation, 2) that of Suggestion, 3) that of Construction. This last, the great principle of the Greeks—whose great philosopher did indeed hold the poem to be "an animal"—has had very careless handling at modern hands. Romanticism has indisciplined the capacity of constructing which, at least, low classicism had. Shakespeare, with his fatal incapacity to visualise organised wholes, has been a fatal influence in this respect." (*Correspondência* 235).

The evidence left in the Maeterlinck edition of Novalis's writings shows that Pessoa was particularly interested in the fragments by the young German poet. In fact, the only section of the volume underlined and annotated is the one gathering the fragments, and a very significant number of them are underlined. Pessoa underlined and annotated several concerning the philosophy of nature and the senses, aesthetics, literature, and Greek mythology. Novalis considers poetry to be an art form capable of integrating everything, and Pessoa's interest in Novalis's idea of poetry is made clear by several underlined passages. They include "il est très compréhensible que tout finisse par devenir poésie" (180) and "la poésie est le réel absolu" ([poetry is the absolute real], followed by Pessoa's annotation "Nota Bene" [Note Well], 185). This interest in the possibilities of poetry is of extreme importance to Pessoa's work, which aims to integrate everything in his literary creation and treats literature as the major and absolute work.[7]Another commonality between Pessoa and Novalis is their reflection on the subtle and vanishing limits between dream and reality, a recurring topic of *The Book of Disquiet* and throughout all of their poetical works. In the Maeterlinck edition, Pessoa underlines the fragment by Novalis stating that we are close to waking up when we dream that we dream ("Nous sommes près du réveil quand nous rêvons que nous rêvons" [77]) and quotes it in the last sentence of his 1928 article on Portuguese provincialism, "O Provincianismo Português" (*Crítica* 371–73).

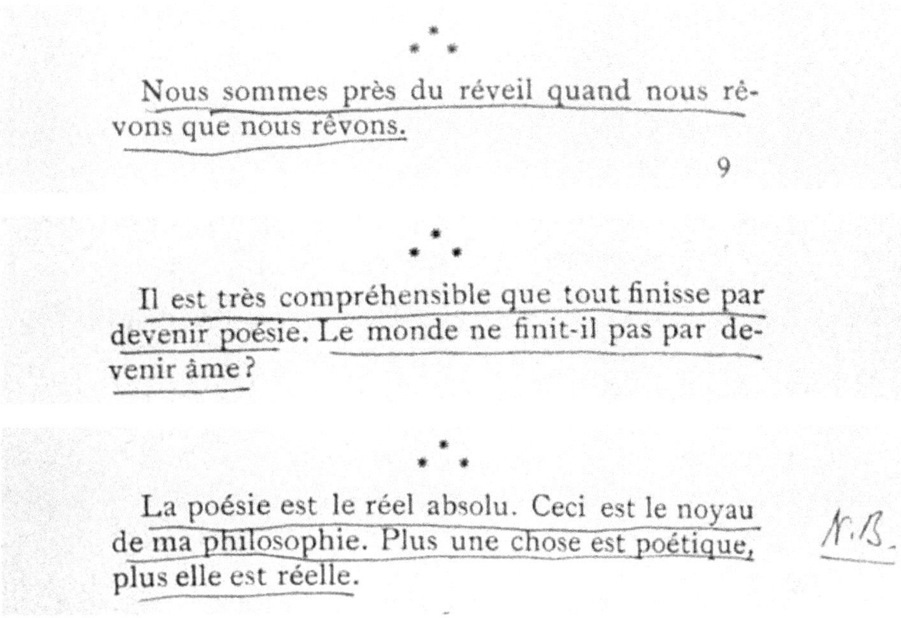

Nous sommes près du réveil quand nous rêvons que nous rêvons.

9

Il est très compréhensible que tout finisse par devenir poésie. Le monde ne finit-il pas par devenir âme?

La poésie est le réel absolu. Ceci est le noyau de ma philosophie. Plus une chose est poétique, plus elle est réelle.

Figure 3. Fragments by Novalis, edited and translated by Maurice Maeterlinck, underlined by Fernando Pessoa. (*Les disciples à Sais et Les fragments*. Paris & Brussels: Paul Lacomblez, 1914; CFP 8-388, pp. 77, 180, 185).

Although explicit considerations on the question of the fragment in itself are not among the underlined passages, it is also clear that this question is not at the center of Novalis' considerations. As Lacoue-Labarthe and Nancy (61) point out, it is through the reading of the fragments, concerning several different topics, and not by a theoretical explanation of its principles that we get a sense of the function and the central motives of the fragment in the *Athenaeum* and especially in the works by Schlegel and Novalis. I would propose that this is also the fundamental sense of the fragment which interests Pessoa, who barely uses the word or reflects explicitly upon the question of fragmentarity.

Further evidence of Pessoa's interest in Novalis' work include a list of poetical works, referring to the name "Novalis" (kept in his Archive at the Portuguese National Library with the signature BNP 48-114^{r}) and an editorial project (BNP 12^{1}-79^{r}; http://www.pessoadigital.pt/pt/doc/BNP_E3_12-1-79r, where Pessoa considers the publication of a Portuguese translation of "The Novices of Sais" and a collection of the fragments, probably taking as source the edition by Maeterlinck, as the similarity of the title and references suggests. The list of works can be

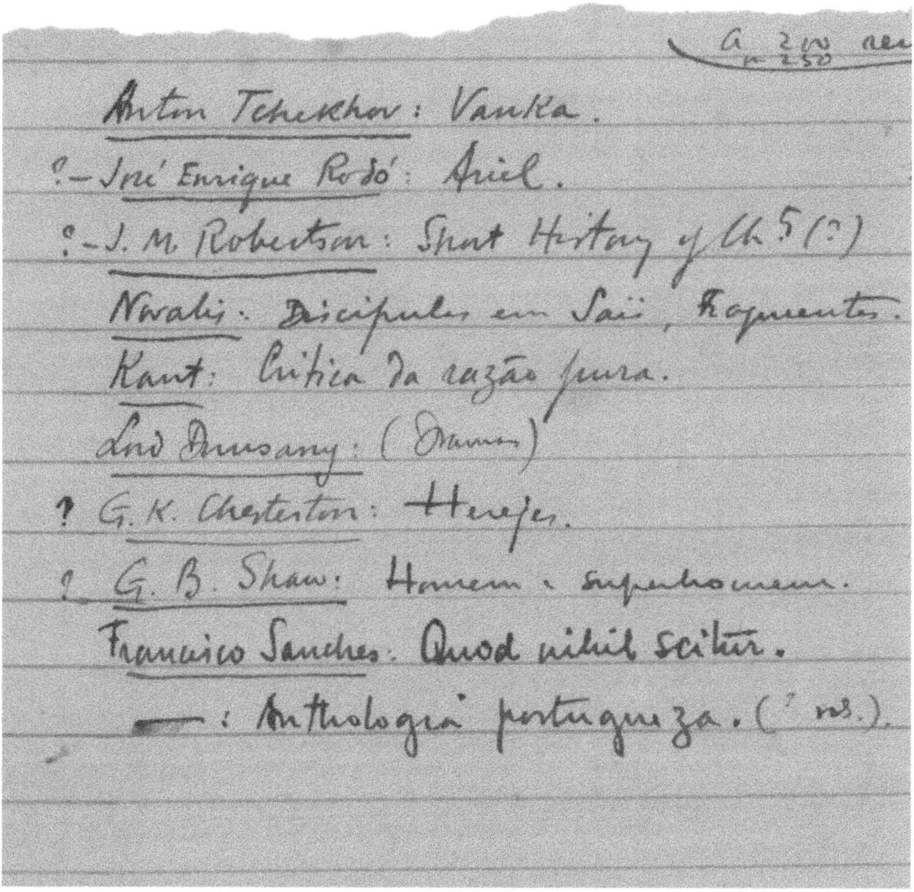
Anton Tchekhov: Vanka.
?—José Enrique Rodó: Ariel.
?—J. M. Robertson: Short History of Ch.s (?)
Novalis: Discipulos em Saïs, Fragmentos.
Kant: Critica da razão pura.
Lord Dunsany: (Dramas)
? G. K. Chesterton: Hereges.
? G. B. Shaw: Homem e superhomem.
Francisco Sanches: Quod nihil scitur.
—: Anthologia portugueza. (? vols.)

Figure 4. Pessoa's project of a Portuguese translation of Novalis, elaborated around 1918. BNP 121-79r; http://www.pessoadigital.pt/pt/doc/BNP_E3_12-1-79r.

dated around 1907 or 1908, and the editorial project was elaborated around 1918, as suggested, in both cases, by the references to titles of works Pessoa was reading or working on in these periods.

Pessoa's *Orpheu* as Fragment and Project

There is evidence that Pessoa, even before his 1915 publications in *Orpheu*, was interested in Novalis's fragments and in German romanticism in general, although Schlegel and Novalis are not usually cited by critics as among the main references of his work. Certainly, Pessoa, Novalis, and Schlegel share some ideas regarding the position of the fragment within their literary work, although

Pessoa does not refer to fragments explicitly or make them a central theoretical topic. Nonetheless, several critics regard him as an author of fragments, both in a material and hermeneutic sense, and associate them with his aesthetic program, which would understand the fragment as a necessary end or as the expression of the impossibility of reaching and expressing a totality (e.g, Santos, Pizarro, and Medeiros). Thus, it remains surprising that Pessoa persistently supports an organic ideal of the literary work, frequently citing the Aristotelian metaphor of the poem as an animal in which the different parts are gathered in an organic whole. There is a notable contrast between this idea of an organic whole and the fragmentary reality of his texts, especially in his archival documents, a disparity that critics have seen as a clash between two different dimensions.[8] Nevertheless, when he was preparing a text for publication, and we know how careful and selective he was in what concerns the publication of his work, he would remove from the text any material signs of incompleteness. Yet while Pessoa's works in *Orpheu* bear no material signs of fragmentarity, they project the sense of an undefined potential totality that goes beyond what has been materialized. Every work by Pessoa emits the idea of a whole that exceeds the written texts, and this is something he shares with the German romantics.

This kind of fragmentarity, which is neither material nor part of a program, is particularly visible in Pessoa's editorial planning, as expressed in notes, commentaries, correspondence, and lists of potential collections of his work. These lists have not only an editorial but also a systemic function, presenting plans of the different parts of the work and establishing relations between them (see Sepúlveda and Uribe). While they are often more elaborate than the actual publications, they give relational meaning to otherwise loose texts. For instance, if we look at the *Orpheu* works in the context of the editorial lists and projects surrounding their publication, we can see that Pessoa left out several of the original elements he had planned to include. What he did choose to publish also gives new meaning to later plans and projects. Before the *Orpheu* pieces came out, he had been considering the publication of a journal to be called *Europa*. The project is mentioned in the correspondence between Pessoa and the poet Mário de Sá-Carneiro, and related plans and notes appear in Pessoa's Archive (*Sensacionismo* 29–37). One of the ideas linked to *Europa* and to texts excluded from *Orpheu* is the publication of a collection of works that would give expression to a new literary and artistic movement he called *intersectionism*, together with a manifesto explaining its principles. He projected this idea in one of his editorial plans for

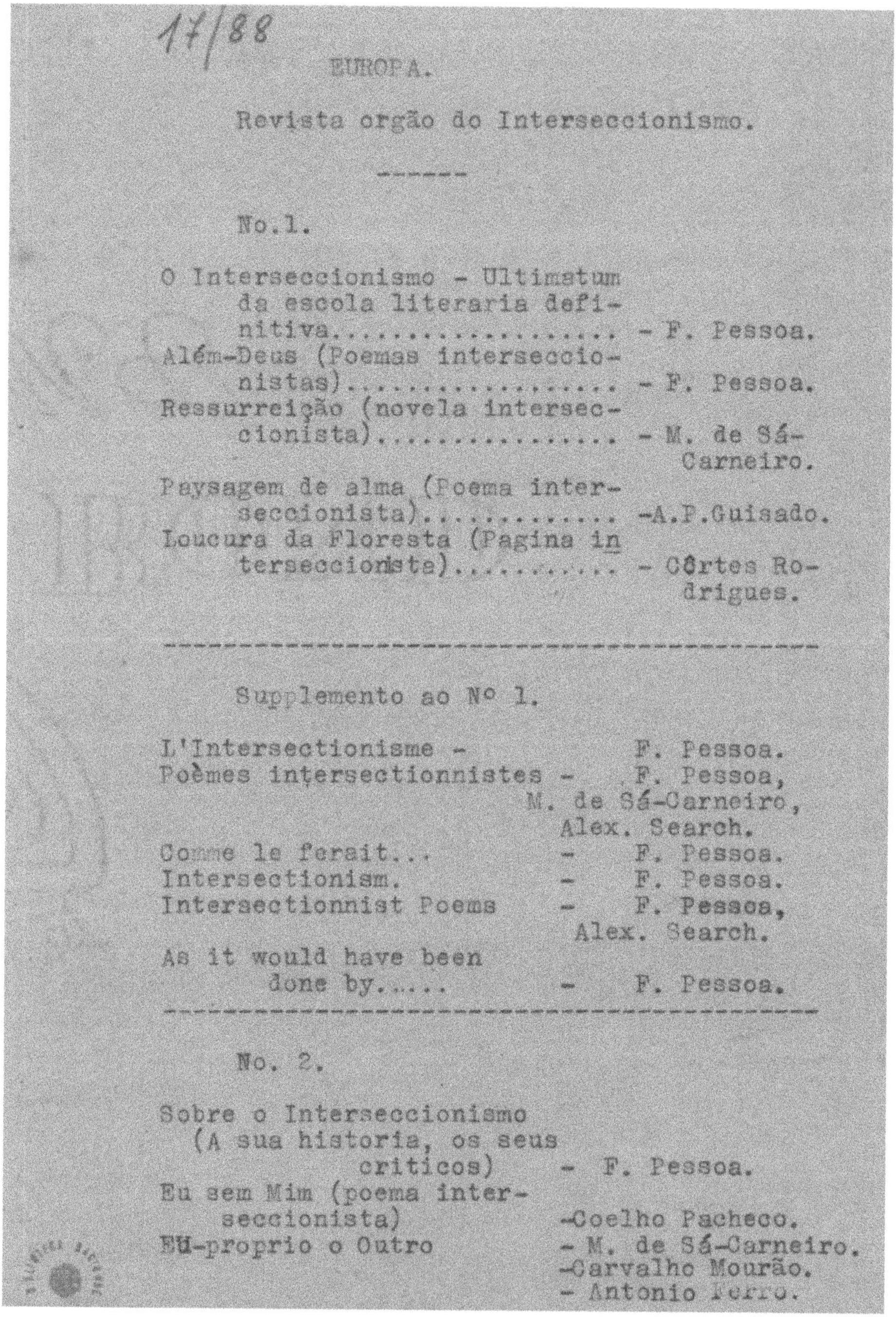

17/88

EUROPA.

Revista orgão do Interseccionismo.

No.1.

O Interseccionismo - Ultimatum da escola literaria definitiva.................... - F. Pessoa.
Além-Deus (Poemas interseccionistas).................... - F. Pessoa.
Ressurreição (novela interseccionista)................ - M. de Sá-Carneiro.
Paysagem de alma (Poema interseccionista)............. -A.P.Guisado.
Loucura da Floresta (Pagina interseccionista)........... - Côrtes Rodrigues.

Supplemento ao Nº 1.

L'Intersectionisme - F. Pessoa.
Poèmes intersectionnistes - F. Pessoa, M. de Sá-Carneiro, Alex. Search.
Comme le ferait... - F. Pessoa.
Intersectionism. - F. Pessoa.
Intersectionnist Poems - F. Pessoa, Alex. Search.
As it would have been done by..... - F. Pessoa.

No. 2.

Sobre o Interseccionismo (A sua historia, os seus criticos) - F. Pessoa.
Eu sem Mim (poema interseccionista) -Coelho Pacheco.
Eu-proprio o Outro - M. de Sá-Carneiro.
-Carvalho Mourão.
- Antonio Ferro.

Figure 5. Pessoa's editorial plan for *Europa* as an "organ of the Intersectionism," elaborated in 1914 or 1915. BNP 48G-32r; *Sensacionismo* 36–37.

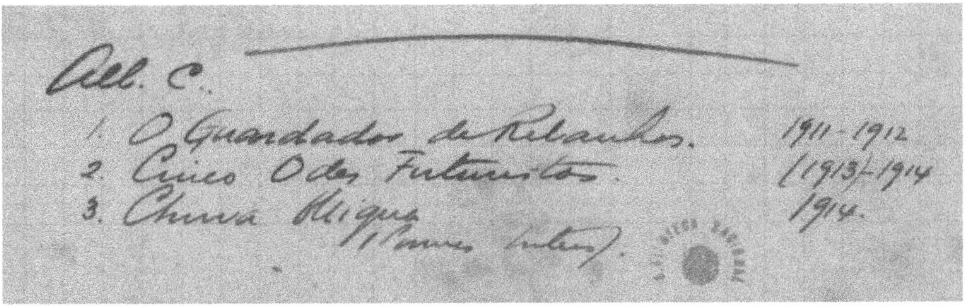

Alb. C.
1. O Guardador de Rebanhos. 1911-1912
2. Cinco Odes Futuristas. (1913)-1914
3. Chuva Obliqua 1914.

Figure 6. Project for publications in the name of Alberto Caeiro, established in 1914. BNP 48-27r;http://www.pessoadigital.pt/pt/doc/BNP_E3_48-27r.

the journal and described it in letters to his friend Armando Côrtes-Rodrigues, who was also a collaborator on *Orpheu* (*Correspondência* 126–27, 132, 140–41).

However, in a letter to Côrtes-Rodrigues, dated January 1915, Pessoa wrote that he had decided to abandon the idea of publishing a collection of works on intersectionism, together with the manifesto, calling the project a *blague* (*Correspondência* 140). That same year, in *Orpheu*, he published the poem "Chuva Oblíqua" ("Slanting Rain"), defining it in the journal as *intersectionist* but not including any further reference to this movement.

In 1914, as we know from several of Pessoa's editorial projects and his correspondence (Sepúlveda, "Orpheu em lugar de Caeiro" 93–95), he had planned to publish a collection of poems by his heteronym Alberto Caeiro, a key figure in his poetry, considered by Pessoa to be the master of his whole poetic creation. One of these projects conceives the publication not only of "O Guardador de Rebanhos" ("The Keeper of Sheep"), the main collection of Caeiro's poems, but also of "Cinco Odes Futuristas" ("Five Futurist Odes") and "Chuva Oblíqua" ("Slanting Rain"), all attributed to Caeiro as author. In *Orpheu*, however, the futurist odes (under another heading) are attributed to the fictional poet Álvaro de Campos and "Chuva Oblíqua" appears under the name of Fernando Pessoa. The first publication of Alberto Caeiro's poems did not occur until 1925, in the journal *Athena*.

Although they are usually seen as representative of Pessoa's work, the pieces in *Orpheu* neglect at least two crucial elements that were important in his planning. The first is the implementation of a new literary movement, which would require the publication of a programmatic text or at least a specific description. The second is the poetry of Caeiro. It is only in 1916 that he publishes a programmatic text, entitled "O Movimento Sensacionista" ("The Sensationist

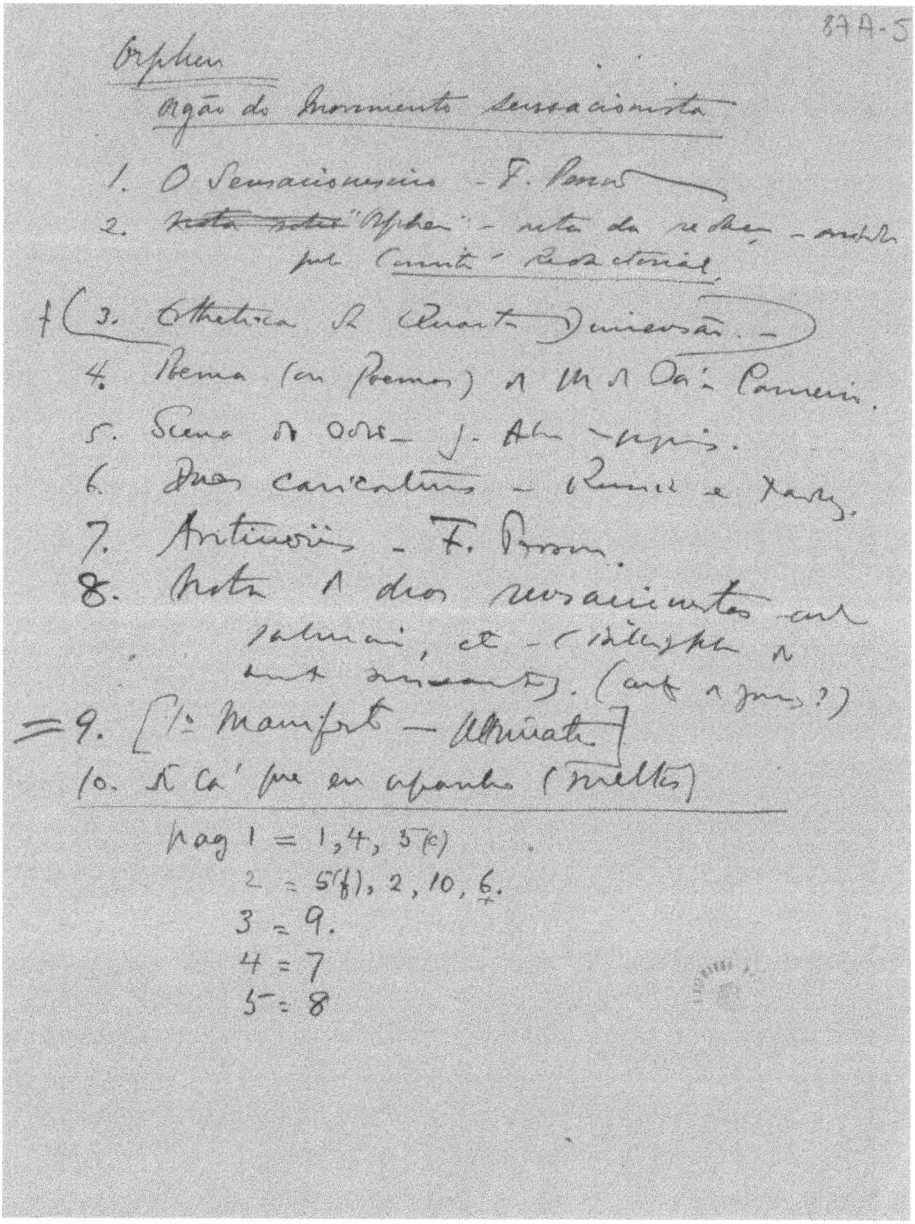

Figure 7 Editorial plan for the third issue of *Orpheu*, elaborated in 1916 or 1917. BNP 87A-5r; *Sensacionismo* 83.

Movement"), which presents *Orpheu* as the decisive "organ" of a new literary and artistic movement, now named sensationism (*Crítica* 127–32). An extensive plan for the third issue of *Orpheu*, never published, reiterates this declaration.

These examples demonstrate how Pessoa constantly shifted among conceptual and organizational possibilities. His editorial projects play a key role in projecting a totality that exceeds his actual writings and publications. From these projects, his correspondence, and his notes, we see that the published work remains part of a larger project, always unfinished. In *Orpheu* Pessoa publishes works that can only be adequately understood if related to aspects that remain to be later described, such as the position of Alberto Caeiro as the master of Pessoa and Campos, or the sense of a new literary movement they represent, only later defined as Sensationism. Texts such as his "Notas para a recordação do meu Mestre Caeiro" ("Notes for the Memory of my Master Caeiro"), published partially in 1931 (*Prosa* 89–139) and his letter to the critic Adolfo Casais Monteiro on the genesis of his heteronyms, written in January 1935 (*Cartas* 251–60), are further examples of systemic formulations that give already-published works a broader meaning.

That meaning is, however, never definitive, as Pessoa underlines in several descriptions of his published work. For instance, in "Tábua Bibliográfica" ("Bibliographic Board"), published in 1928, he states, "Nenhum destes textos é definitivo. Do ponto de vista estético, o autor prefere, pois, considerar estas obras como apenas aproximadamente existentes [None of these texts is definitive. From an aesthetic point of view the author prefers, therefore, to consider these works as only approximately existent]" (*Cartas* 74). In a biographical note written in 1935, a few months before his death, he considers his publications as a whole: "Há que rever tudo isso e talvez que repudiar muito [All this must be reviewed and there may be a lot which must be dismissed]" (*Sebastianismo* 143). Throughout his life, he constantly reviewed and corrected, changing titles and authorship, never accepting a definitive sense of and position for each work within a conceived whole.

Pessoa's and Schlegel's Fragments of the Future

Pessoa rarely uses the word *fragment*. When he does, it is in terms of a regret, a complaint, or a lament at not being able to establish the organic whole that he sees desirable for any literary work. This is the case in a passage about *The Book of Disquiet* in a letter to Côrtes-Rodrigues, dated November 1914: "O meu estado de espírito obriga-me agora a trabalhar bastante, sem querer, no Livro do

Desassossego. Mas tudo fragmentos, fragmentos, fragmentos [My state of mind forces me now to work a lot, without wanting to, in *The Book of Disquiet*. But it's all fragments, fragments, fragments]" (*Correspondência* 132).

The Pessoan text that comes closer to a possible theory of the fragment is the article "O Homem de Porlock" ("The Man from Porlock"), published in the newspaper *Fradique* on February 15, 1934 (*Crítica* 490–92). In it he presents an interpretation of Samuel Taylor Coleridge's description of composing the poem "Kubla Khan."[9] According to Coleridge, an unexpected visit from a man from Porlock disrupted his creativity, and the poem was never finished. Pessoa sees this as a description of the universal experience of poetic writing:

> Tudo quanto verdadeiramente pensamos ou sentimos, tudo quanto verdadeiramente somos, sofre (quando o vamos exprimir, ainda que só para nós mesmos) a interrupção fatal daquele visitante que também somos, daquela pessoa externa que cada um de nós tem em si, mais real na vida do que nós próprios – a soma viva do que aprendemos, do que julgamos que somos, e do que desejamos ser. [All we truly think or feel, all we truly are, suffers (when we are about to express it, even if only to ourselves) the fatal interruption of that visitor who we also are, of that external person every one of us has inside him, more real in life than ourselves—the living sum of what we learn, what we think we are, and what we desire to be.] (*Crítica* 491–92)

This interruption of the visitor is seen as part of every act of expression, as the visitor is defined as "that external person every one of us has inside him". This visitor is also identified as projection and desire ("the living sum of what we learn, what we think we are, and what we desire to be"), as opposed to the reality of "all we truly are," before this "fatal interruption". That is why writing is always "impessoal" (impersonal). As Pessoa notes, "o que de todos nós, artistas grandes ou pequenos, verdadeiramente sobrevive,—são fragmentos do que não sabemos que seja; mas que seria, se houvesse sido, a mesma expressão da nossa alma [what from all of us, big or small artists, truly remains—are fragments of what we don't know; but which could be, if it had been, the real expression of our soul]" (492).

The article points out the necessarily impersonal and fragmentary dimension in every form of poetic creation. This is precisely the sense of the fragment present in Pessoa's publications and editorial projects: the undefined future of a meaning that may be gradually and partially unveiled but always remains to be fully achieved. Fragmentarity is, in this sense, not deliberate but the failure to have full access to "the real expression of our soul." As Pessoa concludes, "do que poderia ter sido, fica só o que é,—do poema, ou dos *opera omnia*, só o princípio e o fim de qualquer coisa perdida—*disjecta membra* que, como disse Carlyle, é o que fica de qualquer poeta, ou de qualquer homem [of what could have been, only what it is remains—of the poem, or the *opera omnia*, just the beginning and the end of any lost thing—*disjecta membra*, which, as Carlyle said, is what remains from any poet, or any man]" (492).

Unlike the romantics, Pessoa does not propose to understand the fragment as a literary genre used to achieve a certain access to reality, truth, or meaning. He sees it as an unfortunate, if necessary, step toward the ideal of an organic, unfragmented whole. That ideal can never exist, and so we find, for instance, in *The Book of Disquiet*, many thoughts on the impossibility of fully corresponding to the ideal, on the necessary imperfection of any work of art. As Pessoa states in the context of a discussion on the organic character of Shakespeare's King Lear, "Não há método de obter a Perfeição excepto ser Deus.... A única obra grande e perfeita é aquela que nunca se sonhe realizar" ["The only method for achieving Perfection is to be God.... The only great and perfect works are the ones we never dream of realizing"] (*Livro do Desasocego* 80; *The Book of Disquiet* 434).

Fragmentarity in Pessoa's work is therefore not an aesthetic program with a specific purpose but the result of a failure, a lack of achievement. The poet traces this notion to the romantics, writing, "Achievement is death, because it is the end. The romantics are self-survivals, perpetual incarnations of their own selves." (*Heróstrato* 153). Like Schlegel and Novalis, he understood the impossibility of fully achieving truth and a totality of meaning This is the first element connecting any of these works, the second one being the acceptance of a necessary temporal dynamic of the literary work, understood as "seedings," in the image of Novalis, or projects, in a sense partially shared by Pessoa and Schlegel. Analyzing the fragmentarity in Pessoa with reference to German romanticism, Carla Gago (232-234) points out how Pessoa shared with the romantics the idea of a totality in preparation and the acknowledgement of the impossibility of its achievement. Like Carla Gago, Irene Ramalho Santos and Paulo de Medeiros see a strong relation between the romantics and Pessoa's work. Focusing on Pessoa's heteronymic project as a whole, Santos notes that "the image of the hedgehog as *fragmentary* completeness in [Schlegel's] Fragment 206 anticipates heteronymic Pessoa," the image of the fragment being one of "a momentary bristling wholeness that precisely as such risks nothingness" (17). Medeiros focuses on the question in his study of the fragments in *The Book of Disquiet*, in which "Pessoa/Soares dá-nos um texto aparentemente fechado em si e 'completo,' que poderia ser publicado como uma narrativa breve [Pessoa/Soares gives us a text apparently closed in itself and 'complete,' that could be published as a brief narrative]." Thus, the text demonstrates, in an exemplary manner, "aquilo que Schlegel denominou como um fragmento absoluto na imagem do ouriço-cacheiro" [what Schlegel referred to as an absolute fragment in the image of the hedgehog]" (88).

Both Santos and Medeiros remind us that at least some parts of Pessoa's work appear to be in themselves closed and complete, bearing no signs of incompletion within the text, in both a material and a hermeneutic sense. Nevertheless, these apparently complete pieces, such as some texts in *The Book of Disquiet* and in his heteronymic productions, particularly those published during his lifetime, can only be adequately understood if related to a greater whole. This sense of a greater whole, a totality of meaning, was persistently present in Pessoa's mind, as he constantly considered how the different texts, as parts of a set of works, might relate to each other and how they gain their meaning only through this relation. As Medeiros recognizes, "o fragmento impõe-se também como fragmento, como texto em aberto que chama a si outros fragmentos, outros textos" [the fragment imposes itself also as fragment, as open text appealing to other fragments, other texts]" (89). Pessoa not only established these relations between different texts as parts of the work but also persistently projected a global sense of this work which would bear no signs of fragmentarity. This constant projection is particularly achieved through his descriptions of heteronymy, of his published works and the ones yet to be published, especially in the mentioned editorial projects. It is this projection of an organic totality that forces us to see Pessoa's work at the same time as fragmentary and as dependent upon a designed unity. The quoted analyses above leave out the mentioned temporal dynamic of the work, expressed in a precise sense of the work as a project, as a common trait between Pessoa and the fragments of the German romantics. These analyses also leave out the absence of a deliberate aesthetic program based on the fragment, in the case of Pessoa, as the main difference separating them.

Schlegel conceived of projects as "Fragmente aus der Zukunft" (*"Athenaeums"-Fragmente* 78) ["fragments *of* or *from* the future"]; in Pessoa's case these projects refer to complete works, *of* the future in the sense that they allude to future achievements and *from* the future as their substance depends upon these achievements. In Pessoa's messianic projection of his work there is no room for the fragment as a pursued entity, but the projected work is *fragmentary* in the sense that it still does not fully correspond, and never will, to the ideal of an organic totality.

Pessoa's editorial projects usually express a perfectly designed whole, never to be fully realized and remaining in this sense always fragmentary. Both these ideas of the project, in Schlegel and Pessoa, share a temporal dimension, projecting in the future an object still to be developed. Both see in their projects a full substance and reality (Schlegel: "an indivisible and living individual"), attributing to the work a progressive sense. They both establish a connection between a reality of the work and a metaphysical dimension. For Schlegel, this dimension is the "transcendental element of the historical spirit"; for Pessoa it is this perfectly designed whole, which due to the unfortunate condition of every writer, was never to be achieved.

NOTES

1. This *Atheneaum* is not the English literary journal by the same name published in London between 1828 and 1921 and featuring works by writers such as T. S. Eliot, Aldous Huxley, Katherine Mansfield, and Virginia Woolf. Pessoa published his poem "Meantime" in the English journal in 1920 (http://www.pessoadigital.pt).

2. Where the source of a translation is not indicated, I am responsible for it.

3. According to Blanchot (526), the fragment of the German romantics bears in itself a meaning that goes beyond totality but does not exclude the idea of a totality of meaning. Blummenberg (256) points out a double function of the romantics' fragment: reference to a lost totality and the expectation of achieving an infinite and unlimited perfection. Lacoue-Labarthe and Nancy (63) note how the separation and isolation of the fragment in this conception recovers a sense of completion, of being self-sufficient.

4. This signature refers to the catalogue of Pessoa's Personal Library, preserved and digitized by the *Casa Fernando Pessoa*, available for consultation and download in http://bibliotecaparticular.casafernandopessoa.pt/. I will refer to further volumes of this library using the respective signatures.

5. Critical literature on Pessoa and German literature focuses mainly on his readings of Goethe and Schiller (e.g., Fischer),leaving aside the importance of Schlegel and Novalis. (Exceptions are Santos, Gago, Medeiros, and Feijó.) Pessoa read German authors, including the romantics, mainly in French translations and via commentaries by French and British critics (Fisher, 55).

6. See Pessoa 166–67 and the considerations of Patrício 154–60.

7. See namely his considerations in the preface entitled *Aspects*; *Livro do Desasocego* 446-451.

8. This clash between the material fragmentarity of Pessoa's writings and an aesthetic idea of the work as an organic totality has been pointed out by, among others, Martins,

Gusmão, Eiras, Patrício, Sepúlveda, *Os livros de Fernando Pessoa*, and Feijó. Martins, Eiras, and Gusmão argue that there is a strong hermeneutical side to Pessoa's fragmentarity, even if it is not based on an explicit program. Feijó (150–54) sees in the absence of a program the evidence of a contingency of the fragmentarity in Pessoa's writings, contrary to the "aesthetic of the fragment" proposed by the German romantics, but also recognizes the poet's consciousness of a lack of achievement. Patrício (163–81) underlines his conscience of the impossibility of achieving a totality of meaning, by constantly adjourning the completion of the work.

9. On Pessoa's reading of Coleridge, especially concerning the poetic writing process, see Castro. On his dialogue with Keat's aesthetic concepts, see Monteiro, Feijó, and Castro.

WORKS CITED

Works by Fernando Pessoa

BNP: Fernando Pessoa's Archive, held by the Portuguese National Library.

Pessoa, Fernando. *Alberto Caeiro. Poesia*. Edited by Fernando Cabral Martins and Richard Zenith. Lisbon: Assírio & Alvim, 2001.

———. *Cartas entre Fernando Pessoa e os directores da Presença*. Edited by Enrico Martines. Lisbon: Imprensa Nacional-Casa da Moeda, 1998.

———. *Correspondência: 1905-1922*. Edited by Manuela Parreira da Silva. Lisbon: Assírio & Alvim, 1999.

———. *Crítica. Ensaios, Artigos, Entrevistas*. Edited by Fernando Cabral Martins. Lisbon: Assírio & Alvim, 2000.

———. *Heróstrato e a Busca da Imortalidade*. Edited by Richard Zenith. Lisbon: Assírio & Alvim, 2000a.

———. *Livro do Desasocego*. Vol. I & II. Edited by Jerónimo Pizarro. Lisbon: Imprensa Nacional-Casa da Moeda, 2010.

———. *O Regresso dos Deuses e outros escritos de António Mora*. Edited by Manuela Parreira da Silva. Lisbon: Assírio & Alvim, 2013.

———. *Prosa de Álvaro de Campos*. Edited by Jerónimo Pizarro and Antonio Cardiello. Lisbon: Ática, 2012.

———. *Sensacionismo e Outros Ismos*. Edited by Jerónimo Pizarro. Lisbon: Imprensa Nacional-Casa da Moeda, 2009.

———. *Sebastianismo e Quinto Império*. Edited by Jorge Uribe and Pedro Sepúlveda. Lisbon: Ática, 2011.

———. *The Book of Disquiet*. Edited and translated by Richard Zenith. London: Penguin Books, 2002.

Books in Fernando Pessoa's Private Library (CFP)

Robertson, John George. *The Literature of Germany*. London: Williams and Norgate, 1913. (CFP 8-470)

Lichtenberger, Henri. *Novalis*. Paris: Bloud & Cie, 1912. (CFP 9-45)

Novalis. *Les disciples à Sais et Les fragments*. Edited and translated by Maurice Maeterlinck. Paris & Brussels: Paul Lacomblez, 1914. (CFP 8-388)

Other References

Ayrault, Roger. *La genèse do romantisme allemand*. Vol. 1. Paris: Éditions Montaigne, 1969.

Blanchot, Maurice. *L'entretien infini*. Paris: Gallimard, 1969.

Blumenberg, Hans. *Die Lesbarkeit der Welt*. Frankfurt a.M.: Suhrkamp Verlag, 1981.

Castro, Mariana Gray de. "Pessoa, Coleridge, homens de Porlock e dias triunfais: sobre génio, inspiração, interrupção e criação poética" *Estranhar Pessoa*, no. 1, 2014, http://estranharpessoa.com/revista-anterior. Accessed June 2020.

———. "Pessoa and Keats" *Portuguese Literary and Cultural Studies*, no. 28, 2015, pp. 143-163.

Eiras, Pedro. *Esquecer Fausto: A fragmentação do sujeito em Raúl Brandão, Fernando Pessoa, Herberto Helder e Maria Gabriela Llansol*. Porto: Campo das Letras, 2005.

Feijó, António M. *Uma admiração pastoril pelo diabo (Pessoa e Pascoaes)*. Lisbon: Imprensa Nacional-Casa da Moeda, 2015.

Fischer, Claudia J. "Fernando Pessoa, leitor de Schiller: uma aproximação à língua alemã" *Real*, no. 1, 2010, pp. 54-70,
http://ojs.real.letras.ulisboa.pt/index.php/REAL/article/view/15/12. Accessed June 2020.

Gago, Carla. "Interstícios — o fragmento em Fernando Pessoa". Dix, Steffen and Pizarro, Jerónimo. *A Arca de Pessoa*, edited by Steffen Dix and Jerónimo Pizarro, Lisbon: Imprensa de Ciências Sociais, 2007, pp. 229-242.

Gusmão, Manuel. "O Fausto — um teatro em ruínas" *Românica*, no. 12, 2003, pp. 67-86.

Lacoue-Labarthe, Philippe, and Nancy, Jean-Luc. *L'Absolu littéraire. Théorie de la littérature du romantisme allemand*. Paris: Seuil, 1978.

Martins, Fernando Cabral. "Breves notas sobre a alta definição". *Românica*, no. 12, 2003, pp. 157-164.

Medeiros, Paulo de. *O Silêncio das Sereias. Ensaio sobre o Livro do Desassossego*. Lisbon: Tinta-da-China, 2015.

Monteiro, George. *Fernando Pessoa and Nineteenth-Century Anglo-American Literature*. Kentucky: University Press of Kentucky, 2000.

Novalis. *Fragmente und Studien. Die Christenheit oder Europa*. Edited by Carl Paschek. Stuttgart: Philipp Reclam, 1996.

———. *Philosophical Writings*. Translated by Margaret Mahony Stoljar. New York: State University of New York Press, 1997.

Patrício, Rita. *Episódios. Da teorização estética em Fernando Pessoa*. Vila Nova de Famalicão: Edições Húmus, 2012.

Pizarro, Jerónimo. *Pessoa Existe?*. Lisbon: Ática, 2012.

Santos, Irene Ramalho. *Atlantic Poets: Fernando Pessoa's turn in Anglo-American Modernism*. Hanover & London: Dartmouth College – University Press of New England, 2003.

Schlegel, Friedrich. *Friedrich Schlegel's* Lucinde *and the Fragments*. Translated by Peter Firchow. Minneapolis: University of Minnesota Press, 1971.

———. *"Athenaeums"-Fragmente*. Edited by Andreas Huyssen. Stuttgart: Philipp Reclam, 2005.

Sepúlveda, Pedro. *Os livros de Fernando Pessoa*. Lisbon: Ática, 2013.

———. "Orpheu em lugar de Caeiro". *Estranhar Pessoa*, no 2, 2015, pp. 86-109, http://estranharpessoa.com/nmero-2. Accessed June 2020.

———, and Jorge Uribe. *O planeamento editorial de Fernando Pessoa*. Lisbon: Imprensa Nacional-Casa da Moeda, 2016.

———,Ulrike Henny-Krahmer and Jorge Uribe, editors. *Digital Edition of Fernando Pessoa. Projects and Publications*. Lisbon and Cologne: IELT, New University of Lisbon and CCeH, University of Cologne, 2017. http://www.pessoadigital.pt. DOI: 10.18716/cceh/pessoa. Accessed June 2020.

Susini-Anastopolous, Françoise. *L'écriture fragmentaire – définitions et enjeux*. Paris: Presses Universitaires de France, 1997.

PEDRO SEPÚLVEDA is an assistant professor in the Department of Portuguese Studies at the College for Social and Human Sciences, New University of Lisbon (NOVA FCSH) and researcher at the Institute for Studies in Literature and Tradition (IELT) of the same institution. His work centers on literary and philosophical Modernity, with a focus on Fernando Pessoa. He coordinates the research project "Estranhar Pessoa" (http://estranharpessoa.com/) and the digital edition of Pessoa's projects and publications (http://www.pessoadigital.pt/).

JAMES HODGSON

Considering Fetishism in João Pedro Rodrigues's *O Fantasma*

ABSTRACT: This essay considers the depiction of fetishism in João Pedro Rodrigues's 2000 film *O Fantasma*. While its unusual and recondite form reflects fetishistic desire in ways that subvert and challenge conventional narrative structures, its presentation of fetishistic sexuality is also embedded in the material world. Thus, the film can be read as an pessimistic statement about the ability of sexual identity politics to effect broad social change. As such, the essay offers a note of caution to recent queer criticism of lusophone cinema.

KEYWORDS: Gay cinema; sexuality; loners; fetishism; João Pedro Rodrigues; *O Fantasma; portuguese cinema*

RESUMO: Este artigo considera a representação de fetichismo sexual no filme *O Fantasma*, de João Pedro Rodrigues (2000). Embora a forma estranho do filme reflete um desejo fetichista em maneiras que subvertem as estruturas narrativas convencionais, o film coloca sua representação de sexualidade fetichista no mundo material. Neste maneira, o filme pode ser lido como uma declaração pessimista sobre a capacidade de políticas de identidade sexual para afetuar mudança social. Portanto, este artigo contribui com uma nota de cautela para a recente crítica queer do cinema lusófono.

PALAVRAS-CHAVE: Cinema gay; sexualidade; solitários; fetichismo; João Pedro Rodrigues; *O Fantasma*; cinema português

João Pedro Rodrigues's first feature film, *O Fantasma* (2000), is something of a puzzle. Putatively, it is a story about social marginalization as experienced by sexual outsiders. Its protagonist, a garbage collector named Sérgio, transforms over the course of the film from a lonely figure who survives on anonymous sexual encounters into a rubber-suited, doglike outcast who lives in a landfill. Interspersed with short sequences of narrative are vignettes that detail his sexual activity; these range from scenes of simulated sex to explicit sex, an aspect of the film that shocked its early audiences (Mercer 18). Critics were disturbed by and conflicted about the film's content, and scholars remain divided about its interpretation, reading it either as a commentary on the social isolation of gay men writ large or as a showcase for psychological collapse.

The film's major plot points can be summarized as follows. Sérgio works on the streets of Lisbon as a garbage collector and cleaner, mostly at night. One night, during his rounds, he helps a motorcyclist, João, sort through some unwanted clothes. This chance encounter sparks Sérgio's sexual interest, and he begins to acquire elements of João's biker outfit, hoarding them in his apartment and wearing them during episodes of sex and masturbation. Sérgio stalks João, first following him to a swimming pool, then breaking into his house and urinating on his bed. In the final sequence, Sérgio dons a rubber suit, breaks into João's house again, and kidnaps him. But instead of sexually assaulting the captive, he abandons him in the street and hitches a ride to a landfill on the back of a garbage van. Running free amid the trash, he eats spoiled food, chases rabbits, drinks from muddy pools, and defecates in a nearby workshop.

The film resists straightforward interpretation. Some reviewers hold that Sérgio, giving in to obsession, kidnaps João and takes him back to his flophouse bedroom, where he rapes him (Messerli; Rooney 66-68). Others believe that Sérgio kidnaps João but is spooked by a car during the abduction and runs off into the night without raping him (Lee 44; Mercer 18). Identifying this ambiguity, the scholar John Mercer suggests that the film is invested in denying the audience access to the events of its narrative and holding us back from its protagonist and his inner world:

> What is most notable about *O Fantasma* is that rather than a particular effect, the film produces a series of denials. In the cold and unknowable Sérgio we are denied a point of identification or recognition within the text. We are denied words, emotions and the emotive cinematic devices that enable us to make the sequence of events easily legible. This in turn means that we are denied a moral compass to navigate us through this ambiguous narrative and in which to situate our responses. We are denied a narrative resolution as the film ends in a manner where outcomes are uncertain. As a result of this denial, we are finally denied the redemptive consolation of love. This denial is really what the film offers us and is the thematic lynchpin around which the narrative is organised and the protagonist's actions are given motivation. Sérgio's erotomania emerges from, and is fed by, denial. (25)

In Mercer's account, the film both invites and denies access to Sérgio's intimate life as part of a broader comment on the sexual marginalization of homosexual desire and those who experience it. Rodrigues continually elicits our interest in homosexual desire while blocking us from witnessing, experiencing, or consuming fully the world we glimpse. He teases us and leaves us frustrated, replicating in the audience the rejection that Sérgio himself experiences.

The scholar Carolina Cucinotta suggests that costuming choices in the film help to mediate Sérgio's narrative of transformation, which is read in terms of a splitting or doubling selfhood:

> De facto, as coisas complicamse na segunda e última parte do filme, quando parece que Sérgio perde o controlo sobre o seu corpo e, consequentemente, sobre as suas ações. A partir da entrada na piscina (onde, umas cenas antes, Sérgio e João tinham tido um contacto direto, apesar do muito frio), a cena da intrusão em casa de João parecenos uma incessante descida em direção à completa submissão de Sérgio ao Fantasma. (123)

Cucinotta sees Sérgio's narrative largely as a battle between a normal ego and an ultimately successful perverse one. This reading, while intriguing, nonetheless frames Sergio's story in terms of a loss of control, which to some degree strips him of agency (his actions are not his own) and arguably pathologizes his sexual behaviour. While Cucinotta makes a useful connection between the costuming choices in *O Fantasma* and Louis Feuillard's *Les Vampires*, noting the rubber suit's similarity to the Irma Vep's costume, her reading suffers from a tendency to view his fetishistic behavior in pejorative terms (125).

I argue, instead, that the film's unusual and recondite form not only sabotages audience engagement but also reflects fetishistic desire in ways that subvert and challenge conventional narrative structures. The portrait of Sérgio's sexuality is qualified by the substantial attention that Rodrigues pays to the material world. Developing Mercer's comments on the relationship between the film's formal elements and its broader political message, I suggest that what might superficially be understood as Sérgio's total sexual liberation at the end of the film is more convincingly read as his consumption by or dissolution into large-scale social, economic, and material processes. The film therefore gestures toward materiality as a potential blind spot in sexual politics.

Bersanian Fetishism

The depiction of Sérgio's sexual life is clearly the film's major focus. It begins with sex; the majority of the narrative events concern his sexual appetites, habits, and activities; and it ends with a sequence that develops from fetishistic roleplay. Mercer has covered much of the film's content in this regard, with an emphasis on reading Sérgio in terms of gay politics. The film, in Mercer's view, is an effort to communicate gay sexuality to the audience—specifically, the difficulty gay men have when their desire is neither recognized nor accepted by wider society. He suggests that this continual rejection is metaphorized in Sérgio's bizarre obsession with João, which he reads as erotomania (a pathological unrequited love).

While I agree with Mercer's central point regarding the significance of sexuality, I believe that fetishism rather than erotomania better explains Sérgio's behavior—most crucially, when he abandons João entirely. Sigmund Freud's well-known account roots the origin of a fetishist's sexual obsession in a traumatic experience of sexual difference (152–57). The account, which strictly concerns the male fetishist, goes as follows: at some point in early life, the male child who will become a fetishist encounters the fact that his mother lacks a penis. This experience is traumatic, in part because it suggests that the child's own penis might suffer the same fate. To cope, the child denies he ever saw the "fact" of his mother's castration. Instead, he holds to the belief that the maternal phallus must still exist and takes the last item or object he saw before glimpsing his mother's lacking genitalia as an impression or memory of a world "in which the woman could still be regarded as phallic." This object becomes the basis of the adult's fetish. In fetishism, however, this denial is not the end of the story, for Freud notes that the child also paradoxically accepts that castration took place. To maintain belief in the maternal phallus alongside the experiential evidence of maternal lack, the child splits his own ego.[1] In part, then, he retroactively imagines the last object he saw immediately before the traumatic site as evidence that the maternal phallus did exist. Over time, the object, whether feet, hair, or an undergarment, becomes imbued doubly with thrilling promise (as it recalls or substitutes for the longed-for maternal phallus) and castration anxiety (because it indicates the "reality" of castration) (156).

Sérgio's sexual activity displays some of the basic fetishistic hallmarks insofar as additional objects are indeed used to supplement or accompany sexual arousal, intercourse, and masturbation. For instance, in the image of sexual activity that opens the film, Sérgio's rubber suit could be taken as the fetish that enables, or at least heightens, his sexual satisfaction. Here I turn to Leo Bersani and Ulysse Dutoit, who argue, in *The Forms of Violence: Narrative in Assyrian Art and Modern Culture*, that fetishism should be viewed in broader terms. They read it as a sexual structure that stems from a dramatic alteration to the normative story of heterosexual development. Normally, as it were, the child takes the sight of the mother's genitals, and the concomitant experience of castration anxiety, as the start of his initiation into a process of repression and identification (the well-known Oedipus complex). The child accepts that the mother does not have a penis; desire for the mother is repressed to avoid similarly punitive action that the father might mete out on the child. In fetishism, Bersani and Dutoit suggest, the child is so traumatized by the sight of the maternal genitalia that his desire is not repressed but fully "detached" or "cut off" from the normal narrative of sexual development. Instead, it swerves or moves on to objects that are not typically invested with desire. "There can be something ridiculously inappropriate in the fetishist's choice of an object. He works, as it were, with whatever is at hand, with the nearest or most accessible thing.... It is, in a sense, a model of desire detaching itself from one image [maternal genitalia/castration] and moving on to other images" (69). Intriguingly, they suggest, fetishism seems to repeat and transform the imagined act of maternal castration into a liberating gesture: "Freud speaks of the fetishist's detachment from any interest in the woman's genitals, and of his displacing that interest onto another object. But this very denial of castration could be taken as a sublimated enactment of it. Desire is 'cut off' from its object and travels to other objects" (69).

Bersani and Dutoit argue that despite the foregrounding of fixation and obsession in fetishism's origin story, Freud's account also points to desire's fundamental mobility: rather than slavishly follow the pathways through which desire is normally channeled, the child is able to tear libidinal investment away from the mother's genitalia and transfer it to other objects. Even though the fetishist is briefly liberated from heterosexual development, only to find his desire fixed even more forcefully onto the fetish itself, this desiring mobility reappears again and again: "For the resolute effort to satisfy the single-minded wish to possess a phallic mother helps to move the child away from the mother, to derange his system of desiring by the absurd, even laughable objects designed to replace the missing phallus" (69). The fetishist starts off with a disturbance to his "system of desiring," which, while not quite a liberated or revolutionary state of being, nonetheless implies the possibility of resisting conventional desiring patterns in some way. Bersani and Dutoit note another advantage to fetishism: a derealization of the object of desire. Unlike the heterosexual male, who in Freud's account of sexuality unconsciously believes that his female sexual partners are objects possessing qualities that will complete him in some way, the fetishist implicitly recognizes the objects of his desire as fantasy objects. He knows that the fetish is not the maternal phallus, even as he imbues it with desire as if it were the maternal phallus. He ambiguously knows, yet refuses to know. Bersani and Dutoit conclude that, rather than desire centered on the phallus (which would presumably manifest as social behavior that promotes the competition for and possession of women), fetishism contains the potential for desire centered on the discovery of "new surfaces": objects that lie outside normative or phallocentric frameworks (72). Their work also suggests that the fetishist bears a certain reflexive capacity or critical distance from the pursuit of his object of desire insofar as he can recognize that whatever it is he pursues will not really complete him, or truly satisfy his wants. While far from revolutionary, fetishism is argued to contain the seeds of a liberatory, agentic approach to the objects in which desire is invested.

These comments shed light on a number of the ambiguous elements in *O Fantasma*. First, the emphasis that Bersani and Dutoit place on the fetishist's object choice as "ridiculously inappropriate" helps us make sense of the prominence of rubbish in Sérgio's sexual activity, which typically focuses on João's discarded clothing (gloves, motorcycle jacket, swim trunks). The fetishist "swerves" or turns away from objects (the genitals) that are normatively desirable and instead invests his desire in objects that are neither desired nor suitable for the investment of desire. What better figure than rubbish, which, by definition, encompasses objects that are no longer interesting or appropriate for desire? João's rubbish, highly inappropriate as an object of erotic attention, becomes Sérgio's chosen fetish. This, in turn, helps us understand why the landfill is given prominence in the film (beyond its startling aesthetic value). As a repository of unwanted objects, the landfill is full of things no longer normatively desirable but potentially available for the fetishist's investment. Given his willingness to scour full bins for things to masturbate with, to collect and reuse as part of sexual play, Sérgio might well see the landfill as a potential fetishistic paradise. Of course, most of his fetish objects once belonged to João, which arguably provides them with a good deal of their erotic significance. But it is worth pointing out that Sérgio turns away from João near the end of the film (as if João no longer obsesses his interest or organizes his desire in the same way) yet nonetheless escalates his fetishistic roleplay by beginning a new life in a landfill surrounded by trash. Here, the strange alien landscape into which he essentially dissolves himself echoes the "new surfaces," which I interpret as referring to novel, unconventional objects of desire. One might read the end of the film as an unconventional moment of sexual liberation or the exercising of sexual agency, given the basic premises of Bersani and Dutoit's model. This leads us to consider if the film works from a queer political perspective.[2] Are the sexual norms of life on the margins of the city so stifling that Sérgio must rebel against them to fully articulate his sexuality? Insofar as it constitutes a rejection of an oppressive social order, leaving his life behind for immersion in the landfill would be a rebellious and politically important move. It also leads us to consider if Sérgio's more general commitment to the expression of a transgressive, fetishistic, and "inappropriate" sexuality also politically radical. Is Sérgio a queer hero? I will explore these questions later in this essay. Certainly, however, Bersani and Dutoit's thesis helps us understand that Sérgio's impulse to run off to a landfill is consistent with his behavior earlier in the film.

Bersani and Dutoit's ideas about the reflexive potential of a fetishistic swerve can help us make sense of significant parts of the film's narrative structure. The film derives narrative tension from Sérgio's growing obsession with João and invites us to read his behavior in terms of a progressive escalation of activity. We presume the narrative climax will involve sexual assault, or even murder, which we understandably anticipate when Sérgio kidnaps João. But this does not come to pass. João's death or rape is avoided when Sérgio breaks off his kidnapping efforts and leaves his victim by the side of the road (disposing of him like waste). Sérgio's decision to break off here is startling: it takes place without much explanation and surely leaves the audience baffled. Certainly, were we to follow Mercer's thesis on erotomania, this sudden turning away from the beloved object becomes a thorny issue. However, it is possible to draw a parallel between João's sexualized destruction at Sérgio's hands and the knowledge of the mother's castration in the fetishist's narrative, as both are violent climaxes framed as narrative conclusions. Like the child, Sérgio approaches a climactic moment of violence but then dramatically swerves away from it toward other objects of desire. The film suggests, at the very least, that Sérgio does not simply follow his desires out to their conclusion but exercises a degree of agency in relation to them. He breaks from a seemingly inevitable and predetermined narrative course. Here, his swerve could be read as narrative violence performed to diffuse or block the possibility of real violence that would otherwise appear to be the probable narrative climax. In Bersani's terms, it is a "sublimating enactment" of castration of a similar kind to that occurring in the fetishist's origin story itself. By turning away from a violent climax and toward a new life in a landfill, Sérgio interrupts a desiring connection made with another person for desiring connections made with more "ridiculously inappropriate" objects (rubbish).

The swerve could even be read as demonstrating what Bersani and Dutoit call the "profit" of fetishism: despite the intensity of the fetishist's fixation on the object, he nonetheless recognizes it as a mere fantasy object and so, theoretically, obtains a degree of distance from or disenchantment with it and, in a broader sense, gains some choice over his own desires. Sérgio has a change of heart, as Mercer mentions, but one that is most likely afforded by fetishism rather than erotomania, as it parallels the "change of heart" (the swerve away from the maternal genitalia) that is central to fetishism's etiology. A Bersanian model of fetishism therefore suggests that Sérgio, obsessed with bizarre material objects, nonetheless implicitly retains some degree of agency over his own desire.

Sexuality in a Material Context

Fetishism is a form of sexuality explicitly entangled with material objects. Likewise, Sérgio's sexual expression is consistently and often literally bound to, articulated through, and supported by specific material objects: from auto-asphyxiation with a shower hose, to masturbating with João's old gloves, to wearing João's swimming costume. But the material world shapes his sexuality, and the film more broadly, in other ways. For example, Sérgio's job as a garbage collector determines a large part of *O Fantasma*. It is the pretext for his encounter with João and gives him an excuse to initiate their first interaction. (When João points out some items that need to be taken to the landfill, he and Sérgio discuss João's motorbike.) The garbage collectors are shown examining the unwanted objects they take away, which gives Sérgio cover for playing around with and then keeping João's possessions. Sérgio's job also serves as a metaphor for his sex life: his nighttime cruising parallels the tasks carried out by the trash collectors, who work unnoticed before the populace has woken and after they have gone to bed. Homosexuality and garbage collecting are nocturnal activities, excluded to the fringes of society and removed from daily life.

Homosexuality was effectively decriminalized in Portugal in 1982; yet at the time the film was released, expressions of homosexuality were still discouraged in public life (de Oliveira et al. 1479). As such, Sérgio's consignment to the shadows echoes a broader, pervasive cultural sentiment. The metaphorical association between rubbish collecting and sex also sites both activities at the bottom of their respective hierarchies: unskilled menial labor and fetishistic or anonymous sex lack respect or value according to dominant social conventions (which privilege professional labor and reproductive heterosexual sex, respectively). In the film, the comparison is often signaled in simple visual language. For example, Sérgio is shown leaving his apartment as a cleaner vacuums in the midground, similarly alone, similarly engaged in clearing the waste of everyday life. Moments later, Sérgio himself is shown sweeping leaves, repeating in a near-identical fashion the cleaner's movements. This reminds us that, for all his sexual quirks, Sérgio is also a menial laborer, low paid and of low social status, and must contend with intersecting disadvantages of economic class and sexual identity. He is isolated but nonetheless shares commonalities with other marginalized individuals.

Class and economic standing affect the kind of sex he can have, where he has it, and his safety. This point has often been neglected in queer scholarship. According to John Binnie, the foundational queer theories developed in the earlies 1990s paid too much attention to meanings in texts and not enough to the production of goods and services, markets and capital accumulation (169). He argues that these latter material features are just as significant, if not more so, for gay and lesbian people in the West: "It must still be stressed that money is the major prerequisite and the greatest boundary for the construction of autonomous, independent assertive gay male subjectivities" (166). Likewise, Mariam Fraser suggests that sexual-identity politics has struggled to incorporate demands for economic justice because it emphasizes recognition and representation over redistribution (121). Elizabeth McDermott points out that while some lesbian women and gay men have secured relative "liberation," the persistent blindness to class in LGBTQ politics means that many have been left behind (66). Living on the margins of society, Sérgio could easily fall into this category. The emphasis that *O Fantasma* places on his material circumstances and his relative impoverishment gestures toward the need for a politics of sexuality to recognize the impact of class. That said, Antonio M. da Silva has argued that Rodrigues's cinema typically associates its characters with abject or marginal areas of urban space, both to indicate their abject social status (as "social pollution") and to show how they resist and challenge the normative frames that manage sexual and gender identity (75). Thus, although Sérgio inhabits the margins in an economic sense, he is able to exercise some agency as he traces his geography out on the nocturnal streets of Lisbon. In da Silva's argument, *O Fantasma* is to some degree about the capacity of those excluded or outcast from society to reclaim space, to carve out their own sexual existence, and to live life on their own terms. Clues in cinematic language, however, suggest that Sérgio's sexual activity is shaped, even restrained, by the physical, material world around him. In a short vignette midway through the film, he is shown having sex with an anonymous man in the street. The shot is striated by the strong geometric lines of the gate that Sérgio grasps for support. Because Sérgio has sex *a tergo* and the shot is poorly lit, it is difficult, but not impossible, to distinguish which arms belong to which man. His partner's face lies just out of focus, so we only see Sérgio's face, his gaze lowered from the camera. Finally, the bars of the gate are organized in pairs, and this, combined with the fact both men grasp the gate, gives the shot a strange repetitive quality, as if the scene were being viewed through a prism. This lyrical cinematic language could indicate a confusion of identity or loss of self experienced by Sérgio during intense sexual intimacy. The scene stresses the visual parallels between the two men, the pairs of arms, and the bars. More striking is the sense that the material world frames Sérgio, even captures him, restricting or at least defining the sex he has. In other words, although the urban landscape furnishes him with opportunities for sexual encounters, cinematic language suggests that it also determines what those encounters look like and that his sexual agency is restricted or limited.

Camera work prioritizes the material world in a number of ways. Often this is straightforward, when the camera fixes on objects over characters. At points Rodrigues foregrounds colorful laundry and shifts the camera focus to relegate the actors to the background; at others, sweeps of concrete subsume the actors; at still others, Sérgio's camouflaged surveillance affords the director an opportunity to present complex arrangements of trees, window frames, actors, and props that work across fore-, mid- and background. One consequence of this focus is that interesting visual correspondences are occasionally made between Sérgio and the material world. About a third of the way through the film, for instance, Sérgio is shown naked after having had sex with an anonymous partner. He leaves the man's apartment by the window, which gives Rodrigues an opportunity to draw our attention toward the visual similarity between Sérgio's set-apart naked legs and the columns of the balcony on which he stands.

Figure 1. Sérgio meets a stranger for sex. © Rosa Filmes.

Here, the erotic or titillating value of the scene—a naked male body—is somewhat offset by aesthetic similarities that emphasize equivalence between Sérgio and elements of architecture. While Sérgio is presented as an object for our contemplation he also seems to subtly flatten into the scenery, which garnishes the shot's erotic charge with a sense of his embeddedness in the world around him. The visual arrangement objectifies Sérgio. It also locates him as merely one object of contemplation among many. The film could even be read as asking audience members to reflexively acknowledge their own role in his sexual objectification. Whatever the matter, erotic contemplation of bodies and aesthetic contemplation of scenery become briefly indistinguishable. Sérgio is not simply imprisoned by the material world but fundamentally part of it, fetishized as an object among objects.

The camera's insistence on the importance of materiality does not just displace or estrange the actors. It disrupts the narrative as well. When the film begins, Sérgio is shown having sex in a rubber suit as a dog barks and whines outside a locked bedroom door. Then we are shown some title credits and a shot of Sérgio working his shift as a dustman. Following this, we see him playing with his dog, Lorde, before he is surprised by a colleague, Fatima. All of this takes place in the film's first few minutes, and up to this point the picture feels relatively realistic. The interaction between Sérgio and Fatima that follows, however, is acutely strange and theatrical. Fatima covers Sérgio's eyes and asks him to

Figure 2. Sérgio spies on João as he watches a movie. © Rosa Filmes.

Figure 3. Sérgio's body mimics the world around him. © Rosa Filmes.

guess her identity; when he responds angrily, she kicks him, and he remains on the floor whining like a dog.

As the acting shifts from lifelike to stylized, both Fatima's violence and Sérgio's doglike submissiveness seem inexplicable. The lack of narrative clues, either in dialogue or in prior material, means that viewers looking for narrative orientation will no doubt respond with bafflement, feeling the "denial" of explanation or grounding

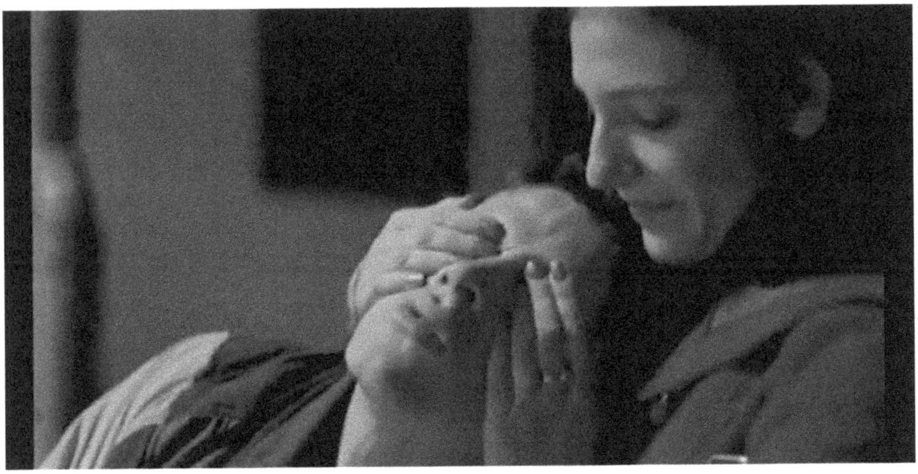

Figure 4. Fatima makes Sérgio guess her identity. © Rosa Filmes

that Mercer discusses. Insofar as this sequence disorients the viewer and disrupts our suspension of disbelief (or prohibits its formation), the staginess could be read in terms of a Brechtian Verfremdungseffekte, or V-effect: that is, a way of preventing the audience from engaging with the film as a piece of entertainment through the encouragement of reflexive viewing practices. Of course, the film has only just begun at this point and has not had a chance to develop any particular political scenario or make specific political insights available to the viewer.[3] What may become more obvious to an audience ejected temporarily from the narrative is the repetition in Sérgio's behavior of elements from the prior scene. We notice how strangely he echoes the submissive behaviour of his sexual partner and how he repeats the whining of the dog trapped outside the bedroom. What Mercer sees as narrative denial could also be understood as the seemingly senseless foregrounding of aesthetic elements: repetition of form over plot development. In other words, the film parallels fetishistic psychic structure. It turns us away from narrative progression and toward its own materiality. Like the proto-fetishist child in Bersani and Dutoit's reading, the audience swerves away from the story's expected course (where narrative sense would be found) toward inappropriate (senseless) objects of apprehension. Following this line of interpretation, the unreal or unnatural shock of Sérgio's doglike mimicry could be seen as an equivalent stimulus to the traumatic sight of the mother's genitals: a moment that interrupts the regular flow of our engagement and redirects our attention to other elements of film composition (its matter).

Figure 5. The screen is dominated by stark lines. © Rosa Filmes.

Narrative progression is foiled in similar ways later in the movie. When walking his dog, Sérgio encounters a police car with a policeman handcuffed in the back; Sérgio opens the door and hesitantly engages in oral sex with him. This is strange because we are given no explanation for the policeman's bound state (we might imagine that it somehow forms part of his own erotic game) or any indication that Sérgio's attention has been invited. Nonetheless, it does not disturb narrative realism as immediately as a later scene does, an episode for which it arguably lays the ground. About two-thirds of the way through the film, Sérgio breaks into João's house and, as he is about to leave, is arrested by the same policeman. Rather than Sérgio ending up in a police station, as we might expect, the arrest turns into an erotic scenario. Here, the audience is diverted from the story twice, first by the commencement of a sexualized interaction, then by the mise-en-scène. Sérgio leans back against a tree while the policeman stands opposite to the trunk on the other side of the frame. This visual composition is crisscrossed by another tree trunk in the midground and the arm and baton of the policeman, both forming strong geometrical complements that divide the frame at forty-five-degree angles.

Not only is the eye distracted by the strong formal components of the shot, but we cannot help but connect this sequence to Sérgio's first encounter with the policeman and view it as both a repetition (an unexpected sexual encounter in which Sérgio is the receptive partner in an act of oral sex) and a reversal (now the policeman is in control while Sérgio wears handcuffs). The film's narrative, a plot about breaking and entering, is interrupted before it comes to its conclusion. We are diverted toward a seemingly ill-fitting erotic scenario in which the viewer's attention is partly taken up by an unlikely sex scene and partly by the formal composition of the shot itself. The erotic relationship seems to be dominated by or subsumed within the aesthetic composition of the shot; the baton of the policeman closely parallels the tree trunk as if the policeman is deliberately posed to produce a sense of visual symmetry for the viewer. Again, a swerve comparable to the swerve in fetishism operates at the level of film form: the viewer swerves away from narrative resolution toward the contemplation of objects (fetish gear, handcuffs, leather, rubber) and the material components of the film.

As these examples demonstrate, sexuality is shown to be embedded in differing material contexts throughout the film. More precisely, these examples show how materiality shapes, stalls, restrains, interrupts, and enables the articulation of sexuality and eroticism. The film makes a consistent effort to show how Sérgio's rebellion is bounded by a broader context. Conversely, the repetition of a fetishistic swerve at a number of key points suggests that Bersani and Dutoit's insights are useful for capturing the film's entanglement of sexuality with the material world.

The Final Sequence: Limitations on Rebellion

O Fantasma's bizarre, lyrical, and dreamlike final sequence brings together the major themes I have outlined: fetishistic sexual activity and an effort to present Sérgio as situated in the material world. This sequence might be read as a rebellious moment for Sérgio, an articulation of his agency, when he breaks free from an oppressive society. However, I see this rebellion as limited. By combining his flourishing sexual exploration with visual evidence of his extreme physical precarity, the film makes a more general comment on the diminished capacity for transgressive and affirmatory gestures of sexuality to affect the status quo. As I have suggested, the final sequence might be initially read as a disconcerting but triumphant moment for Sérgio, as he rejects the society that rejects him and begins a new life outside of its rules. It is worth exploring exactly what sort of triumph this is. When Sérgio abandons João halfway through his kidnapping, he returns the rejection he has suffered throughout the film, becoming the abandoner and—in a way—reclaiming some agency. His subsequent transformation might seem, therefore, to be personally empowering. He casts off social expectations, norms, morality, and relationships for an isolated but ultimately more liberated life. There are obvious parallels with conventional narratives around coming out and sexual self-discovery that frequently form part of a key story about western gay identity (Plummer 2002), although the persistent use of the rubber suit seems indicative of a deeper transformation. We might be inclined to read Sérgio as a queer figure, one whose sexuality critiques, challenges, or rejects the social rules around sexual identity, who stands outside of the norms that control and manage sexuality more broadly (Warner; Bersani, *Homos*).

Sérgio resists interpretation. Is he playing or serious? Is he sane or mad? Is this change temporary or permanent? Is he still human or psychologically beastlike, as some critics have wondered? We are unable to tell for sure. He seems to take the pursuit of a rabbit seriously, for example, as if he really thinks he is a predator chasing prey, but then does not deliver the killing blow and looks at the animal in confusion. Likewise, he seems committed to wearing the rubber suit and gimp mask but later removes the mask. (Does he remove it for reasons of comfort? Why not remove the suit itself? Why not return home?) The uncertainty of his intention (his desire) could occupy the audience's thoughts as the film closes. Bersani and Dutoit's account of fetishism helps explain the ambiguity that surrounds him. The fetishist is beset by ambivalence: he looked away from the mother's genitalia "too quickly": "Having both seen and not seen, he will insist that he saw what he did not see [a maternal phallus] and yet also insist that he saw what he in fact did see [the actual maternal genitalia]. And all this troubled seeing will go on elsewhere—with an irrelevant object perhaps there and not there, perhaps a phallus and perhaps a knee or a piece of fur" (71). This ambivalence of desire depriviliges the phallus, and so long as the fetishist is able to continually seek out new surfaces for his desire, he could be thought of as a "hero of uncertain desire, of undecideability" (71). After Sérgio abandons João, his motivations and desires become seemingly impenetrable, and as such the Bersanian interpretation holds true here. At the very least, as Mercer points out, the audience has to make sense of his actions with very little guidance, and they could plausibly be understood in a number of ways: as part of elaborate fetish play; as evidence of a wish to become closer in form to the trash or to the dogs on the margins of Lisbon; as the embodiment or emblem of the abject social position held by sexual minorities; as a dramatic rejection of the norms around self-presentation; as the uncertain, non-phallic Bersanian fetishist whose unwillingness to compromise his sexual expression defies prescribed cultural imperatives to know himself and rejects the identitarian demand for sexual and psychic intelligibility.

Figure 6. Sérgio disappears into the landfill. © Rosa Filmes.

O Fantasma is not simply concerned with depicting a sexual outlaw, and any argument about the political and strategic validity of Sérgio as a queer or transgressive subject must be qualified by the film's persistent, cross-cutting, thematic interest in material culture. Representations of desire are consistently located in materiality, whether in a literal sense (the fetish object that snares, focuses, and amplifies Sérgio's sexual desire) or in terms of film form (in which the narrative progression is briefly suspended when the film signals its own constructedness). This is no different as the film comes to a close. It is obvious that Sérgio's capers have made him exceptionally vulnerable. While playacting as a dog, he eats spoiled food and becomes sick, which reminds the audience of his bodily vulnerability just as it reminds us that he has human needs (including hunger and health), despite his dehumanized and objectified appearance. Moreover, he is swallowed up by the landfill site.

The film's use of cinematography might lead us to read this as a subversive transgression of social and cultural norms, but it just as easily and perhaps more convincingly provides stark visual evidence of straightforward material impoverishment. For all of Sérgio's rejection of convention, he becomes as disposable as trash. His sexual particularity is located within a material, social, and political system, the material fact of which is shown to engulf him. In this sense, the film embeds life-changing ideas about sexual liberation and self-realization into an indifferent context. To some degree, the pessimism displayed here approaches

Bersani's thoughts on sexual-identity politics, which consider true social change possible only when the underlying affective and relational systems on which social life is built are disturbed or transformed in some way. He is famously critical of efforts to legalize gay marriage, for example (*Is the rectum a grave? And other essays* 85–86), which he takes to be a consolidation of an oppressive sexual and relational status quo. Elsewhere, he argues that, without radically dismantling the hierarchies built into our erotic relationships, "all revolutionary activity will return, as we have seen it return over and over again, to relations of ownership and dominance" (128). Bersani often relies on queer "heroes" of undecidability to illustrate his political visions, the fetishist being a case in point. This has led to criticisms of his work as overvaluing, in Jack Halberstam's words, the potential of "new social forms that supposedly emerge from gay male orgies or cruising escapades or gender-queer erotics or sodomitic sadism or at any rate queer jouissance of some form or another" and as being problematically masculinist, inaccessible, and exclusive (149–50). Some critics have included Bersani alongside other queer theorists who champion transgressive sexual imaginaries but downplay or ignore broader social structures, constraints, and contexts. Steven Seidman puts this point succinctly: "Underlying [queer] politics of subversion is a vague notion that this will encourage new, affirmative forms of personal and social life, although poststructuralists are reluctant to name their social vision.... Insofar as discursive practices are not institutionally situated, there is an edging toward textual idealism" (132).

Of course, neither the film nor Rodrigues ever uses the word *queer*. But with its focus on a rebellious, ambiguous sexual outsider, *O Fantasma* evokes the atmosphere of the debates around the transgressive potential (or not) of sexual expression and sexual freedom. In that light the film could be seen as working to correct the idealism that Seidman identifies in queer politics through its final emphasis on the staggering force of large-scale social, material, and economic processes. As I have argued, the use of Brechtian shock effects consistently reminds us of the matter that makes up the film: its formal composition. In this sense *O Fantasma* works hard to emphasize the significance of the world in which Sérgio moves. But when it essentially dissolves its rebellious sexual "hero" into the overwhelming vistas of a manmade landscape, the film could be taken as alerting us to the fact that the material, social, and economic forces shaping our lives may well be beyond one individual's capacity to affect, no matter how radical, daring, ambiguous, or transgressive we are. This reading has a final implication: on our own, camouflage and assimilation are all we can do, but *O Fantasma*'s pessimism could also function as a redirection (perhaps even a fetishistic swerve) away from the individual toward the importance of a collective response to the problems of contemporary life.

O Fantasma tells two stories about Sérgio: one about his sexual particularity (fetishism), one about the significance of the material context to his life (in the sense of place, economic position, and material precarity). In doing so, the film raises questions about the feasibility of the former to affect and shape the latter. Indeed, the overall impression left by the film is that, despite Sérgio's embrace of his sexuality, the material context is a significant limitation that restricts the possibilities for desiring fantasy, shapes the fantasies he has, and remains unaffected by the most outré gesture of sexual rebellion he can muster. In that sense, *O Fantasma* is a pessimistic film. This is not because of Sérgio's loneliness or the persistence of homophobia. Rather, the film's pessimism derives from his disappearance into the alien landscapes of its final sequence: the enormity of social and political processes represented by the landfill (including globalized, waste-producing, consumer capitalism) seem to swallow up and render moot any efforts to rebel against it. The film's effort to return Sérgio's sexuality to a material context should leave us skeptical both of affirmatory sexual politics, represented by lesbian and gay identity movements, and of the transgressive queer models that followed.

Some general lines for further study are opened up by this paper. First, the connection between same-sex desire and fetishism reoccurs in Rodrigues's work, notably in his 2016 film *O Ornitologo*, which features striking examples of Shibari rope play and urolagnia. A comparative study that assesses his wider corpus for consistencies and variations on fetishism would be important for grappling with how the theme figures in his work more broadly. Second, this essay points to the need for scholarship on the complex entanglement of sex and material culture—in particular, the sense of the limitations of sexuality in contemporary lusophone cinema. Given the uneven but nonetheless dramatic changes in the social acceptance of homosexuality in western countries, it is clear that studies exploring the situatedness of lesbian, bisexual, and gay desires in specific geographical and material contexts will continue to provide necessary, novel insights.

NOTES

1. In this sense the denial is not truly a psychotic denial (whereby the child would totally reject the possibility of castration) or a neurotic repression (whereby the "fact" of castration would be rejected from consciousness but accepted into the unconscious), but something in between. As Freud writes, "He has retained that belief, but he has also given it up. In the conflict between the weight of the unwelcome perception and the force of his counter-wish, a compromise has been reached" (Freud 154).

2. Here I take queer to indicate a perspective or critique that aims to expose and deconstruct norms, values, and beliefs that uphold the privileged position of heterosexuality in contemporary discourse and culture (also known as heterosexism or heteronormativity). See Jagose for an overview of *queer* in this context (Jagose 3).

3. See Johnson for a number of examples in which the V-effect is successfully used in cinema to reveal a political critique (97).

WORKS CITED

Bersani, Leo. *Homos*. Harvard University Press, 1995.

———. *Is the rectum a grave? And other essays*. University of Chicago Press, 2009.

Bersani, Leo, and Ulysse Dutoit. *The Forms of Violence: Narrative in Assyrian Art and Modern Culture*. Schocken, 1985.

Binnie, Jon. "Trading Places: Consumption, Sexuality and the Production of Queer Space." *Mapping Desire: Geographies of Sexualities*, 1995, pp. 182–99.

Cucinotta, Caterina. "Origens Possíveis e Consequentes Desenvolvimentos Contemporâneos Da Longa-metragem O Fantasma, de João Pedro Rodrigues." *GerAção Invisível*, p. 105.

da Silva, Antônio M. "The Portuguese Queer Screen: Gender Possibilities in João Pedro Rodrigues's Cinematic Production." *Rupkatha Journal on Interdisciplinary Studies in Humanities*, vol. 6, no. 1, 2014, pp. 69–78.

da Silva, Simone Cavalcante. "The Space of Queer Masculinities in Karim Aïnouz's Praia Do Futuro." *Space and Subjectivity in Contemporary Brazilian Cinema*, Springer, 2017, pp. 169–83.

de Oliveira, João Manuel, et al. "The Workings of Homonormativity: Lesbian, Gay, Bisexual, and Queer Discourses on Discrimination and Public Displays of Affections in Portugal." *Journal of Homosexuality*, vol. 60, no. 10, 2013, pp. 1475–93.

Duggan, Lisa. "The New Homonormativity: The Sexual Politics of Neoliberalism." *Materializing Democracy: Toward a Revitalized Cultural Politics*, 2002, pp. 175–94.

Fraser, Mariam. "Classing Queer: Politics in Competition." *Theory, Culture & Society*, vol. 16, no. 2, 1999, pp. 107–31.

Freud, Sigmund, and James Ed Strachey. *The Standard Edition of the Complete Psychological Works of Sigmund Freud*. 1964.

Halberstam, Jack. *The Queer Art of Failure*. Duke University Press, 2011.

Hodgson, James. "Possibilities for Queer Revolution in Glauber Rocha's Barravento/ The Turning Wind (1962)." *Studies in Spanish & Latin American Cinemas*, vol. 15, no. 1, 2018, pp. 25–43.

———. "Selfish Mysticism, Queer Utopias: 'Homo-Ness' in Carlos Hugo Christensen's O Menino Eo Vento." *Journal of Lusophone Studies*, vol. 4, no. 1, 2019.

———. "'Você quase ganhou um orquídea viva!': Dissimulação queer e desejo homossocial em Os Cafajestes de Ruy Guerra." *Via Atlântica*, no. 33, 2018.

Jagose, Annamarie. *Queer Theory: An Introduction*. NYU Press, 1996.

Johnson, Randal. *Cinema Novo x 5: Masters of Contemporary Brazilian Film*. Vol. 60, University of Texas Press, 1984.

Lee, Nathan. "Mysterious Skin: João Pedro Rodrigues's Cinema of Carnal Transcendence". *Film Comment*, Jul. 2006: 42–44. Print.

McDermott, Elizabeth. "The World Some Have Won: Sexuality, Class and Inequality." *Sexualities*, vol. 14, no. 1, 2011, pp. 63–78.

Messerli, Douglas. "João Pedro Rodrigues: O Fantasma, Dark Pleasure." Rev. of *O Fantasma*, dir. by João Pedro Rodrigues. *World Cinema Review*, Nov. 2017. Web. 3 Jul. 2018. http://internationalcinemareview.blogspot.com/2017/11/joao-pedro-rodrigues-o-fantasma.html.

Mulvey, Laura. "Visual Pleasure and Narrative Cinema." *Visual and Other Pleasures*, Springer, 1989, pp. 14–26.

Penney, James. *After Queer Theory*. Pluto Press, 2014.

Plummer, Ken. Telling Sexual Stories: Power, Change and Social Worlds. Routledge, 2002.

Puar, Jasbir K. *Terrorist Assemblages: Homonationalism in Queer Times*. Duke University Press, 2017.

Seidman, Steven. *Queer Theory/Sociology*. 1996.

Subero, Gus. *Queer Masculinities in Latin American Cinema: Male Bodies and Narrative Representations*. IB Tauris, 2013.

Warner, Michael. *Fear of a Queer Planet: Queer Politics and Social Theory*. Vol. 6, U of Minnesota Press, 1993.

JAMES HODGSON is an early career postdoctoral researcher based at the University of Manchester, working on sexuality, relationships and personal life. He has published on same-sex relationships in lusophone cinema and has a growing research interest in states of 'being alone' - from loners, loneliness, me-time or alone-time, to solitude and voluntary social isolation.

On José Saramago and Andrea Mantegna

For José Saramago, the Italian painter Andrea Mantegna was clearly a kindred soul. Both began their lives in circumstances as far removed as possible from the "fine" arts of writing and painting, Mantegna as a shepherd, Saramago on a small farm. Neither ever lost that primordial sympathy with nature, however sophisticated their work became, and neither harbored any illusions about humanity after seeing so many sides, so many levels, of human society.

Saramago immediately denies any claim to expertise about Mantegna; he ventures to speak to an audience at the Museo del Prado, he protests, "not with the authority that I lack, but, if such a word is appropriate here, with the abundant love that I have." It is a love built on the purest empathy, and empathy is clearly what compels Saramago to seek out the man as well as his work. As another great painter, Paolo Veronese, told the Venetian Inquisition in 1572, there is a "certain license" granted to madmen, painters, and poets. That same license allows Saramago to venture where professional scholars fear to tread, to try to fathom what made Mantegna see the world so differently from anyone before him. He speaks poignantly about the fatherly relationship that first bound Mantegna to his master Squarcione, turned sour when they both realized the vast gulf between their talents. Squarcione's parting shot, first recorded by the artist-biographer Giorgio Vasari, is infinitely telling:

> "His figures always have the hardness of stones and never the tender suppleness and softness that flesh and natural things have. He would have done better if he had painted marbles."

Mantegna, the self-made man, gave his figures, all of them, the dignity of antique statues, rebelling against the graceful Gothic lines of courtly predecessors like Pisanello, the supreme master of Squarcione's generation, whose knights and ladies gracefully dispose themselves on lush greenswards with perfect manners. Only Pisanello could have cast a medallion of Cupid teaching a lion to sing, reading from a musical score. Pisanello's world was one where chivalry still throve and Arthur was still king of Camelot, but Mantegna, the former shepherd, lived among the stern herdsmen who built ancient Rome. His figures look like statues because they hark directly back to Romulus, Tanaquil, Cloelia, Cincinnatus, citizens of an ancient world that venerated republican virtues rather than the elaborate conventions of courtly life. It is no accident that the least successful of his paintings is *Parnassus*, the allegory he painted for the arch-aristocrat Isabella d'Este as she breathed down his neck.

Saramago concentrates on the grievously damaged chapel that Mantegna painted between 1448 and 1457 for the Paduan notary's widow Imperatrice Ovetari, whose name, "Empress," bespeaks the spirit of an age that had begun to discern dignity in all human beings. The mid-fifteenth century in Italy was an era when girls, and not only aristocrats but also merchant girls, were given exultant names like Splendida, or queenly classical names like Sofonisba, rather than religious horrors like Humiliana or Crocefissa. Imperatrice Ovetari was rich rather than noble, but she felt like an empress nonetheless: she eventually sued Mantegna for painting only eight apostles in her stunning chapel rather than twelve, and lost the case because the magistrates agreed that there was no room to include them in Mantegna's majestic scheme, one of the greatest painting cycles of any century, in any place. Saramago shows his novelist's insight by rejoicing in the fact that humanity devised photography before inventing airborne bombs, so that some record survived of the Ovetari Chapel's frescoes before the Allies destroyed them in 1944, aiming, badly, for the train station. Mantegna's artistic weaponry makes no such mistakes: famously, one of the chapel's images shows an incident from the life of St. Christopher in which the King of Samos, who has ordered his archers to dispatch the saint, receives a deflected arrow in his own eye. That arrow in the eye has long been understood as Mantegna's symbol for the power of perspective. But Saramago attributes to this stern man of the people a still more sovereign power, recalled when he visited the ruined Chapel at the same time as the elderly English couple. Perhaps, Saramago muses, the courteous old man was once part of the RAF squadron that nearly obliterated Mantegna's masterwork, drawn back to repent by the tameless compassion of art. Mario Pereira's translation has captured both the delicacy of Saramago's vision and its steely core.

INGRID D. ROWLAND is a Professor of History, Classics, and Architecture at the University of Notre Dame's Rome Global Gateway. Her latest books are *The Collector of Lives: Giorgio Vasari and the Invention of Art*, cowritten with Noah Charney, and *The Divine Spark of Syracuse*. She is a regular contributor to *The New York Review of Books*.

JOSÉ SARAMAGO
Translated by Mario Pereira

Andrea Mantegna: An Ethic, An Aesthetic*

In a novel published fifteen years ago with the enigmatic title of *Manual of Painting and Calligraphy*, which is narrated in the first person, I imagined that my main character, a mediocre portrait painter traveling through Italy, went one day to the Scrovegni Chapel in Padua, later on leaving a record of what he saw in the pages of a journal that he, the narrator, so to speak, kept, perhaps to reinforce that illusion of verisimilitude that novelists tirelessly pursue even more than the truth itself. After suggesting with no little pretension and complacency that the paintings in Padua lacked the descriptive freshness of *The Life of St. Francis* cycle in Assisi, both of which were painted by the same artist, Giotto, my character, not having to demonstrate any other expertise, passes directly to what he felt and thought, availing himself, it goes without saying, of what the author of the novel, the very one speaking to you now, thought and felt when he went to Italy and was in Padua. My portrait painter, identified in the book simply with the letter H., wrote:

> The figures appear aloof and at times almost priestly. For Giotto they belong to an ideal world of premonition. In a world thus described the divine extends serenely over the concerns and vicissitudes of this world, like some predestination or fatality. No one there knows how to smile with their lips, perhaps because of some flaw in the painter's powers of expression. But the open eyes, with long, heavy eyelids, often light up and exude a tranquil and benign wisdom which causes the figures to hover above and beyond the dramas narrated in the frescoes.
>
> As I strolled through the chapel, once, twice and for a third time, examining the three cycles in chronological order, a thought suddenly occurred to me which I still have not been able to unravel. It was a wish rather than a thought: to be able to spend a night there in the middle of the chapel and wake up before dawn in time to see those groups slowly emerging in procession from the shadows, like ghosts, their gestures and faces, that translucent blue, which must be one of Giotto's secrets, for it is not to be found in any other painter. At least not in my experience.

Let no one imagine I am betraying some deep religious feeling. I am simply trying to find out in the most mundane terms how an artist can create such a world.[1]

Quoting oneself is a narcissistic act that authors always try to justify either by alleging the supposed or actual impossibility in the moment of saying it better or by insinuating that the quotation contains all that could be said on the subject without the need, therefore, of endeavoring to go further, seeking more precision. In this case, the intentions are different. In the first place, this passage situates me at the outset, thanks to an elementary literary device, in the very city of Padua where I would like to take us. In the second place, it leaves a favorable and benevolent idea in your minds, which is that having written a novel fifteen years ago in which painting and painters live and appear in abundance on every page, then perhaps I am capable of speaking to you here today about the life of one of those painters—Andrea Mantegna—and a little bit about his work, not with the authority that I lack, but, if such a word is appropriate here, with the abundant love that I have.

How old was Andrea Mantegna when he, as well, saw Giotto's frescoes for the first time? He was a child, for we know that he had not yet reached eleven years of age when he joined the workshop of the painter Francesco Squarcione in Padua. Before this he had been a shepherd, tending sheep probably for some lord or rural property owner from the village where he lived with his family—Isola di Carturo—which then belonged to the territory of Vicenza and where he had been born in 1431.

How Francesco Squarcione, a painter, a contractor, a collector and dealer of objects of classical art with a shop frequented by humanists from the University of Padua, met the young Andrea, son of the carpenter Biggio Mantegna, we do not know, just as we do not know what remarkable signs of artistic vocation and precocity were shown by the little boy that made Squarcione determine to take him with him. Another mystery is what led Andrea's father either of his own initiative, or as the result of a proposal from Squarcione, to expressly renounce his paternity, for it was as Squarcione's adopted son that Andrea left his native village and went to live until the age of seventeen in the house of the man who would become his father and his master. The clarification of these obscure elements of Mantegna's biography may perhaps have no particular importance for the study of the work of the painter, but it would certainly help us understand the man that he was.

In any case, we know today that the entrance of a child at so young an age into a painting workshop was not exceptional, but that it was a rather common practice at the time. As in the nineteenth century when so much capital would so often be invested in scientific and technological investigation, something quite similar, considering all of the differences in goals and methods, was done in the fifteenth century in the area of artistic activity. The demand for painters, sculptors, architects, and engravers attracted to artistic careers many people who in other circumstances would never have thought about it. A son of peasants or artisans who showed some talent had many opportunities to be noticed and encouraged by a lord or a rich merchant from the neighborhood. Of course, recruitment was much easier among families of artisans—goldsmiths, jewelers, painters, decorators, blacksmiths—that already possessed their own professional traditions and offered their sons the advantage of an early apprenticeship. Until this time, only the Church had sought its artists in the different social strata, only the Church had been capable of gathering within it such a great variety of human types. The fact that this practice now had expanded to civil society, in particular to the world of nobles and wealthy merchants, would have to have, as it did in fact have, a productive effect on artistic expression.

Accompanying his father (the carpenters of that time certainly had an artistic origin), or perhaps on the occasion of what we would call today a guided tour (Squarcione giving a master class to the apprentices in his workshop), Andrea entered one day the Scrovegni Chapel and saw Giotto's frescoes. Upon seeing them, please allow me to repeat the hyperbole, he saw the world that the painter of my novel wanted to see born, and it pleases me now to imagine that, before Raphael would utter the phrase in front of Correggio's *Santa Cecilia*, our little shepherd, still reeking of the flock of sheep that he had grazed, said softly to his soul: "Anch'io son' pittore" (I too am a painter).

He would be one, as we well know, but he would still have for seven more years to pass through the rigorous and difficult experience of workshop apprenticeship, which would go from the total mastery of drawing and perspective to the preparation of paints and the intimate knowledge, through prints and copies, of the painting and sculpture of classical antiquity, which, as we have seen, comprised most of the contents of Squarcione's workshop.

This Squarcione, whose work has practically been lost (we only have by him a signed *Madonna and Child* in Berlin and an altarpiece in Padua), occupies in spite of this a place of exceptional importance in the history of *quattrocento* painting, for he trained more than one hundred and thirty painters in his workshop, where it is thought in all likelihood that the so-called *Paduan* style was born, a style that would culminate in Mantegna and that would spread throughout northern Italy.

Years later, after the break between master and pupil, Squarcione would still tell his most rebellious students: "Ho fatto un uomo de Andrea Mantegna come faró di te" (I made a man of Andrea Mategna, as I will make one of you). Now, if it is true that it was with Squarcione that Mantegna was made into a man, the least that can be said is that Squarcione, taking into account the differences of character, did not make him into the man that he probably had wanted to make of him. And, as for the painter, Mantegna's own genius made him one.

Genius, yes, but also Italy. When the son of the carpenter Biggio was born, artists by the name of Brunelleschi, Ghiberti, Donatello, Fra Angelico, Paolo Uccello, Pisanello, Alberti, and Piero della Francesca were alive in Italy, and one could almost include Masaccio among them, but he had died just three years earlier. At the time, Italy was an immense construction site and an immense workshop where all of the arts flourished with a perhaps inimitable vigor, because this was the era par excellence of the invention of the new from fragments and memories of the ancient, when the reencounter with classical art and its study provoked the rupture that would lead to modernity. It was on the shoulders of those men, of Andrea Mantegna and his generation, that the Leonardos, the Raphaels, and the Michelangelos of the future would stand when their time came.

If this were the theme of the lecture, to give the biographical facts that we currently possess, I confess that I would gladly use all of the time that is allowed to me here describing the seven years of Mantegna's apprenticeship. I should note, however, that there are good reasons to believe that this long period was not entirely peaceful as regards the relationship between the student and the master: we would need no better proof of this than the already cited phrase of Squarcione.

Many very difficult battles, implicit as well as declared, would have been fought in that workshop inhabited by such noble vestiges of antiquity, battles initially caused by the natural clash between an authoritarian temperament, as was Squarcione's, and a proud personality, as was Mantegna's. Moreover, it is not too much to imagine that Mantegna's artistic and creative maturation process, aided by his truly extraordinary intuition, would become, sooner rather than later, a new source of conflict not only in their relationship as men, but also in their competition as painters. The adolescent who at seventeen years of age accompanied his master to Venice was already a complete painter preparing to meet his own destiny that would be characterized by neither servitude nor dependence, except that which came with the social status of an artist of that time, a status that, furthermore, was in the process of transformation and that he would never resign himself to accept with bowed head. It was at the beginning of the following year, in 1448, when Mantegna took the first steps that would carry him into the world of adults and responsibilities: he left Squarcione's house and went to live in another neighborhood in Padua, the *contrada* of Santa Lucia, signing an agreement with Squarcione according to which he could, having already become independent, keep for himself all of the money that he would earn. And the first money he earned was likely what was paid to him for the polyptych, now lost, that he painted around that time for the Church of Santa Sophia.

Having arrived at this point, we should here introduce, to honor and praise the institution of the family, and also to acknowledge the grace of the always ready imagination, an edifying episode: the visit Andrea's parents would pay to their son's new house during which the carpenter Biggio would certainly congratulate himself for the results of his having renounced paternal authority. Perhaps with this episode we would know something more about Andrea's feelings, the assessment that he himself would make of these seven years spent serving and learning. However, we know nothing.

When Andrea, alone at home, because it would take time for him to have his own workshop and students, would finish the day's work perhaps he might visit his other family, Giotto's frescoes, his ancestors from a century and a half earlier, or he might knock on the door of a man who was almost seventy years old, a man called Donatello, who had been in Padua for five years and who would remain there for another five years, to watch him work on the altar of the Basilica of Sant'Antonio in which the miracles of the saint are represented, or it could be that Andrea might in the end take advantage of the fading light of the afternoon to look one more time at the equestrian statue of Gattamelata, recently installed.

Mantegna's vision is one of reliefs, which the eyes touch and surround as though they were hands and which the hands recognize and identify as though they were eyes. Drawing and modeling in light and shade taught him to create on the surface of a wall or a panel the visual impression of volume. But Mantegna seems always to have pursued what we could call a *supreme degree of illusion*, a flat image that the hands refuse to touch from fear of passing through the surface that reason still affirms is there, but that the eyes have already broken through to move beyond: it is our gaze that contemplates us from the vanishing point of a perspective or from the other intangible and irrefutable wall that lies behind the statues that the painting simulates. Squarcione's teaching had imposed on his students, as a model to follow, the extraordinary remains of a revived classical antiquity, but I doubt I would strain verisimilitude too much by imagining that the personality and work of Donatello, who had arrived in Padua two years after Andrea had begun to work with Squarcione, would have powerfully drawn the attention of the young apprentice.

Now, in the exact moment when Andrea, already expert in his trade and free from guardianship, presents himself on the labor market, it so happened that an illustrious Paduan woman, Imperatrice Ovetari, determined to have constructed for herself a chapel in the Church of the Eremitani, which is not far from the Scrovegni Chapel. It is known that at that time when one said chapel, one said painting, and it was because of this that once the masons had finished their part of the work, the painters would move in. The painters charged with decorating one half of the chapel were the Venetians Antonio Vivarini and his partner Giovanni d'Alemagna, whose workshop in Venice was as well-known as the Bellini family workshop. Squarcione's two best students, Andrea Mantegna and Niccolò Pizzolo, who was ten years older than his colleague, were contracted to decorate the other half of the chapel.

(It is appropriate here to offer, in passing, a consideration that will in some way put into perspective what has been said about the abundantly documented bad relations between Mantegna and Squarcione. Since it is hardly credible that Imperatrice Ovetari possessed, on her own, such thorough knowledge of Mantegna's work that she would have confidently entrusted responsibility for such an important part of the decoration of her chapel to a young painter, it seems most likely that it was Squarcione himself who, consulted on the matter, had suggested his two most capable apprentices. We should not forget that Squarcione's importance in Padua at the time was not limited to the realm of the arts, but was also social.)

What was done by the fifteenth century was undone by the twentieth century. On March 11, 1944, the planes came and dropped bombs on Padua. The Church of the Eremitani was struck and part of the frescoes by Mantegna were destroyed and buried in the ruins. This is how my painter from the *Manual* recorded his impressions of his visit there:

> The church of the Eremitani was virtually destroyed and Mantegna's frescoes depicting the life of St James either disappeared or were severely damaged (the

painter was seventeen when he first stood with his paints and brushes before the bare surface of a wall). I look at what remains of Mantegna's pictorial world: monumental architecture, human forms as ample and robust as rocky landscapes. I am alone in the church. I can hear the sounds of a city which has forgotten the war, the drone of aeroplanes and explosion of bombs. Just as I am about to leave, an elderly English couple arrive, tall, dried up, wrinkled, so alike. As if in familiar surroundings, they head straight for the Ovetari Chapel painted by Mantegna and there they stand, lost in contemplation.[2]

Now, I ask myself, what led me to write that the English couple, husband and wife, head to the Ovetari Chapel "as if in familiar surroundings." The logical reason would be that they had already been there before, that they belonged, for example, to that category of cultured travelers who always return to where they have been because it keeps the hope alive that they will come to know it better. But another explanation occurs to me today, one that is certainly more romantic and even more comforting, because it allows for the possibility that a person may repent of the evil that they did and be capable of acknowledging their fault in the place where the offense was committed: it might have been that old Englishman who had manned the destroyer bomber thirty years earlier and who with the thumb of his right hand had pressed the button to drop the bombs. You will tell me that this is too much of a coincidence, and I will respond by saying that life, all of it, is pure coincidence. However, I will have to admit that I am wrong if the planes which on that day had bombed Padua were not, after all, British, but American...

Man, fortunately, first invented photography and only later aerial bombings. Thanks to that foresight, the images that have disappeared left their shadows among us, now that, almost fifty years later, the memory of the actual paintings is fading in the memory of the survivors until it is definitively extinguished with the last one.

All of Mantegna is already here, a style of theatrical though austere solemnity, the sense of the intrinsic minerality of the world, the need to balance this irreducible hardness by appealing to the fruits and the flowers, the garlands, and the graces of an occasionally generous nature. The enormous frescoes of *St. James* (each one measuring almost three and a half meters) were destroyed in thunder and fury, in dust and fire. They described scenes from the saint's life, his calling, his preaching to the demons, his baptism of Hermogenes, his trial, the way to martyrdom, and his death by stoning.

In addition to Mategna and Pizzolo and to Vivarini and d'Alemagna, other painters, such as Ansuino da Forli and Bono da Ferrara, worked in the Ovetari Chapel: so many square meters of wall could not be in the hands of only one painter, otherwise the pious soul of Imperatrice Ovetari would not have been able to experience the rapturous and consoling joy of praying in her chapel completely enveloped in the colors and representations of the lives of her favorite saints, St. James and St. Christopher. The frescoes of the latter saint were painted later, after Mantegna's brief Venetian period, and they were more fortunate, for they escaped the bombing. More, perhaps, than the frescoes of St. *James*, the *Martyrdom and Burial of St. Christopher* arrogantly displays all of Mantegna's perspectival science and, in this specific respect, it can be placed on a par with Piero della Francesca's *Flagellation of Christ*, painted around the same time.

Despite all of the participants and assistance, work on the Eremitani took seven years to complete. This Andrea who passes his eyes over the recently completed frescoes of the Ovetari Chapel is now the main figure of Paduan painting and one of the most important of all of northern Italy. It is certain that he painted the final brushstroke: in 1451, with Giovanni d'Alemagna having died the previous year, Antonio Vivarini finished painting the arch with the evangelists and returned to Venice; in 1453 Niccoló Pizzolo disappears, killed as he returned at night from working on the chapel. Vasari says that he was "afrontato e morto a tradimento" (attacked and killed by treachery), but it is more likely that it had been a fight with swords and daggers like so many others that Pizzolo had been involved in during his life, for he had a fiery and irascible temperament.

With the same violence and the same passion, Mantegna likewise entered and would continue to enter, not only a few times, into fights such as these, for he was no less sensitive than Niccoló regarding questions of honor and precedence. Endowed with little of the Christian virtue of patience, these Renaissance artists easily put their future masterpieces at risk: the slash that could cut the thread of life would also kill the colors and forms that were about to be born. The hand that was still stained with paint from a crucifixion and that was going to deliver the final blow could, in turn, never again hold a paintbrush: they knew this and nonetheless they did not shy away from death, stealer of life and executioner of art.

It was toward the end of his work in the Eremitani when, to escape from the war that Squarcione, already overshadowed by the successes of his former apprentice, had declared against him, Mantegna decided to leave Padua and go live in Venice where the Bellinis, "grandi pittori," in the words of Vasari, and men of culture, welcomed him as an equal. Jacopo Bellini's two sons, Giovanni and Gentile, were nearly the same age as Andrea, but it was Andrea, the youngest, who would leave signs of his strong influence in the paintings of the two Bellini brothers, particularly and persistently in the work of Giovanni. The panel *The Agony in the Garden*, which was painted by Giovanni Bellini in 1465 and is now in the National Gallery London, powerfully recalls Mantegna's painting of the same subject, which is found in the same museum.

It was also among the Bellini family that Mantegna met the woman who would become his wife, the daughter of Jacopo, Nicolasa, with whom he would have five sons, all of them painters, though rather mediocre ones. One of these sons, Francesco, would give him serious grief at the end of his life, for he would be expelled from Mantua for his undesirable behavior. But those days of bitter sadness are still far-off: now Andrea works in the workshop of his new relatives, his father-in-law who esteems him, his brothers-in-law who admire him, and, loosening somewhat the shackles of the imagination, we can see from here Nicolasa approach her groom from behind to watch him paint as the moment arrives for them to walk through the streets and canals of Venice as he had promised, with her as the guide.

Mantegna's marriage to the daughter of Jacopo Bellini exacerbated the hostility that pitted him against Squarcione. Resentful, the old master began to disdain what was also in some way his own work: the style of his apprentice. Here, for example, is the commentary he offered on the frescoes of the Ovetari Chapel: "His figures always have the hardness of stones and never the tender suppleness and softness that flesh and natural things have. He would have done better if he had painted marbles, which have nothing living about them."

Mantegna, whose character was as hard as the stones that were thus imputed to him and who did not easily accept criticism, decided to demonstrate his ability to paint real figures and populated one of the scenes in the Ovetari Chapel with intensely lifelike portraits of characters from Padua's cultural elite, assigning them various roles as protagonists of the martyrdom of St. Christopher. Vindictive, he also represented Squarcione as the miserable, fat, and stupid warrior located behind the saint: the image, however, is not a portrait, but rather a caricature. Mantegna would continue to ridicule his old master on other occasions, in engravings such as *Bacchanal with Silenus* and, especially, in the atrocious allegory that is *Ignorance and Mercury*. Their bad relations account for the fact that at the end of 1455 Mantegna had presented a complaint to the court of Padua demanding payment from Squarcione for the paintings that he had executed during the years when he worked with him.

During his Venetian period, Mantegna painted a cartoon of the *Death of the Virgin* for the mosaic of the Mascoli Chapel in the Basilica of San Marco. In Padua, at the same time as the *Martyrdom of St. Christopher*, he painted for the Church of San Zeno in Verona, where it can still be found, a polyptych of *The Virgin and Child and Saints*. This was his first major pictorial statement outside of the medium of fresco and it shows the persistent influence of Donatello, in this case, of Donatello's altar of Sant'Antonio in Padua from which Mantegna learned and then here applied Donatello's lesson on how to arrange and articulate, plastically, masses and figures.

Earlier, in 1456, Ludovico III Gonzaga, the Marquis of Mantua, had invited Mantegna to work at his court, but it was only three years later, in 1459, after a new request from the lord of Mantua that the painter decided to accept the invitation. The Gonzaga offer him "fifteen ducats of provision per month, housing for him and his family, cereal for six persons, in addition to all of the wood that he needs and still more." The financial conditions are favorable and the affective and cultural environment that will soon surround Mantegna explains why he does not again return to Padua, except for a brief period in 1461.

In Matua with the Gonzaga, Mantegna will be admired and respected much more like a friend than a court painter, and these sentiments, which are first expressed by Ludovico Gonzaga, will be likewise shared and exhibited by the marchioness, Barbara of Brandenburg, as well as the couple's ten children. The meeting between this prince and this painter undoubtedly constituted one of the most extraordinary and moving artistic and human events of the Italian renaissance.

With the move to Mantua, Mantegna begins a new and productive period of creative work. The triptych, today in the Uffizzi, that represents the *Adoration of the Magi*, the *Ascension*, and the *Circumcision* was executed during this first phase of Mantuan activity. Also from this time is *The Agony in the Garden* (National Gallery, London), which quite clearly exemplifies the artist's interest in a scenographic type of representation on different narrative levels with an evident concern for historicity. And *The Death of the Virgin*, of which the Prado is the proud custodian, is also likely from this period, though there are those who assert that Mantegna painted it in 1492, after the trip that he had then taken to Rome. Be that as it may, it is Mantua that is represented in the background of the panel with its towers and walls, its lakes, and the San Giorgio bridge, one of those that Ludovico Gonzaga had built over the marshes that then surrounded the city.

As court painter of Mantua, Mantegna is invited to travel to other places. With the permission of the Gonzaga, he will go to Florence to give advice on the chorus of the Santissima Annunziata, to Pisa to paint a wall of the Camposanto, he will later go to Rome, but wherever he is, he will always long to return to his city of Mantua where they esteem him, indulging his demands and excusing the eccentricities of his character that with the passing of time were becoming more pronounced.

Nothing infuriated him more than the improper appropriation of the fruits of his labor. Upon discovering that the engraver Andrea Zoan, who belonged to his workshop, engraved and sold his drawings without authorization, Mantegna expelled him and forced him, it seems with violence, to hand over to him "the prints and plates." Later, upon learning that the same Andrea Zoan had used for identical purposes the services of another engraver, Simone Ardizzoni, from Reggio Emilia, his wrath turned against him, first with threats, then with persecutions, to the extent that this Simone Ardizzoni had to write a letter to the Marquis Ludovico Gonzaga in which he said: "Since the diabolical Andrea Mantegna learned that I was reproducing the prints, he sent a Florentine to threaten me, swearing that I was going to have to pay for them. And as though this were not enough, I was attacked one night by the nephew of Carlo de Moltone and ten more armed men, Andrea Zoan and me, in order to kill us..." There were no deaths, as far as is known, but the violence only ended when the appropriation ceased. The response that Ludovico Gonzaga sent to this Simone Ardizzoni was the same more or less that he had already given, earlier on, to a gardener who had presented a complaint to him about Mantegna's alleged arrogance: "I am more fond of the tip of the toe of this Andrea than I am of a thousand cowards like you." However, do not think that it was only in cases that involved people of little significance that the Marquis Ludovico Gonzaga came to Mantegna's defense: he was no more receptive to the denunciations of important subjects who protested to him about the harsh character of the master.

As a man and as an artist, Andrea was in full maturity on the day when Ludovico Gonzaga charged him with the execution, on the main floor of the north tower of the Castle of St. George, of the great mural decorations that we call the *Camera degli Sposi*. Other decorations completed by Mantegna at this time have disappeared. However, what has come down to us, the result of a task that we can easily imagine as immense, constitutes one of the most beautiful and perfect works in the history of painting, irrespective of time and place. The date when work began is still being debated, but it can, in any case, be situated between 1465 and 1473. Nevertheless, there appears to be no doubt, if we accept as reliable the dedication painted above the door leading out of the *camera*, about the date of completion, which would be 1474, though some scholars maintain that work on it continued until 1484 or even 1488.

In front of the frescoes of the *Camera degli Sposi* one can better understand, as Giovanni Paccagnini says, "the internal significance that the systematic search for formal perfection, which is present in each one of his works, would have for Mantegna, a search that did not respond to an external formalism, but to a severe ethical conception of expression as conquest that only the virtue of industriousness can attain through an assiduous and grueling exercise." The powerful historical portrait that Mantegna represented in the *Camera degli Sposi* is the highest fruit of this assiduous and ardent search for universal values, one that rejects the ephemerality of the sentiments in favor of the intense yearning, never entirely extinguished in us, for an expression fixed in immutable relations, removed from the perpetual flow of time. There are not many figures, whether painted or sculpted, in the History of Art that so irresistibly summon in our spirit the designation of *eternal*.

Ludovico III died in 1487, but the relations between Mantegna and the Gonzaga did not change in any way. Mantegna found favor with the successor to the house of Gonzaga, Federico, that was the equal to what he had until then enjoyed. And when a son of the painter fell gravely ill in 1480, the new marquis recommended him to a then famous doctor, Gerardo da Verona, who, nevertheless, was unable to save him. It was after this event, and perhaps because of it, that Mantegna painted the St. *Sebastian* that today is in the Louvre and that at the time was taken by Chiara Gonzaga, daughter of Ludovico III, to Aigueperse when she married the Count of Montpensier. Mantegna would take up the theme of St. Sebastian two more times: shortly thereafter in the small panel that can be seen in the Vienna Museum and once more toward the end of his life in the dramatic panel, today in the Ca' d'Oro in Venice, which, according to Fiocco, is an example "of the most abstract linear metaphysics."

The paint in the *Camera degli Sposi* was still wet and Andrea Mantegna had already thrown himself, to satisfy a request from Federico Gonzaga, into the enormous task of painting on canvas the *Triumphs of Caesar* (Hampton Court, London), a set of nine paintings of massive dimensions (in total 27 by 3 meters), intended to decorate a room where theatrical pieces were staged. These canvases, in addition to their evident artistic and decorative quality, can also be seen as a magnificent inventory of Mantegna's manifold knowledge of Roman antiquity, from the clothes and insignias to the weapons and objects, but it is, above all, possible to perceive in them something that without excessive error of generalization we could call the *spirit of Romanness*.

In 1489, Mantegna wrote from Rome, where he had gone at the request of Pope Innocent VIII with the purpose of painting frescoes in a chapel of the Belvedere in the Vatican, to the Marquis of Mantua recommending that he safeguard the canvases of the *Triumphs of Caesar* at the same time as he expressed his hope to be able to continue and finish the work. But it is Francesco II Gonzaga, grandson of Ludovico III, who, in December of this same year, with his marriage to Isabella d'Este approaching, wrote to the pope asking that he authorize Mantegna's return to Mantua for the preparations for the wedding. Quite ill, Mantegna could not make the journey, and he would only return to Mantua nearly a year later, once he had, despite the circumstances, finished work on the Belvedere chapel, which would be destroyed in 1780. In April 1492, there were still two canvases to be painted for the *Triumphs of Caesar*, but Mantegna would not complete the work.

From the representation of the authentic triumph of an emperor, Mantegna turned, in 1495, to the commemoration of the triumph of Francesco II Gonzaga over Charles VIII of France at the battle of Fornovo—a victory that was, however, highly questionable, for Charles VIII was able to withdraw with almost all of his army, which was smaller than that of the victor, and he suffered fewer losses. One year later, the *Madonna della Vittoria*, today in the Musée du Louvre, was exhibited in Mantua with great solemnity in the chapel constructed precisely for the purpose.

Mantegna's life was drawing to a close. Recognized, loved, and respected by all, he was visited in his house by the most important figures of his time, such as Ercole d'Este, duke of Ferrara, and even Lorenzo de' Medici, il Magnifico. Infirm, embittered by grief, Mantegna would continue to paint until he ran out of strength. When, finally, on September 13, 1506, he closed his eyes, never to open them again, he had in his house the *St. Sebastian* (Ca' d'Oro, Venice) and the *Dead Christ* (Brera, Milan), two tragic representations of the interminable sufferings of mankind, two representations as well of the superior and always deferred dignity of human beings.

Élie Faure said one day that the primitive painters always put all that they knew in their works. In his painting, Mantegna not only put all that he knew, but he also put what he certainly was: a complete man in his hardness and in his sensitivity, like a rock that was able to cry.

Lecture delivered at the Museo del Prado, 1992

NOTES

* Originally published as José Saramago. *Andrea Mantegna: una ética, una estética.* Madrid: Casimiro, 2011. Published with the kind permission of Pilar del Río and the Fundação José Saramago.

1. Saramago, José. *Manual of Painting and Calligraphy: A Novel.* Translated by Giovanni Pontiero. (Carcanet: Manchester, 1994), 98-99.

2. Saramago. *Manual of Painting and Calligraphy*, 97-98.

BIBLIOGRAPHY

Camesaaca, E. *Mantegna.* Milan. 1964.
Caravaglia, N. *Tout l'oeuvre peint de Mantegna.* Paris, 1978.
Faure, E. *Historia da Arte.* Lisbon. 1949.
Fiocco, G. *Andrea Mantegna.* Milan 1937.
Gombrich, E. H. *Histoire de l'Art.* Paris. 1990.
Kristeller, P. *Andrea Mantegna.* London. 1902.
Lightbown, R. *Andrea Mantegna.* London. 1986.
Martindale, A. M. *The Triumph of Caesar.* London. 1978.
Meiss, M. *Andrea Mantegna as Illuminator.* New York. 1957.
Tietze-Conrat, R. *Andrea Mantegna.* London. 1951.

JOSÉ SARAMAGO (1922-2010) was the recipient of the Nobel Prize for Literature in 1998.

MARIO PEREIRA is the executive editor of *Portuguese Literary & Cultural Studies.*

Reviews

Maria Manuel Lisboa.

Essays on Paula Rego: Smile When You Think About Hell. Cambridge, UK: Open Book Publishers, 2019.

OFF WITH HIS HEAD

At the end of *Essays on Paula Rego*, Maria Manuel Lisboa writes about a paradox in the artist Paula Rego's work. She notes that Rego has had enormous popular success. Her work sells. She has been accepted by the establishment. Collectors abound. Yet the world that she depicts could only exist with a reinvention of present attitudes to gender, marriage, and the family. Rego's work is always, Lisboa writes, about revenge: against men, against the church, against power, against violence, against conformity. There is conflict in all her work, conflict that the powerful willfully ignore, preferring instead to read her work for its visual command and in relation to the fairy tales and literary narratives that underpin her paintings and prints. Germaine Greer sees this struggle between the visual and the subversive as a violent personal vision fashioned in acceptable decorative terms.

Lisboa has collected here a group of prodigiously researched essays, most of them previously published as *Paula Rego's Map of Memory* (2003) but a few collected from academic journals. Only one is new (a sixty-page study of fairy tales that Rego loves), although Lisboa has extended and edited some of her earlier material. Lisboa is a professor of Portuguese literature and culture at the University of Cambridge, and her essays demonstrate broad knowledge of contemporary theory as well as British and Portuguese literature. In the book she has divided them into two sections: one on the contexts of Rego's art, the other on the work itself. The first section is the weightiest, and its essays are often used as a basis for deciphering the multiple meanings that Rego assigns to her work.

Typically, Lisboa begins each essay by laying the theoretical foundations of her argument. She works from a New Historicist perspective and intends to inscribe the visual text in history. Her defense of this position is outlined as a rejection of a textualist position in which meaning is seen as arbitrary and historical truth is determined as inaccessible. Most of her references are from the 1980s: Derrida, Habermas, Jameson, Bryson, and Schor. She analyzes sixty years of work and concentrates on Rego's productions from the 1980s and 1990s. Throughout, she embeds examples and further commentary in the accompanying footnotes.

In one essay Lisboa writes about Rego's painting *The Policeman's Daughter* (1987), which features family, incest, and paternal power. It is among Rego's best pictures, of interest for its visual solidity and for the themes that circulate among other paintings she made in the same period. Lisboa provides a mental picture of the painting: "A girl or young woman sits in a room by a window without a view, alone except for a black cat, and polishes a man's boot, presumably that of the eponymous policeman and father. Light streams in through the window." Citing Ruth Rosengarten, who has written widely on Rego's work, she notes the sexual tension that provides a reading of incest (the daughter's hand inside the father's phallic boot) and the allusion within the authoritarian boot to state power. To clean someone's boots, Lisboa argues, signifies submissiveness to the point of abjection, an explanation that is important for non-Portuguese speakers. Other writers, Fiona Bradley included, refer to the image of the arm inside the boot in ways that recall Robert Mapplethorpe's photograph of fisting, with its references to anal sex, rape, and incest. Lisboa argues that Rego exposes the fragility of paternalistically defied power: the boot is polished; the male organ is manually stimulated and becomes the hole or anus into which the violating hand and female arm are brutally rammed, a humiliating sexual act. Lisboa is at her best here in a riveting and explicit analysis that reaches to the heart of Rego's provocation.

In 1997, after reading *The Crime of Padre Amaro* (1875) by Eça de Queirós, Rego created a series of sixteen panels and nineteen sketches that superficially illustrate the novel. The connection between the text and the images that followed were independent, one from the other. The anticlericism that Rego had touched on in prior work now became the central idea. Discussing this project, Lisboa calls on post-Freudian psychoanalytic readings to interpret pictures that only have a tangential relation to the novel. Contrary to mainstream Freudian thought, in which the Oedipal complex is said to favor the father over the mother, writers such as Julia Kristeva, Melanie Klein, and Nancy Chodorow see escape from the mother as less ominous than the dominion of the father. The son, who loves his mother and has depended on her from birth for well-being and survival, must abandon her, though he can never fully do so. The female is the good mother, the bad mother, and the powerless mother. As the character Amélia, she is the figure of Padre Amaro's desire. She is powerful and powerless. In *Looking Out*, Amélia stands before a window with her back to us. She sees what we do not and controls what everyone else sees, thereby controlling all: interpretation, the gaze, and the viewer. In a final discussion of a painting done a year later, *In the Wilderness*, Lisboa links the image of a woman kneeling in a foggy seascape to Portuguese imperial dreams dashed by the death of Dom Sebastião and British victory in southern Africa. In the painting, Amélia kneels in an empty seascape, equal to an unsatisfied longing for empire. To this she adds, in her final words on the sins of the fathers, that Portuguese fixation on its lost empire is coexistent with a continuing resentment against the empire builders and the *retornados* who were coolly received in Portugal on their return in 1975 after defeat in Angola and Mozambique. The crime, then, was not only Padre Amaro's lust and the death of his son and the seduced Amélia. The insights that Rego brings to post-imperial Portugal are the truths of discrimination against women and racism against those from the "provinces."

Rego is never direct in her message, and Lisboa deftly guides us through the thickets of symbol and history by calling on feminist and post-Freudian interpreters. She leads us through the fierce debate and referendum on abortion in 1998 and final liberalization in 2007, allowed with restrictions and as a last resort. Rego made a series of ten pastels and fourteen sketches on the topic in which she verbally attacked the alliance between the Catholic church and the state. She also linked female pain, blame, and abortion to Portugal's totalitarian past. "It is unbelievable," she said at the time, "that women who have an abortion should be considered criminals." Lisboa has located the work that Rego made in 1998–99 in the context of voyeurism and the male gaze, feminist theory, and the erotic models that appear in male magazines. Of the eight essays, this one is the most fully and ardently argued, a battleground in which disagreement remains unresolved.

Lisboa's book reaches beyond the work of Paula Rego to engage profoundly with issues that mark our era. Her essays speak to us in various voices, certainly from ideology but also in the movement from the affective, emotional plane to meaning. Rego has discovered a true social sense in history and in our aesthetic response to her criticisms of gender inequality, violence, and hypocrisy. Lisboa finds in this work a basis for investigating history and gender with a consistent eye on the visual culture that has made Rego's art possible.

MEMORY HOLLOWAY is Professor Emerita at the University of Massachusetts Dartmouth.

Marilia Librandi. *Writing by Ear: Clarice Lispector and the Aural Novel.* Toronto: University of Toronto Press, 2018.

Writing by Ear is an ambitious book. It does not merely set out to study the work of Clarice Lispector in an innovative manner; it proposes what Marília Librandi herself characterizes as a (new) theory of fiction writing, based on Clarice Lispector's work.

The premise of the book is as follows: Clarice Lispector's writing engages in a particular relationship with the sense of hearing (experienced both by the fiction writer and by the reader) which justifies a reframing of the concept of "writing" as we conventionally understand it. Different than simply "writing," what Lispector does should best be described as "writing as listening," which Librandi views as a third entity, to be placed somewhere between writing and orality. This proposal implies that the concept of authorship will be revisited as well. The role of listening—traditionally viewed as passive—should now be considered as much a part of writing as the act of (actively) producing *new* words. *New* words which, Librandi would say, are not pulled out of thin air and are not simply *created* by demiurge-like authors; instead, they are partly *heard* and *given* to whomever writes them: "How are we to understand authorship when writers present themselves as objects of reception rather than subjects of production?" (Librandi 7).

This is an exquisitely written and researched book, which occupied the author for years. It gradually grew out of conversations and collaborations with many scholars and students of writing and of Clarice Lispector: "This book is the result of collective work. My name is on the spine, but it has been authored just as much by those who have suffered through and enjoyed the listening/writing process with me"(Librandi xi). The author also claims that the process of reflecting on issues of aurality, which gave rise to the book, started on December 25, 2008, when she and her family "landed" (her words) in the U.S.

The project can also be traced back to work done at Stanford University, where the author taught. There, some discussions concerning "rhythm and writing" took place, organized by a group named "Sense and Sound," in which the scholar

Vincent Barletta, also interested in issues of rhythm, was a prominent participant. However, the *eureka* moment, which was the culmination of this process of experiences and reflections, related to the act of listening (for example, the way our own language sounds when heard through a tapestry of foreign words) was triggered, according to Librandi, by a passage found in Lispector's *A Hora da Estrela* (*The Hour of the Star*). In it, the narrator, Rodrigo S.M., confesses: "escrevo de ouvido," which, in English, could be translated as "I write by ear," or perhaps "I write with what I hear," or still "I write based on what I hear." In Portuguese, Lispector's idiomatic expression, which greatly impressed the author of *Writing by Ear*, could mean that the narrator's approach to writing is a spontaneous one, or that of a non-professional, a self-taught person. Rodrigo S.M. himself reinforces this notion when he confirms precisely what Lispector has stated elsewhere: "Mas acontece que só escrevo o que quero, não sou um profissional (...)" (Lispector, *A Hora da Estrela* 17).[1]

The sensitivity and aural acuity which accompanies the writing process, as Marília Librandi contends, stems from the fact that Lispector, although having written exclusively in Portuguese, was immersed in a world that featured other languages, among them the Hebrew and Yiddish of her childhood and the many European languages (some converted by Lispector into Portuguese, in literary translations) to which she was exposed while she lived abroad as the wife of a Brazilian diplomat. As a Brazilian scholar living abroad, Librandi claims also to have experienced an enhanced sensitivity to her own language after she moved to the U.S., as other languages, particularly English, challenged her, forcing her to strain her *ear*, as she experienced *estrangement* which, conversely, contaminated (or intensified, refreshed) her relationship with Portuguese. This circumstance made her more aware of the role that *listening* played in communication. It is understandable that this fact (experienced in different degrees and fashions by all immigrants) helped Librandi empathize with (and masterfully detect) Lispector's well-tuned writer's ear. Paradoxically, it seems that a renewed mastery of one's own language is achieved when one experiences (if only in part, given the concomitant risks to our vocabulary recall, grammatical precision, etc.) the freshness of a foreigner's ear to words and expressions in one's own native language, to whose beauty, nuances, and contradictions many non-immigrant speakers grow deaf due to habit, a ossified ear, or a lack of experience with other languages.

Librandi claims that what she calls the (oral or) aural quality of Clarice's writing consists of a particularly Brazilian trait seen, in part, in the dominance of the oral tradition in Brazilian culture (in contrast with a less established tradition of literacy) and may be found (*heard*) in several of its best known authors, namely Machado de Assis, Guimarães Rosa, etc.

The book is divided so that it presents the different aspects of this new aural theory (Lispector is here considered as much a theorist as a fiction writer). This allows other scholars to apply it to their respective literatures and cultures, since the field may be, as Librandi views it, in the midst of an "aural turn."

The first chapter, "Writing by Ear," bears the same title as the book and in it the general aspects of the theory are explained. In the second chapter, the author expands on the notion of the aural novel, which could be viewed as a refashioning of Earl Fitz's term "lyrical novel." Then, a more direct analysis of a novel, *Near to the Wild Heart*, is on display in the chapter "Hearing the Wild Heart." Another analysis of a novel is carried out in "Loud Object," a chapter devoted to *Água Viva*. Finally, *The Passion According to G.H* is studied in the chapter "The Echopoetics of GH," where Librandi applies her poetics of resonances to Lispector's book.

I find *Writing by Ear* to be a remarkable achievement because, while deepening our understanding of Lispector's universe, it forces us to move beyond the author of *Água Viva* and face the (not so obvious) fact that fiction writers do follow a particular rhythm when they write. This idea forces us to question the dominance of paraphraseable content (meaning) over internally heard rhythm (sound). And, if nothing else, it also forces us to seriously consider the interdependence of the two. A shocking consequence of this line of reasoning could be the realization that meaning/sense/possibly even story and plot are not such pure, controlled, and deliberate authorial decisions, contrary to what we may have initially thought or been led to think. Any reader of the following sentence, even without an English translation, will notice how Rodrigo S.M's discourse is here propelled (and certainly *shaped*) by the strength and energy of its alliterations and assonances, which leads us to believe that "sound" often tends to precede "meaning," and not only in poetry: "A dor de dentes que perpassa esta história deu uma fisgada funda em plena boca nossa" (Lispector. *A Hora da Estrela* 11).

My only (minor) reservation about the thesis of the book is expressed by the following questions: what writing (particularly "artistic writing") is *not* shaped by rhythm or propelled by an aural thrust? Is that not what writers do and what writing does? (As a student of poetry, where this is more noticeable, I have always suspected this is so.) Potentially, I believe, all writing is strongly influenced by (and dependent on) the act of listening/sound/rhythm, a possibility that Librandi's argument amply allows, by the way, without necessarily placing it explicitly at its center.

Effectively internationalizing the usefulness of the book, Librandi writes that "writing by ear" has relevance "for literatures that tend to maintain an ethical, poetic and political connection with communities deeply shaped by forms of verbal communication that do not rely on the mediation of writing" (18) and that "one of my basic goals for the present book is for it to serve as a conversation starter" (23). And so the conversation has started around this intriguing topic, thanks to this timely book, as was Librandi's intention:

> The presence of hearing/listening in writing calls on its readers to contemplate a sense that has been left largely (if paradoxically) unexplored in previous discussions on the relationship between orality and writing. It is my intention to show that the inclusion of the ear changes the panorama of the discussion. (Librandi 7)

This study does shed new, fresh light on Clarice Lispector's work; on some Brazilian authors, particularly prose writers; and, finally, on Brazilian literature in general and (possibly) on all the writing that almost unnoticeably surrounds us with "its resonant silence, its mute shrieks, its vibrant muteness" (17). This is a welcome and important book.

NOTE

1. Lispector, Clarice. *A Hora da Estrela*. Rio de Janeiro: Rocco. s.d.: "As it happens, I only write what I want, I am not a professional" (my translation).

ANTONIO LADEIRA is an Associate Professor of Spanish and Portuguese at Texas Tech University, where he serves as the director of the Portuguese Program. He holds a Licenciatura in Portuguese Studies by Universidade Nova de Lisboa and a PhD in Hispanic Languages and Literatures by the University of California in Santa Barbara. He taught at Yale University, Middlebury College and, as the recipient of a Fulbright grant, he served as a visiting researcher at the University of São Paulo. His research interests include the study of gender and masculinity in contemporary Lusophone literatures, Portuguese-American writers and immigrant literatures in the U.S. and Canada, poetry in Portuguese, and Clarice Lispector.

Mariana Liz and Hilary Owen, eds.
Women's Cinema in Contemporary Portugal.
New York: Bloomsbury Academic, 2020.

Adapting Delueze and Guattari's ideas of "minor cinemas" for the case at hand, it could be said that female-authored Portuguese cinema suffers a double invisibility on the basis of nationality and gender. In this landmark collection addressing fourteen women filmmakers active since 1974, the year in which the Salazar regime was overthrown by the peaceful Carnation Revolution, the editors and contributors are committed both to acknowledging and transcending the aforementioned invisibility, which clearly applies to many but not all of the directors under consideration—Susana de Sousa Dias has, for example, become a major point of reference in art-house world cinema. Since many studies of Hispanic as well as global cinema(s) make only cursory reference to Portuguese films or Portuguese women directors, the original contribution of this volume (alongside Elena Cordero-Hoyo and Begoña Soto Vázquez's upcoming edited collection *Women in Iberian Filmic Culture: A Feminist Approach to the Cinemas of Portugal and Spain*) is indisputable. Even more commendable, however, is the manner in which the ten chapters of Liz and Owen's book, both individually and collectively, engage readers who (at least in my case) will likely only have seen a fraction of the films under consideration, and aim to convince them that it is worth investing their time in learning more about and watching them.

The impetus for the book came from conferences in 2017 and 2018. Varied female voices working in Portuguese, UK, and U.S. institutions subsequently penned contributions divided into the following sections: "Histories;" "Feminisms;" "Archives;" and "Transnationalism." As Liz and Owen note in their co-authored introduction, the project "involves both examining the conditions of film production, exhibition and criticism, that frame and condition the making and reception of films in terms of gender, and, simultaneously, analysing the narrative, style and aesthetics of these films" (6). A normative as well as descriptive approach is made explicit in Liz's chapter where she comments of two post-financial-crash films with female protagonists how "it is very disappointing that Portuguese women directors reject their role as conscious political agents" (p. 103). Although, as other case-studies make clear, this is not always the case in female-directed films, cinema is hardly exempt from the general tendency by which the Transition from dictatorship to democracy was accompanied by a leap from pre- to post-feminism. The number of women working in the national cinema under Salazar was even less than under Franco in neighbouring Spain, and the history of female cinema in Portugal effectively begins with the return of democratic rule. That does not, of course, imply that the dictatorship has been absent from the corpus of films under consideration or that the relegation of women to the category of second-class citizens was miraculously resolved.

Ana Isabel Soares speaks of the difficulty in accessing the works of Margarida Gil, a documentary filmmaker who seeks to suggest the continuity of gender discrimination and violence from the early modern to dictatorship periods. Patrícia Vieira examines and problematizes the representation of women in relation to their traditional linkage with the natural world with specific reference to *Máscaras* (Noémia Delgado, 1976). A focus on festive rituals involving bulls, alongside the ritualistic slaughter of animals, is shown to document how the coming of age for men is intimately connected with mastery over nature and the female population of a village. The liminal film, Vieira convincingly suggests, "is both a nostalgic homage to a worldview about to disappear with the profound social changes underway at the time and an indictment of that mindset" (p. 116). As Hilary Owen notes in her own chapter, evocatively titled "Monsters, mutants and maternity": "If any single issue united, shaped and defined Portuguese political feminism over the last half-century, it was the decriminalization of abortion" (65). Hence, for example, Paula Rego—arguably the most prominent cultural ambassador for Portugal irrespective of gender—has done paintings on the subject. The atmosphere evocatively conjured by Owen's filmic analysis reveals creative variations on the not-always feminist-friendly slasher and horror genres, with one film pointedly re-appropriating foetal images aggressively deployed in pro-life campaigns.

The complex and frequently contradictory demands placed on female conduct is discussed in Alison Ribeiro de Menezes's eloquent dissection of *Cartas a Uma Ditadura* (Inês de Medeiros, 2006), a documentary about women's letters to Salazar. Charity and homework were venerated, but the fragile state of the domestic and national economy required that working-class women seek paid employment outside of the home. The prime distinction between the section on "histories" and that on "archives" is the tendency for contributions to the latter to be more self-reflective, recognizing the productive ability of film to create and not just reflect on the past, alongside a negation of unmediated access to history. Hence, for example, Estela Vieira's discusses in her study of Margarita Cardoso's *Kuxa Kanema* (2003) and Susana de Sousa Dias's *48* (2010) how both films "critique the positivist conception of the archival image as the source of a complete or absolute historical knowledge" (p. 148).

Such questions are hardly unique to Portugal, and the authors make a spirited case for the national cinema having the potential to contribute to broader debates in and around world cinema(s). Sally Faulkner meaningfully compares and contrasts the careers of Margarita Cardoso and Argentine filmmaker Lucrecia Martel. Although the Portuguese director has cited the more canonical foreigner as an influence, Faulkner contends that her explorations of post-colonialism are not derivative and that the disparity in their respective levels of success is due to material more than aesthetic considerations. Martel is but one source of influence amongst a medley of transnational genealogies from which Cardoso seeks inspiration, including but not limited to literary figures such as Virginia Woolf and Carmen Martín Gaite (the latter a key point of reference, I would add, for some female Spanish film directors such as Paula Ortiz). Liz suggests that the relatively little explored Portuguese capital (Intellect's "World Film Locations" series includes entries on Cleveland, Glasgow, Liverpool, and Prague, but not on Lisbon) could reinvigorate the seemingly exhausted field of studying cinematic cities. Filipa Rosário's analysis of four post "year-zero" films ("year-zero" is taken as 2011 when the post-financial-crisis rescue plan demanded that the state relegate national autonomy to the dictates of international capital) suggests that austerity has been a spur to female creativity, and is symptomatic of an ethos that carries through the volume of simultaneously refusing to embrace victimhood or negate structural inequalities. Intelligent and refreshingly free of typos (a particular achievement given numerous non-native contributors), this book carries out important labour in articulating the aesthetic and ethical advantages of (re-)discovering Portuguese women's cinema at home and abroad for students, scholars, and viewers alike.

DUNCAN WHEELER is Professor and Chair of Spanish Studies at the University of Leeds. His most recent book is *Following Franco: Spanish Culture and Politics in Transition* (Manchester: Manchester University Press, 2020).